4-21-75

AMERICA'S IMPACT
ON THE WORLD

This book is the companion volume to the author's
Impact of Western Man

AMERICA'S IMPACT ON THE WORLD

A Study of the Role of the United States in the World Economy, 1750–1970

WILLIAM WOODRUFF
Graduate Research Professor
of Economic History,
University of Florida

A HALSTED PRESS BOOK

JOHN WILEY & SONS
New York – – Toronto

First published 1975 by
THE MACMILLAN PRESS LIMITED
London and Basingstoke

Published in the U.S.A. and Canada by Halsted Press, a Division of John Wiley & Sons, Inc., New York.

Printed in Great Britain

Library of Congress Cataloging in Publication Data
Woodruff, William.
   America's impact on the world.

   "A Halsted Press book."
   Bibliography: p.
   Includes index.
   1. United States– –Economic conditions.   2. United States– –Foreign economic relations.   3. United States– –Commerce.   I. Title.
   HC103.**W68**   1975   330.9'73   74-23474
   ISBN 0-470-95963-0

To my children: David, Roger, Kirsten,
Mark, Peter, Andrew, Thomas

Contents

List of Tables

(pp. 232–90)

Preface

THIS book is meant to provide a synthesis of America's contribution to the common western achievement in the world during the past two hundred years. In merging the history of the United States into that of the modern world, I have of necessity stressed those aspects that are of world rather than of local or even of national importance. While I am conscious of the variations that exist between the different parts of the United States, I believe that at least in its external aspect it is possible to identify the 'American' impact in the world. And by 'impact' I mean not just the outward thrust of American life but the effect in the world of the colonising inward flow as well. Before the United States could give to the world, it had to take. I am also aware that any explanation of the historical forces that have helped to mould the American character must take account of domestic as well as external forces. Hence, the stress placed in the early part of my book on the circumstances surrounding the nation's inception and its westward expansion across the North American continent.

Because economic history is my major craft, I have emphasised the economic aspects, yet the story I have to tell cannot be confined to any particular branch of history. Unashamedly, in trying to explain the American mind and conduct in the world, I have disregarded the barriers of historical and economic specialism. Specialism to me is not an end in itself but a means to a greater whole. I no more think that the present atomisation of knowledge is normal and permanent, than I think that ultimate and universal history is just around the corner. I can only hope that in approaching my task from what is today an unusual intellectual angle I may add a new dimension to our present knowledge.

About one's approach to history there will always be dispute. About America's need to see its history in a world context there can be no argument. It is especially important for the Americans not only because of their world political responsibilities but also because of their growing role in international commerce, industry and finance. There is ahead of us a struggle between the nation state and the realities of a growing world-wide economic order. Politically, the twentieth century is the age of the nation. In all other respects – in religion, art, science, technology, defence, finance, commerce and business – it is increasingly international and anational. Here lies one of the dilemmas of the modern age.

The trouble is that most Americans are completely unable to see their own history in a world context. Their earlier desire to break with Europe's past bedevils their present thinking. Their belief that they can ignore history and wipe the slate clean and start all over again (as they are now trying to do with mainland China) has caused them to have little sense of proportion regarding the limits of human effort. It is their ignorance of the past – or, perhaps, their abhorrence of the past – it is their belief that they stand outside history which gives them a different sense of the human drama from that held by other people. While their setbacks in Vietnam have done something to change this attitude, they are still reluctant to share the 'vale of tears' of the less fortunate of the world; not for them the stress placed upon the imponderables, the miraculous and the spiritual forces of life that are to be found in Talmudic scripture. Because he believes himself to be in much greater control of his fate than history bears out, the American cannot understand how it is that, after several hundred years of what is called 'progress', the problems facing the world should be greater now than they have ever been. Must there be several more conflicts such as the one in Vietnam, several more leaders felled by assassins' bullets, before the American realises what an important yet what a devious and incalculable thing history can be? It is not only Great Men who make history; it is sometimes lunatics. As long as the Americans confined their activities to the colonisation of part of the North American continent, this weakness – this facility to see things in terms of the moment – did not matter so much; now, when America stands at the centre of the world stage, it is critical for the whole human race.

It is this same lack of historical sense that has deluded the

Americans into believing that they could provide a prescription for the world's economic ills; which is to assume that the United States has the only rational economic system and that all others are the results of ignorance or error. Nothing could be further from the truth. There is no norm, no inevitable goal, which other countries have somehow failed to reach, or for that matter to which they should struggle. If the world has shown an eagerness to accept America's ideas on economic growth and development, it is because the idea of a world of plenty for the common man has filled a vacuum in man's thinking. Other people have their own ideas about religion and politics; what they did not have – until some of them took it from the Americans – was the idea of a universal economic plenty.

However critical some of my comments may appear, I write about the Americans as a friend; I acknowledge my bias. I have known them in peace and war. I have studied and taught their history for many years. I have spent the greater part of my working life since the Second World War among them. I am the child of immigrants myself and, but for the quirks of fate, would have been born and reared on the American side of the Atlantic. My father was one of those who, in the summer of 1914, voluntarily left America to fight in Flanders. A generation later, I took up the fight* where he had left off. Indeed, I have come to the conclusion that there must be a fighting streak in the Woodruffs, for my paternal grandmother Woodruff of Fall River, Massachusetts, had more sons fighting under the Stars and Stripes in 1917 than any other mother in the State.

Finally, by way of explanation, I repeat what I wrote in my earlier *Impact of Western Man*. To those who see 'America' as larger than the United States, I apologise for using these terms interchangeably. My plea is that I have followed the general European and North American practice of identifying Americans with the people residing in the United States.

* I have written of my experiences with the infantry in *Vessel of Sadness*, London: Chatto and Windus, 1970.

Where I have used the term 'North America', I mean Canada and the United States. 'Latin America' for me includes the area from the Mexican–United States border to Cape Horn, as well as the West Indies. When I speak of the western nations, and the West, I am dealing with those people who belong to a general European cultural pattern, regardless of where they were born or where they reside. Thus, the terms 'western nations' and 'the West' include those living within Europe as well as those whites living within the great European settlements of the Americas, Australasia, and parts of Africa.

As with my _Impact of Western Man_, my debt to others in the preparation of this book is great. While I cannot list all those who have helped me in my inquiries I would like to thank the following specialists who were generous enough to read and criticise either the whole or part of the book in typescript or in proof; Professors Henri Brugmans, David Carneiro sen., S. B. Clough, Wolfram Fischer, L. M. Hacker, Yoshitaka Komatsu, Takashi Kotono, Henrietta Larson, Philip Locklin, Charles Morris, David Niddrie, Sir Arthur G. Price, A. L. Rowse, and R. S. Woodbury. Mr Dee Brown helped me with Indian sources. For statistical assistance I am indebted to Professors J. H. Dunning and C. P. Kindleberger. I also received help with figures from Monsieur Becker of the Ministère des Finances, Paris, Herr Bergmann of the Statistisches Bundesamt, Wiesbaden, Mr G. Fogg of the British Department of Trade and Industry, Drs Wolff and Senif of the Deutsches Bundesamt, and Mr Thomas Olmstead. Dr Anson Huang of the Missionary Research Library, New York, provided missionary statistics.

The University of Florida has of course helped me in many ways. I have had the complete cooperation of the university library (I especially want to thank Miss F. E. Apperson, Miss V. G. Francis, Mr S. L. Butler, and Mr J. R. Jones jr.) and the willing and valuable research assistance of Mr David Burch, Mrs Roxanne Dwyer, and Mrs Caroline Comnenos. The latter has shown great patience and resourcefulness in helping to prepare this book for the press. Several drafts of this book were typed by Mrs Charlotte Bannister with unfailing cheer-

fulness and great skill. Last but by no means least my thanks
again to Helga.

Berlin, 1974 William Woodruff

CHAPTER I
Prologue: Origins

FOR those of us who look upon the world with western eyes, America's story begins with Columbus's discovery in 1492. Many years would pass before Europe conceded the existence of a continent that would radically alter its life.

By the seventeenth century, however, possession of the New World was being contested by the Great Powers. While the Spanish flag had flown over land as far north as Oregon on one side of North America and the Carolinas on the other, the Spaniards (and the Portuguese) had been too occupied with the conquest and protection of their possessions in South America to enter wholeheartedly into the struggle for dominion in the north. French ambitions in the New World had been thwarted by European wars and religious strife. Apart from an effort in the Floridas in the 1560s, France did not contend with Spain for dominion of the North American continent until well into the seventeenth century. Indeed, at the outset, while France would have been glad to upset Spanish power, its purpose was to get around the new continent rather than to occupy it. Until 1660 only a few thousand Frenchmen lived in what had come to be called New France. Later in the century, stimulated by the growing ambitions of France under the reign of Louis XIV (1648–1715), the number of emigrants rapidly increased; subsidies were provided and new explorations undertaken. Before the seventeenth century had ended, New France, protected by a number of strategically placed forts, stretched, crescent-like, from the mouth of the St Lawrence to the mouth of the Mississippi.

England, like France, had searched for a northwest passage to Asia. Only as the mist of uncertainty surrounding the existence of the Americas began to fade did its interests in the New World grow. Scarce English funds were better employed in trade or in plundering the Spanish Main than in colonising the New World. For the whole object of early exploration was to acquire wealth, not to colonise land. The discouraging reports of Frobisher and Davis in the 1570s and 1580s, as well as the failure of Sir Walter Raleigh and John White to colonise parts of Virginia (also in the 1580s), had dampened English hopes. While things looked up with the more inviting account of the New England coast presented by George Weymouth and others in the early seventeenth century, the settlement financed by Plymouth, Bristol and Exeter merchants at the mouth of the Kennebec River, Maine, in 1607 ended in failure.

Dutch intrusion into North America began in 1609 with the expedition led by the English mariner, Henry Hudson, who continued the search for a northwest passage to the Indies. By the mid-seventeenth century the Dutch West Indian Company had founded trading colonies on Manhattan Island, in Connecticut, New Jersey, Delaware, and Pennsylvania. The tiny colony of Fort Christina, founded by the Swedes on the Delaware in 1638, was swallowed up by the Dutch in 1655. In the same manner, both Swedish and Dutch colonies were later swallowed up by the English.

Meanwhile France, England, and the Netherlands continued to prey upon Spanish commerce and towns in the southern half of the American hemisphere. As Spanish power in Europe declined in the seventeenth century, inroads were made into Spanish domains in the West Indies and on the South American continent. However, until the revolutions of the early nineteenth century, the power of Spain and Portugal in the Americas remained supreme.

The first successful British effort to colonise North America began with the founding of the Jamestown colony in Virginia by 105 English men and women in 1607. Jamestown, established by a group of London profit-seeking merchants and hence called the London Company, had precarious beginnings; famine, disease, and Indian attacks almost destroyed it at the outset. These conditions were hardly conducive to the flow of free settlers, and, had indentured labour not been available, the efforts at Jamestown might have come to naught. By the 1620s, however, despite the hostility of the

Spanish and the English Crowns – the one because of the colony's existence in Spanish America, the other because the colonists showed a proclivity for two dangerous things: tobacco and popular government – the colony of Virginia had taken firm root.

It was not until the arrival of the Pilgrims at Cape Cod in 1620 that an English colony was successfully established in New England, though half of the 120 settlers who came on the *Mayflower* had died before the spring. By 1642, about 20,000 English settlers had come to the northeastern seaboard of America. To call these people Puritans is to use a broad description covering many kinds of religious dissent. However, most of them were animated by religious zeal. Such men not only came to Plymouth Rock; they also founded colonies at Salem, Massachusetts, in 1628, and at Massachusetts Bay in 1629.

Religious zeal did not play the same role in the founding of the Middle Colonies. The primary aim of the Dutch in New Amsterdam was trade, especially in furs and lumber. The other British Middle Colonies of New Jersey (1664), Delaware (1704), and Pennsylvania originated in royal bequests. Instead of trying to establish a feudal principality, the Quaker, William Penn, made his territory the scene of an experiment in living. Offering racial, political and religious freedom, he attracted migrants of different outlook (especially Quakers from Ireland, England and Germany). America's first 'Melting Pot' did not pass unnoticed by Voltaire and other European liberal thinkers who wrote about Penn's 'Holy Experiment' as the triumph of reason. Alas, a surfeit of brotherly love landed Penn's second son, Thomas, in a London prison for debt. The province that in 1681 had begun as a 'Holy Experiment' ended in 1708 as a mortgage.

In the south, Virginia grew out of the tiny settlement at Jamestown. In 1634, Maryland, founded by the Catholic, Cecilius Calvert, quickly attracted some of the better-to-do English Catholics. As the northern colonies had sheltered those fleeing from the political absolutism of Charles I and the religious uniformity of Archbishop Laud, so Maryland provided a refuge from the intolerance of Northern Presbyterianism. The Carolinas became a refuge for French

Huguenots as well as for English, German and Swiss settlers. The political significance of Georgia, founded in 1732, lay in the fact that it provided a buffer state between the other southern colonies and Spanish Florida. The triangle between the Carolinas, Florida and Louisiana was an area in which competing English, French and Spanish claims had still to be resolved.

While it is easy to exaggerate the role of religious zeal in the birth of the American nation – the 'birthplace' of the nation was as much in Charleston and Philadelphia as it was in Plymouth and Massachusetts Bay – religious zeal was one of the basic forces of early American colonisation; especially so for the various groups of religious dissenters described as Pilgrims or Puritans. The fact that they were God's people of the promise, and that America was God's American Israel meant that they not only had hope for the future, they had a surety about it. They not only knew the errors of the European Babylon from which they had escaped, they knew where they were going. From this inner assurance, from their stern morality and self-discipline, from their middle-class virtues, as well as from their experiences in daily living, came the idealism, vitality, perseverance and toughness of the early settlers' mind. The Calvinistic deists – the men of iron, the Ironsides – who, with the cry, 'Jehovah, and no quarter', triumphed under Cromwell at Marston Moor in the crucial battle of the English Civil War in 1644, were the same people who triumphed on the early American frontier. The early Pilgrim and Puritan settlers were not saintly men (most of us only know them for their supposed bigotry and cruelty); nor were they clever fellows; indeed, they made many mistakes, experienced every kind of set-back until their hopes had been fulfilled. From their success sprang a sense of self-righteousness and moral superiority, and an ability to simplify all issues into the right and the wrong.

Religious zeal provided these early settlers with the spiritual capacity to endure. Success depended on obeying God's rules as revealed in the Bible. To question what had been revealed, to speculate about God's will, was to invite the wrath of a just Jehovah. In time this Biblical-mindedness fostered a literal-mindedness which, in turn, caused the

Americans to become more concerned with the form than with the content of things. It provided them with an extraordinary capacity for written constitutions, programmes, and charters. It helps to explain their concern not with substantive justice but with legal formalism. The later contribution of American jurisconsults, David Dudley Field (1805–94) and Edward Livingston (1764–1836), to the codification of western criminal and common laws was in this tradition.

The spiritual roots and religious zeal of America's early settlers help to explain America's continuing belief (despite the warnings sounded by some of the Founding Fathers) in its mission to the world. To the Greek historian Thucydides, to the Roman historian Tacitus, history was purely secular and human. With the coming of Christianity, however, came a messiah; history, from the beginning to the end, now had a religious and theological meaning. The early Pilgrim and Puritan settlements in the New World were to be a stage in this divine epic. It was the overwhelming desire to create a heavenly society that would be a model for the world that caused John Winthrop, one of the leaders of the early Massachusetts Bay colony, to declaim: 'We shall be as a City upon a hill, the eyes of all people are upon us, so that if we shall deal falsely with our God in this work we have undertaken and so cause Him to withdraw His present help from us, we shall be made a story and a byword through the world'.[1] The early settlements were to be 'the place where the Lord will create a new Heaven and a new Earth . . . a specimen of what shall be over all the earth in the glorious times which are expected'. Only in the light of such sentiments can America's concern with the lot of other people be understood. Gradually, a shift would take place away from other people's religious and political redemption to their material welfare, but the messianic streak would remain.

Despite their sense of spiritual righteousness and their belief in a messianic mission to the world, the early settlers remained acutely aware of the practical problems of life. After all, their problem was immediate: how to survive. Their concern was with the elemental. However spiritually inclined they may seem to have been, they were in fact progressively worldly. Indeed, they took the words of Genesis to heart: 'Fill the earth and subdue it'. To control the universe was not in their eyes diminishing God's dominion; it was fulfilling Biblical revelation. The European Christian belief in a universal order where man's role was fixed gave way to a struggle between the human will and the natural order. Rather than remain prisoners of a cosmic fate, the Puritans intended to take charge of the world and everything in it.

Their actions echoed St Paul's words to the Galatians: 'During our minority we were slaves to the elemental spirits of the universe, but . . . God sent His only Son . . . to purchase freedom for the subjects of the Law'. The ethics of Christian duty – especially Protestant duty – became thrift, sobriety, diligence and hard work. How else could the early settlers have survived in such hostile environment? The emphasis which Protestantism attached to individual judgement encouraged self-reliance and individual enterprise. A new stress came to be placed on wealth, on commerce, and on economic self-interest; yet self-indulgence was discouraged. At work or play, their religion gave a transcendental importance to everything they did. In time, as the hardship and sacrifice of colonial life lessened, the accumulation of wealth failed to be transcended by a god-like purpose; as it did so, the gathering of riches became an end in itself. There was less emphasis on man's wickedness and more emphasis on God's goodness. People talked less about the almost impossible task of a rich man getting to heaven and more about the way in which the ability to accumulate wealth was a sign of virtue.

The birth of the American nation was partly the product of a singular religious experience; it was also the outcome of a world power struggle. Of the contestants, the British had confined their activities in North America to the coastline and to the area north of the Great Lakes; the French, by spreading through the Great Lakes, the Ohio and the Mississippi valleys, had pre-empted the heartland of America; the Spanish dominated the Gulf area and held much of what later came to be Mexican territory; by 1741, the Russians, going eastwards, had crossed the Bering Straits into Alaska. Of these four powers, the two strongest were Britain and France. The struggle between them began in earnest in 1689 with King William's War, and ended with the Treaty of Ryswick (Holland) of 1697 between France, England, Spain and Holland. Important for the American colonists was that it restored all conquests and left the situation in North America as it had been eight years earlier when hostilities began. In 1702 war was renewed between the European powers. This conflict – the war of the Spanish Succession – or, as the colonists called it, Queen Anne's War, concerned the balance of power in Europe. Yet it soon involved the English colonists. Once again, the English tried to take the major French outposts in Canada (Acadia, Port Royal and Quebec); in addition, they sacked Spanish St Augustine in northern Florida. The French responded by penetrating the English colonies from French Canada. The outcome was the Treaty of Utrecht (Holland) of 1713. This treaty, while primarily concerned with affairs within Europe, did, however, uphold British claims to a belt of territory surrounding Hudson's Bay. It also confirmed British possession of Newfoundland and Nova Scotia and the territory occupied by Britain's Indian allies, the Iroquois. Most disturbing to the colonists was the fact that France was allowed to retain New France (Quebec) and Cape Breton Island.

With this settlement it became apparent that the sacrifices made by the English colonists to destroy French power in North America had been of no avail. The French threat remained and grew as they continued to build new forts and strengthen existing ones from the Gulf of Mexico to Quebec. Little wonder that, when hostilities were renewed in 1743 (the year in which the colonists made still another effort to reduce the Spanish fort at St Augustine, Florida), they found the English colonists eager to give battle. The most signal event in the war of the Austrian Succession, or what in America was called King George's War, was the capture in 1745, by the colonists supported by the British fleet, of Louisburg on Cape Breton Island. This was a considerable victory, for the fortress – one of the strongest in the New World – controlled the St Lawrence approaches. Yet the attempts made by the colonists to conquer New France proved abortive. Worse still, at the Peace of Aix-la-Chapelle in 1748 (still another settlement in which colonial affairs, of necessity, were secondary to European affairs), Louisburg was handed back to the French intact. Unlike the colonists, the English government was not concerned to destroy French power in North America but to work out a world-wide balance of power. In contrast to the English attitude, the life and death struggles with the Indians and the French had created in the minds of the early Americans the idea that war was total, righteous and final.

The decisive struggle in North America had to wait upon the French and Indian War (the American phase of the Seven Years War in Europe) that began in 1755 and ended in 1763. The outcome of this contest of arms is well known. Wolfe's victory over Montcalm on the Plains of Abraham in 1759 sealed France's fate. In the following year the French surrendered Canada. Three years later, under the Treaty of Paris of 1763, French power in North America ended. The British, at long last free of foreign wars, could now turn to their own affairs and those of their colonies.

Paradoxically the destruction of French power in New France was instrumental in the destruction of British power in the American colonies. Being no longer vital to the colonists, British power could now be discarded; the enforcing of half-forgotten mercantile regulations, as well as the introduction of new measures by the imperial government in London in the 1760s made this all the more urgent. Particularly irritating was the attempt in 1763 to restrict western settlement and fur trading in the land east of the Alleghenies. Other irritants were the Sugar Act of 1764, which, in trying to raise new revenues, hurt colonial trade and largely destroyed profitable American commerce with the French West Indies; the obnoxious Stamp Act of 1765, which laid a widely felt tax on – among other things – legal documents, contracts, newspapers, playing cards, and dice; and the Quartering Act of the same year, which, under given conditions, authorized the billeting of increased numbers of British troops in public hostels and inns. These regulations (now for the first time strictly enforced) only served to widen the gulf between the mother country and the colonies. A growing number of

Prologue: Origins

9

clashes between citizenry and British soldiers occurred. By 1773, the time of the Boston Tea Party, when citizens disguised as Indians threw a cargo of tea into Boston harbour, there was no turning back in the struggle for independence. The English King was faced by open rebellion; which is what Lincoln would be faced with a century later.

British efforts at conciliation having failed, first blood was drawn at the battles of Lexington and Concord on 19 April 1775. On 10 May, the Second Continental Congress met at Philadelphia. The first real test of strength came a few weeks later at the Battle of Bunker Hill (actually Breed's Hill) opposite Boston on 17 June. It was here that Washington's ragtag army, of which he had had command for only two days and which he did not join in the field until 2 July, was defeated. Undismayed the struggle was continued. On 4 July 1776, the nation declared its independence. Thenceforth, it fought for its life. Its victory at Saratoga in 1777 brought France, and then Spain and Holland back into the war. On 19 October 1781, the British commander, Cornwallis, surrendered his army at Yorktown. In the treaty of peace signed at Paris on 3 September 1783, between Great Britain and the United States, the latter's independence was recognised. For the European powers, the door to the continental territory of the United States had been shut. The imperial ambitions of Britain and France were now deflected to Asia, Africa and Australia.

The fundamental question in the Revolution had not been legislation or taxation, but freedom. On economic and financial matters the British government had shown itself willing to compromise. Those who led the colonists, however, were concerned with independence, and they would settle for nothing less. Distance and the challenge of the New World had increased (under the equalising conditions of a pioneer society) their self-confidence and their egalitarianism. The vast majority of citizens at the time of the Revolution were small farmers, too independent and scattered to be coerced. In such a society everything depended on the voluntary cooperation of the colonists with the imperial government. The 'tyranny' of Crown and Parliament had to be resisted.

At least at the outset the struggle was meant to safeguard the constitutional rights of Englishmen. The fact that the Crown could raise ten corps of American Loyalist troops shows that the issue was not quite so simple as tyranny versus freedom. The only tyranny a lot of people knew was the tyranny of the American mob. One should not confuse this with that of the French mob which established a reign of terror in France a few years later. It was the French Revolution that was the most puritanical of all. Yet more people fled America than fled France; the American revolutionaries confiscated more private property than did the French. Far from being a simple rebellion against tyranny, the War of Independence was America's first civil war, in which an ardent, freedom-loving minority had forced an apathetic majority to accept a new order of things.

Whether it should be called a revolution or not depends on the reader's taste. The Americans were just as Protestant and capitalistic at the end of the revolution as they were at the beginning. Except for the confiscation of royal lands, proprietary estates and the possessions of the 'Empire Loyalists'[2] who fled in great numbers to England, Canada and elsewhere, property remained in the same hands; the class structure was unchanged; the rich and the well-born led American society as they had led it before. Indeed, the American constitution was drafted by aristocrats steeped in European eighteenth-century philosophical, legal, political, religious and economic ideas. The political theory of the Declaration of Independence reflects the thought of John Locke. The concern shown by those who met to draft the constitution in 1787 at Philadelphia – how best to limit the power of popular majorities – reflected the attitude of the American governing class. The constitution that emerged was a compromise between democratic and aristocratic ideas. The application of the democratic principle, though recognised, was limited. Apart from being the new hope of the human race, Republicanism – which is what the revolution is supposed to have established – remained a confused idea.

And yet post-revolutionary America was not the America of 1776. Let anyone who doubts it contrast the outcome of the wars of independence fought in Latin America and North America. The revolution in North America was the rejection of the traditional forms of authority and discipline – the Church, the Army, and the landed aristocracy – forms of authority which continue to rule Hispanic America to this day. Moreover where else had colonists declared themselves free and independent of the mother country? Where else at this time does a new constitution emerge out of the discussion and debate of free men? To have made the first major experiment in constitutional democracy might not have been the primary purpose of the Founding Fathers, but it was the outcome of the struggle for independence. The American revolution may not have possessed the abrupt, violent nature of the French and Russian revolutions that followed it, but its appeal to the freedom and equality of men was meant to be universal. While it is true that egalitarianism (which long predates the revolution) never triumphed even in the equalising conditions of a frontier society, the break with England certainly encouraged it. The twin pillars of aristocratic landholding – entail and primogeniture – were almost completely abolished by State legislatures between 1776 and 1791. The agrarian democracy of the first half of the nineteenth century ensured that the movement would not be reversed. Aristocratic control of public life lingered in the south, also in some of the northern states (Massachusetts, New York, Rhode Island and Connecticut); yet despite some property qualifications, control became more and more democratic as these constitutions were amended or replaced. The new western states that came into the Union after 1800 adopted universal (white) male suffrage. Starting with Maryland in 1810, the other states followed suit. By 1845 only North Carolina had still to adopt adult male suffrage. In contrast to the emphasis placed by Europeans on social status, a new emphasis came to be placed upon the intrinsic worth of a human being. The barrier to progress was no longer seen as Europeans had seen it in terms of human depravity but in terms of traditional hierarchical orders and ignorance. The former had been banished by the revolution; the latter would be overcome by public education.

Thus when Benjamin Franklin referred to his fellow countrymen as '. . . a general happy mediocrity . . .' he was
expressing a conscious ideal of American society. He warned
those Europeans who had no other quality to recommend
them but their status and birth not to go to America. The
stress in America was not on who a man was but what he was.
'. . . God Almighty is himself a mechanic', Franklin said, 'the
greatest in the universe; and he is respected and admired
more for the variety, ingenuity, and utility of his handiworks
than for the antiquity of his family'.[3] In 1835 that shrewd
observer, de Tocqueville, could be convinced that men in
America were '. . . on a greater equality in point of fortune
and intellect, or, in other words, more equal in their strength,
than in any other country in the world, or in any age of which
history has preserved the remembrance'.[4] While abhorring
the mediocrity and social conformity of American life, de
Tocqueville was in no doubt that 'a general equality of
conditions' was the 'primary fact' about the Americans. A
new civilisation was in the making.

Yet de Tocqueville had written while America was still an
agrarian country. The rise of industrialism – especially after
the Civil War – caused a growing inequality of wealth. The
dream of America, expressed at the time of the revolution by
Jefferson and others, was an egalitarian, agrarian, democratic
republic; the reality – despite the fluidity of the classes in the
United States – became a powerful commercial, industrialised, capitalist economy which has helped to create a new
aristocracy of wealth.

The discovery of the American continent ensured the
impact of western man across the entire globe. 'Columbus's
discovery',[5] says one author, 'was thus the necessary counter-
part without which da Gama's new eastern seaway could
never have been exploited'. Spanish silver became available
to pay for the products which the West sought in the East; a
world economy was now feasible. Yet it took some time for
the significance of the New World to impress itself upon the
European mind. A century after it had been discovered,
Henry Hudson sailed up the river named after him, in search
of a passage to Asia.

Once, however, the significance of the new hemisphere had been grasped, it fired the imagination of the Europeans in every field of thought and endeavour. '. . . the discovery of the Americas', said Francisco López de Gómara, historian of the conquest of the Indies, writing in the sixteenth century, was 'the greatest event in human history since the creation, except for the incarnation of Christ'.[6] As a place of shadowy dreams of earthly perfection (witness the writings of More, Rabelais, Montaigne and Bacon), as a never-ending source of religious enthusiasm (witness the effect of visits made to America by the eighteenth-century evangelists, Wesley and Whitehead), as a challenge to existing philosophical and political ideas, as a stimulus given to every branch of science, as an invigorating influence affecting literature and culture generally – in all these ways, the impact of the discovery of America upon Europe was profound. In 1795, the German publicist and statesman, Friedrich von Gentz, wrote:

That Europe itself, from Lisbon to the Volga, has become what it is at this moment; that it has climbed for three centuries from art to art, from science to science, from one plateau of enlightenment, refinement, and freedom to another; that it could send America its new citizens and in them the germs of an immeasurable prosperity; and that it surpassed in breadth and diversity the most prized states of antiquity – all that is due to America and to renewed and strengthened ties with the East Indies more than to any other cause; more, possibly, than to all other causes taken together. . . . The discovery of America and a new route to the East Indies opened the greatest market, the greatest inducement to human industry, that had ever existed since the human race emerged from barbarism.[7]

With the 'discovery' of America, the walls of the Old World had fallen down; a new and greater Cathay had appeared on the horizon. As trade grew, a stimulus was given to the reformulation of economic thought and government policy (witness the writings of Child, Davenant, Petty and Mun); as the spirit of capitalism was further encouraged, the emphasis shifted to the real and the material.

The emergence of an independent United States wrought

significant changes in the hearts and minds of many Europeans. 'America', wrote an ecstatic Van der Kemp from Leyden, in 1781, 'is a land of justice, we are a land of sin'.[8] Writing after the American victory of Yorktown the Abbé Bandole, chaplain to the French Embassy at Philadelphia, extolled the new nation:

You offer the universe the admirable spectacle of a society which, founded on the principles of equality and justice, and now arriving at perfection, can insure to the individuals who compose it, all the happiness of which human institutions are capable.[9]

And, with victory to the Americans secured, Condorcet wrote from Paris in 1786:

It is not enough that the rights of man be written in the tomes of philosophers and in the hearts of virtuous men; the ignorant and the weak must also be able to read them in the example of a great nation. America has given us this example. The act of declaring its independence is a simple and sublime exposition of these rights that are so sacred and have so long been forgotten.[10]

Three years after Condorcet had complimented the Americans on their struggle for freedom, the French Revolution broke out. It is tempting to think (as John Adams and many others certainly did think)[11] that the revolutionaries of 1789 were influenced by the revolutionaries of 1776. Yet, apart from adding a certain vigour to the French movement, it would be unwise to draw too close a relation. In terms of the influence of ideas, it is France not America that inaugurated modern democracy. It was Britain that provided the most influential model of a democratic state committed to the principle of majority rule. However, the 'Spirit of 1776' was not without its influence. It was among the burghers of the Cape of South Africa that unrest was being attributed in 1780 to 'the American spirit'.[12] When later in the 1830s the Boers commenced their historic trek into the interior, they formally declared their desire '. . . to establish our new settlement on the same principles of liberty as those adopted by the United States of America. . . .'[13] American influence is also evident in the constitutions of several Latin American republics, as it is in those of Switzerland, Belgium, Norway and Canada. American republican elements are to be found in the Provisional Constitution passed by the Chinese National Assembly of 1912 and in the Indian Constitution of 1947. Moreover, the colonists' triumph at Yorktown in 1781 stimulated nationalism in the West as Japan's victory over Russia in 1905 would later stimulate it in the East.

Not everyone looked upon the discovery of America and the emergence of the United States as the hope of the human race. Numerous voices were raised in Europe at the end of the eighteenth century questioning whether the impact of America on Europe had been for the general good. In contrast to those who had applauded what had taken place, others were pessimistic. Buffon, Raynal and the Abbé de Pauw argued that all forms of life would degenerate in the New World. Even on the economic plane, there were many who were sceptical about America's influence. The true source of wealth and happiness, said the French physiocrat, Dr Quesnay, lies not in foreign trade with America but in cultivating our own garden (as Voltaire had concluded in *Candide*). Wrote the Abbé Roubaud in 1775:

The opinion was formed that trade – especially distant maritime trade, the most casual, the most perilous, the most costly of all, that ruinous trade that absorbs what is necessary in return for what is superfluous – would produce wealth, simply because it carried from one climate to another the riches produced everywhere by agriculture; and ploughs were thrown into the sea.[14]

From the New World came that 'cursed weed' tobacco, which, given time, would more than offset the physical harm done to the American aborigines through the sale of English rum, French brandy, and Dutch gin. Nor had the gold and silver which 'flowed over Europe in waves' been without its drawbacks. Spreading from Spain to the rest of Europe, it had caused an inflation in prices, accelerated the rate of change in a slow-moving, stable economy, and overturned a financial structure which had stood for centuries.

Foolishly it [gold and silver] was thought to be the wealth of
nations, even to the point of financing them completely; and it
rendered fiscal greed unrestrained. Vices and errors con-
verted it into a universal instrument for all manner of
disorder, and all became politically, socially, and morally
venal.[15]

And the price of economic betterment had had to be met not
only in sweat but in blood.

. . . Perhaps more than twenty million Indians perished in
America; many more men were lost to our own continent. It is
estimated that Spain spewed eight million men over the New
World [Spain's population in 1492 was approximately
9,000,000; in 1694, less than 6,000,000]. Have Portugal,
England, France, Germany, Holland, and other countries lost
any less than that, especially if we count the many victims of
wars and of navigation? Even now, Great Britain is losing
men day after day in order to populate this vast desert. Africa
has already lost nearly 12 million of its own to it, and
continues to sacrifice, each year, more than sixty thousand.[16]

And again, as the Abbé Corneille de Pauw wrote:

Scenes of massacre and of carnage have spread from Canton
to Archangel, from Buenos Aires to Quebec. The commerce
of Europeans having closely bound all parts of the world by
the same chain, these parts are also dragged into revolutions
and the vicissitudes of attack and defence. Asia can no longer
remain neutral when a few merchants have a dispute in
America over a few beaver skins or some logwood.[17]

  Worse in its lasting effect was the exchange of sicknesses
between the Old World and the New. We are not sure
whether syphilis was inflicted upon the aboriginal Americans
by the Europeans or vice versa. We do know that syphilis
spread across Europe like a scourge shortly after the discovery of America. To the English, it was the 'French disease'; to
the French, it was the 'Neapolitan disease'; to the Italians, it
was the 'Spanish disease'; to the Spaniards, it was the
'American disease'. Whatever its origin venereal disease has
remained a curse on the European house from that day to

this. To the New World, the European (quite apart from the diseases introduced by the Africans) brought what proved to be the scourges of smallpox, influenza, tuberculosis and diphtheria.

Finally, a warning about the New World that has a modern ring:

It is the New World, formerly our slave, peopled for the most part by our own emigrants, that will come in turn to enslave us. Its industry, its force, and its power will increase as ours diminish. The Old World will be subjugated by the New; and this conquering nation, after having undergone the laws of revolution, will itself perish at the hands of a people it will have been unfortunate enough to discover.[18]

And so, in Europe, at the end of the eighteenth century, the credit and debit entries in the young nation's account were totted up. To some the United States meant freedom from tyranny, freedom from want, and freedom from ancient inequalities. To others the discovery and development of the United States had undermined and falsified economic order; it had offered panaceas and greater opportunities for extravagance; it had increased the bloodshed and suffering in America, Europe and Africa out of all proportion to the commercial benefits entailed; it had helped to spread diseases across the globe; and, far from the American experience being spritually and religiously invigorating, in return for a worldly mess of pottage it had encouraged religious scepticism, cynicism and indifference. Even the conversion of the native Americans from so-called paganism to the true religion had failed.

Americans at the end of the eighteenth century had neither the time nor the taste to engage in speculations of this kind. 'Experience must be our only guide', John Dickinson had said at the first Federal Convention (1787).[19] The Americans' only wish was to turn their backs on Europe's worries and vices and begin again. It was imperative that they should, for in the American experiment and example lay the hope of the world. With a peculiar innocence regarding the limits of human effort, with a seeming inability to realise that in due season all things must pass, Americans believed, like no other people on earth, in an ever-improving future. Nor was anything allowed to halt their upward march. In its infancy, the nation knew division ('We are fast verging to anarchy and confusion', Washington wrote to Madison in November 1786),[20] counter-revolution, rebellion, threats of secession, treason, war, and economic want; its constitution, not adopted until 1781, had to be replaced in 1789. There was nothing the young nation did not endure, nothing against which it did not prevail.

Thus did the American people embark upon one of the world's greatest experiments in living; thus did America's odyssey begin.

CHAPTER II
America's Empire

FOR the Americans, 'Imperialism' is other people's history. It had nothing to do with a people who had fought a revolutionary war to gain their independence from an imperialist power, and whose leaders for a century and more had openly disclaimed any territorial ambitions in the world. Placing themselves outside history, they looked upon the earlier expansion of the mercantilist states of Europe, as well as their later 'scramble' for parts of Africa, Asia, and the islands of the Pacific Ocean, as evil; whereas their own conquest of a continent was the 'Manifest Destiny' of a people who had inherited 'God's country'.

This moralising attitude towards imperialism contrasts sharply with their own experience, whereby a tiny republic acquired an enormous land empire. American territorial acquisitiveness was indeed felt long before independence. Landownership in North America had always been a bone of contention between the British government and the colonists. The aim of the home government was order; that of the colonists, freedom. London not only wanted to keep its garrison costs within bounds, but it also had made commitments to its Indian allies. The colonists' attitude was expressed by Lord Dunmore, governor of Virginia in 1772:

... they [the Americans] do not conceive that Government has any right to forbid their taking possession of a Vast tract of Country, either uninhabited, or which Serves only as a Shelter to a few Scattered Tribes of Indians. Nor can they easily be brought to entertain any belief of the permanent obligation of Treaties made with those People.[1]

The problem became acute when, after the Treaty of Paris of 1763, England, having obtained all French territory east of the Mississippi, drew a boundary along the crest of the

Allegheny mountains beyond which white settlers were temporarily not to go. Because the Proclamation of 1763 was disregarded by the white pioneers (as it was bound to be), the British government tried to place the territory north of the Ohio river under British control from Canada. In 1774 Quebec's boundary was extended to the Ohio river in an abortive attempt to stem further white invasion (there were probably several hundred settlers west of the Alleghenies in the 1770s). The matter was resolved by the triumph of American arms at Yorktown, which placed all the land between Canada and Florida east of the Mississippi in their possession. Under the peace settlement of 1783, American territory doubled from 400,000 to 888,811 square miles. By then 25,000 settlers were strung out from the Appalachians to the Mississippi and the Missouri.

It now became imperative for the infant United States government to define its own relations with the Indians, which it did in the Northwest Ordinance of 1787:

The utmost good faith shall always be observed towards the Indians, their lands and property shall never be taken from them without their consent; and in their property, rights and liberty, they shall never be invaded or disturbed, unless in just and lawful wars authorized by Congress; but laws founded in justice and humanity shall from time to time be made for preventing wrongs being done to them, and for preserving peace and friendship with them.[2]

In words, at least, one cannot conceive of a more just or enlightened point of view towards a weaker people. The subsequent history of the white man's relations with the red shows that it was Lord Dunmore's words that best described the white man's deeds.

America's next great acquisition of territory was obtained from the French under the Louisiana Purchase of 1803. This territory, west of the Mississippi, had been transferred by France to its ally, Spain, in 1762. Thenceforth, Spain had established its authority in the lower Mississippi valley. As the number of Americans moving into the western territories of Tennessee, Kentucky and Ohio grew, Spanish control of the mouth of the Mississippi and hence over the flow of American commerce became more vexatious. In 1800, Napoleon Bonaparte concluded a secret treaty with Spain whereby Spain undertook to return the Louisiana Territory and New Orleans to France; French power defeated at Quebec might make good its imperial losses at New Orleans. Jefferson, learning of the treaty, was in no doubt that French power should be prevented from returning to the Mississippi valley. Writing to the American Minister at Paris in 1802, he declared, 'The day that France takes possession of New Orleans . . . we must marry ourselves to the British fleet and nation'.[3]

In 1801 negotiations were begun in Paris by American emissaries to obtain a sufficient area at the mouth of the Mississippi to guarantee freedom of navigation and trans-shipment of goods. As the negotiations continued, French power in Europe and the West Indies waned; French interest in the rebirth of a colonial empire in North America died. Indeed Jefferson (having been concerned to purchase only part of the river's mouth) found himself purchasing, for $11·3 million (raised chiefly in London), the whole of the Louisiana Territory – a tract of land comprising 827,000 square miles stretching from the Mississippi to the Rocky Mountains. The new land was roughly the equivalent in size to the already enormously expanded United States. There was no clear understanding whether the purchase included West Florida and Texas; the transaction, whether viewed from the American or French side, appears to have been completely unconstitutional (Napoleon did not scruple to break a secret treaty with the Spaniards never to sell Louisiana to a third power); and, regardless of who owned the territory, Spain still occupied it.[4] For Jefferson, whose earlier hopes had been that the trans-Mississippi lands might one day become a large Indian reservation,[5] it was enough that the 'area of freedom' had been enlarged, an area that one day would be peopled by 'our own brethren and children rather than by strangers of another family'. To that end, in 1804, he despatched Meriwether Lewis and William Clark in the hope of finding a water route from the Missouri to the Pacific coast. Meanwhile

Lieutenant Zebulon M. Pike was exploring the upper reaches of the Louisiana Territory.

However, in the early years of the nineteenth century, America's interests still lay east of the Mississippi in the Old Northwest, along the Canadian border, and in the Floridas. To some Americans, the idea of seizing Canadian territory, which was expected to 'fall like a ripe plum' was much more attractive than pioneering in an unknown trans-Mississippi wilderness. The '. . . Great Disposer of Human Events', said a Kentucky Congressman in December 1811, 'intended those two rivers [the St Lawrence and the Mississippi] should belong to the same people'.[6] Moreover the election of the previous year (1810) had brought to Congress from the agrarian areas of the south and the west a group of 'war hawks'[7] who were determined that what the 'Great Disposer' had intended should be fulfilled – even if the country had to go to war to ensure it. For these and their followers, a war against Great Britain and Canada and on the high seas was to be welcomed. 'This', said Representative Calhoun of South Carolina, speaking of the impending struggle with Britain, 'is the second struggle for our liberty; and, if we but do justice to ourselves, it will be no less glorious and successful than the first. Let us but exert ourselves and we will meet with the prospering smile of Heaven'.[8] On 18 June 1812, war on Great Britain was declared.

In his declaration of war, President Madison listed not American territorial ambitions but four major grievances, namely, the impressment of seamen, the violation of neutral rights and territorial waters, the blockade of ports, and the refusal to revoke the British Orders in Council which were detrimental to American commerce.[9] Impressment is of importance because of the entirely different view taken by the two belligerents. The British held that they were not impressing American citizens (at least, not American-born citizens) into their navy; they were upholding the very old German rule of perpetual allegiance. In the early 1800s, it was as improbable for a man to change his nationality as it was for him to change his skin. In pursuing 'fugitive nationals or deserters', they considered their actions completely lawful.

Understandably the Americans took the view that only by divesting oneself of one's nationality could the New World attract the immigrants it needed. Interference with immigration was, after all, one of the grievances listed in the Declaration of Independence.

The question of neutral rights turned largely on the issue of sovereignty. The United States maintained that all its ships at sea were part of its soil and therefore part of its sovereignty. The British distinguished between the public and private vessels of a neutral country. For half a century now, in order to prevent the neutral merchantmen of another nation from acting as an ally of Britain's enemy, Britain had retained the right to search for contraband. In the Napoleonic wars, search and seizure of American vessels by both the British and the French had been common. The effect of the French Decrees upon American shipping was no less ruinous than the effect of the British Orders in Council. The Americans came to look upon the British as their archenemy simply because, as the British gained mastery of the seas, their searches and seizures of American vessels had become more flagrant and humiliating. The vital issue was an affront to national honour.

Also of importance in precipitating war, was British complicity in stiffening Indian resistance in the Ohio valley. In July 1810, two years before war came, William Henry Harrison, governor of Indiana territory, had cautioned the Shawnee, 'Do not think that the red coats can protect you; they are not able to protect themselves. They do not think of going to war with us. If they did, you would in a few moons see our flag wave over all the forts of Canada. . . .'[10] To this, Chief Tecumseh replied, 'Brother, . . . you have taken our land from us, and I do not see how we can remain at peace if you continue to do so'.[11] At the battle of the Thames, north-east of Detroit in Canada, Harrison defeated a British force and killed Britain's ally, Chief Tecumseh.

In the ensuing struggle between the Americans and the British, America's sea power was gradually broken. On land, far from Canada falling 'like a ripe plum', the battles with the British only served to emphasise the initial weakness of America's military organisation. With Napoleon's defeat in

Europe in 1814, British prospects improved; as Britain redeployed its land and sea forces, hopes for a decisive American victory on the high seas or against British Canada faded. There was, in fact, after two years of warfare, little enthusiasm on either side of the Atlantic. For the Americans, the war offered stalemate; for the British, having just emerged from a titanic struggle with the French, the war demanded new exertions which they were reluctant to make. Moreover they now had a greater respect for America's ability to defend itself. By the time peace feelers were made by the Russian Czar in 1814, both sides were prepared to negotiate.

The Treaty of Ghent (1814), while it restored the peace, said nothing about the reasons why the two nations had gone to war. With the exception of West Florida which the Americans had taken from the Spaniards, all captured territory was handed back. Henceforth, except on the Canadian frontier, the British never tried to impede American expansion again.

The people for whom the Treaty of Ghent had the greatest implications were the North American Indians; for without British help they could no longer resist white invasion. The westward course of American empire was set. Colonised for so long by the British, the United States would now – as the frontier moved on – colonise itself. The Monroe Doctrine of 1823 gave notice to the world that the period of European intrusion in the Americas had ended.[12] Called by the promise of free land, by trade, by silver and gold, by a sense of adventure, by the belief that they were a dynamic, superior people, nothing could stop the march of the Americans to the Pacific. Propelled by overwhelming numbers, by a most extraordinary aggressiveness, by superior arms, by a righteous belief in their cause and their destiny, nothing could prevent them from seeking their own vital interests of power, wealth and security. Judged by their deeds and not by their words, the ultimate arbiter of American policy in the North American continent was naked force.

Nowhere else was this more apparent than in its relations with Mexico during the 1830s and 1840s. Authorised by Spain and later by Mexico, American pioneers had begun to settle in Texas from the 1820s. In the space of ten years, more white settlers had entered Texas than in the previous 300 of Spanish rule. Friction between the two civilisations was not long in forming. There followed the siege of the Alamo at San Antonio in February–March 1836, when Texas insurgents were defeated and backwoodsman Congressman from Tennessee, Davy Crockett, gained immortality. Six weeks later, superior Texas forces overwhelmed a Mexican army led by Santa Anna at San Jacinto; the independence of the Texas Republic was assured.

On the 25th day of January, 1845, Congress annexed 390,000 square miles of Mexican territory. This was the equivalent of the area of the original thirteen colonies, or of France and Germany at that time.

Mexican opposition to the annexation of Texas by the United States, as well as ever-growing pressure by the northern colossus against the Mexican people and their territory, led directly to the Mexican War of 1846–8.

In his message to Congress of 11 May 1846, President Polk asserted that the Mexican War was caused by the armed forces of Mexico having 'invaded our territory and shed American blood upon the American soil'.[13] Some observers saw the war as simply a contrived grab for power and territory on the part of Polk and his associates. The French *Journal des Débats* of the time gave voice to its fear of American expansion: 'The conquest of Mexico', it said, 'would be a wide step towards the enslavement of the world by the United States. . . . Between the autocracy of Russia on the East, and the democracy of America, aggrandised by the conquest of Mexico, on the West . . . *Europe may find herself more compressed than she may one day think consistent with her independence and dignity'.* [14] [Italics original] Others placed responsibility for the war on the shoulders of the slave-owning aristocracy, who saw in Texas the opportunity of acquiring further slave territory. Still others saw the war as arising not out of land hunger but out of America's desire to secure control of the western seaboard.

The basic cause of the war was the unceasing pressure of American expansion; all else was incidental. By the Treaty of Guadalupe Hidalgo of 2 February 1848, Mexico relinquished all claims to Texas above the Rio Grande and ceded New Mexico and California to the United States. The territory (including the present state of New Mexico and California and parts of Utah, Nevada, Arizona and Colorado) added 1,193,061 square miles to the national domain. Ironically the Mexican War was both triumph and disaster, for, while it appeased American ambitions for land and power, it also – in encouraging slavocracy – strengthened the discord lying at the nation's heart.

The spread-eaglism of the American people is also reflected in President Polk's unyielding attitude toward Britain over the Oregon boundary dispute. In the 1840s Oregon included what is now Washington, Oregon, Idaho, British Columbia, and parts of Alberta, Montana and Wyoming. At one time, Russia, Spain, England and the United States all had claims to this region; but in 1819 Spain surrendered its rights, and Russia agreed that its claims would not extend south of latitude 54° 40' N. Henceforth, England and the United States ruled this unsettled region. However, from the late 1830s in growing numbers it was the Americans who occupied the area. In 1844, provided the British would give up the north bank of the Columbia river, the Americans were willing to divide the territory along the 49th parallel. In his first annual message to Congress on 2 December 1845, President Polk, by claiming the whole of the Oregon territory, ruled out any such compromise. The expansionist cry, '54.40 or fight!' was, after all, the slogan on which Polk had been elected. When all the filibustering was over, the two governments compromised by accepting the 49th parallel as their boundary; a further 285,580 square miles were added to American territory; the United States had become a Pacific power.[15]

Two other treaties terminated America's continental expansion. Existing boundary disputes and the need to provide a route for a transcontinental railroad into California (subsequent route of the Southern Pacific Railroad) resulted in the Gadsden Purchase (1853) from a bankrupt Mexican government of 29,640 square miles in what is now southern Arizona and New Mexico. The other treaty concerned Russia's sale of

Alaska to the United States for $7,200,000.* Because the fur trade had declined and also because the general tide of Russian expansion had turned, Russian settlements in California had been abandoned from the 1840s onwards. American Secretary of State Seward was determined that his country should have Alaska. When the Russian Minister Stoeckl visited Seward's home late one night to make known his government's decision to sell, Seward promptly interrupted his card game so that Alaska's 586,400 square miles might be in American hands before cockcrow. The corruption involved was too much for Stoeckl who later asked his government for a transfer so that he might 'breathe an atmosphere purer than that of Washington'. Because the Alaskan Purchase was seen by some Canadians as the first step in the conquest of Canadian territory, it hastened Canadian confederation which came in the same year (1867). According to one author, '. . . Canadian Federation of 1867 was both inspired by the American example and dictated by the fear of American aggression'.[16] The voluntary retreat of the Russians, and the collapse in Mexico (also in 1867) of French efforts to recreate an American empire (under Maximilian of Habsburg, younger brother of the Austrian emperor, Franz Joseph, and protégé of Napoleon III of France), finally ended European ambitions in the North American continent.

Within eighty-five years, American territory had grown from 393,152 square miles to 3,022,387 square miles, or about eightfold. Alaska added a further 586,400 square miles. Accompanying the growth in territory was a growth in numbers from approximately two and a half millions to thirty-two and a quarter millions. What the American people had to fear now was not the European powers but themselves. For, having triumphed in their own hemisphere, they now faced one of the most terrible civil wars of which history has record.

The first blow – that awful act of rebellion, of 'insurrection', as Lincoln called it – fell on 12 April 1861, when Fort Sumter, in Charleston harbour, was shelled. Lincoln's quick

*Less than 2 cents per acre.

response was the call to arms. Twenty-three northern and border states were committed to a battle to preserve the Union. The leaders of eleven southern states quickly joined in a bid for independence. Overnight, the nation was split asunder.

The trail to Appomattox long preceded the shelling of the Federal flag at Fort Sumter. Distrust between the north and south had been growing for decades. In the south, there had emerged an aristocratically-led, rural economy whose interests and outlook were completely averse to those of the increasingly commercial and industrialised north. For forty years before the Civil War, there was no other issue that divided the country as did slavery. The south saw the north as a threat to its existence. It was constantly exploited by Yankee interests; yet it provided, through the Federal tariff system, most Federal income and, through its sales of cotton, most foreign exchange. The north saw the south as an anachronism. Just when the western world had abandoned slavery, the south had increased it; the number of slaves in the United States had increased dramatically from approximately three-quarters of a million in 1790 to more than four million in 1860; just when the productive conditions of the western world had found slavery to be a greater hindrance than a help, the south was claiming that its economic life depended on it. Essentially the conflict was about two ways of life and two different sets of values. The problem was not the conditions of the slave but the political implications of slavocracy. The north did not fight to free the Negro; it fought to preserve the Union.

For Lincoln nothing else mattered. In a letter of 22 August 1862, to Horace Greeley, editor of the *New York Tribune,* Lincoln, who had long believed that slavery was wrong[17] but had never felt compelled to become a reformer on that account, wrote:

My paramount object in this struggle *is* to save the Union, and is *not* either to save or destroy slavery. If I could save the Union without freeing *any* slave I would do it, and if I could save it by freeing *all* the slaves I would do it; and if I could save it by freeing some and leaving others alone I would also do that. What I do about slavery and the colored race, I do because I believe it helps to save the Union; and what I forbear, I forbear because I do *not* believe it would help to save the Union. [Italics original][18]

Whatever stood in the path of achieving that end had to be sacrificed. Had Lincoln been a weaker man; had he fought with his mind only and not as he also did with his heart, he would have allowed the south to secede without bloodshed. Other men did not see the Union as God's supreme effort for American man (had that view prevailed in the eighteenth century, there never would have been a fight for independence from the British); but Lincoln would not yield. In some ways, he had the salt and iron of the early Puritans; he knew precisely what was true and what was false; what should be fought for and what should be abandoned. In insisting upon the principle of unity, he had seized upon the indispensable principle of the American body politic; for the secret of America's greatness was not variety – as was Europe's – but unity. It was Lincoln alone who closed the door to compromise. Oath-bound to protect the nation, it was his awesome responsibility to have to choose between separation and war.

Overseas his decision had an immediate impact. On 13 May Britain proclaimed its neutrality, followed by France and Russia. Lincoln deeply resented England's recognition of southern belligerency (England's Foreign Secretary, Lord John Russell, had called the south belligerents, not insurgents); he feared that recognition of belligerency would be followed by recognition of independence. The south pinned its hopes on Europe's need for cotton. 'Cotton diplomacy' failed partly because large stocks of raw cotton were already on hand in Europe, and also because alternative supplies were obtained from India and Egypt. Offsetting the decline in the cotton trade in Europe was the expansion of other European industries, including wool, linen, iron, shipbuilding and armaments. Moreover Britain's reliance upon American grain, as well as its North American carrying trade, were not to be thrown over in a bid to help the south. Nevertheless the impact upon the Lancashire cotton industry alone was devastating. From 1862 onwards, supplies were never more than enough to keep the industry running at half-time. The total loss incurred by Lancashire has been estimated at more than £10 million (in current value).[19]

Indeed, there were occasions, as with the *Trent* affair in 1861 (which resulted in the deliberate violation of British neutrality on the high seas), when war between the northern states and Britain was close. It is also known that the Confederate victories in 1862 had caused the British and French governments to contemplate intervention and forced mediation. The speech made by Gladstone, Chancellor of the Exchequer in Palmerston's Government, in the autumn of 1862, was intended to prepare the way. There 'is no doubt', he said, 'that Jefferson Davis and other leaders of the South have made an army; they are making, it appears, a navy; and they have made what is more than either, they have made a nation'.[20] Understandably northern opinion was enraged. However, the battle of Antietam, 17 September 1862, in turning the tide of war in the north's favour, settled the issue.

Thenceforth the possibility of foreign intervention faded. In 1862 Lincoln even felt strong enough to issue his preliminary Emancipation Proclamation. This act not only strengthened his position with those who had been calling for abolition; it made it virtually impossible for Britain and France to intervene on the Confederate's behalf. Had they done so they would have appeared to have been upholding slavery. In a sharp protest from Lord John Russell, Britain's Foreign Secretary, on 13 February 1865, the Confederates were no longer respectable belligerents but had become 'the so-called confederate government'.[21] Might had prevailed; for the south, the end was near.

Yet, quite apart from the problem of cotton supplies, it had not been entirely unreal for southern leaders to believe that Britain and France would eventually intervene on their behalf. True, on the anti-slavery issue, there was in Europe a vague sympathy with the north; but slavery was not the crucial issue. More important for the *élite* of western Europe was the fact that the south was aristocratic; it presented far less threat to the cultural and political ideals of the ruling classes of England and France than did the north. Nor did it challenge Britain's industrial leadership. More than anything else, it was the north's role as an aggressor that swung western

European sympathy towards the south. Those who regarded the United States as a growing menace to the civilised world welcomed its disruption. If the Russian leaders seemed to prefer the north to the south, they did so to oppose the British and the French, who earlier had defeated them at the Crimea. The American Civil War affected nothing that was vital in Russian life. Regardless of the legends that have been created, the Russian fleets sent in 1863 to New York and San Francisco were there to safeguard (at this time, there was a threat of war with England over Poland) not American but Russian interests.[22] Had war with Britain come, the Russians would have been in a position to raid British commerce.

While it is conceivable that at the outset of hostilities the sympathy of the ruling classes of England and France lay with the Confederates, there were other voices raised in the northern cause. 'Privilege', said the English parliamentarian, John Bright, 'thinks it has a great interest in this contest, and every morning, with blatant voice, it comes into your streets and curses the American Republic. . . . Privilege has shuddered at what might happen to old Europe if this grand experiment should succeed'.[23] After Lincoln's Proclamation of Emancipation of slaves in the rebel States in 1862 (Antietam made the Proclamation urgent and indispensable), the fight between the north and south shifted in the eyes of many foreign observers to a struggle between slavery and freedom. The freedom of the slaves was a rallying cry that all men could understand. For the more eloquent workers of Manchester – at least for those who spoke for them – Emancipation meant the 'erasure of that foul blot upon civilisation and Christianity – chattel slavery'.[24] Similarly the French cotton workers of Rouen were able to proclaim 'without a moment's hesitation' that the French workers 'would rather go on suffering poverty and hunger than see four million human beings continue to live in bondage'.[25]

Vital to the outcome of the Civil War was the test of arms and the ability to provide supplies. Regardless of its courage and its ingenuity, it was here that the south failed. Only its unflagging, self-sacrificing spirit enabled it to march on from Antietam to defeat in April 1865, at Appomattox. Five days

after the surrender of the Confederate army had brought
stillness to a tortured land, Lincoln was assassinated.

While the northern victory brought no panacea to America, at least Lincoln's major war aim had been achieved: unity
had been preserved. It was an outcome that would affect the
whole western world. Had the principle of unity been lost,
America could never have intervened as it did in two World
Wars. In addition the triumph of northern industrial and
financial capitalism was assured. For the prostrate south and
its plantocracy, there remained debt and ruin. Cotton cultivation, so important for its life, and on which the south had
pinned such vain hopes, now stagnated for more than a
decade; the crop of 1859–60 was not equalled until 1875–6.
In the south, the bewildered Negro was free – to starve; it
would be a long time before the black man would have
anything more than hope. Meanwhile the northern 'carpet-
baggers' swarmed across the land like an army of ghouls;
other northerners came to help the cause of black equality.
Alongside them, for twelve years, the Federal army stood
watch. The south had suffered defeat; the north had been
confirmed in its invincibility.

Abroad, the Union victory caused a considerable increase
in the respect shown for American ideals and institutions. To
some observers, Appomattox was as much a victory for
American constitutional and political arrangements – especially for the democratic spirit that underlay them – as it was
for northern arms. In war and peace, American democracy
had proved itself a viable system. 'One of the characteristics
of this nation', a Russian diplomat wrote home, 'is its
confidence in itself, in its destiny, and in its belief that "the
best government that God ever saw will last forever".'[26]

The London *Spectator* on 17 February 1866, wrote, 'Nobody doubts any more that the Union is a power of the first
class, a nation which it is very dangerous to offend and almost
impossible to attack'.[27] It says a great deal for the growth in
the actual and potential power of the United States that the
Americans were able to bundle Napoleon III's imperialisti-
cally-minded French troops out of Mexico as quickly as they
did – without any Great Power interfering – once the Civil
War was over.

America was respected, not least because the Americans had fought the first modern war. They had devised new weapons such as the breech-loading and repeating rifle, the railway gun, and the machine-gun (which mercifully was not adopted until the war was over). Their iron-plated men-of-war had influenced the change from wood and sail to iron and steam. They had shown themselves able to mobilise an entire nation and its economic resources; they had fought in masses and to the death.

Henceforth America's viewpoint was taken seriously by the world. In the Treaty of Washington of 1871 (a treaty which tried to resolve the outstanding differences between the United States and Britain, and which subsequently resulted in America being paid for the direct damages done by British-built Confederate cruisers during the war), it was American views on the duties of neutrals in time of war that prevailed.

Meanwhile, in war as in peace, the westward movement of the American people had gone on. Split between north and south, the nation never ceased to extend its frontiers to the west. Throughout the war small bands of migrants had continued to group on the banks of the Missouri and the Arkansas and headed west. Once hostilities had ceased, the wartime trickle quickly became a stream; by the 1870s, it had become a river. The road to the Far West was an 'all or nothing' undertaking. Once launched it was difficult to go back. 'Sacramento or Bust'; 'Portland or Bust' were the migrants' mottoes. Many busted. The sight of dead animals, abandoned possessions, and newly-dug graves left the migrant in no doubt as to his possible fate. 'The aged and the young die first', said one migrant. 'The women persevere best and set a brave example'. Francis Parkman, author of a famous account of the Oregon migration, wrote:

One morning, a piece of plank, standing upright on the summit of a grassy hill, attracted our notice, and riding up to it, we found the following words very roughly traced upon it, apparently with a red-hot piece of iron: Mary Ellis, Died May 7th 1845, aged two months. Such tokens were of common occurrence.[28]

The Donner party of migrants, who in the winter of 1846 became stranded in a pass of the Sierra Nevada mountains leading to Sacramento, gained immortality only by eating their dead companions.

Desperate as some of these conditions were, it would be quite false to think that the migrant's lot was all hardship and suffering. The migrants knew how to forge a community spirit and how to enjoy themselves when they could. If they had not been tough and resourceful and a little reckless, they never would have got as far as the Missouri.

Ironically, the names of those who went to sink their roots and build a better land have largely been forgotten. It is those whose purpose in 'westing' was to raise hell who have gained imperishable fame. Such were 'Wild Bill' Hickok, 'Calamity Jane', and the most famous of them all – William Bonney, Junior: 'Billy the Kid', whose 21 years of life were matched by 21 murders. 'To be a saloon keeper' in the west, as Mark Twain said, 'and kill a man, was to be illustrious'. Against the exploits of this group, the more mundane, permanent facts of frontier life have been forgotten.

The basic reasons for 'westing' were not unlike the motives of those who first came to this country from Europe; most migrants wanted to get away from something, or to obtain something they were not already getting.The satisfied never 'wested'. Pushed or pulled, most migrants felt sure that what they sought could be found just beyond the horizon. In 'God's country', there was land, gold and silver for all; and freedom greater than any men had known before. 'We cross the prairie [wrote Whittier, himself too wise to leave home] as of old the Pilgrims crossed the sea, To make the West, as they the East, The homestead of the free!'[29] Said one old westerner in 1890: 'We learned that "God's country" isn't in the country. It is in the mind. As we looked back we knew all the time we was hunting for "God's country" we had it. We worked hard. We was loyal. Honest. We was happy. For forty-eight years we lived together in "God's country".'[30] By then, 'westing' was over.

One of the most powerful stimulants of the earlier westward movement had been the 'strikes' of silver and gold in the

1840s. Beginning with the momentous find of gold at Sutter's Creek, near San Francisco, in January 1848, the 'rushes' for gold, silver, lead and copper followed one after another almost uninterruptedly until the 1880s. This was no steadily moving frontier but a series of mad dashes this way and that – as much from the west as the east – depending upon rumour, upon the movements of the American army, upon the attitudes of the Indian tribes, as well as upon season and transport.

No 'rush' equalled that to the banks of the Sacramento in 1848.

> Oh! California!
> That's the land for me;
> I'm off to Sacramento
> With my washbowl on my knee.

Overnight, once the cry of 'gold' had been heard, San Francisco became a deserted city. Rumour soon had it that the Sierra Nevada mountains were made of solid gold and silver; and, if they were not, there was certain to be a mountain farther on that was. By every possible means, from every continent, people flocked to California, the new land of promise. Off the coast, ships appeared from every part of the world. Soon, 500 of them were lying in the harbour without crews. By 1849, there were more than 50,000 prospectors in the foothills of the Sierra Nevadas. Every nationality and colour could be met with. In six years (1846–52), California's population leaped from about 10,000 to 250,000.

The discovery of gold in the mountains of California was followed by the discovery of gold in the Rocky Mountains. In 1859, gold and silver were found in what became the State of Colorado. The cry now was 'Pike's Peak or Bust!' One hundred thousand 'Busters' reached Pike's Peak in the 'rush' of the first year. The Comstock lode of silver, struck the following year (1860) in Nevada, by 1890 had yielded $340,000,000 of silver. It perhaps yielded more than this to promotors who unmercifully milked unsuspecting investors. Meanwhile other strikes of precious metals had been made in Idaho, Montana, Arizona, New Mexico and the Dakotas. By the eighties most of the mountain rivers and creeks from

Mexico to Canada had been worked out from their sources to
the sea; the digger with his washbowl had been replaced by
expensive equipment owned by vast corporations who hired
skilled 'Cousin Jacks'[31] from Cornwall, England – probably
the first miners to go to the Far West for a wage.

Out of it all, a few 'diggers' emerged richer than the kings of
old: most found that for years they had mined nothing but
disappointment. Disillusioned, some of them returned to 'the
States'; others sought their pot of gold elsewhere in the west
or in Australia. However transient and sometimes melan-
choly the mining frontier proved to be, the fact is that out of
this search for riches – for there never was a more frankly
material civilisation – came settled communities and trade,
churches, and schools (and in sharp contrast to the gang
terrorism and violence that marked the early mining towns),
an ordered, civilised life. Respectability in the West became
respectable. Exit the 'Hangtown gals . . . plump and rosy';
enter the Gothic American woman determined to make the
mining towns of the Far West 'a place fit to bring up children'.
Towns with names like 'Gouge Eye', 'Two Bit Gulch',
'Brandy City', 'Whiskey Digging', 'Deathball Creek', 'Hell's
Delight', and 'Poverty Bar', would die and be forgotten 'in the
lonely places of the West'; their whitening bones would one
day remind later generations of a mining frontier of scattered
settlements that in the second half of the nineteenth century
had swept across and helped to settle the Far West.

For America, the great gold 'strikes' ensured the con-
tinuance of gold as the principal currency metal; they assisted
America's balance of payments; and on a world front they
encouraged the abandoning of a bi-metallic standard of silver
and gold. At an international monetary conference held in
Paris in 1867, most countries voted in favour of adopting the
gold standard. Within five or six years, Sweden, Norway,
Denmark and Germany had done so. For all practical purposes, the United States followed their example (Britain had
changed to a gold coin standard in 1816) when, in 1873, it
ceased to mint the silver dollar.

As the miner and prospector pioneered in the Far West, so
the cattleman pioneered the Great Plains stretching from the

Missouri to the foothills of the Rockies, from the Red river in Texas to Manitoba.

By the late 1860s, encouraged by the overstocking of the Texas range (longhorns brought $4 a head at the end of the Civil War) and the growing demands of America and Europe for meat, thousands of cattle had begun the long drive from Texas to the railheads of Kansas and Nebraska. From the mid-sixties to the mid-eighties, about 5,500,000 cattle made the northward trek. Usually they were pastured and fattened on northern grass and feed before being shipped to the stockyards of Milwaukee, Kansas City, and Chicago (the coming of the refrigerator car in the 1870s enabled shipments to be made to the east and to Europe). As the railroads pierced the plains, the ranching frontier moved farther west.

By the end of the 1860s, the cattle industry depended upon the network of steam railways that carried their produce across the nation. They also depended upon the 'waddy', the cowpuncher, the 'Vaqueros' (what easterners called cowboys), who, for months at a time, drove the longhorns and later the white-faced cattle northwards. His escutcheon was his hat, his shirt, his pants, his spurs, and his pistols. His toughness, his chivalry, his nomadic existence, and his seemingly carefree frontier life obtained for him a permanent place as the supreme American folk hero. Through the mediums of film and television, he became as well known in Tokyo as in Kansas City.

Yet by the 1880s, the hey-day of the cowboy was over. Barbed wire (the 'devil's hatband') and state quarantine laws had curtailed the 'long drives'; the army of farmers and settlers brought by the railways had posed a threat to the cattleman's existence ('Oh, the cowboy and the farmer should be friends'); the enclosing of public land for pasture (in 1888, it was said that some 8,000,000 acres of land had been illegally enclosed for pasture) had reduced the cattleman's kingdom; the ranges had suffered from unusually cold winters and hot summers; the overexpansion of the cattle industry (encouraged by vast ranching corporations *formed from eastern and European capital), and the competitive pressure felt from the railroads on the one hand and from the highly monopolised meat-packing industry of Chicago, St Louis,

Kansas City, and Omaha on the other, had also reduced the industry's profitability. What this industry had meant in terms of increasing the world supply of beef and pork is reflected in the astonishing increase in exports, from an annual average of 26 million pounds (1852-6) to 368 million pounds (1897–1901) for beef, and 104 million pounds to 1·5 billion pounds for pork. Exports of cattle had risen from 1400 to 415,500.

Having helped to settle the great grazing lands of the west, the cowboy had to yield ground to a less colourful if more productive individual – the 'sod-buster', the 'plowchunky', the farmer – many of whom made a home in the plains out of a hole in the ground with sod for walls and roof and buffalo dung for warmth.[32] In the thirty years after 1870, with the aid of the Homestead Act of 1862 (which, in 160-acre lots, threw open the public domain for settlement to a citizen or intended citizen who was the head of a family), with improved rail transport (which carried Americans and Europeans westward), with the help of windmills for irrigation, the heavier and better farming implements and machinery to break the stubborn prairie sod, 430,000,000 acres of the Great Plains were occupied.[33] There resulted an avalanche of grains and flour. Between 1852–6 and 1897–1901, the average annual exports of wheat and wheat flour grew from 19 to 197 million bushels; there was a similar rise in the exports of corn and corn meal from 7 to 192·5 million bushels.

Even this new vast domain in the American west could not satisfy America's land hunger. Eager pioneers pushed into western Kansas and Nebraska. Nebraska's population jumped from 123,000 in 1870 to over 1,000,000 in 1890; that of Kansas, in the same years, rose from a third of a million to 1,500,000. The farmer trod on the rancher, and the rancher and the farmer together (aided and abetted by all the other interests; railroads, mining, timber and real estate companies) trod on the original owners of the land – the Indians. By the late 1870s, an intense and organised campaign had developed to throw open all Indian territory in the west to the whites. In the 1870s and 1880s, the seizing of Indian territory was only prevented by the use of Federal troops. Yet no authority could stop the westward movement of the migrant. Eventually on 2 March 1889, Congress agreed to transfer certain unassigned lands at the heart of Indian territory to the public domain. Less than two months later, on 22 April 1889, at the sound of a gun:

the clear, sweet notes of a cavalry bugle rose and hung a moment upon the startled air. It was noon. The last barrier of savagery in the United States was broken down. Moved by the same impulse, each driver lashed his horses furiously; each rider dug his spurs into his willing steed, and each man on foot caught his breath hard and darted forward. A cloud of dust rose where the home-seekers had stood in line, and when it had drifted away before the gentle breeze, the horses and wagons and men were tearing across the open country like fiends. . . . Some of the men who started from the line on foot were quite as successful in securing desirable claims as many who rode fleet horses. . . . One man left the line with the others, carrying on his back a tent, a blanket, some camp dishes, an axe and provisions for two days. He ran down the railway track for six miles, and reached his claim in just sixty minutes. Upon arriving on his land he fell down under a tree, unable to speak or see.[34]

A flood of 50,000 white settlers poured like an avalanche into the last great Indian reservation. By nightfall, under conditions of utter pandemonium, almost 2,000,000 acres of land had been claimed, most of it to be sold again. Within half a day, Guthrie and Oklahoma City, each with an instant population of 10,000, had come into being.

The opening of Oklahoma in 1889 was followed by white settler invasion into one western Indian reserve after another. In 1891 the white agricultural frontier burst across the Sac and Fox, Iowa, Shawnee and Potawatomi reserves east of Oklahoma Territory. In 1892, Cheyenne and Arapaho lands farther west were invaded. In 1893 the Cherokee Outlet was occupied by white settlers in search of land. Three years earlier, in 1890, the United States Census Director had announced the end of the frontier with the words, 'There can hardly be said to be a frontier line'.[35] Through tears, sweat and blood, the real west, stretching from the Mississippi to the

Rockies, had been occupied by the white race. The curtain
had fallen on one of the greatest acts of colonisation.

With the passing of the frontier, the American dream of a
rural, land-owning democracy died. The reality for most of
those who had searched for 'God's country' was debt and
tenancy. With few material resources, it only required a
couple of bad harvests for solvency to give way to destitution.
Indeed, in the late eighties, many homesteaders had given up
the struggle against fire, debt, drought, and had become part
of a widespread retreat from the inhospitable plains. On the
arid or semi-arid plain, 160 acres, adequate elsewhere, had
proved to be too small an acreage on which to survive. From
1880 onwards, through the monopolies in real estate, railways, timber and mining, the little man was being squeezed
out of the public domain. Kansas lost 180,000 people between 1887 and 1891; in 1891 alone, 18,000 eastbound
prairie schooners were counted crossing the Missouri river
bridge at Omaha. Between 1889–93, more than 11,000 farms
had been surrendered to mortgage companies, many of which
were themselves bankrupt. As an anonymous Kansas homesteader lamented:

> But hurrah for Lane County, the land of the free,
> The home of the grasshopper, bedbug and flea,
> I'll sing loud her praises and boast of her fame,
> While starving to death on my government claim.[36]

A Kansas housewife wrote to the Governor of her State on 29
June 1894: 'I take my pen in hand to let you know that we are
starving to death. . . .'[37] As a champion of the farmer's cause
(William A. Peffer, United States Senator) put it: the railroad
builder 'took possession of the land'; and the moneychanger
'took possession of the farmer'.[38] For some time yet, the great
cities of the east and the mid-west would continue to absorb
all the migrants Europe could send. But the dream-age, when
a poor man need only walk into the sunset to obtain the good
earth, was over.

To the aboriginal Indians, the movement of white Americans from the Mississippi to the west coast was the last,
desperate chapter in a struggle that had gone on for more than

300 years. Repeatedly the boundaries of the Indian reservations had been encroached upon; the white man's word broken. 'Many, if not most, of our Indian wars', said President Hayes in a message to Congress in 1877, 'have had their origin in broken promises and acts of injustice upon our part'. Neither the Proclamation of 1763, that recognised the Indians' right to their land; nor the Northwest Ordinance of 1787; nor the opinion of Chief Justice John Marshall, rendered in 1832,[39] had halted the onward rush of the white man.

By the 1830s the whites had resorted to open coercion. Amost 100,000 members of the five civilised tribes of the southeast were exiled to the Indian Territory (Oklahoma) west of the Mississippi. But even there they found no peace. The perpetual title to this territory assigned to them became a dead letter. Instead the whole Indian community west of the Mississippi found itself increasingly squeezed between the mining, the ranching, the farming, and the railway frontiers. Indian land was invaded, the game killed, forts built. It did not matter whether the tribes were utilizing the land as efficiently as the white man or not, or how moderately prosperous their agricultural economies had become: nothing mattered except getting the Indian out of the way. Black Elk, an Oglala Sioux leader, recounted the invasion of Sioux lands between 1863 and 1890 thus:

... everyone was saying that the Wasichus [white men] were coming and that they were going to take our country and rub us all out and that we should all have to die fighting. . . . Once we were happy in our own country and we were seldom hungry, for then the two-leggeds and the four-leggeds lived together like relatives, and there was plenty for them and for us. But the Wasichus came, and they have made little islands for us and other little islands for the four-leggeds, and always these islands are becoming smaller, for around them surges the gnawing flood of the Wasichu; and it is dirty with lies and greed. . . . That fall [1883], . . . the last of the bison herds was slaughtered by the Wasichus. . . . The Wasichus did not kill them to eat; they killed them for the metal that makes them crazy. . . . Sometimes they did not even take the hides, only the tongues. . . .'[40]

By 1883, about 13,000,000 buffalo had been killed.[41]

   In desperation the Indians had struck back; onto the Great Plains rode the American army ('Dog face', to the Indians). From 1862, an almost constant military campaign was fought. Yet for all its numbers and superior arms, the American army did not sweep across the western plains with the same speed as, at an earlier point in history, the Asian hordes had swept to the outposts of Europe. By the skilful and courageous use of one of the finest light cavalry known to history, the Indians were able to deny the white man total victory for twenty-five years. The Cheyenne–Arapaho War of 1861–4 was accompanied by the First Sioux War of 1862–7. The discovery, in the sixties, of gold in the sacred Black Hills of the Sioux, together with the encroachment of the railrods, caused the Sioux tribes to unite, under Sitting Bull and Crazy Horse, with the Cheyennes. There followed the Second Sioux War of 1875–6, a last, vain attempt by these tribes to retain their communal lands. 'One does not sell the earth', said Crazy Horse. But to buy and sell individual private property in land was indispensable to the white man's life. Six thousand 'braves' were committed to battle. Meanwhile, also in the 1870s, in the Pacific Northwest, the Nez Percé tribes under Chief Joseph had fought their way to within sight of Canada. Defeated almost on the border, the Nez Percé were exiled to Oklahoma, only to be swept aside by the white invasion of 1889–93. In the 1870s, war had spread to the Apache (who raided and fought in small bands led by men like Geronimo) in Arizona and New Mexico. The last great clash was the Ghost Dance War of 1890 with the Teton Sioux of the Black Hills.

   Across the years (1860s–90s) are written the battles of New Ulm, Sand Creek, Washita, Rosebud, the Little Big Horn, Salt River Canyon, Wounded Knee, and a score of others. Sometimes the Indians won temporary relief, as Crazy Horse did for the Sioux and the Cheyenne at the Battle of the Rosebud in 1876, or when Sitting Bull annihilated Colonel Custer and his troops at the Battle of the Little Big Horn; but eventually the white tide returned to engulf them. For the red man, there was no escape, no compromise he could make, no terms he could accept save death or exile. It was the opinion of General Philip Sheridan, commissioned after the surrender of the Confederate forces at Appomattox in 1865 to 'pacify' a wide section of the frontier, that 'There are no good Indians but dead Indians'.

In the atrocities committed against each other, there is nothing to choose between the conduct of one side or another. The quiet of a scholar's study is the place for reason, not a battlefield. No quarter was given to woman or child. 'There was one little child, probably three years old, just big enough to walk through the sand . . .' recalled Major Scott J. Anthony, giving evidence before a committee[42] that enquired into the Sand Creek Massacre of 1864 (perpetrated not by the regular Army but by a civilian militia.[43] '. . . the Indians had gone ahead, and this little child was behind following after them. . . . I saw one man get off his horse, at a distance of about 75 yards and draw up his rifle and fire. He missed the child. Another man came up and said, "Let me try the son of a bitch; I can hit him",' the Major said. 'He got down . . . but he missed. A third man came up and . . . fired, and the little fellow dropped.' Lt Cramer's testimony was: '. . . The women and children were huddled together, and most of our fire was concentrated on them. . . . I told Colonel Chivington . . . that it would be murder, in every sense of the word, if he attacked those Indians. His reply was, ". . . Damn any man who sympathizes with Indians!" . . . he had come to kill Indians, and believed it to be honourable to kill Indians under any and all circumstances'. And Lt J. D. Connor: '. . . in going over the battleground the next day I did not see a body of man, woman, or child but was scalped, and in many instances their bodies were mutilated in the most horrible manner'. Black Elk said of the 'Massacre' of Wounded Knee of 1890 in the Dakotas, 'We followed down along the dry gulch, and what we saw was terrible. . . . it was one long grave of butchered women and children and babies, who had never done any harm and were only trying to run away. . . . I did not know then how much was ended. . . . A people's dream died there. . . . the nation's hoop is broken and scattered. There is no center any longer, and the sacred tree is dead'.[44]

In time, the white man's wish was granted. By the 1890s, peace had returned to the west; the longest civil war was

over; most Indian chiefs were dead; the few that remained
were exhausted. 'I am tired of fighting', a great Indian warrior
and statesman said. 'Our chiefs are killed. . . . The old men
are all killed. . . . The little children are freezing to death. My
people, some of them, have run away to the hills and have no
blankets, no food; no one knows where they are, perhaps
freezing to death. I want to have time to look for my children
and see how many of them I can find. Maybe I shall find them
among the dead. Hear me, my chiefs, I am tired; my heart is
sick and sad. From where the sun now stands, I will fight no
more forever'.[45] Yet his people, decimated, torn apart, scattered to the winds, did not die. Those who survived clung to
life with the same tenacity they had shown when fighting the
white invader. In time, they began to multiply (Indians in the
United States now number more than 800,000)[46] and, as they
did, they won acceptance (in word if not in deed) as brothers
in the white man's house.[47]

Thus did the white man's aggressive civilisation prevail;
thus did the common man win 'God's country'. For while the
conquest of the American west was an act of epic proportions,
it was essentially the work of ordinary, unpretentious individuals like the folk heroes, Kit Carson and Dan'l Boone.
There emerged the legends and traditions of the sod-house
frontier, the Pony Express, the Lonely Rider, the Western
Stagecoach, the Conestoga Wagon, the handcarts of the
Mormon 'saints' *en route* to Utah, the little red school house,
and the small white church.

It was a scene that echoed the thunder of animals' hooves,
the crack of the buffalo whip, and the assassin's bullet. It
heard the war whoop of the Indian braves and the cavalry
bugle's call to arms. Across it all, sounded the note of the
lonely fiddle and the din and tumult of the 'digger' and the
cowboy coming to town for whisky and doings.

The eventual transformation of the American wilderness
into farms and towns provided a legacy of spiritual optimism
and exuberance. It confirmed them in their belief as the
Chosen People. It made the American familiar with conditions of boom and bust. It taught him to think big: where was
there a river, a desert, or a mountain that he couldn't cross, an
enemy that he couldn't defeat? Not least, it left a social

tradition of nomadism. Never had there been such a 'restless, roving, rummaging, ragged multitude'.[48] The fluidity and turbulence of the frontier shattered the European peasant's static view of life. Unlike the colonisation by the Europeans of the other great temperate areas of the world, America let loose a human whirlwind that no authority could temper. Hence, the dichotomy in America's history between the idealism of the official voice and the facts of frontier life. The price of rapid, disorderly colonisation was waste and suffering (in contrast to the more orderly if slower development of Canada and Australia). Its rewards were wealth and opportunity for the western world on an unprecedented scale.

By the 1890s, the continental expansion of the United States was complete; its natural frontiers had been rounded out. The United States now occupied an area of 3·6 million square miles, the equivalent of Europe's total (including European Russia). Certain of its States, such as Texas and California, were larger than the largest European countries. Increasingly now, Americans felt that their manifest destiny called them across the seas.[49]

Encouraging them in their overseas expansion was the belief in their role as God's Chosen People. 'God,' said Senator Beveridge of Indiana, '. . . has made us the master organizers of the world to establish system where chaos reigns. . . . And of all our race He has marked the American people as His Chosen Nation finally to lead in the regeneration of the world.'[50] Or, as Herman Melville put it: '. . . we Americans are peculiar, chosen people, the Israel of our times; we bear the ark of the liberties of the world'.[51]

Chosen or not, the outcome would be the triumph of the Anglo-Saxon race. In his book, *Our Country* (1885), Josiah Strong wrote: 'This race [of Anglo-Saxons] . . . having developed peculiarly aggressive traits calculated to impress its institutions upon mankind, will spread itself over the earth. If I read not amiss, this powerful race will move down upon Mexico, down upon Central and South America, out upon the islands of the sea, over upon Africa and beyond.[52] Earlier, Darwin had written in *The Descent of Man* (1871): 'There is apparently much truth in the belief that the wonderful progress of the United States, as well as the character of the

people, are the results of natural selection: the more energe-
tic, restless, and courageous men from all parts of Europe
having emigrated during the last ten or twelve generations to
that great country, and having there succeeded best'.[53]

The sense of moral righteousness – the dichotomy between
word and deed – permeates American conduct abroad as it
did during the period of continental expansion. President
Cleveland in 1893 could refuse to submit a treaty of annexation of Hawaii to the Senate on the grounds of 'international
morality':

It has been the boast of our Government that it seeks to do
justice in all things without regard to the strength or weakness
of those with whom it deals. . . . I mistake the American
people if they favor the odious doctrine that there is one law
for the strong nation and another for a weak one, and that
even by indirection a strong power may with impunity despoil
a weak one of its territory.[54]

Yet *The Nation*, writing in 1894, could say, 'The number of
men and officials in this country who are now mad to fight
somebody is appalling'.[55] It was partly the din kept up by the
yellow press in 1898, coupled with the mysterious destruction
of the U.S.S. *Maine* in Havana harbour at this time with the
loss of over 250 lives, that forced President McKinley to yield
to war clamour despite the fact that Spain had already agreed
to every condition for peace. There followed the invasion of
Cuba and the Philippines, the annexation of Hawaii and other
islands (Puerto Rico, Guam, Wake and Tutuila), and the
military and commercial invasion of China.

McKinley could quiet his conscience with a dream which
enabled him to look upon the Philippines as 'unfit for
self-government', and compelled him to 'uplift and civilize
and Christianize them'.[56] Theodore Roosevelt was in no
doubt that the Spanish–American War, in which he played his
own conspicuous part, was 'the most absolutely righteous
foreign war of the nineteenth century'.[57] However righteous,
the outcome was to suppress Filipino aspirations for freedom
and independence. Right had to yield to might in Roosevelt's
acquisition of the Panama Canal Zone in 1903. Force was
threatened in the United States–Canadian Alaskan Boundary Dispute of the same year. Yet, when Roosevelt again

sought the nomination for Presidency in 1912, he ended his speech: 'We stand at Armageddon and we battle for the Lord'. To which his followers responded: 'Onward Christian soldiers, marching as to war. . . .'*

America's supreme moral outlook was especially evident in President Wilson's conduct at Versailles in 1919. Clemenceau is purported to have asked, why did Wilson need fourteen points when Christ himself had managed with ten. The truth is, Wilson was able to distinguish right from wrong, good from bad, in such a simple American way as to be offensive to his European counterparts, many of whom thought him a hypocrite. The thread of historical *naiveté* runs through all that the Americans have done. Secretary Kellogg's Pact of 1928, which outlawed war but provided no facilities for enforcing peace, was completely ineffective in policing the world. President Roosevelt's attitude towards Stalin during the Second World War, as well as President Eisenhower's relations with the Russian General Zhukov in 1955,[58] are different aspects of the same story. What this *naiveté* has cost the world since 1945, it would be hard to say.

Since the Second World War, the emphasis has shifted to the economic side of imperialism. (See Chapters IV and V.) According to the Marxist point of view,[59] the Americans, having satisfied their territorial ambitions through acquiring a land empire in North America, now seek power through the extension of their economic interests abroad. American business, in its search for profits, has reached a stage where it can only survive by increasingly exploiting world markets, world capital, and world resources. It has in fact become anational. Especially has American foreign business activity been stimulated by the need to safeguard the supply of indispensable raw materials. In 1972, 40 per cent of total foreign United States direct investment was concerned with the exploitation of world mineral resources. Global companies such as Exxon have more than half their total assets abroad.

Yet to say that the scramble for territory before 1870, and the scramble for markets, raw materials and outlets for

*The previous year Senator Taft and several Congressmen had caused a storm in Canada, and the outright rejection of a reciprocal trade agreement, when they spoke of it as being the prelude to annexation.

investment after 1870, are the main forces behind American expansion is surely oversimplifying things. The idea that the only alternative for America to the choking of the domestic market was foreign aggrandisement is to place too great a stress on the inner necessity of capitalism to expand or die. The Americans are undoubtedly a market-oriented people, but one can make too much of that point. Even on the score of territorial aggrandisement, which we have spoken of at length, there is another side to the American medal. Despite all the filibustering that went on at the time, Canada remained free. Texas was refused admission to the Union for a decade; and Polk was eventually content to deed the northern part of Oregon to England. The wonder about Mexico is not that the Americans took so much of its territory but that they did not take the lot. The *Ostend Manifesto* of 1855, aimed at seizing Cuba, did not result in Cuba's annexation but in the repudiation of those who drafted it. To acquire Alaska, members of Congress had to be bribed. Hawaii had to wait fifty years and the war of 1898 before it was annexed. (And that is precisely when a powerful anti-imperialist movement in America arose.) Is it likely that a country which could give back freedom to the Filipinos, and offer it and have it rejected by the Puerto Ricans, would contemplate ruling the world? The basic cause, it seems to us, behind American expansion (as that of the other Great Powers) was not economics but politics. The struggle for power has had greater importance in world history than the search for profits. (Does anyone believe that America's present outer-space adventures have been prompted by American capitalists seeking to carve out vast new markets on the moon?)

The Americans may have been more idealistic and ethical in their outlook; more convinced than others that they had a mission to the world – a mission that, as the twentieth century progresses, moves increasingly from the spiritual and the political to the secular and the economic. They may have assumed that whatever territories they acquired would accept the American way of life. Basically, however, they have been involved with the same problems of disparate power that have confronted the other imperial nations. They have differed from the rest chiefly in ascribing a purity of motive to themselves that no people can possess.

CHAPTER III
Americans in a World Context

THE discovery and settlement of America set afoot a migration and mixing of the world's people that is without precedent.[1] Of the tide of Europeans that flowed westwards, no country took more than the United States.[2] In the past two hundred years, Americans have increased their numbers almost fiftyfold – from four million in 1790 to 200 million in 1970.[3] This fiftyfold increase was ten times greater than the increase in world population during the same period; indeed, until the 1930s, the influx of migrants into the United States played a greater role in increasing American numbers than did the natural increase of its people. One can only conjecture what Europe lost in providing America with a constant stream of adult, and sometimes highly skilled, people.

The bulk of these immigrants came from Britain, Ireland, Italy, Austria-Hungary, Germany, Spain, Russia, Portugal and Scandinavia. Until the 1880s, those coming from northwest Europe predominated. By 1914, however, about three-quarters of the immigrants entering the United States came from southern and eastern Europe. Essentially the United States provided a safety valve for Europe's excess numbers. Those displaced by the radical changes in western European agriculture and industry in the nineteenth and twentieth centuries obtained relief by emigrating to the New World. Necessity and hope spurred them on. Until the development of American industry at the end of the nineteenth century, land was the greatest lure. The outcome was reallocation of world resources. Labour and capital were taken from where they were relatively plentiful to where, in the early United States, they were relatively scarce. Economically, at least, the world – that is, the European world – was better off.

Great as the human concourse to the New World was, Europe's overall numbers continued to rise. In fact, between 1750 and 1900, they are high compared with the average annual rate of world population growth.[4] Even Italy's population, whose migrants between 1846 and 1924 totalled 9½ million, continued to grow (from about 24 million in 1850 to 38 million in 1920). Ireland was the exception; as a result of terrible famine and economic distress, numbers fell from 8 million in 1846 to under 4½ in 1901.

The effect in Europe was to depopulate certain regions rather than to cause a decline in overall numbers. In the eighteenth century, a silence fell upon the Scottish highlands after the crofters had left. The Canton of Bern in Switzerland feared an almost complete depopulation. Six counties alone, out of the thirty-two in Ireland, accounted for almost half of the total Irish emigration up to 1900. By then, it was estimated that from one-fifth to one-quarter of the total male labour force of Greece had left for the United States. The exodus of the Italian peasantry to America in the early 1900s, we are told, ' . . . left villages deserted, fields uncultivated, and herds unwatched . . . wages doubled and in some instances tripled as desperate landlords attempted to stem the flood'.[5] In 1908 an Italian-American wrote of his travels through southern Italy: 'We passed through Positano, a quaint town perched on the hillside, which has been abandoned by its male inhabitants, all of whom are in America'.[6] Similarly

. . . Half of the village of Trivigno in Luciania had gone to America by 1906. In the same year Laurenzana, which had once boasted a population of 7300, contained only 3000. Most striking among the larger centers was Alcamo in Sicily, seat of a very heavy migration to America, which lost 20,000 of its resident population of 51,000 between 1901 and 1911. Among whole provinces, Campobasso (Abruzzi) fell by 16,000, Potenza (Lucania) by 16,000, and Trapani (Sicily) by 10,000.[7]

It was conditions such as these that eventually awakened the social and national conscience of many Europeans to the losses that the exodus entailed. In Scandinavia, Italy, Greece and Germany, societies were formed to curtail emigration.[8]

Instead of driving people off the national soil, efforts were made to obtain improved social insurance, land laws, and taxation.[9] Emigration was no longer looked upon as the draining off of the more undesirable elements of society – the unwanted misfits – but the direct loss of the children a country had taken the trouble and the cost to rear; the sapping of its productive and military strength. A country ought to be able to devise a policy whereby its citizens could be retained. Moreover given the right standards of agricultural and industrial technology, it might be possible to bring back some of those who had already left. The power of the free market to buy and sell labour on a world scale should be controlled. America had taken enough of Europe's sons and daughters. By 1922 even liberal Britain had begun to subsidise emigration to its Empire. But by then America was showing signs through its new restrictive immigration laws that the 'melting pot' was full.

The discovery and colonisation of the New World also affected the people of Africa and Asia. As a result, about one-third of all people of African descent now live outside Africa.[10] Moreover unlike Europe (and Asia) whose numbers grew between 1650 and 1850, African numbers declined. Rough estimates put the number of those enslaved to work in the New World in the period 1510[11] to 1890[12] between 15 and 20 million.[13] Slaves were used to meet the growing world demand for tropical produce from Brazil, the Caribbean (especially sugar), and, later, the American south (tobacco, rice, indigo and cotton).

Nothing equalled in importance the growth of cotton cultivation. By 1808, the number of slaves entering the United States had fallen considerably. The growing antipathy toward slavery and the decline in the profitability of southern staples offered hope that the trade in human beings might decline. Then came the Industrial Revolution with its insatiable demands for raw cotton, and a dying slave trade was revived.[14] Its brutalising effect on black and white would leave its mark for generations to come.

Slavery also changed the nature of Africa's trade with the rest of the world. By the nineteenth century, the old African commodities of exchange had been eclipsed by the trade in human beings. Quite apart from the devastating effect of firearms and rum, the flooding of African markets with cheap British cottons and metals discouraged the development of African handicraft industries. Slavery drained many African tribes of their life and talents.

America's need for African slaves was an almost total loss to African society. Coastal and near-coastal areas were forced to develop a monoculture in human beings, out of which only America and Europe, and some of the slave-trading states of west and east Africa, stood to gain. None of the wealth carried away by the Europeans ever returned to enrich Africa. Instead, there resulted a state of political anarchy without parallel; many of the coastal people became 'enmeshed in a spiral of mounting violence'.[15] States such as Benin, Dahomey and Asante 'diverted their energies from the peaceful development of politics, arts and culture to preoccupation with slaving wars and wanton destruction'.[16]

Yet, important as America's impact on Africa was, slavery was not some enormous evil inflicted by the white man on the black. The white man undoubtedly caused slavery to appear in districts where hitherto it had been unknown – but he enlarged an already existing practice among blacks, and between blacks and Arabs that stretched from antiquity to the present day. It was the leaders of west African tribes who, continuing to snare their fellow-blacks from further inland, resisted abolition to the end. In the highly centralised monarchy of Dahomey, the slave trade was a state enterprise.

The catalyst causing the movement of Asians to America was not cotton but gold. The gold 'rushes' of the 1840s–50s caused the number of Chinese immigrants to jump from eight individuals in 1840 to 50 in 1848, 25,000 in 1852, and 35,000 in 1860.[17] The total in 1870 was 64,000, most of them young, male, agricultural peasants coming from the farming districts of Kwang Tung in south China. Their intention was to obtain enough to support their families in China, as well as to provide themselves with a small 'nest-egg' with which they might return. Social prejudice prevented the emigration of upper-class Chinese and of women.

In addition to working on the gold fields of the Far West, the Chinese helped to build the railroads and provide labour in the cities. Growing opposition to them, however, culminated in the Chinese Exclusion Act of 1882, when there were 132,000 Chinese in the United States. Continuing discrimination and rough treatment (including a massacre of nineteen of them in 1885) reduced the figure to 74,954 (30,868 of them American-born). In 1943, mainland China became an ally of the United States; as a result, the Chinese Exclusion Act was repealed. However, the new quota only allowed for 105 Chinese immigrants annually. In 1965, to accomodate certain Taiwanese as well as refugees from the Asian mainland, the number was increased. Yet the effect on China was inconsequential.

The Japanese followed the Chinese. From 1868 to 1924, approximately 200,000 of them entered the United States. Like the Chinese, they provided cheap labour, but, unlike them, they sought to remain in Hawaii and the United States permanently. Race prejudice decided otherwise. From 1908 onwards, efforts were made to squeeze them out.* As Asians they were further discriminated against by the introduction of the Quota Acts of 1921 and 1924. Japan's response was to observe a 'Day of National Humiliation'. Worse was to come. In 1942 the Supreme Court approved the 'relocation' in semi-concentration camps of 112,000 of the west-coast Japanese, two-thirds of them United States citizens by birth.

Of the other groups coming from Asia and the Pacific – Turks, Armenians, Syrians, Arabs, Palestinian Jews, Filipinos and Hawaiians – only the Palestinian Jews, because of their religious ties with Israel and with other American Jews, can be said to have had much influence on their homeland.

The Quota Acts of the 1920s, in curtailing European and Asian immigration increased that from the American hemisphere. In 1970 the Mexicans (with five million) were, next to the Negroes, the nation's second largest minority. But here again, their impact has been felt more in the United States than in the immigrant's country of origin.

*In 1919 at Versailles President Wilson opposed a Japanese motion prescribing race equality.

The opposite is true of the Canadians. So great has been the lure of America that only 10 per cent of the immigrants entering Canada between 1851 and 1950 stayed there permanently. In 1930 there were more than three million people born of Canadian parents living in the United States.

An exception must also be made for the drain of talents and skills (the so-called 'brain drain')[18] from the other continents to America since 1945. (Between 1949 and 1967, about 100,000 doctors, scientists and technicians came from abroad.) As with immigrants generally, the lure was better economic prospects. The result was a clear economic gain for the United States and an equally clear loss of training costs and future potential to others – especially to countries in the underdeveloped world.

Many of those who were drawn to the United States subsequently returned to their native land, taking something of America back with them. Such were the 'birds of passage' (who came and went from the United States in their millions from the 1880s onwards) whose chief aim was to obtain sufficient wealth to afford a better existence in Europe ('he who crosses the ocean buys a house'). Hence, 40 per cent of the total immigration into the United States between 1890 and 1910 (12½ million) returned to Europe, most of them for good. Fifty per cent of the Finns who came returned. Of Greek immigrants in the period 1908–23, about 46 per cent went home.[19] Of the almost two million Italians who came between 1902 and 1921, 60 per cent were repatriated.[20] At the end of the nineteenth and during the first two decades of the twentieth century, national organisations in Sweden and Norway encouraged the flow.[21]

So many of these immigrants eventually returned to the land of their birth that they were given special names. In Italy, they were known as 'Americani'; in Ireland, 'returned Yank'; in Greece, 'Brooklis' (Greeks who went to America were thought to live in Brooklyn). Other names existed, such as 'Yankee-des' or 'okay-boys'.[22] Because they slipped back unnoticed into the urbanised, industrial life from which most had come, there was no special name for British repatriates.

While some of these migrants returned to their homeland disillusioned, others were able to tell wondrous tales of the rich land across the seas (sometimes at a commission of so much per head for those they could encourage to try their luck in the New World). Exaggerated or not, America became a byword for riches and social and political equality. Repatriates returned with a new sense of class equality and of the need for universal suffrage, as well as a new tolerance for other people's religions. Many carried the struggle for democracy and freedom (including black freedom) from the New World to the Old. Some bore with them American attitudes toward teetotalism and prison reform. Not a few occupied important positions on returning to Europe.[23] Their influence on the agriculture and industry of continental Europe, however (except for the Swedish-Americans who bought farms in Scandinavia), appears to have been slight. The Italian repatriates to central and southern Italy were content to purchase a little of their native soil (often at inflated prices and in such small quantities as to increase the parcellisation of the land),[24] build a house of their own, and sit

. . . like gentlemen at home or in the *piazza* telling stories of the wondrous land beyond the ocean. They were marked in various ways: by derbies and overcoats, by cigars and gold chains, by American slang and curses, and by an air of affluence and worldly wisdom.[25]

American emigrants returning to their ancestral home were black as well as white. Paul Cuffe (a half Negro and half Indian American Quaker) carried black immigrants to Sierra Leone in his own ship in 1816.[26] A large number of American Negroes who had fought on the British side in the War of Independence had preceded them. With the assistance of the American Colonisation Society (founded in 1816) and the personal intervention of President Monroe, other Negroes followed. By the 1820s, under the leadership of a white American, Jehudi Ashmun, and Joseph Jenkins Roberts (a Virginian of mixed white and black ancestry), black Americans were going to Monrovia (the scene of an earlier unsuccessful attempt at colonisation), later to be called Liberia. Thenceforth, until Liberia was proclaimed an independent republic in 1847, white and black Americans were active in building up Liberia's community of freed slaves. The armed conflicts which the new black immigrants had with local tribes were openly assisted by the United States Navy. A digest of laws was provided, foreign commerce was assisted, and a democratic constitution adopted. Yet at the time of Liberia's independence in 1847, immigrants from the United States and their descendents were fewer than 3000. By then the movement had lost its impetus. The emancipation of the American Negro in the 1860s put an end to it. Yet America's economic impact on Liberia during the past 100 years has grown, not lessened, as the history of the rubber, iron ore, and shipping industries bears out. In no other African country has America had more influence. Liberia's early American origins partly explain why in 1914 it was one of only two African countries free of European tutelage.

In contrast to the groups of resident aliens who came and went from the United States in droves, American citizens have made their way abroad since the earliest days of the Republic. In 1900 there were 91,219 of them. Between the two Great Wars the figure rose to approximately half a million. By 1970, as a result of America's economic and political expansion, there were 1,737,836.[27] Only recently, however, have Americans migrated (as Europeans did in the nineteenth century) to start a new life elsewhere. In the five years, 1965–70, about ten thousand of them emigrated to Australia.

Since independence, American activities abroad have been widespread. One author writes:

By the mid-nineteenth century, many individual Americans in the East had made a contribution, for good or ill: the vivacious Asahel Grant, for instance, without whom a slaughter of several thousand Christians in Kurdistan might not have taken place; Eckford and Rhodes, whose shipbuilding skill rehabilitated the Turkish navy; Dwight and Goodell, who helped engineer a precarious toleration for the tiny Protestant minority among the Turks; Robinson, who laid the groundwork for the study of the archaeology of the Holy Land; Lynch, the first successful navigator of the Jordan River; and the Yankee traders whose hustling efficiency made Turkish opium available in such profusion in the Far East.[28]

The rapid growth of American commerce in the eighteenth and nineteenth centuries increased the number of American merchants and businessmen abroad. By the 1830s, business agents of every kind (in trade, transport, banking and insurance) were to be found across the world, particularly in western Europe. By then, there was no major trading port or whaling station on any continent or island that did not have its American representative. Early Yankee proclivity for turning a profit anywhere is illustrated by Jonathan Lambert and Richard Cleveland who took possession of the deserted island of Tristan da Cunha in the South Atlantic with the hope of selling provisions to passing ships.

In the twentieth century (particularly since 1945), the number of American businessmen living abroad (some working for themselves, most of them representing United States-based business and industrial enterprises) has grown rapidly. Americans now control much of the world's electronic industry, auto-making, chemicals, farming machinery, and oil refining. Many corporations, such as Exxon (formerly Jersey Standard Oil), Ford, and Dow Chemical, are global; some of them with the majority of their assets abroad. In 1967, 4200 American corporations controlled 14,000 foreign business enterprises.[29] It is the professional and technical employees of these United States global, multi-national corporations, together with business managers and officials, who today make up the largest occupational group (especially if we include their families) of American civilians employed abroad.

The American businessman abroad has helped to create new forms of industry, new and higher standards of technical and commercial efficiency, and new opportunities for employment and economic growth and development. However, not everyone sees this as a good thing. Some Europeans and others feel that they are in danger of becoming the commercial (and political) vassals of the United States.

Fifteen years from now [says one European], it is quite possible that the world's third greatest industrial power, just after the United States and Russia, will not be Europe, but American industry in Europe. . . . What threatens to crush us today is not a torrent of riches, but a more intelligent use of skills. . . . This war – and it is a war – is being fought not with dollars, or oil, or steel, or even with modern machines. It is being fought with creative imagination and organisational talent.[30]

The American businessman abroad is concerned with the production of material goods, with economic efficiency, and with higher levels of living; in short, with ever-growing affluence and the fundamentals of technology. Not surprisingly, while America's business presence in the non-western world is growing, these aspects of Americanisation have had less appeal and effect where traditional ethics and social organisation have been at variance with the west.

Especially important has been America's spiritual impact upon others,[31] exercised chiefly through the Protestant missions (but also uniquely for America through the religious revivalists who have influenced the English-speaking world since the days of Jonathan Edwards). The first genuine missionary society in colonial America was the Society for the Propagation of the Gospel in New England, formed in 1649, whose object was the conversion of the Indians of Massachusetts. Even earlier the Charters of Virginia and Massachusetts had mentioned the propagation of religion. In the eighteenth century, with the Protestants of western Europe, the Americans became increasingly conscious of their missionary obligation. Influenced by German and British example, the American Board of Commissioners for Foreign Missions was formed in Massachusetts in 1806.[32] Serving chiefly the Congregationalist, Presbyterian and Reformed Churches, the Board sent out its first missionary, Adoniram Judson, to Burma in 1813; the second, John Scudder, reached Ceylon in 1819. Thenceforth, as the west penetrated larger parts of the earth, the Gospel was carried by these and other Protestant churches (Baptists since 1814, Methodists since 1819). Two American Protestant missionaries, David Abeel and Dr Elijah C. Bridgman, reached Canton in 1829.* Two others reached Java in 1834 – Henry Lyman and Samuel Munson – but were both martyred on arrival.[33] Under the guidance of black Americans, Africa became a missionary

*The famous surgeon missionary Peter Parker arrived in 1834.

field in the 1820s. The blacks received no better reception than the whites who followed them, and, healthwise, they lasted no longer. Yet, by the 1830s–40s, American Protestant missionary outposts had been established in the Cape Province as well as at the mouth of the Gabon River[34] and in Liberia.

While the task of these missions was to convert the heathen, the Gospel was also carried to those of other religions, as well as to Protestant immigrants in South America, Oceania and South Africa. In 1836, Jane Wilson, the wife of one of the South African missionaries, was the first known white woman to die and be buried in the Transvaal. In the post-Civil War period, a number of American women Protestant missionaries were sent abroad having equal status with the men.

For some Americans the capture of souls was pursued with the same competitive zeal as was given by others to the capture of markets. Each of the many American Protestant sects fought an individual battle for converts. The allegiance they tried to win was not to a corporate community (as the Catholics did) but to a particular Church. Incomprehensible to the leaders of the foreign societies where they proselytised, they avoided being identified with their country's political and military power. If they followed in anybody's footsteps, it was in those of their European Protestant predecessors or of their own Yankee traders. 'What a reproof', said abstemious American missionary Eli Smith who, on arrival in Tiflis in 1830, stumbled upon a hogshead of New England rum. Yet they could not divorce themselves entirely from the actions of their government. It was western military might that in the 1840s and 1850s opened the Chinese and Japanese doors to them; as it was Spain's defeat in the 1890s that enabled them to enter the Philippines, Puerto Rico, and other parts of the Spanish empire. Indeed, while such examples are rare, it was a Protestant missionary, S. Wells Williams, who served as interpreter with the 1853 Perry expedition to Japan and who, five years later in 1858, helped to draft the Treaty of Tietsin.

By 1925 the United States was providing almost one-half of the world Protestant foreign missionaries (14,043) and 65 per cent of the necessary finance ($45 million). The corresponding figures in 1969 were 70 per cent (33,290) of the total Protestant missionary force and about 80 per cent ($349 million) of total finances.[35]

Not only had figures risen and America's missionary role increased; the deployment of missionary forces had changed. In 1925, about 43 per cent of the Americans were serving in east Asia; a little over 16 per cent of them were in south Asia, chiefly in India. Until the triumph of the Chinese communists in 1949 caused a decline in Asian activities, the United States predominated in China as the British Protestants had predominated in India. Forty-five years later, in 1970, three-quarters of the total North American Protestant missionary force was equally divided between Africa, Asia and Latin America. The number of Protestant missionaries in Latin America had grown during the decade 1959–69 as those in Asia had declined. In the early 1970s, Brazil led the world. Next came Japan, followed by the Philippines.

Although, in 1969, American Protestant missionaries outnumbered the Catholics three to one, the latter have also increased their strength since their Catholic Foreign Mission Society was founded in 1911. Its first members sailed for China in 1916. In 1968 they numbered about 10,000.[36] In the late 1960s, the Americans were providing more money than any other nation to finance Catholic missions. In their acceptance by the Papacy, American Catholics had come a long way since Leo XIII's Encyclical of 1899 condemning certain 'American doctrines'.

Until the rise of the Chinese communists, Asia had always been the major area of missionary effort for America's Catholics. Recently, however, they have appeared in parts of the world normally the preserve of European missions. In 1970, with about 4000 American Catholic missionaries, Latin America led all other continents.

The effect of these Protestant and Catholic missionaries is not to be gauged by the few converts they have made relative to the size of native populations, or by the way in which they have met the religious needs of their Christian communities. Their influence has been much more widespread. In particular the Protestants have always been concerned with a worldly as well as a heavenly goal. The secret of the Protestant ethic was, after all, action. Hence their stress upon education, health, hygiene, manners, dress, work training and general behaviour. From the stress placed upon education, came the Protestant-founded schools and colleges to be found on every continent, especially in Asia. It was from such roots that the famous American University of Beirut, and Robert College in Istanbul, sprang. Other examples are St John's College, Shanghai and the Isabella Thorburn College for women, Lucknow. In Tokyo American Protestants founded Rikkyo in 1874, Aoyama Gakuin in 1883 and Meiji Gakuin in 1886 – all of which later became universities. The University of Peking was begun under the auspices of American Benedictines in 1925. Often it was in these colleges that a country's future leaders received their first formal education.

All missionaries have helped in enlarging our knowledge of cultures long since changed, in preserving native languages from extinction, in codifying the laws and in diffusing productive techniques. It was, for instance, the missionaries' turning-lathe that captured the attention of the chief of the Zulus in 1836, not the Gospel. Sometimes, as with China, they have given a foreign country a unique place in the conscience of their fellow-countrymen. Until the emergence of the great philanthropic foundations, such as the John D. Rockefeller Foundation established in 1901, the transfer of American medicine (at least half the drugs listed in the pharmacopoeia of Europe are of American Indian origin), surgery, nursing and public health, was also the work of the religious missions.

A secularised version of the American Christian missions is the Peace Corps[37] established as an agency of the United States government on 1 March 1961. In his special message to Congress, President Kennedy said:

I recommend the establishment of a permanent Peace Corps – a pool of trained American men and women sent overseas by the United States Government or through private organizations and institutions to help foreign countries meet their urgent needs for skilled manpower . . .[38]

Soon the agency had hundreds of volunteers in training or on assignment in Africa, Asia and Latin America. These included teachers, physicians, mechanics, engineers, land workers and many other specialists. Ten years later, in 1971, about 50,000 Peace Corps members had worked abroad (Table 1).

Seen in historical perspective, the Peace Corps is really much older than the hopeful days of John F. Kennedy's administration. It tapped the same voluntary tradition and used the same concept of stewardship as the Christian missions had done before it. In 1961, philanthropy, humanitarianism, optimism, belief in progress and terminal solutions were old on the American scene, especially a belief in empiricism and practical consequences, which has been evident in American history since the First Federal Convention of 1787. Whatever aspect of American life we turn to – even in the diffusing of its ideas in education, in which the work of William James (1842–1910) and John Dewey (1859–1952) was most important – we can never escape the pragmatic and progressive twist.

Moreover the stress placed upon worldly goals has always been a characteristic of the lay Protestant, as we saw it to have been of the Protestant missions. Seventeenth-century John Eliot had proposed that the Indians be taught 'letters, Trades and Labours, as building, fishing, Flax and Hemp dressing, planting orchards, etc.'[39] In the eighteenth century Dr Samuel Gridley Howe of Massachusetts (having fought in the struggle for Greek independence from the Turks) concerned himself with improving the standard of living of the Hellenes by the use of improved agricultural techniques.

In the 1870s, the Massachusetts agronomist W. S. Clark assisted in the founding of the agricultural college at Sapporo, Japan.* As for world peace, this would best be served, said the Reverend Charles Jefferson in 1910, not by weapons 'but the good will of islands of human beings around the world, healed in our hospitals, taught in our schools, and baptized in our churches'.[40]

If there is anything peculiarly American about the Peace Corps, it is its anti-communist bias. Like foreign aid, the Peace Corps was meant to be an instrument of foreign policy. Strangely enough in linking the diffusion of skills and techni-

---

*Similar assistance was given by Americans in the founding of the Agricultural Institute of Allahabad, India, in 1905.

ques with the political and social content of the American way of life, America was merely doing in 1960 what it had hoped to do a hundred years before; except that the nineteenth-century ideological enemy was Monarchism, not Communism. Now that the activities of the Peace Corps are being dramatically curtailed, it is worth asking not whether it has helped to defeat Communism but whether or not it is the intimate relation which young Americans have had with the people of other lands that, more than anything else, has justified its existence.

During the last three decades, as the American presence has grown in the world, the ranks of the Foreign Service Officers[41] and diplomatic personnel have also greatly increased, especially by numerous administrative, financial, economic, technical, and military and naval experts. Important American financial and economic advisers (working either in a private or a public capacity) included Jenks, who went to China in 1904, Dawes, who was Chairman of the Dawes Committee for Europe in 1923, Milspaugh, who advised the Persian government in the 1920s and the 1940s, and especially Kemmerer, who probably exercised most influence on the financial policies of foreign governments during the interwar years.[42]

Americans have not only changed the arena in which diplomacy has been practised; its informality (what is called 'shirtsleeves' diplomacy) has helped to change diplomatic protocol. Time-honoured precedent and custom have had to compromise with American ideals of efficiency and equality. As President Nixon's and Dr Kissinger's activities bear out, the Americans, in diplomacy as in anything else, will not be constrained by convention. Dramatic examples of the political and cultural power exercised by the diplomatic community (and the allied occupation forces) were the changes that took place in Japan and Germany after the Second World War. In less time than it took the Founding Fathers, the Americans turned out a new Japanese constitution, introduced political and social equality and the concept of civil rights, reorganised the education system, and sought to create a model democracy based upon the American experiment.

No less dramatic were the changes introduced into the economic sphere. The industrial and banking cartels which had dominated Japanese and German trade and industry were dissolved, and – despite the fact that the Japanese had no tradition of prohibition of monopolies like the United States – there was introduced an anti-monopoly act modelled after the United States antitrust laws.

More prominent, if not more influential in the world, have been the tourists[43] who have gone abroad for pleasure. Europe has always been their mecca. Beginning with a few hundred after the Napoleonic Wars, the number going to Europe in the 1840s was about 30,000 per annum. 'I saw that no other people on earth', wrote Nathaniel Hawthorne at the mid-century from his post as American consul in Liverpool, 'have such vagabond habits as ours.' Restless, and with sufficient wealth to satisfy their curiosity, the number continued to grow throughout the 1850s and 1860s. Aristocratically inclined fellow-countrymen living in Europe resented the growing invasion. 'Vulgar, vulgar, vulgar', was how Henry James described the swarms of Americans in London in 1869. 'Innocents Abroad' they may have been in Mark Twain's phrase, but to Henry Adams in Paris there was very little to recommend the growing hordes of Americans 'who stare and gawk and smell'. Yet nothing could reduce their ranks. By the 1890s, more than 100,000 were touring Europe. Improved sea-travel and conducted tours had removed most of the discomfort. Growing volume had reduced costs. By 1914, by which time tourism had become an important source of foreign exchange for Europe, a major complaint of American tourists was that wherever they went they were sure to meet other Americans.

While the two world wars and the depression of the 1930s caused a lull in tourist activity, the movement has always been renewed at higher levels than before. During the past twenty-five years, aided by air travel and growing affluence, the increase has been unprecedented. Measured *per capita,* many other nations spend more than the United States; yet the number of American tourists going to Europe alone in 1970 was approximately 3,000,000; they spent about $1,310,000,000. The total number of American foreign tourists in 1970 was approximately 5,000,000; the total disbursements $6,153,000,000. Of the $17,400,000,000 representing world-wide international tourism earnings in 1970 (estimated), the United States contributed $5,090,000,000 (excluding fares paid to foreign-flag carriers). One out of every $3.40 spent for international travel was an American dollar. This was a net outgoing in 1970 of $2·5 billion and a significant portion of America's balance of payments deficit for that year. One suspects that the overall economic effect of this money cannot have been much less than that of the whole American foreign aid programme. Moreover tourism is relatively free of political implications, it does not require an enormous bureaucracy to administer it, and the economic is only one of its many beneficial effects.

Nothing has altered the world's view of America in recent times so much as the use of American military might abroad.[44] Between 1948 and 1970, partly from its own seeking and partly from the force of events, America had a defence policy (one that is undergoing marked change in 1973) that entailed the policing of all continents. As a result, global commitments of the United States army extended from Alaska through the islands of the Pacific to south-east Asia, and from western Europe through the Mediterranean. The United States today has more than fifty military alliances with nations stretching across the world. Great military organisations such as NATO in the northern and ANZUS in the southern hemisphere were American-inspired. Since 1949 the United States has fought in Korea and Vietnam, launched military interventions in Lebanon (1958) and the Dominican Republic (1965), and – if its critics are to be believed – covertly attempted, with the aid of its Central Intelligence Agency, to overthrow several governments including the governments of Iran (1954), Guatemala (1954), Cuba (1961), Indonesia (1965), and Chile (1973). 'This has become a very small planet', said Secretary of State Rusk, speaking in May, 1965. 'We have to be concerned with all of it – with all of its land, waters, atmosphere, and with surrounding space.'[45] A few years ago, the only long-term influences exercised by the American armed forces abroad were in the Philippines and the

Caribbean. In 1939, President Franklin D. Roosevelt was derided for saying that the American frontier was on the Rhine; today, it stands on the Elbe and the China Sea. Until the Second World War, the peace-time defence expenditures of the American people were relatively small ($1 billion in 1940); in 1970, the figure had risen to $81 billions.

The irony of the situation is that, while the American armed forces abroad have been concerned to make the world safe for the western democratic way of life, their efforts have often resulted in making the world a much less safe place than it was. The number of lives taken by American troops in Asia since 1948, added to the devastation caused by the widespread use of military technology, has not drawn the world closer to Americans; it has, in fact, alienated much of the world from them. Since the Korean War, there has been a growing fear in the world of an extension of their power and influence.

The nineteenth-century land of hope (especially to the white world), is becoming identified by its critics with the powers of darkness. Yet the Americans did not choose to wield power on this scale. It was their misfortune to come to power in an age of global convulsion.

The discovery and colonisation of America caused a redistribution of people and territory in which the aboriginal people of America and Africa lost and the Europeans gained. A greater Europe was created outside Europe. The subsequent migration of the white Americans to the Pacific, coupled with the march of the Russians to the China Sea, ensured white hegemony around the globe and foreshadowed the clash of eastern and western interests at Mukden in 1904 and at Pearl Harbor in 1941.

The exodus of Europeans to the New World would have been sufficiently important if, like some of the earlier migrations of history, the Europeans had been drawn westwards and then forgotten. Instead, the colonisation of America changed the scale and the course of world commerce, agriculture, and industry. The two worlds – the Old and the New – became so interrelated that they only made sense when considered together. Before the First World War,

America was already emerging as the colossus of the world. In the two Great Wars, its economic strength was decisive.

Since 1945, the commercial and technical influence of the American people has come to exceed that of any other western nation. Known abroad in the eighteenth and early nineteenth centuries for their sense of mission, for their political and religious freedom and the realisation of humanitarian ideals, rather than for their ability to strike a business bargain, they are now known for their prowess in business, science and technology. The freedom preached by the managers and technicians of America's commercial and industrial empire in the 1970s is the freedom from material want. Their hallmark is no longer a new vision of man – though their habits and manners tend to create a new life style – but economic efficiency.

Compared with the earlier exodus from Europe which (diffusing a civilisation in its entirety) created a very different world, the cultural influence of Americans abroad – even allowing for the television and the film – has struck less deep; not least, because America itself is a young country and its influence has had to be imposed on much older and often hostile civilisations. (Not to this day has it succeeded in assimilating the Indians whom it conquered.) Its cultural influence has been greatest in the European world; and this because the ideas it has diffused have not been entirely new to Europeans. The ideas of worldly progress, of rationalisation, of calculation and mechanisation, for instance, which the Americans put abroad, did in fact spring from the Old not the New World. What the Americans have done is to present these ideas on a new scale and with new emphasis. Yet, however superficial some aspects of Americanisation may appear to be, it would be foolish to minimise the extent of America's commercial and military influence on the future of the whole world.

CHAPTER IV

America's Influence on World Finance

THE fact that the West came to look upon money as a sign of God's providence (in contrast to the ancient view that regarded money as barren) greatly assisted the accumulation of western wealth. In all the great works of antiquity, the crucial factor was not wealth but labour (which, according to the labour theory of value, some people equate with capital). One has only to look at the great public works in China and India to realise that, for many people in the world, labour, unassisted by machines and capital equipment – ant-like in its teeming thousands – was and still is the crucial factor.

The astonishing thing about recent history is the amount of money or mobile capital that has been accumulated by the people of western Europe and North America, much of which they have loaned to each other.[1] America itself began with a mortgage. Without the financial backing of English capitalist merchants, the *Mayflower* would never have sailed. Only with the help of European funds did much of the United States transportation, foreign trade, and land development get under way.

Helping to explain the accumulation and movement of wealth on both sides of the North Atlantic was the growing interrelation and interdependence of the Old World and the New. This complementarity prompted greater specialisation, which, in turn, increased the profitability of economic life and provided the countries of western Europe (especially the United Kingdom) with a surplus of capital that could be profitably re-invested abroad.

International investment[2] in recent times has grown largely as the result of the extraordinary expansion of western man,

which is borne out by the distribution of 'world', i.e. chiefly
western foreign long-term[3] investments. In 1913, the total
was $45 billion (it had been $4 billion in 1864). The United
Kingdom accounted for about half and Europe for almost
the whole of these foreign investments. Outside Europe, the
chief borrowers were North America, $10·9 billion; Latin
America, $8·9 billion; Asia, $7 billion; Africa, $47 billion;
and Oceania, $2·2 billion. (Table II.)

The two nations dominating this general picture in 1913
were the United Kingdom and the United States; the one, the
greatest creditor, the other – in its colonising stage – the
greatest debtor. Like the Dutch, who had led in the money
markets of the western world before them, both
nations – nominally at least – were Protestant and capitalistic. In monetary terms, America's debt to the outside world
grew at a rate faster than that of any other nation. In 1789, its
outstanding debt to Europe, chiefly Britain, was about $60
million; by the late 1830s, this figure had more than quadrupled; by 1857, it was about $400 million ($150 million
short and $250 million long term). By the First World War,
European investments in the United States had reached $7
billion, representing no less than 14 per cent of international
indebtedness at that time, 22 per cent of European foreign
investments, and about 91 per cent of total foreign investments in the United States.

Behind these figures lies the story of early America's
financial dependence upon European governments and private investors. Without French money and supplies, the
Americans could hardly have achieved independence
when they did. By 1793, the Americans owed the French
$6–7 million. A decade later, in 1803, they purchased the
Louisiana Territory from Napoleon with $11·3 million, ob-
tained largely from London, Amsterdam and Paris money
markets. Constant financial help was given by European
merchant houses to Americans engaged in foreign trade. This
short-term mercantile financing had considerable influence
on America's balance of payments. Indeed to win freedom
from English finance took far longer than to win freedom
from the Mother of Parliaments. Perhaps not altogether a bad
thing, when one considers the benefits not only of the money

itself, but also of the invaluable British merchant experience that accompanied it.[4] Financing much of America's foreign commerce in the nineteenth century was the short-term London sterling bill of exchange. In 1837 British commercial credit in the United States was estimated at $100 million. European funds were also invested in America's banking organisation; by 1841 foreigners owned most of the stock of the Bank of the United States.

Beginning with the Erie Canal in 1825, considerable investments were made by Europeans in road and canal building. State indebtedness for public works between 1820 and 1840 increased from $128 to $200 million. The discovery of gold in California in 1848 gave a fillip to the entire American economy and, in doing so, stimulated the flow of European funds to the United States. From the mid-century, there was a dramatic increase in the growth of European investments in both the private and the public sectors.

No single item of foreign investment in the United States before 1914 exceeded the importance of railroads. In 1853 Europeans held a quarter of the nominal value of railroad securities; by 1890 perhaps a third. Even as late as 1914 railway bonds accounted for more than half of all outstanding investments in the United States.

Important European investments were also made in trade, mining, ranching, agriculture and industry, as well as in the provision of government and public services. The greatest outlet for capital investment, however, has always been the building industries and the construction of dwelling houses,[5] and it was here that native funds predominated. Fortunately so, for the great ports and cities that sprang up first along the shores and then in the interior were as important in helping to colonise the great temperate areas of the earth as the steam locomotive. In United States history, one makes little sense without the other.[6]

Whether the demand for venture capital made by the United States diverted European resources abroad that might have been better employed at home is anybody's guess. No doubt, the money could have been spent on improving the economic lot of the western Europeans rather than in improving the rising parts of the world; had this happened, there might have been greater social harmony and economic competence in Europe. But this is to assume conditions that did not apply. The fact is, the money was used to make a profit, to safeguard an existing investment, or to protect some political stake. The market was King.

The outflow of European funds in fixed-interest bearing securities (in contrast to the later preponderantly private business investments made by the Americans) hardly seems to have starved European business and industry of capital. Between 1870 and 1913, British investors placed abroad about 40 per cent of their gross capital formation, largely in fixed-interest bearing securities; yet it can hardly be argued that, because of this, British industrial development languished.[7] Most capital needs could be met from profits, or by a loan, or by enlarging a partnership.

What we do know is that the demands of the Americans and others for European capital caused the foreign issues market to become most profitable to European banks and issuing houses; partly as a consequence of this, the European foreign investment market came to be better organised than the domestic market. But this is hardly saying that America's gain was Europe's loss. In so far as foreign investment meant a greater freedom for capital (and labour and skills) to move to where it could, economically speaking, be best employed and in so far as foreign investment was able to release undreamt of quantities of food and raw materials, the whole world stood to gain; some parts of it, it is true, more than others. The real significance of capital exports for the United States was that they enabled the development of that country to proceed at a faster rate and with much less hardship than might have been the case if it had had to depend upon itself. In so far as these exports spared America the development costs of the technology it borrowed from Europe, it was enriched.

America's overall position as a lending nation since 1913, compared with the other lending nations of the world, is traced in Table II. This Table provides only the broadest outline of the changes taking place, yet it reveals the dramatic rise of the United States as a creditor nation. By 1913, with its own national capital market organised, America had more than $3 billion invested abroad, while investment by foreigners in the United States were more than $7 billion. By 1938 United States investments abroad were estimated at $11 billion (excluding government war debts), and investments by foreigners in the United States at $7 billion. In these years (1913–38), America's position had changed from that of a net debtor (on long-term) to that of a net creditor. Similar figures for 1960 were $18·4 billion invested in the United States, and $45·4 billion invested by the United States abroad. By 1970 the American figure stood at $104·7 billion. The amount invested by the rest of the world in the United States was $48·8 billion (most of it from western Europe). The difference lay not in the totals, but in the employment of these funds. Whereas direct business investments accounted for only 30 per cent of the European figure, they made up three-quarters of American private business investments abroad. Overall, for the hundred years 1870–1970, American private foreign investments multiplied one thousand times. Since 1945 the United States has in fact supplied (put more precisely we should say organised the supply of) more than half of the world's needs for foreign capital.

Table III shows how these American investments were divided between Private Direct Business Investments abroad and Private Portfolio[8] Investments. Negligible in 1869, these direct foreign business investments by 1897 had exceeded $600 million, and by 1913 had become more than $2 billion. By 1970 they had reached $78 billion. Three years later, in 1973, they were not far short of $100 billion (compared with Britain's $15 billion). Even this staggering figure (most of it accounted for by a few hundred United States-based multinational firms) represents a mere 6 per cent of United States private domestic business investments.

The changing ratios of American Direct and Portfolio Investments shown in Table III leave no doubt about the extraordinary proclivity of the American investor for direct business investments. The British foreign investment market matured at a time when the demand was for fixed-interest bearing public securities. In America, such portfolio securities were generally confined to internal rather than foreign development. Individual calculation of profit opportunity was the characteristic that marked both British and American foreign private investment; the difference between them was not in objectives but in the organisation of their funds.

Table IV/A shows the geographical distribution of private American investments abroad in 1914. At this time, investments in Mexico and Canada predominated. The most important were in transport, mining and agriculture. By 1914, while the bulk of American private foreign investments were still in the Americas, there had been a shift towards Europe. Subsequent changes in the distribution of American private funds can be traced with the aid of the other parts of Table IV. Overall, from 1897 to 1970, Europe gained most; its share of total American foreign lending increased from 21 per cent to 31 per cent. Britain and Germany have accounted for most American investments in Europe, Britain's total being by far the largest. Canada also accounted for a large part of American direct foreign investment. In fact, western Europe only became more important than Canada in 1969. The Canadian figure reached 30 per cent of the total in 1936 and has since remained in that vicinity. Latin America's share rose and fell in the interwar years. By 1950, with 39 per cent of the total, it had reached a level which it had not had since 1936. However, in the past two decades, the figure has declined to 19 per cent. The largest items for Europe and the Americas were manufactures, petroleum and transport. Mining and smelting, important items in American investments in Canada and Latin America, were relatively unimportant in Europe.

Concerning investments in Asia, by 1929 these accounted for 5 per cent of the United States total. By 1970 the figure was 7 per cent. In 1929 the order of importance was petroleum, manufactures, trade and agriculture. In 1970 the bulk of American capital in Asia was invested in petroleum and manufacturing. In 1929 China, Indonesia and the Philippines were the most important areas. In 1970,* with petroleum equalling all other United States direct Asian investments, capital (about half of the total) was concentrated in the oil-bearing lands of southwest and eastern Asia.

There must have been very little American money in Africa in 1914; even by 1929 it was only 1·4 per cent of the United

---

*In that year oil revenue to the Arab countries was about $25 billions.

States total of foreign investments. By 1970, however, the figure had reached 4½ per cent. Investments in British South Africa (later the Republic of South Africa), Libya and Liberia have accounted for most. Petroleum is America's present greatest investment in that continent. In 1970 it accounted for about 60 per cent of the American investments; trade, the big item in 1898 (about 20 per cent), is no longer reported separately.

The figures for Oceania (chiefly Australia and New Zealand) were 2 per cent of American foreign investments in 1929, 4½ per cent in 1970. In 1961, for the first time, United States–Canadian new direct corporation investment in Australia (£65·4 million) exceeded United Kingdom investment (£55·6 million). Manufacturing, petroleum search, mining, and trade have always been important. In addition, since the Second World War, Americans have made inroads into the Australian food-producing industries, and land holding. Acquisition of Australian land by American individuals and corporations went on steadily throughout the 1960s, but in the sixties and the early seventies it had become a veritable land rush. At the beginning of 1972, between 60 and 70 per cent of Australia's approximately half million square miles of the Northern Territory was held by Americans for cattle grazing and agricultural ventures under long-term leases. This is roughly comparable to foreigners holding title to two-thirds of Ohio, Indiana and Illinois. Accompanying the land boom has been a mining boom. American companies have invested more than $800 million (most of it at the end of the sixties and the beginning of the seventies) to explore and develop Australian coal, iron, bauxite, copper and nickel. In 1970 there were about 450 American companies operating in Australia.

Taking an overall view of the uses made of American private capital abroad in the period 1897–1970, the two most important fields were mining and manufacture. Mining (the most productive early foreign investment) rose to a peak of 27 per cent of the total in 1908. By 1970 this cumulative total had fallen to 8 per cent. Petroleum, another extractive industry, increased its share from 14–15 per cent in 1908 to

28 per cent in 1970. In 1914 American investments in foreign manufacturing stood at about 18 per cent; by 1970 it was 41 per cent. The figure rose fastest between 1957 and 1964. In 1972 the distribution of United States foreign business investments showed about 40 per cent in manufacturing, 30 per cent in oil, and 10 per cent in other mining ventures.

The course of investments in the other major groups, public utilities (including transport), trade and agriculture is traced in Table IV.

Except for the years 1877–9 and 1881, and a short period at the end of the nineteenth and the beginning of the twentieth century (1898–1901 and 1905) when special conditions prevailed (such as the repatriation of British funds in the 1870s, or the formation of giant corporations at the turn of the nineteenth century), the United States consistently borrowed more than it lent abroad. In its total commercial relations with other nations (i.e. allowing for trade and shipping charges, banking and insurance, etc.) it was a net debtor nation until the First World War. It emerged from that conflict – at least for a period – as the leading creditor nation of the world.

Even before America's entry into the war in 1917, the allies had been compelled to exchange more than $2 billion of their American holdings for vital war supplies. An additional $2·6 billion of supplies had been provided by the United States government in war loans. With America's entry into the war (as the private foreign loan market dried up), the United States government took upon itself the responsibility of financing the supplies needed by its allies. In 1917 $9,581,000,000 were made available to European governments. By 1919, excluding war loans, the level of United States holdings abroad had risen from $3·5 billion in 1913 to $6·5 billion (Table III). In contrast, the European powers had either lost all their foreign investments (Germany) or had had them greatly reduced (France and Britain). In addition, American postwar private investments abroad continued to grow during the 1920s until in 1930 they amounted to $15 billion.

The war not only reduced Europe's credit standing relative

to that of the United States; by accelerating the growth of American direct business investments abroad, it also helped to change the character of world investment. Between 1919 and 1930, foreign business investments about doubled. America's ability to raise capital had become so great that in the same period (1919–30) its foreign public (portfolio) investments almost trebled. The centre of international finance had begun to shift from London to New York City. At the end of this period, its investments abroad were about equally divided between portfolio and direct business investments (Table III).

The increase in foreign business investments in the 1920s is explained by the fact that there was a limit to what the domestic investment market could profitably absorb. Also business was becoming global. American industry, with its enormous capital outlays, was having to adapt itself to world conditions. Having expanded across a continent, it now began to expand across the world. The need was as much psychological as economic. In 1900 it was estimated that about 28 overseas branch factories employed American capital and techniques; in 1910, the figure had increased to 70, and by 1929 to 179. Important in the 1920s was the spread of branch factories making automobiles (the sixth Ford car built was shipped to Canada), power generators and other electrical equipment, communication systems, and agricultural machinery. Great mining and pulp companies also spread across the white-settled world. Other factors prompting the new global order were improved communications, the diffusion of American technical knowledge and patent rights, rising tariff barriers, and the growing need to obtain and control increasing quantities of the world's basic raw materials, especially oil. The distribution of United States direct investments by country and industry groups as it existed in 1929 is set out in Table IV.

In addition to increasing the proportion of direct business investments during the interwar years, the Americans also changed the character of world investment and economic relations as a result of their policy on war debts and German reparations. Put simply, the Americans, during the war and after the armistice, had transferred resources to their allies of more than $10 billion. Britain's indebtedness to America was not far short of half this total. When the war ceased, the Americans expected to have their loans repaid with interest at 5 per cent. For western Europe, such a hope was completely unreal. In December, 1918 British leaders proposed to President Wilson that existing war debts between the allies should be cancelled. Provided the United States would cancel its claim upon Britain for about $4 billion, Britain would cancel the debts due to it from its allies of about $10 billion. France shared the British view. In no position to accept the financial logic of the Europeans, President Wilson stuck to America's financial claims. The outcome was dreary. In 1922 America's debtors accepted obligations of over $11·5 billion, payable over a sixty-two year period at an average interest rate of 2·135 per cent. Under these agreements, principal and interest totalled in excess of $22 billion. As most of these debts had been incurred in desperate conditions that did not encourage the purchaser to haggle over prices, one can only conjecture how much of these staggering sums represented not the transfer of armaments and provisions but war-time inflation and profiteering. In no period of American history prior to the First World War were so many fortunes made so quickly. The real contribution in the common struggle against Germany, however, was paid not in supplies but in flesh and blood,[9] and on this score the Americans escaped lightly. In 1923 the British Foreign Minister, Arthur Balfour, made a last appeal for the cancellation of all war debts and reparations. President Coolidge's response, 'They hired the money, didn't they?' is the best illustration we have of an outlook which saw nothing wrong in separating the financial and political interests of the nation.

And so, with America at the helm, the postwar financial madness continued. The allies continued to press Germany for the reparations (fixed at $33 billion) in order to be able to pay the United States war debts to which most Europeans felt the Americans were not entitled. Under great strain, Germany's financial system collapsed. In 1923 the French and the Belgians made a vain attempt to collect their money by occupying the Ruhr. Also in 1923, in an attempt to seek a

solution, Congress scaled down America's financial demands.
In 1924 the Americans even loaned the Germans gold (the
new settlement was linked with the name of a Chicago
financier, Charles G. Dawes) which was immediately handed
to France and Britain who, in turn, gave it back to the
Americans. This ingenious way of avoiding the financial
reality of the postwar world was undone once the Americans
ceased to hand out gold. There followed a further scaling
down of German reparations in 1929 (this time the work of a
Wall Street financier, Owen D. Young); an obligation which
Germany could accept only by floating bonds in the United
States, on which, in 1931, Germany finally defaulted; this
despite the establishing of the Bank of International Settlement in 1930 and the Hoover moratorium on payments of
reparations and war debts declared in 1931. The situation was
aggravated by the fact that throughout the boom period of the
1920s the high rates of interest obtained in New York for
short-term funds caused a further influx of foreign capital.
The high rates offered by New York houses also increased the
costs of making service payments to American creditors, and
encouraged further speculation in the United States. The
market value of all shares listed on the New York Stock
Exchange alone had risen from $27 billion in 1925 to $87
billion in 1929. The Great Depression followed. (By March
1933 the New York Stock Exchange listed $13 billion
shares.) The Debt Default Act of 1934 (Johnson Act), in
prohibiting loans to any government in default in its payments
to the United States (with the exception of Finland, all foreign
debtors had formally defaulted on war loans on 15 June
1934), shut the door to any further help the United States
might have been prepared to give to foreign governments.

By 1934 the mad escapade of war debts and reparations
had come to an end. Only Finland and Cuba eventually paid
in full. The sad chapter ended with recriminations on both
sides. The Europeans accused the Americans of being 'Uncle
Shylock'. Not only had they been grasping; their intransig-
ence over the war debts and their financial inexperience had
made the world's problems worse than they might have been.
At America's door was placed responsibility for Europe's
postwar financial and economic woes. Naturally many

Americans took a different view. They felt that the older European powers had taken advantage of their generosity. With the Dawes and Young Plans in 1924 and 1929, they had tried to bring order out of Europe's financial chaos; in the interests of peace, they had liberally scaled down the war debts owed to the United States and had foregone their legitimate rights as creditors. Of one thing they became increasingly convinced: not to be duped so easily again. As the war clouds in Europe began to gather, America withdrew behind its ever-rising trade barriers and the provisions of the Neutrality Acts passed by Congress between 1935 and 1937.

More important than apportioning blame is to appreciate to what extent the climate of international investment had changed from what it had been in the century before 1914. In the first place, America's ascendency as the world's leading creditor nation had been much too rapid even for its own good; the extraordinary affluence of certain groups had led to much imprudent lending; a great deal of the money poured into Europe and Latin America in the interwar period, especially in private portfolio investments in foreign government loans, was as good as lost from the beginning. A level of indebtedness was incurred which it was impossible to repay. Measured by any economic or financial criteria, these loans could not hope 'to earn their keep', let alone repay the interest and capital. 'I venture to challenge', wrote one authority in 1932, 'a denial from any responsible person acquainted with the public borrowings of the years 1926–28 of the assertion that, with the exception of loans recommended by the League of Nations and the central banks, the *bulk* of the foreign loans in these years to public authorities in debtor countries would better not have been made'.[10] The truth is that in comparison with Britain's experience in the nineteenth century the whole investment situation had changed. It had been one thing for the Old World to go to the aid of the New in the nineteenth and quite another thing for the New World to try to go to the aid of the Old in the twentieth century. British investments had created the things it wished to buy, as well as the wealth out of which its investments could eventually be repaid. Its open ports, its free-trade policy, and its willingness to go into the red on its balance of trade with others (though not on its overall balance of payments, which included many other items than trade) helped to seal Britain's bargain with the rest of the world. In contrast, even where investments had been wisely placed, America did not have the same need to buy the products its foreign investments were helping to create.[11] The fact was that America's need of other people's goods and services (the only way that debts can be repaid) was limited. Little wonder that in the 1920s the problem of war debt repayment had proved so insuperable.

The changed conditions in which the Americans were operating – and for which they were only partly responsible – had shown themselves earlier in the collapse of raw material and food prices in the 1920s. The sterling bill of exchange – hitherto the most important channel of short-term capital movements – had also been gradually abandoned as the most reliable means of financing foreign trade. Similarly the gold standard had been set aside and the nineteenth-century mobility of people, capital and commerce impaired. In these conditions, freedom of trade gave place to national autarchy. By the eve of the Second World War, except for the large-scale movements of liquid funds from country to country, often effected by cable, in search of security (the movement of so-called 'hot money'), the flow of foreign long-term investment had, for the time being, virtually ceased.

The losses sustained by the American foreign investor – though not by the issue houses, some of which had done extremely well out of the flotation of foreign issues – were immense. In the 1930s almost $11 billion of foreign investments were wiped out. The paradoxical thing was that, while America was losing its money abroad, world economic and political conditions in the years 1937–40 were causing a flight of capital to the United States. The flight became a panic during the Munich crisis of 1938 and after the Stalin–Hitler pact of 1939. In 1940, before the trickle had become a flood, America's (gross) overseas investments were worth almost $4 million less than they had been in 1930; over 80 per cent of the fall in value can be explained by the liquidation or depreciation of portfolio investment. Direct investments, however, proved more resilient than portfolio investments; indeed, in the late 1930s, United States direct investments abroad rallied. By the end of 1940, at $7·3 billion, they had almost regained their 1930 level ($8·0 billion). An estimate of the United States international investment position in 1938 (given in Table II) shows that, while the total was still much below that for the United Kingdom, America's role had grown since 1913, especially in comparison with France and Germany, whose shares in world investment had fallen considerably in the interwar years.

In so far as the Second World War propelled the United States to the centre of world financial power, it accelerated the trends in international investment already visible before 1914. Even without the Second World War the vast natural potential of the United States would have forced Americans to the forefront. Yet by 1945, wartime obligations, the accumulation of trade credits by foreigners, and the cost of armed services abroad had eaten into the foreign balances of both the United Kingdom and the United States. Since then, however, there has been a remarkable resurgence in international capital movements, with the United States in the lead; a resurgence which has disproved the fears expressed in the early 1940s about the future of private investment.

The astonishing speed with which United States direct business investments have grown in the postwar years is shown in Tables III and IV. In 1950 the total was in the region of $12 billion. By 1970 it had grown to $78 billion (as against the $13 billion of foreign business investments in the United States). In 1973 it was not far short of $100 billion, a figure that exceeds the gross national product of most nations in the world. To be exact, using 1970 figures it exceeds the gross national products of all countries except the United States, the Soviet Union, Japan, West Germany, France and Britain.

The percentage distribution in 1950 showed investments in Latin America (always thought of as a United States sphere of influence) to be 39 per cent of the total. Canada (which some American companies treated sales-wise as another State of the Union) followed with 30 per cent, and western Europe with 15 per cent. Since then the importance of Europe, especially since the establishment of the Common Market in 1957–8, and Canada has grown. In 1968 United States companies owned 43 per cent of the capital of all Canadian manufacturing industry. American ownership of Canadian mining undertakings was much the same.

The situation in 1971 was as follows: Europe, $27·6 billion; Canada, $24 billion; Latin America, $15·8 billion; other areas, $18·6 billion. About 60–70 per cent of these cumulative totals of United States direct investments were in the developed world, where evidently the risks are least and the profits best. For instance, in 1971 United States-based multinational corporations accounted for 13 per cent of all capital investment in manufacturing in the United Kingdom, France, West Germany, Belgium-Luxembourg, Mexico, Brazil and Canada. The interesting fact is that most of this money did not come from the United States at all, but was raised in the country where it was used.

Relative to Europe, Canada and Latin America, the opportunities for direct investment in Asia and Africa are small. The combined direct investments in these two continents in 1970 did not equal those of Latin America. Considerable amounts can be found in certain countries such as Japan and South Africa, yet they do not add up to much when compared with world totals. Hence, while it is true that the United States owns about three-quarters of foreign capital invested in Japan, this is only about 2 per cent of the American total abroad. Japan has followed a deliberate policy of keeping the American figure low, and restricting foreign investments to productive purposes.

The course of private direct investments in foreign manufacture, petroleum, mining and other industries since 1914 is traced in Table IV. For the past twenty-five years investments in manufacturing have constituted the largest field abroad. Their importance increased threefold between 1960 and 1971. In the latter year out of an American foreign total of $86 billion, $35·5 billion were invested in manufacturing industry; $24·3 billion were invested at this time in petroleum and $26·3 billion (a good deal of it in mining ventures) in other industries. At this time (1970–1) United States foreign concerns controlled about 80 per cent of Europe's computer business, 90 per cent of its micro-circuit industry, 40 per cent of its automobile making, 50 per cent of its transistor industry, 65 per cent of its telecommunications, 65 per cent of its agricultural machinery, and 45 per cent of its synthetic rubber industry. American direct business investments are also important in Europe's heavy industry and in petrochemical manufacture.[12] Estimates of United States investment in certain industries in France, Britain, West Germany, Canada and Australia are given in Table V/A–V/E. The overall position in 1972 shows that about 40 per cent of the approximate $100 billion of foreign direct business investments were in manufacturing. At that time the Americans were investing in foreign undertakings six or seven times the amount foreigners were investing in the United States.

No matter what economic indicator we turn to, whether we compare domestic exports with total sales of United States-based multinational firms (in 1972, $49 billion against $200 billion), or domestic exports of manufactures taken alone compared with those sold by foreign business affiliates (Table XXI), or the sales of foreign-based firms with the sales of domestic manufactures (Table XXI), or the plant and equipment expenditures of home and foreign-based manufacturing concerns (Table VI), they all point to the same conclusion: that United States direct investment in foreign-based manufacturing firms since 1957 has grown at a more rapid rate than domestic manufacturing activity. It appears to have been a profitable course of action. Whereas the earnings on foreign direct investments grew from $1·8 billion in 1950 to $8·7 billion in 1970, the profits of domestic non-financial corporations (after taxes) grew only from $21·7 to $30·7 billion. Foreign earnings as a percentage of domestic earnings in these two years were 8 per cent and 28 per cent respectively.[13] Some of this is to be explained by the different general business conditions obtaining at home and abroad (1970 for instance was a bad year in the United States but a boom year elsewhere); some of the difference arises from the way the figures have been put together – calculated a different way it is not difficult to show that the average profitability in manufacturing for America's affiliates abroad was not much unlike the parent company. Generally speaking,

America's foreign business investments have paid off quite handsomely. The extent to which they have secured markets for the Americans which they might have lost to other nations is something (outside of theory) about which we cannot be sure. Obviously, the competitive position of most United States-based firms has been improved by going abroad, or they would not stay there. But the conditions affecting each industry vary so widely that they demand separate investigation.

The extraordinary expansion of American business abroad has provided some of America's critics with what they consider to be the most telling evidence of economic imperialism. They point to the fact that American business abroad, in liquid funds as well as industrial capital, can mobilize a financial power beyond the control of any government. They show how the Americans take possession of other people's money. It is said that during 1966–70 sources other than the United States provided over 80 per cent of the fixed and working capital of all United States-based affiliates. Whereas in 1971 United States direct investments abroad rose by over $7·8 billion (to a cumulative total of almost $90 billion), foreign direct investments in the United States rose by only $400 million (to a cumulative total of about $14 billion). Even in the developed world, such as in western Europe, the fear that Americans are becoming the new Caesars is real. Yet it is very easy to be carried away with these figures and to exaggerate America's influence in the world. Europe, for example, is a long way from being monopolised by the Americans. The American invasion of Europe has in fact been going on for more than a hundred years, yet in 1970 United States firms owned no more than 5 per cent of European corporate assets. Americans have invested heavily in Europe primarily because of Europe's growing affluence. But they did not create it; they have added to it (not least by organising European funds and Europe's skilled labour) and have benefited from it by exploiting the enlarged consumer markets. As a commercial people addicted to mass-production and mass-distribution, they were able to appreciate the advantages of scale before the

Europeans. Today, while Europe is not without its giants, more than half the world's largest businesses are American. The turnover of the twenty largest American corporations almost equals the gross national product of West Germany. In the manufacture of automobiles, General Motors, whose turnover equals that of the thirteen largest German companies,[14] dwarfs all its European rivals. In terms of size, weight, and punch, the business battalions of the Americans are without their equal. (Table V/F and V/G.)

Even so there are a number of small foreign United States companies whose success in electronics, optics, acoustics, solid-state and high energy physics, instrumentation, metallurgy and aerospace research cannot be explained in terms of size alone. Size and weight did not prevent a number of large corporations failing in their attempts to establish themselves in European industry in the postwar period.

Certainly, the argument that America's success abroad is due to a superior technology needs to be looked at critically. The fact that the United States spends so many billions of dollars on research and development (in 1970 about $18 billion) proves very little. Most of this money is spent on the defence industries, nuclear energy and space. It was European scientists who first split the atom. Europe used nuclear energy in industry before the United States. It was Europeans who first discovered and developed radar, penicillin and the jet engine. Europeans were able to match American efforts with the production of the first successful computer in 1953. Europe has a long list of recent technical successes in machine tools, in aeronautics (swing-wing and vertical take-off planes and hovercraft), in pharmaceuticals, in laser technology, in cryogenics, in office machinery (fluidics and holography), in glass processing, in steel production, and in colour television and casette tape recorders. The new rotary engine (just developed in Europe) might well revolutionise the automobile industry. Perhaps not on the same scale, but the Europeans sell their patents to the Americans just as the Americans sell theirs to the rest of the industrial world. Indeed, while there are not so many European firms operating in the United States as there are American firms operating in Europe, there are examples of European houses competing sucessfully within the United States. In the past few years, British, Dutch, German and Swiss companies have taken over certain branches of American domestic industry. The breakdown of European investments in the United States in 1970 shows the leading items to be manufacturing: 46 per cent, petroleum: 23 per cent, and insurance: 17 per cent.

The explanation for all this lies partly in the nature of the industry itself – oil, aluminium, chemicals, copper and steel, and rubber, seem to encourage a world-wide outlook, in contrast, say, to textiles and brewing. Also, when an industry gets so large that it has millions or billions of dollars invested in fixed plant and machinery, it has to take some steps to ensure a reliable supply of raw materials.

We feel quite sure that nationality has little to do with it. In fact, in the closing decades of the nineteenth century, it was the American press that was talking about a British business invasion, and not the other way round. Indeed it is possible that as late as 1950 foreigners held more business assets in the United States than American citizens held outside their country. Nationality, like technology, must play some part in the invasion of a nation's territory by the businessmen of another country. Yet the vital factors, as we see them, are the mental attitudes of the individuals concerned and the scale of the effort. If we may shift attention, does anyone believe that the Americans have replaced British oil interests in the Middle East since the 1940s because of nationality or superior technology? To talk about superior nationality is silly. As for technology, overall technological superiority lies on neither side of the North Atlantic. Weight and business acumen are what matter; and in these things, at this point in history, the Americans have few rivals.

Curiously enough, while so much of the business invasion of Europe since 1945 can only be explained in terms of seizing new investment opportunities (the bulk of them let it be said with Europe's own money), which evidently were thought to be more profitable than investments made in the home market, many of the industries in which the Americans excel in Europe today are the same kind of industries – the mass-production of capital-intensive consumer goods – in which they excelled a hundred years ago. Then, it was the sewing machine and the typewriter; now it is the automobile and the computer. The Americans have always concentrated their effort on the more dynamic, faster-growing and usually more profitable sectors of a country's economy. Yet, they have not concentrated – at home or abroad – on high technology industries because they are somehow smarter than others, but because they are richer than others. These are the things which the Americans have specialised in for a hundred years or more. Similarly, the amount spent on research and development, relative to others, springs more from the need of the capital-intensive industries in which (in size at least) they have excelled for so long. Other people are equally scientific and equally productive as the Americans. But they have different mental outlooks, different resources and different market structures.

Complementary to the creation of American foreign business organisations has been the establishment of an American banking network around the globe. In 1918 United States banks had established branches in sixteen countries, primarily in Latin America and Europe. Growth was slow in the 1920s and 1930s, although United States banks did appear at this time in east Asia. Because of the closing down of branches in Germany and Russia, there was little overall growth between 1918 and 1939. However, as America's political and economic power grew in the post-Second World War period, its banking organisation expanded abroad at an accelerating rate, often by buying into subsidiary organisations. By the end of 1970 branches were located in sixty-six different countries. Between 1950 and 1970, the number of bank branches abroad increased from 95 to 536. The total assets/liabilities of these branches more than quadrupled between 1966 and 1970 (from \$12·4 to \$52·6 billion). Europe, which accounted for three-quarters of the assets, Latin America and east Asia were the three most important areas of growth. As many of these banks were deeply involved in the financing of foreign industry (much of it under the control of United States-based multinational firms), it

became increasingly difficult to say where America's foreign
financial power ended and its industrial and political power
began.

One outcome of the expansion of American private business, especially banking business in Europe since the Second
World War, has been the creation of a vast reservoir of dollar
resources referred to today as the Euro-dollar and the
Euro-bond market. Even though our main concern here is
with long-term investment – with the international capital
rather than the international money market – it is necessary
to say a word or two about what has become the largest, freest
market for short-term funds that the world has seen. The
development of the Euro-currency market since the Second
World War, in which the dollar is only one of many currencies
traded, has caused a dramatic shift in financial power and
control away from the central banks of the different countries
to the international money market. The integrative role of a
single financial centre – such as Britain held in the nineteenth
century – has passed to the Euro-currency and the Euro-
bond market.

Most Euro-dollars are dollars on deposit in banks in
Europe. Euro-bonds are loans of the normally short-term
Euro-dollars made for five years or more; most are traded
like any other bonds on the principal stock exchanges of the
world (except those of the United States).[15] In effect the
Euro-dollar market is a banking system operating (largely by
telephone) with dollars outside the United States.[16] Hence
dollars that return to the United States cease to be Euro-
dollars.

Those who laid the foundations of this market had no idea
that it would become the giant of today. In fact it all began
very modestly in the autumn of 1957 when, following the
Suez crisis and the subsequent restrictions placed on the use
of sterling to finance non-British trade, a number of London
bankers began to make use of European dollar resources.
Shortages of sterling simply prompted the use of overseas
dollars.

Several things turned the 1957 trickle into a flood.[17] First of
all there was a growing and unprecedented demand for (and
supply of) dollars in Europe. Deposits of dollars in European

banks were encouraged by the emergence of a deficit in the United States balance of payments during the 1950s. Improved political and economic conditions in Europe in the late 1950s, coupled with currency convertibility and unrestricted repatriation of earnings, also helped. In addition the attempts made by the United States and European governments to devise national monetary policies – especially the attempts made by the American government to increase the cost of borrowing by foreigners on the New York market – caused a disparity in interest rates to develop in favour of the Euro-dollar market. Government intervention in 1965 and 1968 to strengthen America's balance of payments position added further impetus.

Not least important was the market's efficiency. Because it is almost free of national restrictions, and also because of the economical way it is run, the Euro-dollar market is able to pay more for money borrowed and charge less for money lent. Interest rates have been consistently higher than those obtained by time deposits in New York banks. Money simply migrated to where it could maximise its income. By 1968 the market had spread to continental Europe, Canada and Japan; markets in other convertible currencies, including the Japanese yen, had appeared alongside the market for the Euro-dollar. Yet, as in 1957, London had remained the principal market,[18] the Euro-dollar the chief currency, and the provision of trade credits the Euro-dollar's most important single employment.

By 1970 about $46 billion Euro-dollar loans were outstanding. So great had these foreign holdings of dollars become that they were regarded by some as a threat to America's balance of payments with the rest of the world. By 1960 the liquid dollar obligations to foreigners had outstripped the gold reserves of the United States (Table X). As America's balance of foreign payments continued to deteriorate throughout the 1960s, efforts were made to stem the flood of dollars to Europe. On 10 February 1965 a voluntary payments programme was introduced to encourage the repatriation of business income from abroad, as well as to expand exports. Foreign-based businesses were urged to meet more of their long- and short-term capital needs from foreign

rather than domestic resources.[19] Within a few months,
American corporations had borrowed $340 million in
Europe against the issue of dollar bonds by their subsidiaries
there. There was a repatriation of funds from European-
based companies and banks. Actually, as the 625 United
States corporations affected were quick to point out, the
figures for 1966 ($3·14 billion sent abroad in direct private
investments; $4 billion returned to the United States in
foreign income), provided sufficient evidence that private
foreign investment already was contributing toward a health-
ier balance of payments position.[20] Moreover, while United
States private business operations in Europe in the postwar
period have undoubtedly played a large role in the growth of
the Euro-dollar market, there have been many other
agencies – governments, central banks, corporations and private individuals alike – who for profit or security reasons have
kept their dollars outside the United States and in doing so
have fostered the growth of the market.

In any event the voluntary payments programme of 1965
failed to stop the outflow of capital to Europe. On 1 January
1968 mandatory limits were placed on foreign investments,
and companies were required to repatriate a specified percentage of foreign earnings. It was this measure which increased
the tendency for American foreign businesses to issue securities or company bonds abroad (something rarely done
before mid-1965).[21]

By the spring of 1971, several special factors (the growth of
American foreign business and tourism, the cost of war,
domestic inflation, more favourable interest rates in Europe
and a rising volume of imports from there) had combined to
release a flood of dollars far exceeding the world's demands.
Triggering the whole thing was the decline in the total
demand for dollars. As demand fell off (however we explain
it) the scarce dollars of the immediate postwar years – the
so-called dollar gap – became a glut; the greater the flood, the
less the dollar's value relative to other European
currencies – especially relative to the undervalued West
German mark. The Europeans and Americans operating in
the international money market for profit considerations
were encouraged to change overvalued Euro-dollars for

America's Influence on World Finance   91

undervalued West German marks (or Euro-marks), and to a
lesser extent other currencies. In 1971 the United States
government sought a temporary solution by issuing special
securities for sale to the overseas branches of American
banks. The banks used $1·5 billion Euro-dollars in buying the
certificates. Also in 1971 the Export-Import Bank of
Washington eased the pressure in Europe by borrowing a
further $1·5 billion Euro-dollars from American branch
banks. These measures removed some of the excess reserves
of dollars held in Europe, but the flurry of monetary speculations was soon renewed. Because of its central role in the
world economy which it had held since the Bretton Woods
agreement of 1944, and also for reasons of prestige, the
United States refused to devalue the dollar. The more its
balance of payments position with the rest of the world
worsened, the more unreal this attitude became. Speculation
against the dollar grew throughout 1971; the less value placed
by the money market on what appeared to it as an overvalued
dollar, the more value placed on gold[22] and other currencies.
On 15 August 1971, the dollar was devalued by ten per cent.
In December 1971 (with the Smithsonian Agreement), new
currency rates were set. However, instead of America's
position improving it worsened. Throughout 1972, every
weakness in America's domestic economy was reflected in the
dwindling value of the dollar. In February 1973 another
massive run was made on the dollar in the international
money market and America was forced to devalue again. The
dollar-dominated world of the late 1940s, 1950s and 1960s
had come to an end.

   Present-day attitudes to the Euro-dollar market are sharply divided.[23] Praised or damned, the fact is that while the
world's demand for dollars relative to certain other currencies
is declining, American dollars have created the largest financial market operating outside any nation's jurisdiction. An
overall estimate of the short-term liquid funds of all private
businesses and private banks operating on the international
money market in 1971 (most of them United States owned
and controlled) was in the region of $268 billion. This is a
staggering sum, and one with which no government or
international monetary authority can cope. These vast and

highly mobile funds not only facilitate international business and maximise gain, they also present a serious threat to the financial organisation and the monetary policy of many countries. It needs only the sudden movement of one per cent of sums of this kind to bring on a monetary crisis. No government can be sure that the control of its economy by monetary policy will not be jeopardised by movements of international money. This is what happened to West Germany in 1960–1. The German government's intention to tighten credit by raising interest rates was completely thwarted by the phenomenal influx of funds from abroad, chiefly from the United States.[24] It was a shift of $6 billion from the Euro-currency market into Germany that triggered the second devaluation of the dollar in February 1973. No one seems to know whose money it was. The only thing definite is that the move not only triggered the second devaluation but gave somebody a profit of $400 million. Little wonder that those who helped to create the Euro-dollar market are having second thoughts about the market's future. What most haunts government financial advisors and central bankers is the size of the mobile funds over which – try as they may – they have little or no control.

Whatever its hazards the growing international market for dollars and other currencies has at least supplemented traditional methods of raising short- and long-term capital. The significant thing is that it has broken down the traditional barriers that separated the money and the capital markets. It has also helped to reduce disparities between national markets in the demand for and supply of capital. It obviously meets a considerable need which was not being met. So long as the market remains adaptable and countries tolerate the movement of these enormous sums in search of maximum gain, the market will survive. Outside the totalitarian States there is little that freely elected governments can do to prevent the movement of short-term capital organised in this way. Indeed, as never before, national governments in the West are faced by an international monetary power that, while it might not undo nationalism, can certainly topple a national government. It is not a question of the supposed wickedness of the gnomes of Zürich, or of Frankfurt, or of

London, or of New York. It is a question of facing entirely new phenomena in which the relations between the national State and the international money market have still to be worked out.*

While direct business investments abroad and the use of Euro-dollars and Euro-bonds, and other short-term international funds, have had an important effect on the postwar long- and short-term capital market, there has also been a resurgence of private portfolio long-term capital movements. However, with the exception of bonds issued by the World Bank in the late 1940s, of Canadian bonds sold in the United States, and the special help given by the New York investment market to Israel, it was not until the late 1950s (when the French franc was devalued and the pound sterling made convertible) that the revival in the foreign bond market took place. Henceforth, encouraged by European recovery and the integration of the European economy (the European Common Market began operations in 1958), American interest in European bonds grew. For the first time in almost thirty years, European banks and other institutions found the New York bond market ready to buy long-term bonds for Americans and Europeans at relatively low transaction costs. Fear of inflation and dislike of the tax collector (bond income is easily traced), rather than a shortage of savings, help to explain why Europeans floated their bond issues in New York (where the supply of liquid capital was growing) rather than in Europe. Between 1950–4 and 1955–9, private American long-term lending, largely in bonds, grew from $256 million annually to more than three times that amount. For the same years, the annual average of American direct business investment doubled. By 1960, the total of new bond issues (domestic and foreign) on the New York market was more than twice the combined total for all continental European markets. The annual average for the years 1960–4 amounted to $1·4

*In one sense the problem is not entirely new. As early as the sixteenth century the national monarchies became aware of the need to control national credit. As a result, the role of the Fuggers of Augsburg and the Florentine merchant bankers (whose outlook was international) was restricted. Similarly, the new seventeenth-century Bank of Amsterdam was designed to serve Dutch national interests.

billion.[25] The total of new foreign issues for 1962 came close to an all-time peak reached in 1947 – most of them subscribed from outside the United States, and particularly from Europe. Unlike the flow of Euro-dollars, which appear to have been sensitive to changes in interest rates, the conditions in the bond market appear to have been influenced by other factors, such as domestic monetary policies which severely limited foreign issues on the European market. Of the $325 million of new European bonds sold in New York in 1962, Europeans took up $130 million.[26] The book value of long-term portfolio investment in the United States by foreigners increased from $4·6 billion in 1950 to $35·9 billion in 1971. Of the approximately $5 billion of international bonds issued outside the United States in 1971, seven-tenths were Eurobonds, three-tenths were the traditional type of foreign bonds. The course of United States portfolio investments abroad is traced in Table VII.

The other great change in international investment in recent times is the growth of what is commonly referred to as 'Foreign Aid'. As 'half-brother' to the world, the American has a long history of giving private help to others.[27] A good deal of the money brought by migrants to the United States, for instance, was offset by the remittances made by them to their relatives in Europe. The Swedes were receiving an annual sum of $3,000,000 as early as 1882.[28] During the years 1922–7, the figure was approximately $9,500,000 – in some years the equivalent of Sweden's payments of old-age pensions. A similar annual figure ($10,000,000) was received by Norway for the years 1912–13.[29] An investigation held by the Italian government in the 1920s showed that a total of two billion dollars had been remitted to Italy between 1901 and 1923, 80 per cent of it coming from the United States.[30] This money gave temporary relief to many a hard-pressed home, tided many a little farm over a crisis period, and provided millions of emigrants with the funds to reach the New World.[31] In addition private help has been given through the numerous organisations such as the missions, the American Red Cross (founded in 1882), the Jewish Joint Distribution Committee, the Friend's Service Committee, the Near East

Relief Committee, the Rockefeller and the Ford Foundations, and the Carnegie Corporation. There have been few
calls for private relief in the past hundred years that have gone
unanswered.

Government aid, however, dates back only to the help
given to the Irish in 1847 and 1880, and to Venezuela after
the earthquake of 1912. A few years later, several bilateral
financial transactions were conducted between the American
and German governments; and in the 1930s, as part of its
'dollar diplomacy', the American government established the
Export–Import Bank of Washington which could lend to
foreign governments as well as to private enterprises. But
these public acts were exceptions to the rule that foreign relief
and investment were matters for the private individual, not
the State. Only with the end of the Second World War was
that policy reversed. Since then, foreign aid of all kinds has
become increasingly a matter of government action and, to an
unprecedented extent, an instrument of foreign policy.

In this, America follows an old tradition.[32] The alliance of
finance and diplomacy entered the modern age with the
merchant princes of the Renaissance. Seventeenth- and
eighteenth-century French and English statesmen were
skilled in the use of money to serve national interests. It was
said of the French monarch, Louis XIV (1643–1715), that he
was 'the treasurer of needy sovereigns'. Nations have always
bought allies (except Sparta, whose allies had to pay for the
accommodation) and silenced would-be aggressors with
money. Nor, while some Americans would doubt it, is there
anything new in those who receive aid biting the hand that
gives it. It has always been so. As Machiavelli says in *The
Prince*, 'friendships gained with money, not with greatness
and nobility of spirit, are purchased but not possessed. . . .'[33]

What is new about America's experience during the past
thirty years is the amount of aid given; also, what the
Americans have expected to get out of it. While many people
have thought that they might save the world's soul, only the
Americans have suffered the illusion that with enough money
they might save the world's economy. The relatively new-
found beliefs that financial assistance and economic development are somehow inextricably linked, and that a richer

world will be a safer world, are ideas that are both recent and peculiarly American.

These ideas did not really gain currency until the Marshall Plan of 1947, under which, in the next five years, a number of European countries received $12 billion of supplies.[34] They were further recognised and strengthened by President Truman's programme of technical assistance to other lands, begun in 1949. Until then, America was more concerned with acts of mercy, or stop-gap measures to defend the 'Free World' against Communism, as witness the rushing of arms and economic aid to Greece and Turkey in 1947. When Congress passed the Mutual Security Act of 1951, Communism was still the chief foe, but economic development had by then found more advocates, and massive government foreign aid had come to be accepted. President Eisenhower's attempts in the 1950s to shift the emphasis in foreign aid from giving to investing, i.e. from grants to loans, as well as to shift some of the burden of foreign economic development away from the taxpayer back on to the shoulders of the private investor, was looked upon by some as a backward step. By then foreign aid was so deeply entrenched in Washington that no President could have had much effect upon it. Indeed, by the time President Kennedy came along, government agencies giving foreign aid had become so numerous that he was obliged to create the overall Agency for International Development (which by 1965 had more than 5000 highly-skilled technicians abroad, assisting foreign development). It is significant that the term Mutual Security was supplanted by the term International Development.

Whether given to protect the United States and its allies or to promote international development, the precise quantity and nature of foreign aid in the period 1945–70 can only be guessed. There are instances of double-counting, and some information, for security reasons, has been deliberately concealed. But taking the figures for what they are worth, we find total United States government foreign assistance, military and other, in the period 1945–70 was $125 billion. A breakdown of this figure shows Europe receiving $43·3 billion; Near East and South Asia, $27·6 billion; Latin America and Western Hemisphere, $10·1 billion; Africa,

$4·1 billion. Until 1962 France and Britain led the aid list (in total amounts received). Since then, there has been a marked shift to Asian countries. No correlation can be drawn between a country's numbers and the amount of aid received. Since 1948, twelve countries (out of a total of 111 that have received aid) have accounted for about half the money spent. Prior to 1960, most assistance was given to western European nations. Currently most aid (military and economic) is being given to the nations surrounding the Russian and Chinese land-mass. (Table VIII/A.) Details of United States foreign assistance expenditures for 1971–3 are given in Table VIII/B.

Although this aid is officially classified as either military or economic, there is really no way of separating one from the other. If we take the classifications at their face value, the immediate postwar years of the Marshall Plan account for the largest amounts of economic aid. Military assistance ran at its highest level from the late 1940s to the mid-1950s. Since the mid-1960s, the proportion of aid devoted to economic and social purposes has increased. In the period 1946–70, military programmes took $40 billion of the $125 billion spent.[35] The figures for the year 1970 were: $1700 million, economic aid; $700 million, military aid. In dollar terms, as a percentage of Gross National Product, aid has declined from about 2 per cent in 1946–58 to about ¼ per cent in 1968–70. In the same period, the G.N.P. increased more than fourfold. In fact, in 1970 the United States was contributing a smaller percentage of both its G.N.P. and its National Income to foreign aid than many other nations.[36] And whereas in 1960 about 65 per cent of this money was in grant form, by 1969, 69 per cent was in loan form bearing interest. A figure given for 1966 shows that 90 per cent of all foreign aid was tied to the procurement of United States goods and surpluses.[37]

Because these funds have been used as an instrument of foreign policy, they cannot be explained in terms of philanthropy or economic need. Thus, in the period 1951–4, Yugoslavia obtained $325 million in foreign aid, while Latin America (with more than ten times the number of people) received $101 million. Similarly between 1945–64, whereas West Germany received $3,659 million in grants, India and

Pakistan (with a population ten times greater) received $149 million. In the absence of a coherent philosophy of foreign aid, it is difficult to speak of the programme's success or failure. Nor do we know how much of it is invalidated by corruption and log-rolling.[38] In Israel, Greece, Formosa, Tunisia and the Philippines, some of the economic benefits of foreign aid are self-evident. But these successes are offset by equally dismal failures elsewhere; hence the belief held by many Americans that they are history's first 'Fight Alls, Pay Alls and Lose Alls'.[39] Certainly, there is not much economic development to show for the $150 billion (or is it $250 billion)[40] spent. Indeed, it is doubtful if the Americans have been any more successful in saving the world from its economic woes than they have been in spreading Christianity or political democracy.

Complementary to bilateral aid has been the assistance given by the many international agencies established since the end of the Second World War (Table IX). Believing that the revival of an adequate private capital market in the postwar period was impossible, the United States took the initiative in 1944 in laying the foundations of the World Bank and the International Monetary Fund; the former was intended to make long-term capital available to member nations; the latter was meant to provide the necessary funds to settle short-term imbalances in international payments. The capital of the American Export–Import Bank (founded in the 1930s) was also increased in 1945 by $3 billion, to be used in intergovernment loans for reconstruction (Table VIII/B).

Great as the work of these and other agencies has been (not least those of the United Nations Development Fund, to which the United States has made substantial contributions), the backbone of international investment in the West has remained the private investor. By 1954 United States foreign private investment had exceeded the value of foreign aid. Thenceforth most of the long-term capital reaching low-income countries has come from private sources.

Despite the hostility shown by some past civilisations to commerce in general and finance in particular, money has always played a role in the life of mankind. The more specialised and commercially oriented a people has become, the greater that role has been. Never has it had greater significance than it does in the life of the highly capitalised West today. Only by borrowing from the Old World was the European family able to settle the New. As the integration of the white-settled world proceeded, capital became more abundant and mobile than it had ever been. Given the right terms, private, profit-seeking capital willingly assisted the productive and (where military and naval equipment was concerned) destructive forces of many people. In time, vast sums of European wealth were mobilised and put to use in every continent. As a result of this process, by the end of the nineteenth century the United States had become the world's greatest debtor nation.

Yet the money the Americans borrowed, in financial terms at least, was put to excellent use. With its help the human and the technological resources of Europe were transferred to the New World. The outcome was a special bounty for the whole western world. So much so that by the 1890s the Americans could afford to place large sums abroad. Assisted by the rapid expansion of their own economy and the stimulus provided by the First World War, their foreign assets soon exceeded their liabilities. In the interwar years, the United States became the world's leading creditor nation.

Since the Second World War, American money has greatly helped the non-Communist world. The crucial factor determining the flow has been the search for profit. Except for private philanthropy and postwar foreign aid, profit and security considerations were just as important in the distribution of twentieth-century capitalist American investments, as they were in those of nineteenth-century capitalist Britain. The Americans differ from the British and the other western creditor nations in the quantity of capital they have accumulated and the manner in which (through direct business investments) they have employed it to extend their business and industrial empire throughout the world. It is the scale of their business investments, their special nature, and above all else their business acumen and aptitudes as a commercial people, that distinguish them. The significance of American investments in the European-settled parts of the world is not that they introduced industries that without them would never have existed, but that their capital enabled existing industries to grow at a more rapid rate. After the Second World War while Europe was trying to restore its losses the Americans gained almost a monopoly in the production of capital-intensive consumer goods. Europe's recovery and the establishment of the Common market in the late 1950s has done much to reduce America's overwhelming superiority.

In so far as they have introduced industries that the indigenous people, left by themselves, would not have had, America's impact on the non-western world has been more pronounced. The money they have placed in low-income countries has made a considerable contribution to the capital, incomes, foreign exchange, revenue, employment, trade and standards of technical efficiency.[41] Yet, relative to the amounts needed, even these sums are often too small and too concentrated for them to have a dramatic effect upon the poorer parts of the world. Indeed there are some economists who believe that American private investment in the low-income countries has done more harm than good.[42] Most of it is in the extractive industries (concerned with syphoning off natural wealth and resources to the Western world) or in consumer goods industries and hotels, which the poorer countries can ill afford. In contrast the construction of public works (such as transport and power) or the development of manufacturing or heavy industry (that might provide a further stimulus to economic growth) have been neglected. Because of the risk involved, low-income countries have to pay more for money than developed countries, and there is a faster rate of return of dividends from the poor world to the United States than there is from the rich. Moreover, the grandiose schemes propagated by the Americans during the 1960s for the economic growth and development of the poorer world encouraged many poor countries to borrow money which they cannot hope to repay. The promised growth has not materialised, but the debt is there. Also, what we know about the impact of American corporations operating in the underdeveloped world tells us that they assist the balance of payments position of the United States more than that of the host country. In these circumstances, despite the growing political independence of the low-income countries in the postwar period, the gap between the rich and the poor of the world can only widen.

The truth is that some of the low-income countries possess neither the wealth, nor the technical traditions nor the social environment necessary for success. The purpose of the international corporation, in entering the underdeveloped world, is not to stimulate economic development but to find profitable markets. As a private organisation, it has to charge more for money and services where the risks are greatest. In fact, it is not the monetary cost of American capital that the underdeveloped world resents most (this is usually small compared with the cost of hiring local capital); it is being 'monopolised' and 'bossed around' by Americans, individually and as a nation. The basic problem for the poorer nations of the world is how to obtain an improved technology and at the same time retain their national pride. While the chief purpose of private capital is economic, the chief resentment against it in the world today is psychological. The presence of the American foreign investor is seen and felt abroad today as his · nineteenth-century anonymous British predecessor never was.

About the future of foreign investment and the international money market several things might be said. Despite the fact that the influence of the American multinational corporations and American banks abroad is growing, there is nothing immutable in America's present financial position in the world. Its overwhelming position in foreign investments and the international money market is a very recent post-Second World War phenomenon; it arose out of special conditions and it could just as quickly disappear.* What we are dealing with is an entirely new phenomenon. The American presence in the investment and money markets of the world has become so great as to challenge national sovereignty. Yet the integrative role in world finance which London held in the nineteenth century has not passed to Washington. It rests today in the hands of the international capital market and the

*The measure passed in December 1973 by the Canadian House of Commons to control foreign investment (principally U.S. investment) would have been unthinkable a decade or two ago.

international money market, and by and large it is outside the jurisdiction of any government. The short-term assets and huge dollar holdings of American corporations and overseas branches of American banks in 1971were not far short of $200 billion. Not least to avoid loss rather than to obtain profit, these funds had a hand in generating the monetary crises that have enveloped the dollar during 1972–3. These things may be very short-lived – indeed the size and power of American capital abroad may prove its own undoing – but unless a compromise can be worked out between the interests of the nation and the interests of the international capital and money markets, a head-on collision between the politician and the businessman would seem to be inevitable. There is a changing attitude on the part of the American people towards the individual, capitalist, free enterprise system whence came so much of their wealth. The greater their monetary problems, the more likely we are to see restraints placed upon the employment of private short- and long-term funds. The present Space Age has already witnessed a change in the American attitude towards investment as a whole. America's rockets to the moon are not the modern equivalent of ancient man's pyramids and temples, but they are for the Americans an unusual non-commercial use of capital.

Nor can we overlook the important changes that might be brought about in world investment by the action of the United Nations. The United Nations' Development Decade of the 1960s, in which the Americans took a prominent part, while it failed in its goal to invest one per cent of the accumulated national incomes of the industrial nations in the developing world, might be the shadow of things to come. The trouble is that the industrial nations are now less dependent than they were on the primary producing areas of the world. The tendency is to invest with each other. As long as there is freedom of choice, most American investors will continue to place their money in the more profitable white-settled world. The problem is compounded by the fact that – where the world's economic problems are concerned – most governments (rich and poor) speak with two voices: one voice calls for a global effort, the other insists on national autonomy. As long as one nation's political goals differ from those of its neighbours, we shall go on living in a world of economic disequilibrium. It is this which made the Smithsonian Financial Agreement of 1971 (hailed by President Nixon as 'The Greatest Monetary Agreement in History') so impotent. The difficulty lies not in plans and schemes to reform the world's monetary system; the libraries are full of them. The difficulty lies in resolving the problems created by the different outlooks and the different interests. We assume a uniformity of outlook between the economist and the politician which does not exist. We assume that what is good for one nation will necessarily be good for another. We assume that what we are dealing with is money, whereas what we are dealing with is power. Equity and altruism never have determined the economic policy of sovereign states, and there is little sign they will do so now.

Ultimately the future of the low-income countries depends upon themselves. Foreign capital can help or hinder development, but it is not so important as mental attitudes. Capital by itself does nothing. The United States was greatly assisted by European funds; Japan managed to develop almost without them. Each example of development is particular and intensely human. How a people react to a situation depends on what kind of a people they are, which, in turn, depends on their history and their environment. Where the American effort to help the underdeveloped world has failed, it has done so because – like so many other American efforts in the world – it was conceived in the absence of history.

CHAPTER V

The Impact of American Technology

WHILE the word 'technology'[1] was little used by the Americans in the eighteenth century, in comparison to the term 'the Useful Arts', the role of applied science has been basic in the formation and progress of the American commonwealth; for the United States is the only nation to have taken shape at a time when a technical, power-driven civilisation was spreading from Europe to the rest of the world.

With the outbreak of war with England in 1775 technology began to play a conscious role. '*British tyranny*', said Timothy Matlack in 1780 to the American Philosophical Society, 'restrained us from making Steel to enrich her Merchants and Manufacturers, but we can now make it ourselves as good as theirs'.[2] Eventually resolution, inventiveness, and ingenuity – and not a little luck – won for the colonists their political (and later their industrial) independence. Henceforth, as the arts of peace were renewed, the momentum of technical development grew. The process was slow and piecemeal and should not be exaggerated. In 1806 Robert Fulton was able to find only one mechanic in the whole of New York able to make a time-fuse torpedo.[3] In 1820 Daniel Treadwell could not find a single steam engine in Boston and had to work his recently invented printing press by horses. Gradually, however, there were developed the weapons, tools, and improved systems of transport and communications without which the nation and economy are inconceivable. Only thus were the cotton textile manufacturing plants of Samuel Slater's New England created and bound to Eli Whitney's cotton-producing south. It was improved technology that eventually linked the food-producing areas of the American west with the great urban centres of the east. The territorial division of labour among the three great sections of the country – the northeast, the south, and the growing west – was fostered not only by foreign demands but by improved technology. The conquest and colonisation of the American continent, the extraordinary speed with which wealth was accumulated (and consumed), the emergence of a system of mass-production and a national market – all these things were dependent upon the improved technology of European and American society. It is not surprising that the early accounts of the development of the economy have tended to exaggerate technology's importance.[4]

Peculiar to the development of American technology was its basic aim. It was not enough that technology should help to free the young republic from Britain's grasp, that toil should be lightened, and that wealth should be increased; technology was meant to express the political and social content of the American way of life. Only through the development of the useful arts could the material success of republicanism and civil liberty be ensured and its example followed. Progress in technology and progress in equality and liberty were meant to march hand in hand. (The ancient Greeks, Anaxagoras and Aeschylus, had had similar feelings about the relation between progress in technology and democracy.)[5] Only thus could the American people fulfil their mission to the world. 'Every order of things', Robert Fulton argued in 1807, 'which has a tendency to remove oppression and meliorate the condition of man, directing his ambition to useful industry, is, in effect, republican'.[6]

That the American way would be a pragmatic, common sense, utilitarian way was evident from the very beginning. Regardless of the unity that marks western technical methods and traditions, American technology, in response to the needs of a different environment, underwent a subtle change. The modification of firearms from European smooth-bore musket to a rifled firearm more suitable to American conditions is abundantly clear.[7] Axes (symbol of the frontiersman), hatchets, mattocks, pickaxes (tools in clearing the land); hoes, spades, shovels, sickles, ploughs, garden rakes, and hay forks (needed to husband the land); saws, hammers, augers, chisels (needed to build shelter); and likewise the tools of the blacksmith, the cooper, and other artisans – all underwent a gradual change in the New World. The paths of western European and American technology diverged – even before the revolution – not because of English edicts forbidding Americans to develop their country as they thought fit, but because their outlook and their needs were different. For the Americans, the criterion that mattered was usefulness. 'You know', said Thomas Jefferson, writing to Thomas Cooper in 1812, 'the just esteem which attached itself to Dr Franklin's science, because he always endeavored to direct it to something useful in private life'.[8] 'Inventive genius,' argued Jacob Bigelow, the Harvard professor in applied science in 1816, should be concentrated on improving '... the facilities of subsistence, and the welfare of those among whom we live. ... The researches of most of our ingenious men have had utility for their object.'[9]

It was the stress placed upon utility (rather than upon individuality, or beauty, or traditions), coupled with the fact that early America had much more work to do than there were skilled hands available to do it, that caused the American people to begin a love affair with the machine that has gone on until the present day. The nineteenth-century Yankee was drawn to machines, as people of other civilisations were drawn to the arts, administration, religion, music, or metaphysics. Said the British engineer Joseph Whitworth, in a report to the House of Commons in 1854,[10] 'Workmen hail with satisfaction all mechanical improvements.' This 'eager resort to machinery' by American workmen, Whitworth thought, went far to explain the extraordinary development and the prosperous condition of the United States. However we explain it, there grew up in early America almost a psychological and moral compulsion to use machinery. Given the unhindered use of machinery, given democratic and social opportunity, especially given a public system of education, American man would surely find his El Dorado.

Not everyone saw in the growth of machinery and the triumph of industrialism the dawn of a wantless world. Alexander Hamilton's view of an industrial civilisation may have triumphed over the Jeffersonian dream of a rural democracy, but it is wrong to think that it triumphed easily. Many early American voices spoke out against the machine. In 1813 Oliver Evans' steam sawmill at New Orleans was in fact destroyed. Similarly those who introduced the English Cartwright loom had to overcome much opposition. 'Labor-saving machinery,' said Philadelphia workmen in the 1830s, was 'Europe's curse and America's dread.'[11] Yet it was de Tocqueville who saw most clearly the implications of a growing machine economy in the United States:

Every new method that leads by a shorter road to wealth, every machine that spares labor, every instrument that diminishes the cost of production, every discovery that facilitates pleasures or augments them, seems to be the grandest effort of the human intellect. . . . You may be sure that the more democratic, enlightened, and free a nation is, the greater will be the number of these interested promoters of scientific genius and the more will discoveries immediately applicable to productive industry confer on their authors gain, fame, and even power.[12]

For de Tocqueville, the outcome was not in doubt. Democracy and the machine together would produce 'a state of accomplished mediocrity'. His opinions on the essential incompatibility of democracy and science (pure and applied) would be echoed by writers down to the present day.[13]

The stress placed upon utility was said to explain the relative backwardness of early American science. 'It is astonishing', wrote the Abbé Guillaume Raynal in 1774, 'that America has not yet produced a good poet, an able mathematician, a man of genius in a single art, or a single science';[14] which provoked Ezra Stiles, President of Yale College in 1785, to claim that America had contributed as much to science in 'the last half century as in all Europe'.[15] Hurt pride prompted Thomas Dobson (who between 1790 and 1798 reprinted the *Encyclopaedia Britannica* at Philadelphia), to be a little overgenerous in his assessment of American achievements when he said that 'the United States of America have produced their full proportion of genius in the science of war, in physics, astronomy and mathematics, in mechanic arts, in government, in fiscal science, in divinity, in history, in oratory, in poetry, in painting, in music, and the plastic art'.[16]

Most of these commentators saw what they wanted to see. It is possible that we exaggerate the attention given by the early Americans to the useful and the pragmatic,[17] as we tend to overdo the worship of the machine. Far from being concerned merely with the useful not a few early American scientists were able and willing to enter into 'refined philosophical speculation' with their European colleagues. The truth is that colonial America produced a number of men who became scientists in their own right.[18] Leading all others in the late colonial period and the early years of the republic were Benjamin Franklin (1706–90), famous for his contributions to experimental science, especially for his work on electricity; the expatriate Benjamin Thompson (1753–1814), known for his experiments on the nature of heat as a form of motion; James Bowdoin (1726–90), who, among other contributions, corrected Franklin's theory of electricity; David Rittenhouse (1732–96), a Philadelphia clock and instrument maker who built the first planetarium in the colonies and made important systematic astronomical observations; Benjamin Rush (1745–1813), distinguished for his contributions to experimental medicine and his pioneering work on mental health; and Amos Eaton (1776–1842), who was outstanding in the field of natural history. Charles Wilson Peale's Philadelphia Museum of Natural History (established in 1784) boasted Jefferson as one of its Presidents. Out of the intellectual and scientific ferment caused by these and other eighteenth-century American scientists (who have been called 'Gentlemen dilettantes') was born the American Philosophical Society (1743), the American Academy of Arts and Sciences (1780), and the American Academy of National Sciences (1812).

How these developments in industry and science compared with those being made elsewhere in the western world is evident from the reports of the various international exhibitions held throughout the second half of the nineteenth century. The first was the 'Great Exhibition of the Works of

All Nations', held in London in 1851. Of all the American exhibits, none received as much praise as Cyrus Hall McCormick's reaper (only McCormick received a much-coveted Grand Medal as well as a Council Medal).

The American horsedrawn, mechanical reaper was, in fact, the most significant invention introduced into farming between 1830 and 1860, for it speeded up the production process precisely at the point where grain could either be harvested quickly and successfully, or ruined. The cutting bar and reel which bent the grain back against the bar were not new. What was new was mechanisation. According to some observers, it created in agricultural technology the same momentous change that the 'Spinning Jenny', and the power loom had produced in textile technology. The functionally simple, cheap, light and strong American ploughs and other agricultural tools also compared very favourably with the more expensive, cumbrous European products. More than anything else it was the successful demonstration of American agricultural implements and machinery – especially the reapers and draught ploughs – that caused British observers to realise that the 'adolescent Republic across the Atlantic' was rapidly coming of age. Said London's *Punch*,

> . . .
> By Yankee Doodle too, you're beat
> Downright in Agriculture,
> With his machine for reaping wheat,
> Chaw'd up as by a vulture![19]

Next in attracting attention was Samuel Colt's revolver, of which the *New York Herald* of 20 October 1851 said '. . . will kill eight times as quick as any weapon formerly in use'. Indeed, the Colt revolver threatened – along with the other firearms exhibited by the Americans – to revolutionise military tactics.[20]

If adoption of an invention is a measure of its success, then nothing achieved world acclaim in 1851 more than the American sewing machine. Invented by Thomas Saint, an Englishman, in 1790, for sewing leather, the sewing machine was re-invented in the late 1820s by a French tailor, Barthélemy Thimonnier, and again in the 1830s by the

American Walter Hunt (who never applied for a patent), and in the 1840s by Hunt's countryman Elias Howe. It was Howe's shuttle principle (demonstrated in London in 1851), in the hands of that business genius, Isaac Singer, that revolutionised sewing as a domestic activity throughout the world. The age of mass production of footwear and clothing had dawned. To the American manufacturer, the mass market is what mattered; paramount were the convenience and the buying habits of the many, not the few. Said a Boston observer:

> John Bull, you laugh in proud emotion
> At our small wares sent o'er the ocean
> .... But ......
> We beat you, John, at all that *pays*.[21]

Other exhibits demonstrating the character and the accomplishments of American technology were mass-produced locks and clocks; machine tools and presses; rubber goods; cotton drawing frames, which by saving labour increased production 10–15 per cent; saw gins for cleansing cotton; spinning machines; Lowell's self-acting lathe and power loom; Woodbury's wood-planing machine; David Dick's press from Pennsylvania, especially designed for the manufacture of heavy tools and machine parts. Also shown were American textile and iron products, vehicles, preserved foods (unaffected by heat or cold), photographic equipment, the Morse telegraph (which had opened the telegraph era in 1844 with the words, 'What hath God wrought'), printing presses, surgical instruments, locomotives from New Jersey, pianofortes, violins, glassware, chemicals, and scientific instruments for use on land and sea. Alongside all this were the wheat, the cotton, the flax, the timber, the fruit, the hams, the copper, the iron ore, the precious metals, the textiles, the clothing, and the footwear of a burgeoning America. Despite the quality and the number of America's exhibits in London in 1851, to most Europeans America was still a raw, new nation across the seas.

The twelve major international exhibitions that followed[22] went a long way to change that attitude. The first of these, the New York exhibition in 1853, was meant to show that Brother Jonathan could equal – if not surpass – anything, at least in mechanics, that his one-time master John Bull could do; even to the building of a second Crystal Palace of iron and glass. Once again, in New York as in London, the aim of American industry was evident: to provide simply constructed, unadorned machines that could find mass employment. Whatever the item, the basic aim was to produce most with the least human effort. Nothing impressed spectators at New York in 1853 so much as the American Corliss and Nightingale steam engine that faultlessly powered every machine in the exhibition.

American technology was again on display two years later in Paris (1855). However, of the 1200 United States exhibits expected, only 54 arrived. 'Who would have believed', wrote a French observer, 'that this great American people, which seems to have atrophied all the artistic part of human nature in order to concentrate on agriculture, industry, and commerce, who would have believed that this great nation . . . would have so fallen down in the great exhibition of 1855!'[23] Yet the Americans easily took first and second prizes for agricultural machinery. The McCormick reaper cut an acre of oats in 22 minutes, compared to the 66 minutes taken by its English rival. The American thresher threshed 740 litres of wheat in half an hour, while the next best (English) machine threshed only 410. Yet the significant thing at Paris in 1855 was not the triumph of one agricultural machine over another, but the machine's triumph over hand labour: skilled threshers, using hand flails, threshed only 60 against the American machine's output of 740 litres.

Also recognised at Paris was America's skill in manufacturing indiarubber products. Only an inventive genius such as Charles Goodyear,[24] with the coveted French Cross of the Legion of Honour, awarded to him for the originality and quality of his vulcanised rubber wares, could finish up in a Paris jail for debt. Other awards were made to American exhibitors for their weapons, oscillating engines, sewing machines, woodworking machines, and scientific instruments. The fact that wood was relatively plentiful at this time in the United States accounts for the greater use made of it; and, having worked with it so very much, the Americans naturally set to developing their own particular kind of woodworking machines and techniques.

Once more, in London in 1862, it was the practical, mechanical things – the steam ploughs, the milking machines, the reapers, the sewing machines, the mass-produced weapons, locks and clocks, the carriages and the locomotives – in which the Americans excelled. Attracting particular attention was the Porter-Allen high-speed steam engine. Designed by Charles T. Porter, it ran at 150 revolutions per minute, against English machines that ran at 50–60 revolutions per minute. And it did this without a condenser. Alas, for the Europeans, a steam engine without a condenser and, therefore, without the need for an air pump, was simply unthinkable.

Exhibitions in Paris (1867), Vienna (1873), and Philadelphia (1876) followed. The exhibition of 1867 was the first for which determined efforts were made to obtain a Congressional appropriation. It can come as no surprise to the reader to learn that what was at stake was not the reputation of American technology but the American form of government and civilisation; Americans were duty-bound to show the world, crusade-wise, the superiority of their civilisation. As General Nathaniel Banks of Massachusetts put it to Congress in 1866: '. . . it is in our power to represent the social and political character of the country in such a way as to attract the attention of other nations . . . and thus place before the world an enlarged view of the condition and the prospect of American civilisation.'[25] Congressman Henry Raymond of New York looked upon the Paris exhibition of 1867 as a contest between the products of labour under democratic liberty and those under monarchical despotism.[26] Every effort should be made by Congress to assure that democratic liberty won. Time and again in the second half of the nineteenth century, this argument was repeated. 'God in His wisdom', said Representative McCreary of Kentucky in 1888, 'established this Republic in order that it might stand out before the world as a model by which other lovers of liberty might fashion their governments – as an illustration of what freemen may accomplish in a "government of the people, by the people, and for the people".'[27]

However, in the American system of government, it is not words that matter so much as votes; and, especially where the appropriation of funds is concerned, the ability to manipulate committees. Perhaps because they had spent so much time talking about it, American exhibitors at the Paris Exhibition of 1867 got off to a bad start; despite the pious pleadings in Congress about democracy, they also got off without government funds. In fact it was only after the third week that the American part of the 1867 exhibition took on any semblance of order. Even then, American large-rifled cannon, which the world was eager to buy and which the United States in its recent Civil War had proved it could make and use most effectively, were not shown. The iron and steel exhibit was meagre and bore no relation to the scale of American production or United States achievements in metallurgy. Criticisms were also aired about the poor workmanship of American exhibits. Even in the mass production of portable arms, it was argued (true enough by the Belgian Commissioners who probably resented an American finger in the armaments pie, anyway) that the Liége armories could turn out better weapons.

Yet there was praise at Paris in 1867 (as always) for American agricultural machinery (reapers and mowers in particular), for Cyrus Field's Atlantic cable (re-installed in 1866 across the Atlantic after its failure in 1858), for David Hughes' printing telegraph, for the Grant locomotive, for the Sharp machine for making screws, for the Sellers' planing machines, for the Corliss reciprocating engine, for small arms (for the Winchester repeating rifle, which the Confederates had said enabled a Yankee to 'load up in the morning and shoot all day'), and, among other industrial exhibits, for American-designed woodworking machines. For these, as well as a host of industrial consumer goods such as clothing, footwear (the Civil War had further encouraged the mass production of shoes and uniforms), and carpets, the Americans had few equals.[28]

In contrast the exhibition at Vienna in 1873 probably did the American image in the world more harm than good. 'The American department was the least creditable part of the Exposition ...', wrote Charles Francis Adams to his countrymen.[29] At least the American Commissioners found some comfort in reporting that, if the other people's exhibits

were anything to go by, American machine designs were
being widely copied in Europe.

America's triumph at its Centennial Exhibition held in
1876 at Philadelphia more than offset its poor showing at
Vienna three years earlier. The Philadelphia Exhibition was,
in fact, a landmark in the history of American mechanics.
Believing by now in their own 'manifest destiny' and in the
possibility, if not the certainty, of human progress; unified by
the sword into one nation; rich beyond belief in natural and
human resources; held together by a common culture and an
extensive system of transport and communications, America
was, in fact, fast becoming the most powerful nation on earth.
All signs pointed to this end. In agriculture, in industry
(especially in the output of the growing metallurgical industries), in the expansion of its continental empire, in inventiveness, in finance, in commerce, in its rapidly growing numbers,
in its job-conscious rather than class-conscious working
people, in its breed of resourceful (if sometimes ruthless)
entrepreneurs (of whom 'The Public Be Damned' Vanderbilt
was only one of many) – in all these ways, America epitom-
ised the theme of the exhibition: Power. '. . . Nowhere else',
said the *Atlantic Monthly* for July 1876, 'are the triumphs of
ingenuity, the marvels of skill, and invention so displayed. . . .
Surely here . . . is the true evidence of man's creative
powers.'[30] There were agricultural, mining, textile, clothing,
footwear, stone- and wood-working machinery; there were
typewriters, adding machines, printing presses, locomotives,
road and railway cars, telegraphs and cables – even Bell's
recently patented telephone – saws and tools, and an exhibit
dealing with the youthful United States petroleum industry.
Nothing was revered more than the great Corliss steam
engine dominating the Machinery Hall. Said the same corres-
pondent:

The Corliss engine does not lend itself to description; its
personal acquaintance must be sought by those who would
understand its vast and almost silent grandeur. It rises loftily
in the centre of the huge structure, an athlete of steel and iron
with not a superfluous ounce of metal on it. . . . Yes, it is still in
these things of iron and steel that the national genius most

freely speaks; by and by the inspired marbles, the breathing canvases, the great literature; for the present America is voluble in the strong metals and their infinite uses.[31]

For six months '. . . without haste, without rest, and with equal pulse,' the machine propelled 8000 other machines around it and became, 'the marvel of all spectators.'[32] While there were examples of unusual ornateness of machines and furniture, by and large, exhibits remained true to the functional simplicity, the standardisation, and the practical quality usually to be found in American equipment.

Philadelphia was unusual in that it was the first international exhibition to ban alcoholic refreshment; the first to have a Women's Building; and, even more bewildering to some strangers to the American scene, the only exhibition thus far to have a 'Miss' engineer in charge of machinery. The only really sour note was struck by a Belgian who tried to spoil everything by accusing the Americans of money-grubbing habits.[33]

It was evident to all that in the development of its industrial arts and skills America had come a long way since 1851. By the 1870s, the American lathe, planer, gear, screw-cutter, and milling machine (all indispensable to an industrial revolution based upon metallurgy) were the equal of the British tools – if not better. Britain's Henry Maudslay and James Nasmyth were matched on this side by Joseph Brown, Charles Norton, and others. Moreover by 1876 American machine tools,[34] while they were as precise as any other, were concerned with the mass production of interchangeable parts,[35] a system of manufacture credited to Eli Whitney[36] (and Simeon North), who began firearms manufacture in 1798–9 in Connecticut. The method soon spread to other branches of industry, and even as early as the Great Exhibition in London in 1851 was being referred to as the 'American system'.[37] The turret-lathe (a multiple tool holder) as well as the universal grinder, for instance, were peculiarly American inventions aimed at mass production.

Between 1876 and 1900 there were six more major international exhibitions.[38] At Paris in 1900 the United States was second only to France both in the number of its exhibits and the number of awards received. 'Brother Jonathan' was no longer riled by what others said about his 'small wares'; he was, in fact, confident that, small or large, his wares and his machines were the best in the world.

In demonstrating the technical achievements of the American people, these international exhibitions not only helped to change America's image at home and abroad; they also encouraged the expansion of its business houses and manufacturing plants to other lands.[39] Directly as a result of the first London exhibition, McCormick made a licensing arrangement with a British house for the making of his reaper in England. Before the end of the century, American agricultural machinery manufacturers had established branch factories in Europe, Canada and Latin America.[40] Colt was encouraged to start a branch factory in London. (Earlier, in the 1840s, John Hall of the national armoury at Harper's Ferry had transferred his skill in weapon manufacture to Britain's arsenal at Woolwich outside London.) For sewing machines, the world's appetite knew no bounds. The Singer organisation sold its French patent to a Paris house in 1855; by 1868 it had established its first factory abroad in Scotland; by 1874 more than half its total output was being sold outside America; by the mid-eighties its sales network and foreign plants were world-wide. In 1856 American rubber manufacturers began their invasion of the European market by operating a Scottish branch of the industry.[41] Also diffused abroad were improvements in cotton, wool and footwear manufacture.[42] With these went the techniques of preserving food, of making chemicals, soaps, drugs, film, explosives, typewriters, elevators (improved by Elisha G. Otis in the 1850s and electrified by F. J. Sprague in the 1880s–90s), printing presses, and machine tools. American steel technology was important in the origins of the industry in Canada, Mexico, India, South Africa and Australia. Since 1857 a number of United States companies had manufactured locomotives, heavy guns, and other machinery at St Petersburg for the Russian government.

In the commercial application in what were, in origin,

largely European electrical inventions, the Americans were
remarkably successful. By the 1870s the Bell Telephone
Company's chief competitor in England was the American
Thomas Edison Telephone Company. Merging their interests
in London in 1880, American factories making telephone
equipment became world-wide. Western Electric's first factory abroad began operations in Antwerp in 1882, the same
year that the American Edison Electric Light Company's first
generator began operating in London. Other famous American telephone and light companies that were soon to operate
on a world scale were Thomson-Houston, Brush Electric, and
General Electric Corporation.

In going abroad, Americans were merely taking advantage
of the law of international specialisation. More than anything
else, they had become adept at producing mass-market
oriented, relatively sophisticated consumer goods for which a
large market already existed in the United States. Without a
large market and the comparatively high incomes of the
American people, these products never would have been
manufactured on this scale. The only societies abroad which
could make use of American manufactures, the only societies
where branch factories were planted, were themselves high-
income societies. Essentially Americans carried their business and industrial activities abroad because it paid them to
do so, and also because their business enterprise refused to be
confined to national boundaries. It was as natural for some of
these undertakings to turn to Mexico, Canada and western
Europe as it was for them to try to exploit the growing
opportunities of the American west; in fact for a good deal of
the nineteenth century, western Europe was closer, cost-wise,
than parts of North America.

In the extractive industries, many techniques originated in
the United States in the nineteenth century. Widespread were
systems of open-cut mining. Contributions were made to
Malayan tin-mining, and the mining industry in India and
China. Similarly the application of machinery and modern
methods to copper mining was largely pioneered by Americans. At the end of the nineteenth century, the exploitation of
copper resources in Chile and Mexico was dominated by
United States corporations employing their technology.

American influence was also felt in the Katanga copper-bearing region of the African Congo. By the outbreak of the First World War, various flotation or extractive techniques (to separate one metal from another, and the metal from the ground-up gangue) had been introduced to parts of Latin America, eastern Asia, India, and southern and central Africa.

America contributed to the mining industry of South Africa, both with techniques and equipment. The 'rocking-cradle' with a sieve-meshed floor, 'the universal equipment of all diggers in Africa', was introduced by Jerome Babe (hence its name 'Baby') from Louisiana.[43] Babe was evidently one of those resourceful individuals who found it profitable to sell Remington rifles in the morning and mining machinery in the afternoon. Two American geologists, Gardner Frederick Williams and his son, Alpheus Fuller Williams, managed the largest diamond company in the world at Kimberley for almost fifty years.[44] One of America's most famous mining engineers, John Hays Hammond, had a similar influence on the Rand. In 1895, having taken a leading part in the abortive Jameson Raid aimed at overthrowing the Boer Republic, Hammond narrowly missed gaining immortality for the wrong reasons, i.e. by being executed. But for Kruger's mercy, he would have been.[45]

It is said of the Australian Gold Rush of the 1850s that 'From the outset American supplies of mining equipment . . . were considered of better quality than the English, and here demand was usually in excess of supply . . . so many new things were introduced by the Americans at this period that they gained a special name of "Yankee notions".'[46] Australians even came to know the talents of a young mining engineer, Herbert Hoover, who would one day be President of the United States.

Meanwhile other Americans were helping to lay the foundations of still another branch of the mining industry whose repercussions would be far greater than those of both silver and gold. Yet it was only with the drilling of the Drake oil well in Pennsylvania in 1859 that petroleum for illumination was produced in America on any scale for the first time. By then, Americans (and western Europeans) had improved rotary drilling by using industrial diamonds. However, it was not until the appearance of the automobile at the end of the century that the importance of petroleum and its derivatives increased. In 1913 William M. Burton and Robert E. Humphreys of the Standard Oil Company of Indiana invented a high-temperature, high-pressure cracking still which could reduce oil to the required consistency. By then American oil companies had begun to stake out their claims and introduce their production methods, including their techniques of drilling and refining, to the oil fields of other continents.

America diffused many plants and agricultural practices to other continents.[47] In the eighteenth century, England is said to have obtained a greater variety of trees from America than it had procured from elsewhere in the previous thousand years. Among other plants diffused in the world were corn, the potato, the tomato, tobacco, cotton, the sugar cane, alfalfa grass, papaws, pecan nuts, new varieties of loquats, the Smyrna fig (rediffused like the important Bahia orange) from California, and plague-resistant stocks of vines to replace European and African vines devasted by phylloxora in the 1890s.

By the First World War, almost comet-like, the United States had become the industrial and agrarian leader of the world. Never has any country equalled America's capacity for producing and consuming wealth as the United States did in the half-century before 1914.

At this time, it led in the most basic of all staple industries – the provision of food – as well as in the supply of industrial fibres and metals. The value of wheat and wheat flour exports from the United States had increased more than twentyfold in the years 1850–1915.[48] In crop yield per acre it lagged behind Canada and Australia, but not in output per man hour. It was the leading meat supplier until the end of the nineteenth century; its meat exports grew from 1000 hundredweight of frozen meat in 1874 to one-and-one-third million hundredweight of 'chilled' meat in 1899.[49] Indeed so abundant did American supplies of food become that some branches of European agriculture – particularly the English and the Danish – were transformed under the pressure of their competition. Many of Europe's agricultural workers made the re-adjustment by migrating to the far distant frontiers of the United States.

America's domestic production of pig iron (the 'food' of modern industry) had also leapt from 2·2 m. tons in 1870–4 to 31·5 m. in 1914. By 1913, its output exceeded that of Britain (10·4 m. tons) and Germany (19·3 m. tons).[50] There was a similar dramatic increase in the output of steel. By the 1860s, the largely duplicative methods of making steel, the William Kelly process (American) and the Henry Bessemer (British) had been adopted in the United States. In 1870–4, Britain led with about 500,000 tons. The figures for Germany, the United States, and France were 300,000, 140,000, and 130,000, respectively.[51] There followed a number of European developments beneficial to the United States. These were the introduction in the 1850s and 1860s of Friedrich Siemens' Gas Regenerative 'Open Hearth' Furnace; and, in the 1870s and 1880s, of the Gilchrist and Thomas 'Basic Process' (partly anticipated by the American Jacob Reese ten years before), which enabled the production of steel from ores with a high phosphorous content such as those of the United States and French Lorraine. By 1913 America led with an output of 31·8 m. tons. Germany was next, with 18·9 m., then Britain, with 7·8 m. However, unlike Britain, who sold a great deal of its steel to others, the greater part of America's iron and steel output was consumed at home. As for copper, the other basic mineral of nineteenth-century industrialisation, by 1913 the United States accounted for 55 per cent of world output of the smelted metal.[52]

By the turn of the twentieth century, America also led in the output of coal and oil. Whereas in the early 1870s Britain had mined three times as much coal as the United States (120 m. tons against 43 m.), by 1913 the United States produced 509 m. tons and Britain 287 m.[53] By 1902 the United States had also regained from Russia the leading place among the world's oil producers.

In the supply of raw cotton, America was without equal. The famine caused by the Civil War had shown to what extent the world depended upon its supplies. As for its manufacture, if we take the mill consumption of cotton in 1913 as a measure of size, America's 26·6 per cent of world consumption exceeded the British 20·3 per cent.

The metal and engineering industries also provide evidence of America's rise before 1914. By then, so far as total output is concerned, the United States had surpassed Britain; America's exports of machinery and engineering products – much of them mass-produced using interchangeable parts – had also drawn nearly level with the British and the German. The situation in 1914 was that, besides their contributions to the development of the traditional industries, the Americans developed the tools and the metalworking techniques required by the newer, capital-intensive consumer goods industries in which they excelled.

In 1914 the United States showed signs of leading in the so-called Second Industrial Revolution (dependent upon scientific progress, especially in physics and chemistry), as it already led in the First Industrial Revolution (dependent upon coal and iron and the mechanisation of traditional industries such as textiles). Witness, for instance, the developments in the automobile, the electrical equipment (particularly household appliances), the chemical (including the development of synthetic textiles especially nylon), and the rubber and plastic industries. By 1914 America led in all these new branches of manufacture – most of all in the automobile industry (Chapter VI). It was in these new industries that America's major global impact, through its multinational corporations, was made.

In the field of pure science, nineteenth-century America had an outstanding physicist in Joseph Henry (1797–1878), whose experiments formed the basis of the modern electromagnet. The one great scientist who easily stands comparison with his European contemporaries, was the mathematical physicist Josiah Willard Gibbs (1839–1903). It was his theory of thermodynamics that helped to lay the foundations of modern physical chemistry and chemical engineering.

The First World War stimulated the trends long evident in the American economy towards standardisation, mass production, industrial research, and scientific management (including production incentives). The father of scientific management, Frederick W. Taylor, had published his book, *The Principles of Scientific Management*, in 1911, two years before Ford's moving assembly line had gone into full-scale operation (E. K. Root had employed an assembly line in the Colt Armory at Hartford, Connecticut, before him). It was the pressures towards increased industrial efficiency caused by the First World War that led European industrial and military leaders to seize upon Taylor's efficiency techniques. In a circular dated 26 February 1918, the French war leader Clemenceau declared it 'an imperative necessity' for all heads of military establishments to study Taylor's works.[54] 'Taylorism' and 'Fordism' that followed it were, in fact, a scientific, systematic formalisation of the entire productive process. In discarding empirical for scientific knowledge, they revolutionised man's attitude towards industrial production. Individual man was not the end of life; production was. Lenin was shrewd enough to recognise what 'Taylorism' implied. In an article dealing with 'The Urgent Problems of Soviet Rule', which appeared in *Pravda* for 28 April 1918, the Russian leader urged that Russia '. . . should try out every scientific and progressive suggestion of the Taylor system.'[55] Paradoxically, the goals of the Russian and American industrial and business leaders were growing closer.[56] What Taylor and Ford gave to the world was a new technology (one might say, a new social philosophy) of production (in organisation and incentives); one that was born of the social and political philosophy of the American people.

The efforts of Taylor and others to increase the efficiency of the American economic system did not prevent its collapse in October 1929, with momentous consequences for the western world. In the United States production slumped (the Gross National Product fell by almost half between 1929–32); labour became redundant (by 1932 there were 13 million unemployed); foreign investment and technical development stagnated. On a world front expediency and economic autarchy ruled. In the Hawley-Smoot tariff of 1930, America tried vainly to protect its industries from the world's economic woes. Despite the empirical measures introduced by Roosevelt from 1933 on, the economy showed no gains in the rate of growth between 1929 and 1938. Not until the late 1930s was business confidence restored, and only then because preparations for a new and far greater war were beginning to make themselves felt.

In many respects, the Second World War had effects similar to those of the First. It has been estimated that in 1944 the United States war production was twice as great as that of Germany, Italy and Japan (the Axis Powers) combined. Throughout the war years, jeeps, tanks, heavy artillery, ammunition, aircraft, ships, food, and other provisions flowed in a constant and swelling stream from American farms and factories to every part of the 'free world'. Because of its extraordinary fecundity and productive capacity, America not only maintained abroad an enormous army, navy and airforce; it fed and supplied its allies as well.

Such a productive effort could not have been made without progress in pure and applied science. Of necessity the emphasis in American industry shifted from stressing the 'know-how', the pragmatic and the empirical, to stressing the scientific, the 'know-why'.[57] By the 1940s, pure science was playing a role in American industrial development which would have been quite inconceivable in the late nineteenth century. Science also contributed to many changes in agriculture, including the introduction of new insecticides, fertilisers, herbicides and hybrid plants. Before 1923, when Robert A. Millikan (1868–1953) obtained America's first Nobel prize in physics, there had been no awards to Americans for chemistry, medicine or physics. Thereafter Americans took one in five Nobel prizes for chemistry, one in four for medicine, and one in three for physics.

The tremendous productive effort of the Second World War not only fostered certain branches of science; unlike the First World War, it left behind unexampled prosperity. Whether measured by price movements, industrial employment, the rate of growth of output, income levels, or trade balances, all American indicators pointed toward healthy economic expansion. By 1945 the growth rate had almost doubled the 1913 level.

Since 1945, at least in monetary terms, there has been an enormous increase in productive capacity, especially in the more rapidly growing industrial and service sectors. From 1948 to 1970, while the average annual hours of work remained practically constant, the G.N.P. in current dollars rose almost fourfold. In 1958 prices, the Gross National Product rose from $324 billion in 1948 to over $529 billion in 1962, and to over $789 billion in 1972, when it accounted for about 30 per cent of world G.N.P. As for income, with about 6–7 per cent of the world's population, the United States today accounts for about one-third of world income; and there are signs that this concentration of wealth is increasing rather than diminishing. As a percentage of national income, manufacturing grew from approximately 5 per cent in 1799 to 30 per cent in 1970, when America led the world (followed by the U.S.S.R.) in the output of manufactures. By 1972 the United States had yielded pride of place to U.S.S.R. in the output of steel (133 million tons against Russia's 140 million tons). Meanwhile, income from agriculture shrank during the same period from approximately 40 per cent in 1799 to 3 per cent in 1970. In 1971 $5\frac{1}{2}$ times as many persons were employed in manufacturing as in agriculture;[58] farm population was about 5 per cent of the total.[59] The nation's greatest weakness was its growing reliance upon foreign supplies of oil. Although in 1972 it led with 11·2 million barrels a day, it was consuming 17·4 million. Russia at this time produced 8·6 million barrels a day but consumed only 7·6 million.

The most dramatic change so far as employment is concerned (emphasising the primacy of politics), is the extent to which America's most rapidly growing industries – aircraft, missiles, electronics, chemicals – have all become heavily dependent upon defence contracts. Even more dramatic is the continuing increase in the service industries.[60] By 1970 the number of people employed in service industries (including government), which had probably doubled in importance between the 1860s and 1960s, exceeded the combined total of those employed in agriculture, manufacturing, mining and construction. In 1972, against the 19 million people employed in manufacturing, the service industries (including government) employed more than 25 million. In 1973, service industries accounted for about 40 per cent of national income, making the United States predominantly a 'white-collared' economy.[61]

More important from a world point of view has been the postwar growth of American business abroad. Since 1945 many corporations have become global; those already global when the war ended have extended their activities in the postwar years. In the United Kingdom alone, in 1970-1, American corporations sold goods worth nearly £6 billion, accounted for nearly 13 per cent of the total production of manufacturing enterprises, employed almost one-tenth of the total labour force, and produced a fifth of all manufacturing exports.[62] This postwar invasion of Europe by the Americans was described by English Prime Minister Harold Wilson as 'industrial helotry'; by Charles de Gaulle as 'a lien weighing heavy upon our national patrimony'; and by West Germany's Finance Minister, Franz Joseph Strauss, as *Ausverkauf* ('sell-out').

The course of American business abroad since 1914 is traced in Table IV (parts A–D). Geographically speaking the bulk of the American operations are in the western world, especially in western Europe, Canada, Australia and South Africa. Regarding the employment of these funds, the figures show that in 1970 American foreign business activity was concerned overwhelmingly with manufactures and mining (including petroleum). In Africa, Asia and Oceania, mining (including petroleum) was the major activity. It is apparent from these business investments that outside the western world the thing that matters to the Americans is oil.

Within the western world, Americans lead in space technology, nuclear energy and aeronautics. They dominate oil, automobiles, telecommunications and electronic machinery (including computers and office machinery), boot and shoe machinery (United Kingdom), detergents, sewing machines, photo-copying equipment, vacuum cleaners, and certain prepared foods (i.e. breakfast cereals and baby foods); they have a substantial influence in other branches of the food industry, in razors, rubber tyres, household equipment (i.e. washing machines, refrigerators, etc.), in watches, clocks, safes, locks, agricultural machinery, cameras, and portable power tools; they are important in cigarettes, synthetic fibres, thermoplastics, telegraph and telephone equipment, chemicals, mining and other machinery, elevators, ophthalmic instruments, heating, cooling and ventilating equipment. (Table V.)

The names and the main activities of the largest 100 United States manufacturing and petroleum affiliates operating in the United Kingdom in 1970–1 are provided in Table V/D. Of the total number of foreign subsidiaries operating in the United Kingdom in 1971 (710) the United States accounted for 432.[63] The first ten are concerned with transportation. Allowing for variations (for instance, American mining and land development corporations play a greater role in South Africa, Canada and Australia than they do in Europe), one finds the same stress upon transportation and its ancillaries elsewhere.

In this respect much of the basic industrial technology which the Americans have been employing is not new to Europe. What is new is the scale of the American effort and the sophistication of their products. Indeed, it is tempting to draw a parallel between American foreign activities one hundred years ago and now. There is the same concentration of effort on the 'newer', capital-intensive consumer goods industries (then, the sewing machine; now, the automobile), the same eagerness and business acumen to exploit a commercial opportunity at home or abroad, the same tendency towards mass production, initially meant to serve the needs of the enormous United States market, but which eventually spilled over into a world market, and the same ability to obtain the necessary domestic or foreign capital. What has changed over the years is not the principal but the weight and extent of America's influence in the world.[64]

Throughout this period the thing that has mattered has been the American genius to react aggressively to a business opportunity – rushing in where others fear to tread. Witness the rise and fall of an American investment empire in Europe in mutual funds between 1955 and 1970. To an unusual degree, Americans are risk-takers; and they know how to out-compete others, very often with other people's technology and other people's money. Moreover, they not only see business opportunities to which other people are blind; they see nothing incongruous in getting ten million people to eat the same packaged cereal for breakfast; economies of scale and efficiency are what matter, not variety. They have also been assisted by their high-powered sales organisation – whether for investments or breakfast foods, by their managerial control and accounting procedures, by the size and growing financial power of their business empire – which enabled the American giants to outcompete the last independent French-owned computer firm and British-owned Rolls-Royce, by their ability to get behind the tariff barriers of the Common Market, and by the fact that Europe – because of the fratricide it has practised in the present century – undermined its own strength. Very important in all this is America's growing reliance upon other people's raw materials. The crucial factors, as we said at an earlier point, are the Americans' attitude to business, and the scale of their undertakings.

In the last resort the movement of American business abroad can only be explained in terms of profits. In this they are following a tradition as old as the East India Company (1600). Instead of accepting the limitations of the domestic market American corporations have gone global, penetrating the more profitable areas of the world. Markets (rather than the cheaper labour supply of Mexico, Hong Kong and Taiwan, which they have also tapped) have been their goal. They have invested in the Western world because it has the highest standards of living. It is a matter of cause and effect: partly the investments have helped to create the wealth; largely, we believe, it has been the growing wealth of other white communities that has encouraged the American business invasion. The search for profits also helps to explain why so little American manufacturing industry is to be found in Asia (except where their military power has predominated, as in South Vietnam), Africa and Latin America. Some businesses, such as banking, may prosper there, but markets large enough and with income enough to absorb American mass-produced, capital-intensive manufactures are not to be found there on the same scale as they are in Europe and Canada.

Undoubtedly technology is the secret of the extension and unity of America's civilisation. Without it, Americans could not have colonised the New World. So successful did their efforts prove that for many science and technology came to embrace all human actions and to provide the answer to all human questions. It is this faith – coupled with America's material success – which has caused so much of the world to emulate the American example.

Yet American tools alone have not determined its destiny. Science and technology are only a part explanation of how it came to be where it is. Its great wealth, which Katherine Lee Bates had the wisdom to call 'the fruited plain', came from its total situation and its total environment. Indeed much of the high tide of its progress over the past century must be put down to the bringing into cultivation of vast, new fertile regions, to the tapping of enormous new mineral deposits, and to the introduction of new forms of transport and power. Not least important, it came from the extraordinary degree of interdependence that grew up between the economies on both sides of the North Atlantic. It was the wealth thus obtained and so rapidly put to use to industrialise and urbanise great parts of America (and western Europe) that enabled its people, however temporarily, to set aside the basic 'law' of political economy – diminishing returns. But that was a finite phase of history, dependent upon historical circumstances and good fortune.

So successful have Americans been that it has caused them (and those others – such as the Russians and the Chinese – who wish to follow their example) to exaggerate the role of industrialisation as the primary cause and the true source of economic well-being. They have assumed that, because industrialisation became the dynamic factor in the northern hemisphere at one period in history, it must necessarily become the dynamic factor elsewhere today. There is a false assumption that industrialisation is the cause and not the effect of economic development. The trouble is that industrialisation has become the new alchemy. (It plays the role that chemistry played in the Middle Ages.) Because industrialisation (numerically at least) shows the most rapid rate of 'growth' or maximum income, whereas agriculture, the means by which we live, is referred to in current economic dogma as 'the least productive sector of an economy', it is regarded as the most desirable process of change regardless of its relevance to the total economy of a country or that country's historical situation.

Since the Second World War the American business empire, aided by its seemingly limitless resources, has proliferated. The outcome is an international business unit of such size and power over production, markets, labour and finance as to challenge national sovereignty. More pervasively, through their influence on world business, the Americans have changed the mores and the living habits of others. Wherever we find them abroad their stress is upon mass techniques. Only thus have they been able to turn things of curiosity into items of mass production and consumption, with tremendous effect upon the daily living of countless millions. The worst aspect of this process has been what the French call 'cocacolization'; the best, as the Americans might counter, is to have given choice where previously choice did not exist.

Meanwhile the rest of the world is far from becoming a satellite of America. It may well be that American-dominated, global business organisations will succeed on a world scale where all other international organisations of the past – religious, social and political – have foundered. Yet it would be foolish to conclude from the present growth in the number of multi-national corporations that nationalism – one of the most decisive forces in helping to shape the modern world during the past 300 years – has suddenly been undone by the American businessman and his technology.

CHAPTER VI

America's Contribution to the Conquest of Distance

THE conquest of time and space lies at the heart of the American saga. Born of a struggle by a seafaring race to conquer the high seas of the world, the Americans have encompassed distance as few others have done. They were the first to think in terms of the conquest of a continent rather than a country. Their great distances and their growing commercial ties made rapid communications indispensable. Even when their continental destiny had been fulfilled, they knew no rest until they had ventured into outer space. Their rhythm of life, moulded as it is by their attitudes to time and space, is fast and intense; so much so, that it has caused them to identify the conquest of distance with the march of human progress.

The medium that moulded the early American character was not a moving frontier across the land, but the sea. Said John Quincy Adams, then United States Minister to Russia, to Alexander I, Tsar of all the Russias, in 1810, 'My countrymen, Sire, are so familiarized with the ocean that they think not much more of crossing it than of going over a river.'[1] The sea was the early colonists' greatest field of adventure and economic activity, their greatest source of wealth and power. Long before independence, colonial-built ships had entered the rivers of Europe and Africa, and the whaling vessels of New England – of Nantucket, New Bedford, Marblehead, and Province Town – had already won world renown.[2] As long as American shipwrights (with their skills and abundance of good timber and naval supplies) could build ships at half the cost of similar vessels laid down in England, nothing could stop a maritime and commercial race like the British from buying them.[3] Almost a third of the ships engaged in the British carrying trade in 1776 (exclusive of the trade between the West Indies and North America) had been built in the colonies.[4] Indeed, when hostilities with the British began, the colonies quickly established their own navy which, in 1777, numbered 34 cruisers mounting 412 guns. The maximum number of privateers was reached in 1781 with 449 vessels carrying 6735 guns.[5]

Notwithstanding the losses sustained in the struggle for independence, the Americans were quick to recover their position on the high seas once the war was over. Before the end of the eighteenth century, in terms of shipping tonnage and foreign trade, they had probably become the first commercial nation in the world; American vessels were to be found in all oceans; in 1789 more than two score of them were engaged in the 'China Trade' beyond Cape Horn.[6] By 1790, with the return to Boston of the 213-ton square-rigged American ship *Columbia*, they had circumnavigated the globe. Shipping in the Indian Ocean was further encouraged by the Jay Treaty of 1794, which legalised American commerce with British India.[7]

The years 1792–1807,[8] when most of Europe was at war, were most prosperous for American shipping. Tonnage grew from 564 million to 1268 million; of the ships arriving in United States ports, those owned and registered in America increased from 63 to 92 per cent.[9] In those years handsome profits were reaped by neutral America transporting the products of the French, Dutch and Spanish colonies, as well as supplying the imports of Britain and France.

Alas, these favourable conditions did not last. By 1807 relations between the United States and Britain and France had deteriorated to such an extent that open war on the high seas was imminent. Not prepared to risk war for 'this protuberant navigation, which has kept us in hot water from the commencement of our government',[10] Jefferson recommended to Congress the imposition of an embargo on the movement of American ships. The result was almost the ruin of the industry. 'The grass', said a British traveller of the time, 'had begun to grow upon the wharves [of New York].'[11]

The recovery that followed the repeal of the Embargo Act in 1809 was short-lived; for in 1812 the United States went to war with Britain. Gallant as its little navy of twenty-three vessels of all classes proved to be, however incredible the losses inflicted upon His Majesty's ships by the skilled and resolute use of the American privateer – between 1812 and 1814, thirteen hundred prizes were taken, valued at $39 million – the contest was an unequal one in which the Americans suffered most.[12] Gradually, as French sea power succumbed to British might, Britain was able to shift its fleet across the Atlantic, until eventually American shipping had either been destroyed or blockaded. By the autumn of 1814, the lighthouses strung along the American coast no longer flashed their friendly lamps. The only shipping they could help was British. And this time, unlike at Yorktown in 1781, there was no French fleet lying off in the darkness, ready to turn the scales in America's favour.

So great were the young nation's powers of recovery, so aggressive its merchants, that by the 1820s it had passed from defeat at sea to the beginning of a golden age. United States tonnage entering American ports increased from approximately three-quarters of a million in 1819 to 1½ million in 1840 and to 6 million in 1860. The approximately half million tons registered in foreign trade in 1831, by 1862 had grown to about 2½ million; a figure not surpassed until the First World War. Moreover the influence of American shipwrights was not confined to the United States. It was Americans like Henry Eckford and Foster Rhodes who, working in Turkish yards, helped to restore the Ottoman fleet after its destruction at Navarino, Greece, on 27 October 1827.

Indeed the war had not long been finished before America had launched the largest and fastest wooden sailing vessels in the world. In 1818 the American Black Ball Line had inaugurated the fast sailing packet service on the North Atlantic routes. Other American lines soon followed, giving regular service to Europe and other parts of America. By 1845 more than fifty American vessels were plying their way, to and fro, across the Atlantic. Sailing packets (with a three or four weeks' passage, dependent on whether they were east or west bound) had halved the time of the Atlantic crossing. By then, the fastest American sailing ships, which in the 1840s had come to be known as 'clippers', were crossing the Atlantic in about two weeks.[13]

The first clipper, *The Rainbow* (750 tons), built in New York in 1845, was American in design and construction.[14] Clippers were ruggedly built and ranged in weight (after 1850) from 1000 to 1600 tons (though the *Great Republic*, burnt in 1853 before it had time to be launched, was 3300 tons). Streamlined to offer minimum resistance, and commanded by skilled and daring seamen, their enormous areas of canvas (often widespread when others had theirs furled) thrust them through the highest seas at unprecedented speed. Encouraged by rising freight rates, and with thousands of dollars in bets at stake, new shipping records were established. In 1850 the *Sea Witch* made a voyage from New York to California, reaching the Golden Gate in 97 days. In 1851 the famous *Flying Cloud* (spars carried away, sails blown out, and the mainmast cracked) reduced this figure to 89 days, 21 hours. The 436 miles covered by the clipper *Lightning* in one day, as well as the 21 knots set by the *James Baines* (1856) in one hour have never been beaten by any sailing vessel. (These are speeds beyond most present-day cargo vessels.) The most famous builder of clipper ships was the Nova Scotia-reared Donald McKay. Trained as a shipwright in New York (where clipper building began), McKay moved with the industry to Newburyport, Massachusetts, and then to Boston. From the Boston yards came the most beautiful and fastest ships that have ever sailed.

In the design of the clipper, speed – not cargo space – was paramount. Once the cry of 'gold!' had been heard in 1848, all was sacrificed in the race to the western gold fields. From April 1847 to April 1848, four vessels had cleared Atlantic ports for San Francisco; in 1849, the figure had grown to 75. When the gold fever had passed, increased demands for fast transport came from France and Britain to carry on their wars in China (1840s–50s), Russia (1853), and India (1857). By 1850 some clippers were obtaining $60 per ton of forty cubic feet, compared with the $10–12 being paid to slower vessels. But then, in California, beef and pork were bringing $40–60 a barrel; tea, coffee and sugar, $4 a pound; playing cards, $5 a pack; and cowhide boots, $45 a pair. So profitable was the clipper trade to the American shipping industry that vessels could pay for themselves with one voyage. This was true of

The Sea Serpent and forty-seven other clippers carrying provisions and migrants to San Francisco in 1851.[15] Even ships intended for the China trade (which had opened for the Americans with the sale of furs and ginseng in 1784) were sent round the Horn with freight for the California market, and thence (once the English Navigation Acts had been repealed in 1848) to Hong Kong to load tea for London. The first American clipper to carry tea direct from China to London was the *Oriental*, which departed from Whampoa on 22 August 1850 and arrived at London on 4 December: 104 days later. The profits made from this record run equalled two-thirds of the cost of building the vessel.[16] American clippers (breaking the British East India Company's monopoly in tea) sailed from Canton to New York and Singapore to New York in 84 and 86 days respectively. The clipper *Natchez* once sailed from Canton to New York in seven weeks. Because these fast vessels were able to rush the China tea crop to New York and London before it was spoiled, they were able to command rates double those of the slower English ships. (Of the approximately 58,000 tons of foreign shipping lying at Canton in 1855, 24,000 tons were American, 18,000 British.) However, for coffee the opposite is true: until the First World War, United States sailing vessels carrying Sumatra coffee to New York were given a bonus for a long voyage. The longer the voyage, the deeper brown the coffee (from sweating in the holds) and the higher its market price.[17]

Important American scientific contributions to the improvement of navigation in the first half of the nineteenth century were made by John Fitch (1743–98) who published his navigational aid, the *Columbia Ready Reckoner*[18] in London in 1793; by Nathaniel Bowditch (1773–1838), astronomer, navigator and mathematician, whose *The New American Practical Navigator*, first published in 1802, is still published; and by John Willis Griffiths (1809–82) who wrote the first scientifically based textbook on naval architecture, *Treatise on Marine and Naval Architecture*, 1850. Even more famous is Matthew Fontaine Maury (1806–79), whose *The Physical Geography of the Sea*, published in 1855, earned for him the title of 'Pathfinder' of the oceans. It has been estimated that Maury's work (by reducing the time of many sea voyages) saved American and British shipowners $12 million annually. Cyrus West Field (1819–92), in laying the first trans-Atlantic cable in 1858, acknowledged Maury's genius when he said, 'Maury furnished the brains, England gave the money, and I did the work.'[19]

So intensely did the Americans concentrate on improving the wooden sailing ship that they neglected the use of iron and steam. While John Fitch probably was the first to introduce steam navigation to the United States (in the 1830s), the man who is known to every American schoolchild is the clever mechanic and astute businessman, Robert Fulton, who launched the first financially successful American steamboat (the *North River*, later known as the *Clermont*) on 17 August 1807, on the Hudson. Rapid projection rather than basic invention were the keynotes of Fulton's success.[20] Important in opening up the waterways of America's western empire were Nicholas J. Roosevelt (1767–1854), whose steamboats plied the western rivers in the early decades of the nineteenth century; Henry M. Shreve (1785–1851), who in 1817 designed and successfully operated the *Washington* in its journey from New Orleans to Louisville. A shallow-draft steamboat with a paddle wheel set in the stern, his vessel could operate in 20 to 30 inches of water or 'in a heavy dew'.[21] Between 1816–45, 1500 passengers and crew were killed from steam-boiler explosions alone; a greater toll of life than all the Indian scalp raids put together. Hardly surprising, the American paddle wheelers became known as 'floating coffins'. In 1855, by which time western steamboats were about to be superseded by steam railroads, there were 727 (tonnage 170,000). The number of steamboats on the Great Lakes had also grown to 369 in 1860. By then, the travel time from New Orleans to Pittsburgh had been cut from 100 to 30 days.

Meanwhile the interior of the continent had also been opened up by canals. The first important one was the Erie, longer than all England's canals put together, completed in 1825. The value of goods shipped to the west by way of the

Erie Canal and the inland lake system increased almost tenfold between the mid-1830s and the mid-1850s. The mileage of United States canals grew from 1277 in 1830 to 3698 in 1850. Of great importance to the growth of lake shipping was the Sault Sainte Marie Canal built between Lake Superior and Lake Huron in 1855.

On the high seas the American sailing ship *Savannah* (350 tons) was, in 1819, the first ship to cross the Atlantic with an auxiliary steam engine of 90 horsepower.[22] In the 1830s, American paddle steamers were going from the eastern seaboard to Cuba, Mexico and New Orleans; in the 1840s, they began to ferry gold-seeking Americans to and from the isthmus of Panama. Before the middle of the century, American steamboats were also operating in France (a steamboat of Robert Fulton's design had been launched on the Seine in 1803, and others on the Saône and the Rhône between 1827–50), in Latin America (in Nicaragua, Mexico, Argentina and Chile), and in the Chinese river and coastal trade.[23]

From 1847 to 1858, the famous American Ocean Steam Navigation Company (New York–Bremen) and the Collins Line (New York–Liverpool) were operating regular government subsidised steam services across the Atlantic. The Collins Line's first ship, the *Atlantic*, sailed in 1850. A decade later, primarily as a result of dreadful accidents (in which Collins not only lost his ships *Arctic* and *Pacific*, but his wife, his only daughter, and his youngest son), the company was defunct. An important factor was the Federal Government's reluctance to match the subsidy given by the British government to the rival Cunard Company.[24] Unlike British political interests which were unanimous in recognising the vital role of the mercantile marine in Britain's national life, Americans were divided. Why should the south and the American mid-west foster what they regarded as purely northern interests? As a result, by 1859, against Europe's thirty-one vessels, only a handful of American steamships were making regular voyages across the Atlantic. Assisting the growth of the foreign lines was the passage money sent by immigrants already living in the United States. Forty per cent of the aggregate total of $250 million of individual remittances received by the Irish in Ireland between 1845 and 1900 was thus earmarked.[25]

American steamers in the Pacific fared better than those on the Atlantic. They were largely engaged in the protected coastal trade (the growing eastern and western seaboard trade of America via Panama had been construed as coastal trade and was therefore restricted to American vessels) and between 1848 and 1858 sea-borne traffic to the Pacific coast had enjoyed boom conditions. In those ten years, twenty-nine steamers were put into service. The Pacific Mail alone carried 175,000 passengers to California and brought back an estimated $200 million of gold. The 'American monopoly' of steam-shipping in Chinese waters was broken only by the British – in the 1870s. As late as 1910 the United States had three large passenger steamships in service, all three competing satisfactorily with the Canadians and the Japanese.[26]

America probably reached the zenith of its nineteenth-century sea power in 1851 when its total tonnage was 3·7 million as compared to 4·3 million tons for the whole of the British Empire. In only seventy to eighty years, a fledgling nation had come close to displacing Britain as the greatest sea power. Alas, the spectacular growth of the American sailing-ship industry in the 1840s and 1850s was followed by an equally spectacular decline. By the mid-fifties (nearly all the California clippers were built between 1850–4), the rush to California was over. Speed was no longer needed as it had been earlier and shippers were not prepared to pay premium rates for it. By then the new Panama railroad (opened in 1855) had begun to deprive the clippers of some of their most lucrative traffic. China had also proved a disappointment. Changing American fashions had caused a fall in the silk and tea trade; American sea otter furs, which the Chinese still wanted, had been hunted almost to extinction. More importantly steam – in which Britain led – was claiming a larger share of ocean freights; between 1850–60 the share carried by steamers had doubled from 14 to 28 per cent. Nor had the West Indian trade (thrown open to American traders from the 1830s) expanded enough to offset any of these drawbacks.

By the late 1850s the fastest clippers had either been driven to death or impoverished by the combined effect of mounting costs and falling freights (freights which in 1850 had stood at

$60 per ton, by 1857 had fallen to $7·50);[27] the problem of excess tonnage had become acute. For some ships a temporary solution was found in the less remunerative and slower grain, guano or wool trade, or by surreptitiously engaging in the Chinese coolie trade[28] (forbidden by Congress in 1862). The coolies were shipped to the Chincha Islands off Peru (to dig guano) or to Cuba in conditions not far removed from slavery. Some shippers even made a profit by carrying the last of the African slaves to the Americas. Whatever expediency was resorted to, by 1857 the boom in American shipping was over.

The outbreak of the Civil War in 1861 ensured that the decline would be accelerated. Shipping tonnage was reduced by almost one million tons during the war years.[29] Because the government would not allow ships that had taken refuge under other flags while the war was on to be brought back into American registry when the war was over (a restriction lifted only in 1897), American-registered ships could only be obtained by building them in the United States. But the government's tax and tariff policies, coupled with the rising cost of labour and the fact that Americans did not have the same advantages in building steamships as they had earlier when building wooden sailing ships, made the construction of ships in American yards uneconomical. (Table XIII.)

The basic cause of the relative decline of the mercantile marine between 1850 and 1913 (Table XII) was probably the shift that had taken place in the nation's interests and values. As one author put it, 'the doom of the American merchant marine was sealed with the Louisiana purchase . . .'[30] Increasingly, the nation's effort was concentrated on inland and coastal shipping, as well as on the development of the railway network, the opening up of western territory, and the increase of manufacturing, urban development, and mining. It was these things which caused money, enterprise and skill to forsake the high seas. Thus to the recommendations of a committee appointed in 1869 to investigate the decline of the shipping industry, Congress was largely lukewarm; notwithstanding the extent to which America depended – for people and commerce – on the shipping lanes that joined it to the Old World.

The feeling held by most of its leaders that ocean-going shipping was something best left to other nations prevailed until the needs of the First World War were felt. The criterion was what would pay best in monetary terms. It could hardly be anything else when so much of American life was determined by what suited individual interests best. For the rest of the nineteenth century America remained the only Great Power unwilling to maintain its strength on the high seas.[31] In the war with Spain in 1898 the fleet had had to rely upon British transports and naval auxiliaries. When in 1907 Theodore Roosevelt sent the 'Great White Fleet' around the world to show the flag, he also had to send fifty-odd foreign merchant vessels to supply it. By 1914 the bulk of the western world's freight was being carried in British steamships; American ships were carrying only 10 per cent of the country's foreign trade. In sharp contrast was the growth in domestic shipping between the eastern and western seaboards of the continent following the piercing of the isthmus of Panama in 1914.[32] The canal also stimulated European shipping to and from North America's west coast, and gave Europe and Australasia a new and shorter Pacific sea-link. America succeeded in 1914 where, in the 1880s, the French had failed, because they were able to overcome Panama's greatest hazard: disease.

In 1914 America was almost entirely dependent on the ocean-going shipping of other nations. Before its entry into the war in 1917 one billion dollars had been paid to foreign ship-owners for their services. The ship-building programme of 1917–19 cost another three billion dollars, with very few ocean-going vessels to show for the money while the war was on. When it ended, the Federal government returned to the *laissez-faire* policy that had predominated before 1914. In 1920 (when America's ocean-going tonnage was about ten millions), the Emergency Fleet Corporation (established in 1917) was dissolved; many of its 1500 vessels being disposed of for what they would bring.

With the outbreak of the Second World War, the nation found itself once more completely unprepared. Again the government bore the cost of hasty new construction. Between

1940 and 1950 the tonnage registered in foreign trade grew from three to nineteen million tons. A subsequent fall after 1955 caused the government to subsidise the industry in the interests of national security. But this did not prevent – any more than after the First World War – a decline in ocean-going tonnage. By 1960 the high figure of 1950 (19,154,000) had fallen to 14,737,000. The percentage of United States commerce carried by U.S. flag and foreign flag ships in 1970 is shown in Table XI. At this time, the United States carried less than 6 per cent of its own seaborne commerce; Liberia – at lower costs – carried 26·9 per cent of American cargoes, most of it in American-owned ships flying a flag of convenience. The object of the Merchant Marine Act of 1970 was to remedy a situation whereby more than nine-tenths of United States foreign commerce was being carried in vessels (many of them American-owned) bearing other nations' flags.

Yet what private capital refused to do as private entrepreneurs it was compelled to do as taxpayers. In 1954 the government launched the first atomic-powered submarine, the *Nautilus*, and in 1959 the first atomic-powered merchant ship, the *Savannah*. In that year the St Lawrence Seaway was completed, opening the heart of the American continent to ocean-going shipping.[33]

Less attention was given to ocean shipping after the Civil War because the Americans were concentrating their efforts on colonising the American continent. In this task railroads played a vital role.

The first railroad operating as a common carrier in the United States was the Baltimore and Ohio opened in 1830 and intended to tap the trade of the Ohio valley. Under construction at the same time was the South Carolina railroad, running from Charleston, South Carolina, to Hamburg on the Savannah River, over 100 miles away. Opened in 1831 and completed in 1834, this track was the longest in the world. The locomotive, the *Best Friend of Charleston*, was American designed and built. However, even Charleston friends are not always what they seem, for the *Best Friend* blew up in June of that year, injuring several passengers.

Undeterred the Americans soon had the *Phoenix* on the rails; but this time the locomotive was separated from the passengers by a barrier car loaded with cotton bales.

By the 1840s, with over 3000 miles of track, the railroads were no longer considered primarily feeders to other forms of transport, but the chief agent in the country's progress and improvement. Under their impetus, the old rivalries of the cities on the Atlantic seaboard (including Boston, Charleston, Savannah and Baltimore) to be the first to control the interior, were renewed. By the 1850s, railroad mileage had tripled to 9000 miles, and the first so-called trunk lines were in operation. One of these lines ran from Boston to the St Lawrence River at Ogdensburg; another consolidated line ran from New York to Lake Erie (Dunkirk and Buffalo) and thence across the plains of the midwest to Chicago and Lake Michigan. From the southern ports of Charleston and Savannah, trunk lines struck out for Chattanooga and Nashville, Tennessee; these southern lines striking northwest were soon joined by other lines coming southwest from Richmond and Norfolk, Virginia. Other railroads quickly spread across the midwest (the first line reached the Mississippi in 1854) and ran down the river to the Gulf. Between 1850 and 1860, about 8000 miles of railroads were built in the southwest. The result was to direct the flow of produce away from New Orleans and Mobile to the ports of the eastern seaboard which provided the most direct access to the all-important transatlantic trade. New lines were built from the Gulf to resist this trend. But the trade from the north and the southwest continued to be drawn eastwards. By 1860 there were 30,000 miles of railroad in the United States; by then railroads had become the most important form of national transport. While the commercial panic of 1857 and the Civil War did much to interrupt large-scale railroad building in the United States, between 1860 and 1865 a further 5000 miles of railroads were added; more than 3000 of which lay west of the Mississippi River.

With the end of the Civil War the westward movement gained new momentum. There followed the great age of the transcontinental railroads. Three lines had been built from the Mississippi to the Pacific by 1884, and five by 1890. The first of these gigantic undertakings was the Union Pacific Railroad, created by Congress in 1862. With the southern voice stilled by war, only northern interests were considered. Beginning at Omaha, Nebraska, in 1866, with an unlimited supply of immigrant labour to help it (many of them Irish), the Union Pacific made its way westward across Nebraska, Wyoming territory and Utah. Meanwhile the Central Pacific line, working from the western seaboard and assisted by an army of Chinese coolies, had climbed the grades of the Sierras, crossed the arid valleys of Nevada, until eventually amidst prayers by the Reverend Todd ('We have got done praying', was the message sent by the telegraph operator to the American nation),[34] it joined the Union Pacific at Promontory Summit, Utah, in 1869. This joining of coast to coast with a band of steel greatly appealed to the imagination of the American people; so much so, that it was celebrated not with the Irishman's whisky or the Chinaman's tea, but with champagne. Both officials whose job it was to drive home the final spikes having missed their blows, it was left to an unknown labourer to join America together.

Other transcontinental lines followed: in 1864 Congress had chartered the Northern Pacific. Completed in 1883, the route went from Duluth on Lake Superior, and St Paul, westwards across Minnesota, through the Badlands of Dakota, up the Yellowstone valley of Montana, on through Washington to Portland, Oregon, and Puget Sound. The first transcontinental line driven across southern territory was the Southern Pacific, authorised by Congress in 1866. This was built along the Gulf coast across Louisiana, Texas, New Mexico, Arizona and California. In 1882 it joined New Orleans with Los Angeles. It was then continued up the San Joaquin valley to San Francisco. Between 1869 and 1884, the second of the southern lines, the Atchison, Topeka and Santa Fe Railroad, was built from Kansas City, Missouri, up the Arkansas, through the centre of Kansas, across the corner of Colorado, through the Rockies at Raton Spur to Santa Fe. It was continued through New Mexico and Arizona – the country of the Apache and the Navajo – until in 1884 it found an outlet on the Pacific at San Diego. By 1890, by which time there were 72,000 miles of railroads west of the Mississippi, five major lines connected the Far West with the railroads of the east. With the exception of the lines running from Los Angeles to the Canadian border, all the major trans-Mississippi lines ran from east to west.

In so far as the trans-Mississippi lines were instrumental in joining the Atlantic and the Pacific oceans, they ensured that the political unity obtained by war would be continued. Undoubtedly they facilitated the westward migration of settlers from home and overseas. They not only attracted migrants from Europe, they carried them to the frontier, sold them land on credit, taught them new agricultural techniques, helped them to build towns, and provided an outlet for the growing mineral and agricultural wealth of America. While the railways hastened the death of much wildlife in the trans-Mississippi west, they increased the cultivated resources available for foreign trade; they also helped to mobilise the human and financial resources needed to settle America. No other agency affected the history of the trans-Mississippi west as they did.[35] To some extent, they reversed the order of settlement, first came a railroad and then a town. In thirty years, with the stimulus of better transport, places such as Omaha, Kansas City, Independence, Duluth, Oakland, Portland, Seattle and Tacoma had become great cities. They undoubtedly assisted in the growth and development of the trans-Mississippi States.[36] On the outbreak of the First World War, total mileage was more than 250,000;[37] by then there existed an integrated railroad network across the nation.

American railway technology[38] was not confined to the United States. Soon after the first English locomotive had been imported (the *Stourbridge Lion* for the Delaware and Hudson Railroad in 1829) and had proved too heavy for America's early trackwork and bridges, several locomotive builders appeared in New York, Philadelphia, New Jersey and Massachusetts. As a result the famous American type of locomotive was developed (described as 'long, rakish, elegant if a bit spindly').[39] Those of William Norris and Matthias Baldwin were soon in demand in Europe, and it was Norris who in the 1840s organised the locomotive and car shops for the Austrian State railroad. During the 1860s the Americans devised air brakes and the Pullman sleeping car; in the 1870s there followed the refrigerator car and the railroad coupler. Later came the Westinghouse brake system (1887), the steel frame (1903–6), and the development of electric and diesel oil propulsion. From the 1850s onward, with the expansion of business interests abroad, American railroads were built in Mexico,[40] Canada and Chile (primarily for mining), in Cuba (for sugar), in Panama (to cross the isthmus), in Nicaragua, Costa Rica, Guatemala and Venezuela (primarily for tropical fruit and oil), in Peru, Brazil and Argentina (to link the interior with the ports), in Africa (as an outlet for the Republic of the Transvaal to the Indian Ocean),[41] and in Eastern Europe (centered on St Petersburg). Their effect in Latin America[42] and Canada was closely connected with the search for mineral wealth.

Seen from a world standpoint, American railroads not only ensured the Anglo-Saxon colonisation of great parts of the North American continent; by joining the Atlantic with the Pacific, they forged one of the vital links that helped to ensure white hegemony around the earth through the temperate latitudes of power. For the Americans they brought about an increased awareness of Asia. In 1909 President Taft and his Secretary of State, Philander C. Knox, pressured the Chinese government to include United States banking interests in a European consortium organised to finance railroad concessions in China.[43] The American transcontinental railroads set an example that would soon be followed by Canada, Russia, Australia and South Africa.

America's contribution to the development of other forms of transport and communication came as a direct result of its own needs. The telegraph, which by 1860 had spanned the entire American continent, made 'One nation under God' a reality. Being the first instant communication over great distance prior to the telephone, it had a revolutionary effect on the dissemination of news, of business and military intelligence, and traffic control of America's vast network of railroads. Samuel Finley Breese Morse (1791–1872) was not the first to conceive the idea of an electric telegraph, but he promoted and applied the idea in America and abroad more than anybody else. In 1838 he devised the Morse Code which became known throughout the world and for which he was later rewarded by many governments. It was another American entrepreneur, Cyrus West Field (1819–92), who promoted the first Atlantic telegraph cable in 1858 and later in 1866. By 1903 there had been laid a network of telegraph and underwater cables around the globe.*

With the further introduction of radio, telephone, the motion picture, and television, the twentieth century relations of man have been transformed. Today television (especially as it has become the greatest channel of the American film), dominates all other forms of mass communication.[44] Nothing has caused greater uniformity in culture, commerce, education and entertainment. Here partly lies the source of the growing challenge to the nation state.

No twentieth-century transport is more closely identified with the Americans than the automobile. Despite the fact that the basic inventions were European in origin, it was the Americans who put them to commercial use on a larger scale than anyone else. First marketed successfully in 1893, American passenger car registrations had by 1910 reached one-half million; by 1929, twenty-three million. Before Ford's Model T appeared in 1908, an automobile cost about $1500; the Model T sold at $825; by 1925, largely because of assembly line techniques and the economies of scale, it was priced at $260. By 1929 automotive exports had surpassed in value American exports of cotton, which had held first place in the foreign trade of the United States since the early nineteenth century. It was never to be as high again. Instead there followed a dramatic shift on the part of the American automobile industry to foreign assembly and manufacture. Today Americans own more automobiles (as they own more of most other things of a capital intensive nature) than the rest of the white race combined. If we allow for the cars manufactured by them abroad, then their position is truly a dominat-

---

*The cable and telegraph systems combined helped to bring about a more effective world marketing system. For example, Minnesota prices for wheat became much steadier once they could be compared with Liverpool prices.

ing one. In 1952 they were making three-quarters of the
world's automobiles and almost one-half of all the trucks and
buses. In contrast, Asia at this time, which had more than half
the world's population, had only 3 per cent of the world's
automobiles. In 1971 American domestic production of
motor vehicles was about one-third of world production, but
by then much of America's production was in Canada and
overseas. With few exceptions, such as Volkswagen, Fiat,
Renault and British-Leyland, all the largest European automobile firms are now American-owned or controlled. The
industrial and financial empires of General Motors, Ford and
Chrysler dwarf all the rest.[45]

The automobile has joined the world together as the
railways never did. (Much of the inspiration, the engineering
and technical skill, the finance and the driving force behind
the building of the Pan-American Highway, which by 1976
will link Alaska to the Straits of Magellan, has been American.) It obviously has affected all aspects of the other major
industries, including metals, engine construction, glass,
petroleum,[46] rubber, and motels (a unique American contribution to travel). Its ever-growing demands have caused a
world shortage of oil. There is no other industry that has
contributed so much to the growth of the multi-national
corporation. Not only have new and vigorous sectors of other
people's economies been created, but those economies have
come to depend as never before for their economic well-being
on this one form of transport.

In providing individual transport on a mass scale, the
automobile industry has been the greatest cause of urban
sprawl, of pollution, of congestion, and (through traffic
accidents) of physical disability. In transforming the physical
and social habits of many societies, it has dissolved many of
their traditions and customs. Not least, it has encouraged the
quantification of life and has increased the psychological
adaptation to time, as well as the mobility of the individual.

In the contribution they have made to the development of
the aviation industry, the Americans have been pre-eminent.
Like most other innovations in transport and communications, aviation grew out of the joint effort of Americans and
Europeans, and it was upon the basis of their experiments

that the first successful flight was performed by Wilbur and Orville Wright, at Kitty Hawk, North Carolina, in 1903; two years later, in 1905, the Wrights flew an unprecedented twenty-four miles in thirty-eight minutes.

With aircraft, as with the telephone, radio, automobile and television, the American genius expressed itself in turning a curiosity into a mass-produced product. Yet growth was relatively slow. Without the continuing support of the American military, and the dramatisation of the new form of transport provided by Lindbergh's solo, nonstop flight from New York to Paris in 1927, it would have been even slower. With no world empire commitments, such as those held by the British and the French, the Americans did not pioneer in some of the early air routes between Europe and the other continents; yet the first passenger service across the Pacific (1935) and (allowing for earlier German dirigibles) the North Atlantic (1939) were both inaugurated by the Pan American Airline Company. Indeed, by the 1950s, United States commercial companies were flying more passenger miles than the other nations combined. For a period after the Second World War the British led in commercial jet transportation. By the 1960s, however, the Americans were taking the lion's share of world aircraft business and had established a number of altitude and speed records.

On a world front there are few aspects of life that the aircraft industry has not affected. In the physical sciences it has caused important changes in engine construction (jet), fuels, metals and controls (radar); for better or worse, it has linked the more remote parts of the earth with the more developed western centres; it has helped to make national borders obsolete; it has necessitated new types of defence; it has loosed a flood of American (and other western) tourists upon the world; it has outmoded and largely replaced other forms of transport (hence, partly, Britain's selling of the *Queen Mary* and the *Queen Elizabeth*); it has quickened commercial transport; and, finally, it has become of such size and national importance that its progress has become a matter of keen national rivalry.[47]

In the story of America's contribution to the conquest of distance, there is no more stirring chapter than that which tells of American-man's flight to the moon.[48] In every way, especially in the triumph of the human spirit, this is the greatest and the most exciting adventure of them all. It is a stupendous, world-wide drama that began with the launching of the first American satellite on 31 January 1958 – four months after the Russians launched the first satellite – and ended on 20 July 1969, when Neil Armstrong took 'one small step for a man, one giant leap for mankind'.

We are no more able to predict what the outcome of this particular adventure into the unknown will be than Columbus could when he first sighted the island which he named San Salvador. Certainly the Americans have not 'conquered' outer-space. That they can never do; anymore than they can conquer nature or life. What they have done is enter a new era in the exploration and understanding both of the universe and of man. The door of the vast solar system has been opened; man's curiosity being what it is, it will not be shut. Even in practical terms, he has already felt the benefits on earth from the data being made available by orbiting satellites.

We are similarly unable to compare these events with what has gone before. Never before in the conquest of distance have we faced infinity; never before have we dealt with such speeds and with such distances; never before has there been such a concentrated, immense, complex technological effort (involving the expenditure from 1961 through 1970 of 41 billion dollars). These are not differences in degree from what preceded space exploration; they are differences in kind. Indeed, the differences are so great that they must not only cause the American people to ask what goal in space exploration they should now seek as a nation, but also what goal they should seek as men. Well might Buzz Aldrin, on his way home from the moon, read to a world audience words drawn from the eighth Psalm of the Old Testament: 'When I consider thy heavens, the work of thy fingers, the moon and the stars, which thou hast ordained; what is man, that thou art mindful of him?'

To a greater extent than is true of most other nations, the history of the American people has been a struggle with space and time. Historically speaking, Americans have always been on the move. Other than the Bedouin of Arabia, or the members of a persecuted race such as the Jews, what other people is there in the world today so many of whom die where they were not born; what other people is there who find it so hard to remain in one place for long?

The American not only has an extraordinary urge to move; as a matter of absolute necessity, he* must get from one place to another in the minimum time. Whatever form of transport or communication we are considering – on land, on or in the sea, or in the air – speed has always been the vital factor. He has a different rhythm of life which moulds all that he does. Quick, fast movement is what he is famous for; to some Americans, it is almost their reason for being. The first impact of an American corporation abroad is the quickening of pace. In saying, 'time is money', they imply that the purpose of life is movement and speed. Hence, the real shock to the Americans of Russia's first Sputnik was the shock of hurt pride; another people could be first and fastest. More than for any other reason, the Americans were determined to be on the moon first so that the Russians would be second.

How the Americans have come to be as they are in their attitudes to distance and time is partly their western heritage and partly the challenge provided by their own unique, comet-like passage of history. Do we have to search for an occult reason why the Americans march to a faster beat? Their whole history explains it. The nation itself is the child of exodus. The country was discovered and colonised by people on the move, many of them adventurous and restless. Discontent and dissatisfaction accompanied the Americans in their long hard march across America. Unlike the people of other lands – many of whom know only their family, their tribe, their village – the horizon of most Americans is the whole vast United States, and they will settle for nothing less. Unity – physical, geographical, political, social and mental – is as vital to the American as diversity is to the European. In one sense, in their mobility, they are like the nomadic people of other times and places; in another sense, shorn as they are very largely of the traditional ties and local customs that bind

---

*Or she, for it was Elizabeth Cochrane Seaman, 'Nelly Bly', who first broke the fictional record of Phineas Fogg in Jules Verne's *Around the World in Eighty Days*.

other people together, they are utterly dissimilar. The tie that most closely binds so many Americans to where they are is neither ancestry nor tribal lore; it is the need to gain a livelihood. For some, it is a tie that is easily broken if a better livelihood is offered elsewhere. In fact until now the whole American experiment has cried out against roots, against the past, against permanence and continuity.* Add to these things, America's great wealth – for the urge to move rapidly and the will to shorten distance are nothing without the means to pay for them – and we can better appreciate why the Americans have made the extraordinary contribution they have to the conquest of distance.

Whether these things will continue, we cannot say. Values change according to time and circumstance. In fact they are changing before our eyes. The United States Government's refusal to continue with the supersonic aircraft programme is, so far as we know, the first example of its kind in American history. This is not all. With earlier developments in transport and communications (regardless of their scientific contribution), the possibility of commercial exploitation was always one of the strongest impulses of action. But with the coming of the first Sputnik and the outer space exploration that followed it, there has come about a dramatic shift in emphasis from commercial opportunity and gain to national rivalry and survival; there has also been the change from dealing with distance and challenges which the mind could grasp, to dealing with infinity.

The sobering thought that occurs to us as we cast our eye over past and present efforts to conquer distance is that in progressively removing the barriers of distance – in making a much smaller world – the Americans have also removed the shield which for so long provided them with national security and protection.

*The desire to move on, to break camp, to try again elsewhere lies deep in the American. His literature from Twain and Melville to Dos Passos and Steinbeck bears this out.

CHAPTER VII

America and World Commerce

DESPITE the social defences erected against the unchecked working of the market economy,[1] a belief in the justice and power of the market place is central to American life. In this sense, the Americans have remained true to their original intention in coming to this land: not to loot and leave but to settle and trade.

Outside America, their greatest area of trade has always been the Atlantic basin. Their first trade – the fur trade – was the lure which drew them inland and helped them to create an empire in the new world. Income from the early sale of furs and fish[2] (which allowed Catholic Europe to observe its meatless Fridays) and other colonial produce enabled them to survive in the wilderness. Out of the proceeds of Anglo-American trade, their first seaport cities – Boston, Philadelphia, New York, Baltimore, Charleston and New Orleans – were built. Indeed by 1776 there had been woven an interrelated commercial fabric between the Old World and the New of such complexity and strength that it was able to withstand the worst strains of the Revolutionary War.

Mercantilist England's control of American trade was not without its advantages to the colonists. England not only marketed (within western Europe or elsewhere) what they produced; its merchants financed and supplied what the colonists needed. Indeed, in the ten years, 1761–70, all the continental colonies except the Carolinas had a balance of trade deficit with England, i.e. they were taking more than they were giving;[3] which is what is to be expected of a young country getting onto its feet. The lucky thing for America was that English merchant bankers were prepared to finance the difference.

Especially fortunate was Britain's willingness to give an exclusive position to American tobacco. First sent from Jamestown in 1613, by the early decades of the eighteenth century tobacco accounted for almost half of American exports to Britain and about one-third of its total exports to all countries. By 1775 England was taking 100 million pounds (four-fifths of it for re-export by British merchants, chiefly to continental Europe). Britain also provided a market for southern rice, indigo, and naval stores (tar, pitch, rosin, turpentine, hemp, masts and yards). Until cotton appeared at the close of the eighteenth century, tobacco remained the leading item in America's foreign trade. None of the items coming from the other colonies at this time (dried codfish, whale and cod oil, lumber, ships, flour, potash, grain, livestock, furs and skins, and pig and bar iron) equalled the importance of tobacco and cotton. Despite the fact that from the 1850s most of the South's cotton crop was being shipped directly from Charleston, Savannah, Mobile and New Orleans, the commission charged by English and Yankee middlemen and shipowners often turned a southern trade surplus into an unfavourable balance of payments; hence the south's belief that it was being exploited by the north, especially by the bankers and merchants of 'that monster city' New York.

In return for these exports, English merchants provided, either directly or indirectly, most of the tools, equipment, hardware, and first quality iron (the best iron in the eighteenth century, together with hemp and flax, came from Russia[4] and Sweden), clothing and furnishings, drink (coffee, tea, rum and wine), molasses and sugar, needed by the colonists.

Moreover through a complicated system of multilateral trade involving the Americas, Europe, and Africa, all claims and balances could be settled through England. There thus grew up a system of trade between the three continents in which the colonial merchants and shippers were largely free to buy and sell where it suited their interests best. In this way, America was able to regularise its trade with the West Indies, Europe and Africa. To the Indies, the Americans took chiefly food, especially 'refuse' cod,[5] and brought away sugar, molas-

ses and fruit. To Europe, they took colonial produce including distilled rum from Rhode Island; which, in a roundabout
way, was exchanged for manufactures and equipment. To
Africa, they carried rum, brandy, tobacco, flour, lumber,
weapons, gunpowder, sperm-oil candles, cloth, brass wire,
trinkets, crockery, and bar iron. In the 1840s, Commodore
Matthew Perry, who a decade later would open Japan's door
to his country's commerce, added the following items which
might be traded on the west African coast: brown sugar,
hams, cheese, tin buckets, ladies shoes, gloves, paint, palm-
leaf hats, brass kettles, paper and ink, ribbons for bonnets,
silk stockings, and '5 dozen cotton umbrellas'. They brought
away slaves and whatever African produce was offering,
including ivory, palm oil, dye-woods, skins, pepper, coffee,
gold dust, and gum copal.[6]

At the time of independence, the colonies were sending
about a quarter of their exports to the British West Indies,
and receiving about a third of their exports therefrom. By
then, partly because of ocean currents and prevailing winds, a
good deal of American trade followed a clockwise direction:
from the West Indies to the colonies, from the colonies to
Europe and/or Africa, and then back to the West Indies. It
was this trade that resulted in more Negroes than white
colonists crossing the Atlantic before 1800, most of them
destined for the sugar plantations of the Caribbean.

Though forbidden to trade directly with Asia, colonial
merchants worked the Mediterranean and Turkey trade
under the British flag. Beginning in the 1780s, United States
traders were seen doing business in China, India, the Philippines, Sumatra, Arabia and Iran. By the 1830s, in order to
satisfy China's demands for furs and the world's demands for
oil, American ships had pursued the sea otter, the seal, and
certain kinds of whales almost to extinction. In 1846 American ships comprised more than three-quarters of the world's
aggregate whaling fleet of almost a thousand vessels. The
whale and the skin trade not only realised unbelievable profits
for those who directed it (between 1793 and 1807 the
Americans shipped $3\frac{1}{2}$ million seal skins to Canton and on one
voyage made $53,118 on an investment of $7867);[7] it also
carried the American flag into every ocean of the world. It

was Captain Nathaniel Brown Palmer in the *Hero* out of Stonington, Connecticut, who in November 1820, 'discovered' the land jutting out from Antarctica toward Cape Horn, part of which is still named after him.

While official statistics take no account of either slavery or smuggling,[8] a flourishing American slave trade continued throughout the colonial period. Indeed smuggling and contraband trade not only bulked large in seventeenth- and eighteenth-century American trade, it was, in fact, endemic to the whole western world.[9] It ensured, so far as the colonists were concerned, that British mercantilist regulations would be observed more in the breach than anything else. Thus, British regulations (begun in the 1650s with the intention of protecting British shipping from the far more efficient shipping of the Dutch) did not prevent New England traders from exchanging southern tobacco for Spanish (Canary) wine, regardless of the fact that, under the regulations, the tobacco should have gone to England, not Spain; and that the wine should have come from England's ally, Portugal.

Similar regulations concerning other articles enumerated by Parliament in 1660 and 1705 (sugar, indigo, rice, molasses and naval stores, all of which should have been shipped from the colonies to England) were also evaded. Widespread evasion was practised against the Acts of Parliament of 1721 and 1764, which added many other items to the list of articles to be traded only with England. We are told that in the latter year (1764) about four-fifths of the molasses imported into Rhode Island had evaded the duty imposed by the Molasses Act of 1733.[10]

There is plenty of evidence of contraband trade between New England and the Dutch and French West Indian sugar islands. No regulation devised by the British Parliament prevented the colonists from exchanging their fish, salt meats, cereals and timber for needed specie or illicit molasses, sugar, silks, laces, brandy and gin. For much of the eighteenth century the sugar islands of the Caribbean were the mainspring of European colonial trade, and it was in the Caribbean that the best 'pickings' of contraband trade were to be had.

But, then, in the eighteenth century, nobody went to hell for smuggling. Indeed there was just as much of it on one side of the Atlantic as on the other. In the early 1700s New York's port trade could increase 300 per cent, while its revenues declined by half. In the late 1700s William Pitt was able to tell Parliament that, of the thirteen million pounds of tea annually consumed in England, duty had been paid on less than half. Smuggling, both private and governmental, became such a fine art and so widespread during the French Wars (1793–1815) that, in the absence of smugglers' memoirs, it is very difficult to know who was cheating whom.[11] The protests of British merchants on the West African coast in the 1820s against the inroads made by American traders show that nothing could stop an uninhibited Yankee in search of a profit. Shut out of British possessions by official measures, the Yankees quickly resorted to smuggling.

It was the English Parliament's insistence on its taxing power after the financially crippling Seven Years War with the French and the Indians, and its enforcement of hitherto half-disregarded trade laws aimed at smuggling, that cut into a most profitable American commerce and helped lay the foundations for the struggle for independence. The signatures of John Hancock and other merchants on the American Declaration of Independence suggests that at least some of the fervour surrounding the Boston Tea Party can be explained in nominally illicit dollars and cents.

Although the Declaration of Independence of 1776 and the war that followed it are regarded as important turning points in the early history of the United States, these events had little effect upon the foreign trade of the American people. To break the political bonds that held them to the forum at Westminster was one thing; to cut the commercial ties that joined them with metropolitan London was another. The services of the mercantile and financial centre of the western world were not to be dispensed with that easily. In any event the American merchant was not interested in flag-waving but in convenience and gain; and these could best be found in London. As John Adams wrote from Europe in

1785, 'The Britons boast, that all the prophecies of the loss of the American trade from the independence of the United States, have proved false';[12] which may partly explain why the British were not prepared to make trade concessions to the Americans in the postwar period.

Peace not only meant that the Americans were now free to trade openly with whom they pleased; it also meant that their produce (particularly tobacco) could no longer claim an exclusive position in the British market; it meant the temporary loss of the trading privileges they had enjoyed in the British West Indies; it meant (once the protective shield of the British Royal Navy had been withdrawn) that their shipping (unless it sailed under a British 'flag of convenience' which many did until the British forbade it in 1811) would become fair game for all who wished to plunder it, especially in the Caribbean and off the North African coast;[13] it meant the loss of British shipbuilding orders; finally, peace also meant that the bounties on indigo, naval stores and lumber, which had profited the colonies, would be discontinued.[14]

All these things provided only temporary setbacks to American foreign commerce. (Income from the American export trade in the late 1780s was not much less than it had been in the early 1770s.)[15] Moreover it was soon to feel the tremendous stimulus of the French Wars.[16] Between the years 1789–1860, American foreign trade did in fact grow sixteen-fold, from $43 million in 1790 to $688 million in 1860 (Table XIV). In this period, United States foreign trade grew at a faster rate than that of the British and greatly exceeded the rate of increase of America's population (though in 1860 the value of United States foreign commerce was only about one-third that of the British). Accompanying this growth was a phenomenal increase in American domestic trade between 1799 and 1850, from about $133 million to $2 billion.

Despite the development of American industry in the period 1790–1860, the United States continued to rely on the supply of British manufactures and equipment. Except for certain years, America took more of other people's goods than it was able to supply. It made up the difference in several ways: by invisible exports (i.e. shipping, financial and commercial services and remittances made by immigrants to their families in Europe), by money it was able to attract in foreign investments and by the export of specie and bullion. The figures given in Table XIV show total imports to have increased more than fifteenfold. The leading items were textile manufactures, raw wool, and flax. Imports of iron and steel products were also important (Table XV). The principal commodity imports – as distinct from manufactures – were sugar, coffee, rum and wine.

Nor was there any great change during the years 1790–1860 in the source of these things (Tables XVII and XVIII). Partly to find an alternative to British-controlled trade, New England merchants had, since the 1780s, brought tea and silk from China.[17] The very first treaties forced upon China (1844) and Japan (1854 and 1858) by the Americans were commercial treaties. Since the early years of the nineteenth century – in exchange for coffee, pepper, tea, sugar and rum, delivered to Smyrna in American vessels – Yankee traders had established a near monopoly of the Turkey–China opium trade.[18] So much so, that some Chinese were under the impression that Turkey was part of the United States. In absolute value, the China trade reached its peak in 1850–5. During the French Wars, iron and shipping supplies (cables, rigging and sails) had been obtained from Russia.[19] But relative to British trade all these items were small; especially when, after 1814, Britain became the chief source of high quality iron.

According to Table XVIII, other changes in imports during the years 1821–60 were an absolute increase in America's demand for West Indian sugar, as well as Brazilian coffee (Americans were switching from tea to coffee); and a decline – because of changes in fashions – of the China silk trade. In 1836, long after the slave trade had been declared illegal by Congress (1808), whole cargoes of slaves were being shipped from Africa, via Havana, to the United States. As many as 15,000 Africans were taken annually to Texas alone.[20] So openly was the law flouted that the slave trade grew instead of declined. It is possible that more slaves were brought into the United States in 1859 than in any year when the trade was legal. The price of a young, healthy male slave was $1800 on the New Orleans market in 1860.

There also grew up at the end of the eighteenth century a small but 'legitimate' trade with West and South Africa. With the whites of the Cape (which became an important point for ships trading with the Far East and the Indian Ocean), lumber from Boston and wine from the Cape Province were two of the most important items of trade. 'Wine is rising in price,' reported Governor Janssens from the Cape to his Dutch superiors in Holland in 1803, 'the good qualities having been advantageously sold in the south of North America.'[21] A few years earlier in 1789, Hasket Derby, returning to New England from Calcutta, had sold $1500 worth of Calcutta cloth at the Cape and purchased 253 ostrich feathers.[22]

In the years before the Civil War, there was also a dramatic increase in total United States exports. Tables XVI and XIX reveal the extent to which America increased its role as the world's greatest supplier of food and raw materials. (In addition, in the 1850s, about two-thirds of California's gold production of $630 million was exported.) Of these exports, cotton was King. Accounting for only about 14 per cent in the first decade of the nineteenth century, by 1851–60 cotton made up approximately half the total. On the eve of the Civil War in 1860 it comprised 60 per cent. If we add rice, tobacco and sugar, then three-quarters of these exports were being produced by the south. Ironically (for the south), it was the income obtained from the sale of cotton that helped to finance northern development and set the nation's course to Appomattox.

Cotton not only played a leading role in the changing fortunes of the United States, it affected the life of the whole Atlantic basin. In 1860 England's leading export was the same cotton, now in a manufactured form, that the American south had earlier exported to Britain. It is this dovetailing of the American and the European economies that helps to explain the rapid colonisation of North America by the white settlers.[23] In 1860 Europe was not only ready to buy four-fifths of what America wanted to sell; it was also able to provide the human, financial and technical resources necessary to develop the New World.

In so far as the American Civil War placed undisputed political power in the hands of those who favoured rapid industrialisation,[24] Appomattox witnessed the triumph of one culture over another. The 'truth' that rang out from 'The Battle Hymn of the Republic' was a northern 'truth'. By the end of the nineteenth century, the north's triumph was complete.

No longer restrained by southern political power, northern industrialists were able to employ Federal laws to foster their own interests. Especially was this true of the increased tariff protection obtained by the Act of 1864. By 1885 the output of the manufacturing industries had surpassed that of agriculture. By 1914 (again encouraged by the increased tariffs of 1890 and 1897) it was twice as great. On the outbreak of the First World War America produced one-third of the world's manufactures. Its output of coal, iron and steel was far greater than that of any other country. And alongside the spectacular development of manufacturing industry there was an even more extraordinary development of trade, finance, health, transport, public utilities and government service, which employed almost one-third of the labour force. The fourteen-fold increase in domestic commerce (from about $2 billion in 1860 to $28 billion in 1908) was phenomenal. While it is not until the last quarter of the nineteenth century that we can justifiably speak of a United States 'common market', America is probably unique in the extent to which such a large volume of consumer goods came to be bought and sold on a national scale so early in its history. The fact that it was a new society meant that there were no deep-seated traditions or built-in habits and tastes which might have delayed the acceptance of mass-production and mass-consumption techniques.

The great internal developments taking place in America in the years 1860–1914 were accompanied by equally important developments in foreign trade which grew about sixfold (Table XIV). Though still an overall debtor nation, America increased its share of world trade (as it is presently calculated) from about 9 per cent to 11 per cent.[25] In these years, the balance of trade went in America's favour. Encouraging this was the colonisation and further development of the enormous and varied natural wealth of the United States (much of which was exported), the continuing immigration of Europeans, the growing convertibility of currencies (the United

States officially adopted the Gold Standard in 1900), and the improvements in world transport and communications. The rest of the world (especially Europe) settled its balances with the United States multilaterally, by offsetting American claims with the claims or credits held against other nations. Important 'invisible' payments were made to Europe for shipping, financial and commercial services, immigrant remittances and tourist spending.

Between 1860 and 1914 America's growing reliance upon other people's raw materials is reflected in a fivefold increase in imports (Table XIV). Especially important were wool, silk, timber, pulp, fuel, minerals, skins and hides, and rubber. Sugar and coffee, the principal food and drink imports in the 1860s, occupied the same place in 1914. While Europe remained the greatest trading partner, accounting for more than half the total United States import trade in 1860 and 1914, increased demands for Asian silk, sugar and rubber caused Asia's share to rise from 8 per cent in 1860 to 16 per cent in 1913 (Tables XV, XVII and XVIII).

United States exports in the same period increased more than sevenfold. In the closing decade of the eighteenth century they had averaged $44 million; one hundred years later they averaged $1 billion (Table XIV). By 1874, encouraged by the movement of the frontier as well as by the expansion of industry and commerce, America was selling more than it was buying in the world. It was this export surplus that enabled the United States to meet its obligations as an overall debtor nation. The most striking changes were the increase in the sale of manufactured goods (the world volume of which had increased threefold between 1880 and 1913) and the relative decline in the sale of raw materials. Whereas in 1860 about two-thirds of the value of United States exports had consisted of raw materials and food and about one-tenth of manufactures, by 1911–20 raw materials had fallen to about 22 per cent, and finished manufactures (which had taken the lead in the 1880s) had risen to 37 per cent (Table XVI). After the Civil War, the exports of machinery and petroleum also began to grow at an increasing rate. However, the three leading export items remained cotton, wheat and meat, products vital to the changes going on in western Europe at this time.

Cotton remained the leading export until the 1930s, though its share declined from 50 per cent in 1851–60 to 15 per cent in 1911–20. (Yet agricultural exceeded non-agricultural exports until 1922.) Because of the setback of war, exports of cotton for 1880 were only slightly above those for 1860. Conversely the exports of wheat continued to grow. Encouraged by the westward movement as well as by Britain's industrialisation and its free-trade policy, they increased from about 9 per cent in the mid-century to 21 per cent in 1861–70; they continued to grow throughout the second half of the nineteenth century until in 1901 a temporary peak was reached with 239 million bushels. (The cost of transporting a bushel of wheat from Chicago to London in the fifty years before 1900 had fallen from about 40 to 10 cents.) This was to be the highest figure until 1917. Corn reached its peak in 1897, with 212 million bushels. If, to these exports of grain and flour, meat and meat products are added, it is not difficult to understand why certain countries in Europe, faced with this growing avalanche of food from the New World (including Canada and Argentina), which caused prices to fall sharply, were forced to reorganise and further protect their agricultural industry (between 1869 and 1887, the acreage sown to wheat in England was almost halved), but at least they were spared the trials of Ireland's potato famine.

Relative to other continents, Europe's share of America's exports began to decline from the 1880s onwards. This was particularly true of Britain, whose share fell from a half to a quarter. To some extent, the loss of British markets was offset by gains made in Canada and other parts of the Americas (Tables XVII and XIX). The predicted gains in trade with Asia had never really materialised in the nineteenth century. In 1900 less than one-tenth of the value of United States foreign trade was being done with Asia, Africa and South America combined. China's trade was about 3 per cent.

The outcome of this ever-widening Atlantic economy – until 1914 we might call it the economy of Greater Europe – was a remarkable increase in the wealth (in output

and in per capita income in goods and services) of the western
people. This was the result of world colonisation, which
provided seemingly limitless natural resources. It also resulted from the growing specialisation of the American and
European economies, as well as from the developments in
ocean-going transport.

The course of world trade in the interwar years reflected
the general disarray of western civilisation. There was little
real growth in world trade between 1913 and 1939. In the
latter year, it was (at $46 billion) little more than it had been
in 1914 ($38 billion). Corrected for price changes, the
volume of world trade did not recover its 1913 level until
1927; it rose by about one-fifth until 1929; collapsed during
the 1930s; and in 1936 was about 2 per cent greater than it
had been in 1913.

In its foreign trade America fared no better than the rest.
Becoming a creditor nation in its overall obligations to others
for the first time during the 1920s, it maintained its export
surplus by making a growing quantity of dollars available to
other nations through loans and by paying for foreign services
of one kind or another. Yet its foreign trade followed the
same erratic course taken by world trade generally. Stimulated by the unprecedented demands of the First Great War,
it increased sharply to a peak in 1920. the following year
(1921) exports were halved. A decade later, in 1930, foreign
trade was (at about $7 billion) half of what it had been ten
years previously. By 1939 it had fallen still lower, to $5·5
billion. Fortunately the collapse of foreign trade was not a
life and death matter for the economy as a whole. America
had other wealth to fall back upon;[26] and, where employment continued, its standards of productivity remained
high.

It was in the interwar years that America's ever-increasing
reliance upon other people's raw materials became evident.
Between 1860 and 1940, as industrialisation progressed, raw
materials had risen from one-tenth to a third of total imports.
Conversely imports of manufactured goods fell from one-half
to one-fifth. Leading imports, in order of value in 1939, were:
crude rubber (to feed the automobile industry), coffee, wood

and paper products, sugar, raw silk (which experienced a decline in importance owing to the manufacture of synthetic substitutes), wool and manufactures and tin (Table XVIII).

It was during the same years (1914–39) that Europe ceased to be the main source of America's imports (Tables XVII and XVIII). In this period, while Europe's share was almost halved, Asia's share was almost doubled. While America's reliance upon European manufactures was declining its reliance upon the crude rubber supplies of southeast Asia and the raw silk supplies of Japan was growing. The upshot for Europe (especially Great Britain) was a depression in its chief exporting industries. The outcome for Asia was increased American demands, but the prices of both crude rubber and silk (because of the conditions of world commerce) were also depressed. In the interwar years America's reliance upon Canadian wood and paper pulp continued to grow. The sharp increase in Latin American exports to the United States (especially for petroleum from Venezuela) had to wait until after 1939 (Tables XV and XVIII).

Between 1914 and 1939 exports fluctuated even more sharply than imports, from $8228 million in 1920 to $3177 million in 1939 (Table XIV). Of these exports, manufactured goods followed by raw materials remained the two leading items. But whereas raw materials had been two-thirds of total exports in 1851–60 by 1940 they had fallen to about one-tenth. Increasingly now America needed its raw materials for its own domestic industry. Moreover it was able to offset the decline in its exports of raw materials by an increase in its sales of manufactured goods. By 1931 exports of machinery had replaced raw cotton as the leading export, a position which cotton had held since 1803. By the 1930s, in contrast to its dominating nineteenth-century position, the production of cotton was between one-quarter and one-fifth of world total. Leading exports in 1939 were: machinery, petroleum, raw cotton, automobiles and parts, iron, steel, copper and its manufactures, and chemicals (Tables XVI and XIX). Despite its lessening importance Europe remained America's greatest customer, taking 41 per cent of its exports in 1939, about one-third less than in 1913. Meanwhile America expanded its markets for manufactured goods in

Latin America and Asia (Tables XVII and XIX). In these areas during and immediately after the First World War it was able to take advantage of the upset caused to Britain, France and Germany by the European conflict.

In some ways the war only hastened the trend towards autarchy that was already under way. The desire for national aggrandisement and economic self-sufficiency (which reappeared in force in Europe in the 1870s and was strengthened still more by the First World War) had been there all the time. To assume that there was harmony in world trade in the prewar period under British leadership and disharmony in the postwar period when the Americans had power is to distort the facts. A good deal of the harmony which we see in retrospect in British-led world trade is probably illusory; indeed much of pre-1914 western life appears harmonious when compared with the turbulent half century that followed it.

Europe's and America's troubles in the postwar period sprang more from the structural change that had taken place in the relations between the Old World and the New. America's appearance at the end of the nineteenth century as the industrial and commercial giant changed, perhaps for all time, the complementary nineteenth-century state of affairs[27] whereby European manufactures and machinery were exchanged for American raw materials and food.[28] By 1914 the territorial division of labour and capital upon which the prosperity of the western world had been based no longer held good. In so far as the First World War served to accentuate America's lead in the world economy it assisted this trend.

The combined effect of these factors caused world commerce to become increasingly an implement of international power politics and a tool of national vested interests. It also prompted the western nations to re-erect the tariff barriers that had been removed in the second half of the nineteenth century and to abandon the hard-won principle of currency convertibility.

America's efforts, as the leading trading nation, to halt these trends were signally unsuccessful. Having agreed at the

Geneva Conference on Trade in 1927 that 'the time had come to put an end to the increase in tariffs and move in the oppposite direction', it then produced, in the Hawley–Smoot tariff of 1930, the most protective fiscal measure any administration had devised. This act was the signal for the raising of tariff levels elsewhere. Similarly Franklin D. Roosevelt could sound a ringing challenge to the western world in 1932 to free its trade, yet by refusing to discuss currency stabilisation (vital in halting the further disintegration of the world economy, and which his administration had already agreed to do), he sealed the fate of the World Economic Conference in London in 1933. The beggar-my-neighbour policy of currency devaluation in the world was allowed to continue unchecked.

Almost as if to offset the unfavourable impression they had given in London in 1933, a year later (under the Trade Agreement Act of 1934) the Americans began a bilateral scaling down of their own tariff levels. However, because of the widespread use of quotas to control imports this gesture did little to help world trade. The balance of payments problems of the western nations remained unresolved. Indeed it was at this time that Britain was forced to reverse its traditional free-trade policy. Nor did the flight of capital from Europe to America at this time do anything but complicate an already impossible situation. So topsy-turvy had the economic affairs of the western world become that America – the supposed leading creditor nation of the world – was eventually receiving more capital than it was making available. Given time these economic problems could have been resolved. But Europe had very little time left. In September 1939 it plunged once more into a world-wide war.

When the Second World War ended only the United States had the material resources necessary for world leadership. Its exports of goods and services in the immediate postwar years (1946–9) dwarfed those of other nations. Moreover, unlike after the First World War, the Americans did not shirk their world responsibilities. On the contrary, they took it for granted that they would have to lead the 'Free World'. There seemed to be nothing they would not do to ensure Europe's recovery and the restoration of world trade. To this end, between 1945 and 1952, they made available more than $30 billion worth of supplies (most of it as outright gifts).

This change in outlook is reflected in its commercial negotiations with its allies during and after the war. Earlier, under agreements made in 1941 (the Atlantic Charter) and 1942 (the Mutual Aid Agreement), the Americans had stressed the need for the restoration and freedom of world trade. It is they who took the initiative that resulted in the meetings held at Bretton Woods, New Hampshire, in 1944 – attended by many nations – which resulted in the establishment of the International Monetary Fund and the World Bank. Under the Bretton Woods system all currencies were officially denominated in terms of gold (although they were actually pegged to the dollar). As the dollar was fixed to gold it served as a standard of value for all currencies. No sooner had peace come than in December 1945 new proposals for the expansion of world trade were put forward by the American government. This time the pitfall of war reparations was avoided. Imaginative political thinking on a world scale was particularly evident in the Marshall Plan, made public two years later, in 1947. While few Europeans would concede that the difference between recovery and bankruptcy was the $12 billion worth of supplies provided by the Americans between 1948 and 1951,[29] this aid undoubtedly acted as a catalyst for the forces working for European recovery and unity.

The Marshall Plan was America's postwar economic leadership at its best. Other ideas were not so readily taken up by western Europeans. The sharp differences of opinion that existed between the Americans and the British, for instance, about the International Monetary Fund and the World Bank are well known.[30] However, as long as the Americans held financial power it was their view that prevailed – sometimes with disastrous results. Their action in making convertibility of sterling one of the conditions for a British loan in 1947 resulted in the exhaustion of British reserves and subsequent devaluation.

While in the postwar period the Americans have not been able to rid themselves of their strong protectionist traditions, nevertheless, at United Nations trade meetings in France (1949), England (1951), and Switzerland (1955–6), concessions were made to other countries that did achieve considerable reductions in the prewar United States tariff levels. And this trend was continued by the Kennedy administration in the 1960s under the United Nations General Agreement on Tariffs and Trade. Under this agreement in 1967 fifty nations, including the United States, agreed to reduce tariffs by about one-third over five years. This undertaking covered 80 per cent of world commerce. The trouble is that it did not take account of other (non-tariff) barriers to trade.

Confused as the rest of the world may be about America's intentions in foreign trade, it cannot be held responsible for a decline in world trade. Far from it. With certain ups and downs the postwar years have witnessed a remarkable recovery and expansion of international trade. Between 1953 and 1970 world trade grew from approximately $167 billion to $639 billion.[31] Much of this can be put down to improvements in world transport and communications, to the growth of multi-national business, to the great regional trading blocks that have appeared – such as the European Economic Community – but some of it was the result of American initiative and action. By 1958 the U.S. had substantially increased the gold and dollar holdings of other trading nations. Indeed, throughout the entire 1950s, total spending abroad exceeded foreign total spending in the United States. Yet in contrast to the situation that prevailed in the nineteenth century (when most international trade consisted in exchanging food and raw materials for manufactured products), the greatest increase in trade was between the already developed countries of western Europe and North America.

In 1950 America replaced Great Britain as the world's leading importer. In 1959, for the first time in the present century, it bought more goods and services in the world than it sold. Significant was the growing reliance upon other people's raw materials, especially for forest products (much of them devoted to bombarding a literate public with ephemeral publications like newspapers and magazines), minerals, and petroleum. By the 1960s, despite the fact that it was the leading producer, petroleum was one of its largest imports. By then about one-seventh of the minerals used came from abroad.[32] These not only included strategic industrial minerals such as cobalt (important in missiles, glass-making and automobiles), nickel, chromite, and manganese (almost all of which are imported), or tungsten (more than half of which is imported), but also some of the most widely used minerals such as iron, copper, lead, zinc and bauxite. Even for iron there has been a dramatic change in the past thirty years. In 1937–9, its reliance upon foreign iron amounted to about 3 per cent of its domestic production; in 1971, despite the fact that it was the second leading producer, the figure had grown to 46 per cent. Similar figures for copper were −13 to 5 per cent; for lead, 0 to 45 per cent; for zinc, 7 to 129 per cent; for bauxite, 113 to 618 per cent; and for petroleum, −4 to 39 per cent.[33] By 1954 the nation (according to President Eisenhower's Commission on Foreign Economic Policy) had passed 'from a position of relative self-sufficiency to one of increasing dependence upon foreign sources of supply [which] constitutes one of the striking economic changes of our times'.[34] In 1970 more than half of the strategic industrial materials used came from abroad. Dependence for raw materials used in the manufacture of particular products, such as the nuclear reactor or the jet engine, is even greater. At that time half of America's imports came from the western hemisphere; most of the rest came from western Europe and Japan. Leading items from Canada were basic minerals, wood and scrap iron; from Latin America came fuel, foods and drink (Table XVIII). The claim that imports are flooding into the United States from foreign affiliates of United States multinational corporations is not supported by the facts. In 1971 only about 7 per cent of the goods produced abroad by the multinational corporations entered the American domestic market.

America's growing demands for the produce of the rest of the world is of special importance to the poorer nations. The United States is the principal buyer of Bolivian tin and Chilean copper, as it is of the minerals of Mexico and Peru. It is the largest foreign market for the coffee, sugar, fibres and fruit sold by Brazil, Colombia, Ecuador, Haiti, the Dominican Republic, and Guatemala; also for Uruguay's wool and Venezuela's oil. For some of these items, dependence upon the United States market is almost total. In recent decades the terms of trade (that is, what a country can receive in return for what it exports) have generally been moving against the primary producers of the world.[35]

United States purchases are also important for Malayan rubber, for fibres from India and Pakistan, for oil and rubber from Indonesia, copra, sugar and wood from the Philippines, tobacco from Turkey, and rubber from Thailand. For South Korea, Formosa and South Vietnam, American markets are indispensable.

Although Africa has in the past been oriented almost entirely towards western European markets, American purchases of coffee are important for Angola, Ethiopia, Ghana, Ivory Coast, Kenya, Malagasy Republic and Uganda. The United States is also an important buyer of rubber from Liberia, as well as minerals from the Republic of South Africa. Despite the United Nations embargo, it still buys much-needed chrome from Rhodesia.

America's chief markets for its own products are in the white-settled world (Tables XVII and XIX). Because of war and inflation its foreign sales increased threefold during the 1940s. In the 1950s, with the recovery of the other western nations and Japan, the increase in sales declined. Despite the fact that great quantities of raw materials and food have been given away under the various aid programmes of the postwar years, manufactured goods (including chemicals) predominated. In 1970, three-quarters of its exports were manufactured goods (Table XXII). Indeed, the trade figures for 1972 white world. Canada and Latin America took almost half of them. Even so, it was in 1970 that West Germany replaced the United States as the world's leading exporter of manufactured goods (Table XXV). Indeed, the trade figures for 1972 showed Japan's and Germany's balance of trade in manufactures as $19 and $16 billion respectively; whereas the United States had a deficit amounting to $7 billion. But for the fact that American exports in high-technology goods were able to hold their own in world markets, America's deficit would have been greater still. In 1971, for instance, the trade surplus in high-technology goods was about $9 billion; but the overall deficit in low-technology goods was about $15 billion.

What comparisons between the exports in manufactures of the great trading nations do not tell us is the extent to which other people's exports are in fact the products of American affiliates. While foreign output of most of the United States multinational corporations is sold in the countries where it is produced (particularly is this true of manufactures), yet in 1970 United States foreign firms and their affiliates accounted for 20–25 per cent of world exports. Roughly the same proportion applies if we separate world exports of manufactures from the exports of other commodities. On the other hand for a highly industrialised country such as the United Kingdom, percentage-wise at least, the impact is less. In 1970, United States firms in the United Kingdom accounted for only 10 per cent of that country's exports. The important thing is that throughout the 1950s and 1960s, the sales of manufactures by American branch factories and affiliates abroad were increasing at a faster rate than either the foreign sales of the parent company in the United States or total American exports (Tables XX and XXI). Their exports of manufactures were probably growing at faster than the world rate. Indeed, all available figures for the past quarter-century suggest that the most dynamic part of American manufacturing industry is not in the United States at all, but abroad.

Moreover domestic exports cannot be considered outside the support given by the American government. So important has this financial assistance become (as a percentage of exports financed by foreign aid) that it represents more than two-thirds of certain agricultural commodities and up to one-third the exports of others (Tables XXIII and XXIV). For the exports of cotton (America's chief raw material export in 1970), rice, wheat, tobacco and soya beans, government assistance has become vital.[36] And, as most products are required to be shipped in American vessels, foreign aid has helped to sustain the relatively high charges of the United States shipping lines.

Foreign aid has not only affected America's export pattern; it has drastically affected the import patterns of many countries accepting aid. For instance, it has promoted trade with Asia much more than with Latin America. This is true of India, Pakistan, Korea, Formosa and South Vietnam, as it is of Israel, Turkey and Iran. Moreover where aid has been given in the form of loans rather than outright grants, an increasing proportion has to be used in debt service. The extent to which this is swallowing up the inflow of capital to the poorer countries is a cause of grave concern.[37] It would not be difficult to defend the action of the American government in subsidising (in the form of foreign aid) much of its foreign trade; but it would be quite impossible to argue that its action, however conceived, could lead to the liberalisation of trade. Neither in the liberalising of trade nor in the rich countries helping the poor countries has American eloquence been matched by American action.

It is impossible to understand America's role in world trade these past two hundred years without appreciating the extent to which its discovery and development were part of a common western experience. It was English resolution and arms that first won for these early groups of settlers the right to exist as separate communities in the New World. It was England's defeat of the Spanish Armada in 1588 which gave it full command of the North Atlantic. It was trade with England and continental Europe that allowed the first settlements to survive and grow. So vast and so complementary did that trade become that it enriched both the Old World and the New. However misguided Europe may think America has been, Europe is richer, materially speaking, for America's bounty.

Relative to its numbers, America was trading more than most other nations a quarter of a century after independence. And not only did its production and commerce continue to grow with astonishing speed, but its character underwent profound change. As it became the industrial as well as the agrarian leader of the western world, its complementarity in trade with Europe (whereby it exchanged its primary produce for manufactures and capital equipment) gave way to a new complementarity (whereby, increasingly, one kind of manufactured goods was exchanged for another). It was America's capacity for economic adaptation that eventually enabled it to replace Britain as the leading trader and banker of the world. Indeed so rich and powerful did the United States become that after the Second World War it was able to maintain its balances with other nations only by giving some of its wealth away while paying some of its citizens not to produce more. No other nation in world history has ever become so rich so quickly or has been so embarrassed by what it has produced.

While American developments can only be understood as part of a greater western experience they have to some extent been unique; hence the difficulty of trying to interpret America's role as a leading trading nation in terms of a British norm, especially in terms of British classical trade theory. Its chief concern in trade – particularly these past hundred years – never has been with the outside world but with America. Indeed, since Alexander Hamilton's protectionist *Report on Manufactures* of 1791, all American traditions have pointed not to the liberalisation of trade but to the protection of the far more important continental home market. Despite the tariff concessions made by the Americans over the years, no industry has ever lost its protected home market to foreign competition (though there are many who believe that under the influence of America's multinational corporations that policy is being abandoned). It is this preoccupation with a continent rather than with the world that helps to explain why there never has been a free-trade party in the United States. It took the Great Depression of the years 1929–33 for Americans even to begin to realise to what extent the changing fortunes of world trade could affect them for better or worse.

The dichotomy that exists in American outlook between domestic and foreign interests, between the welfare of home industry and the liberalisation of world trade, makes it hazardous to predict what its future trade policies will be. At least we know that the traditional voice of America – the one that represents not 5 but 95 per cent of America's national income – has always spoken in terms of dollars and cents for home industries. Unlike the British House of Commons which has always been looked upon as a school for statesmen, Congress is an assemblage of politicians many of whom have local interests at heart. The need in America today is for a largeness of outlook; the political reality, alas, is sectionalism. American statesmen may talk about the birth of a new world, but reality for the American politician is re-election. What America's foreign trade future will be no one knows. With an overall deficit in its balance of payments for some years (Table XXVIII); with its 1972 deficit the largest in its history; with its first deficit in its balance of trade since 1893; with its gold reserves halved during the past fifteen years; with the Europeans (Communist and Non-Communist) moving away from America toward their own regional trading blocks; indeed with the whole world moving towards new coalitions or groupings of nations based upon racial or regional economic ties and interests; with the dollar suspect and under attack; with America obtaining a declining percentage of world trade; with the rise of new forms of tariffs abroad that endanger American exports; with insufficient capital to meet its own needs, let alone those of the world; with the international monetary system (according to some) on the edge of collapse; with so many people accusing America (because of the erratic swings of the United States balance of payments and its growing domestic inflation) of being responsible for the world's trading and monetary ills; with no longer the power to persuade or compel others to follow its lead; with all these things happening, America is much more likely to concentrate on keeping its trading head above water than on trying to create an harmonious trading world, or on trying to close the gap between the rich and the poor. Their immediate intention is to reduce their spending on defence and aid. They are also trying to improve their trading relations with other nations through negotiated treaties (this they did in 1970 for several products, including textiles, steel and petroleum). In addition in 1972 they took the initiative to improve their trading relations with China and Russia; though the gains here are much more likely to be political than commercial. Not much improvement can be expected unless America can do something about its own domestic inflation, its relatively higher labour costs, and its falling productivity standards, which are pricing its domestically produced goods out of the market. Hence, partly, the growth of foreign-based business. Highly significant is the fact that its rate of productivity growth, which in 1950 began to lag behind certain European countries and Japan, has worsened. Between 1965 and 1970 United States productivity rose only by 1·7 per cent per year against 4·5 per cent in western Europe and 10·6 per cent in Japan. This was the smallest increase in productivity of any industrial nation in the western world.[38]

However unpleasant some of these facts may appear, we should not be mesmerised by them. The fundamental balance of payments position of the United States with the rest of the world (considering its long- and short-term liabilities and assets) is strong. If a titan like the United States is worried then there is not much hope for tiny Israel. Many of the setbacks listed above are temporary; others are not so desperate as they sound. For instance, while inflation is undoubtedly a growing problem in the United States, it is not so great a problem as it is in most other western countries. As for devaluation of currencies, compared with the experience of the other great trading nations, the Americans are relatively new to the game. It would be ridiculous to argue that devaluation of the dollar is good for the United States (devaluation is not a sign of strength but a sign of weakness) but the dollar has been occupying a position relative to gold and the other currencies to which it is not really entitled – at least not on performance. Moreover, in so far as devaluation has made many Americans appreciate for the first time that their currency is no more invincible than their army, it could have a salutary effect. Considered purely from a commercial point of view, the devaluation of the dollar also means the appreciation of the mark, and especially the yen; which again could improve America's competitive position in world markets. As for productivity, nothing fails here quite so much as success. Productivity standards are falling in the United States partly because America is becoming a service economy where productivity is hard to increase. If we were to isolate productivity for manufactures, mining and construction work from the service industries, an entirely different picture would emerge. Overall growth rates in productivity, like all the other overall growth rates in economics, need to be handled with extreme care. For instance most of America's trade deficit in 1972 (the United States passed from a $7 billion trade surplus in 1964 to a $7 billion trade deficit in 1972), was with Japan. Most of its other trade problems were with Canada. Indeed in 1973 the deficit is beginning to turn into a surplus. Be that as it may, disequilibrium in international trade and exchange crises are something that America and the other nations are going to have to live with for a long time to come. The leaders of the great trading nations are not concerned to build a world economic utopia. Most of them are in fact fighting a day to day battle for political survival. As long as they are concerned with national advantage – as of necessity in the present political arrangement they must be – the political and economic interests of the different nations will continue to diverge.

Whatever the course of future American action, it will be a poorer world for many if its position in world trade deteriorates; for its foreign trade, while it may play a secondary role in the welfare of its own economy, is vital to that of many other nations. The outlook would be especially bleak for the underdeveloped world. It is in this respect that Americans, in their present moment of power, bear special responsibility.

CHAPTER VIII
Epilogue

ALMOST two hundred years ago, a new nation emerged on the American continent dedicated to the freedom and equality of man. No nation ever began its life with greater aspirations to human betterment, or grew in power and influence to world stature with such astonishing speed.

From an economic point of view the birth and growth of the new nation caused a redistribution of the world's wealth and people; it also meant the far more productive use of the natural resources of America, out of which the western world was enriched.

From a spiritual point of view, as Thomas Jefferson said, the United States was 'acting for all mankind'. Hence, from the earliest days of the Republic, the Americans were concerned to extend their religious and political beliefs to others. Indeed, while all western Christian nations have had a missionary urge, none has universalised its experience into a general theory of spiritual, political and economic progress as much as the Americans have done. In spiritual matters the message was that of Christ. True the American message was a little more worldly than the rest, but essentially the compassion was that of the Nazarene. In politics the Americans urged the merits of a democratic form of government based on a wide, popular franchise. In material things, with other Europeans, they set abroad a new view of money and wealth. Far from regarding money as sterile they came to look upon it as a vital instrument in the creating of a better world.

So adept did the Americans become in creating surplus wealth that their domestic and foreign capital soon came to dwarf that of any other nation. Whereas ancient civilisations were known for what they could achieve through the organisation of labour, America came to be known for what it could achieve through the organisation of capital. Like no other nation, it placed its faith in business, in industrialisation, standardisation and quantification.

In this perhaps lies the heart of the American matter; for America is not so much originality as process. The secret of its success does not spring from its ability to ask why, or whether it ought, but rather to know how. For the American, the know-how is the know-all; hence, partly, their passion for technology. Their confidence in getting to the moon was much greater than their reasons for going there. Of all people, the Americans are the most 'oughtless'.

This undue concentration on the process rather than the purpose of life has had many implications. It has caused a new stress to be placed not on being but on becoming. Not on ends but on means. Not on permanence but on change. It is this stress on movement, on change, on speed, that has introduced to the world a new rhythm of human behaviour. The American beat, whether at work or play, is sharp and metallic; it is restless and without repose. Its effect was to cause the continents to shrink; to dazzle the world with the wonders of science; to cause the first atomic explosion; and (with the Russians) to 'conquer' outer space. Its rhythm of life has not only given a new emphasis in the world to physical mobility; but, with the help of films and mass-media, it has encouraged social mobility as well.

Whether the beat of American life stems from the extension of the powers of the individual, or whether the individual was moulded by the beat of American life, we are not sure. Certainly the scope that it came to give to the individual – by means of which it was able to release the pent-up energies of the European world – distinguishes it from the collective spirit of other civilisations. Never have individual initiative and the individual's acquisitive instinct been freed on the scale that they were in America; never has there been such material success. Little wonder that their motto became: 'What is not, can be'. So successful did the experiment prove, that it caused Americans to believe that history in all its aspects is progressive; that all change is for the better.

Yet America was not only living proof of the western idea of worldly progress. It was supported by a view of spiritual progress as well. Indeed the paradoxical thing about the

American's radical assertion that he was in charge of his earthly lot is that the basis of his claim was spiritual. More than anything else America's explosive force in the world is to be accounted for not by its science or its machines but by its religion. Christianity was dynamic and progressive in worldly matters in a way that other religions had never been. In seeking a worldly goal, America's immigrants were convinced they were also serving God.

Out of this amalgam was born a dream that inspired the early white Americans to heroic efforts; that became the basis of their self-confidence and optimism; that provided them with their idealism and their humanitarian outlook towards others. Shorn of the weight and cares of the past this dream allowed them to look upon life with an extraordinary innocence and simplicity. America was not history; it was aspiration; it lived not for the past but for the future.

The outcome is a civilisation of which most white Americans are justly proud. Where is there another society on this scale that has succeeded in combining liberty, efficiency and unity as they have done? What other people believe as they do that the common man is capable of self-government? Who has tapped the energies and talents of the common people with greater effect? Who has provided a greater impetus to free expression of opinion, or worked so hard for sexual and racial equality? Who has had a greater belief in the power of education for all? Which people has offered others greater hope or given so much of its wealth away? Where else has a nominally Protestant society showered such munificence upon Catholicism and world Jewry? No country has contributed more to the conquest of distance. None has quickened (through the efforts of its global corporations and its private investors) the economic progress of so many countries in modern times. America is the land that taught the rest of the world that it need not starve. Indeed so rich did many of its people become that they fell into the error of believing that the spectre of want had been banished for all men for all time, everywhere. Other men spoke of their country as motherland, or fatherland; only Americans said theirs was 'God's country'.

Why then, if all these things are true, has the American dream, like the European dream of the 'noble savage' that preceded it, begun to fade? Why do so many Americans wish to disassociate themselves from the values of their society; especially as they are the heirs to America's material abundance? Part of the answer lies in the fact that America has come of age at a time when the rate of change is greater and faster than it has ever been.[1] Like other western nations the Americans are overwhelmed by the dramatic quality and incomprehensibility of what is going on around them. Man's power over nature has exceeded his power over himself. It seems to many that man is no longer spiritually, mentally or morally able to control what he has created. Added to this is the present disgust felt for the rottenness and corruption of public life, and the unbelievable magnitude of organised crime and drug addiction. It has resulted in a topsy-turvy world in which the means and ends of life are becoming confused. Moreover no nation has ever had to accept world responsibility so quickly. And the events in Vietnam (unlike the more limited and swiftly victorious contests of its earlier history) have seriously challenged America's belief in its invincibility. Most of the people north of the Mason-Dixon line do not know what it is to have suffered defeat.

Important as these things are in explaining America's present mood, they are not so important as her disregard of the past. It is the Americans' inability to make allowance for the past in the present that has led them to offer idealistic, universal solutions to the world's ills based on a completely false analogy with an American 'norm'. To change things for the better, other societies simply needed the right ingredients; the right ingredients have always been American ingredients. The rest was easy. In promising economic development for all, they have never questioned that the material advance of the United States might have sprung from non-recurring historical circumstances; that the world might be too vast and too complex a place for them to have anything but the slightest effect upon it. On the contrary, they have assumed that life on this planet is simple and predictable, whereas it could hardly be more complex and uncertain.

The sad part about it all is that it raises false hopes in the world. It permits Americans to set up completely unrealistic, unattainable goals, and then wonder why they cannot reach them. It is this defect, this ability to wander out of history, which enables them to wander out of reality, which permits cabinet ministers, even Presidents, to talk about a wantless, workless, warless world as if it were just around the corner.

It is this simple attitude to the complexities of life that has led the Americans to confuse words with deeds. Right through their history, from the *Novus Ordo Seclorum* of the Great Seal, through the proclamations and edicts regarding Indian rights, through Wilson's fourteen points, through the 'Pact of Paris' of 1928 (where the fundamental relation between nations, the struggle for ascendency and power, was disavowed), through the 'Atlantic Charter', through the Roosevelt, Truman, Eisenhower, Kennedy, Johnson and Nixon administrations, the American people have been the people of the slogan, of the new label, of the promise, of the form. Their history is littered with idealistic abstractions such as 'The New Freedom', 'The Square Deal', 'The New Nationalism', 'The New Society', 'The New Deal', 'The Fair Deal', 'The New Frontier', 'The Great Society', and so on. While the effect of these things has been slight, it has not stopped them hungering for more. The remark made by England's Florence Nightingale, that 'Declarations are not self-executive', badly needs to be taken to the American heart. The truth is, they have never really understood the complexity of causation (that is why they have to cling to 'breakthroughs', and 'explosions', and 'miracle' this and 'super' that – hence their play 'Jesus Christ, Superstar'). What they have done, in effect, is to take the power of man to one extreme, as the Middle Ages took the inadequacy of man to another. Life, for the Americans, is a calculable series of events. It explains their love for the synthetic rather than the real. Nothing seems to impress them more than to walk on artificial turf or to stand at Florida's Disney World in the middle of a celluloid apple orchard.

Added to the American's ability to disregard the uniqueness, the ambiguity and the complexity of human life is the dichotomy that has always existed in the American mind. It is this which enabled them to talk about the self-determination of the Indians while conquering them, to espouse the liberal-isation of trade while raising tariffs, to talk peace while making war. Regardless of its early intentions, America has proved to be not only fundamentally moral, but materialistic; not only revolutionary, but conservative; not only democra-tic, but oligarchical; not only idealistic, but pragmatic; not only altruistic, but commercial; not only individualistic, but uniform; not only politically active, but politically naïve; not only universal, but isolationist. It is this American dualism, this ability, for instance, of President Calvin Coolidge to say, with the same breath, that 'the business of America is business', and 'the chief ideal of America is idealism', that baffles those who study its history. Without hope, even without dreams, there would have been no glory in the American experiment. Yet the easiest way to ensure that hope will die at the hands of despair is to make completely unrealistic assumptions about life.

It is this which makes it impossible for so many Americans to appreciate that the limits of conscious choice of action are narrow; that so much of life is an option of difficulties; that so much of their history has been a struggle between their original endowment and their destiny (how they began and what they intended and how things have worked out). Life for the Americans, as for anybody else, has been full of surprises. Lincoln knew this, as all great Americans have known it: 'I claim', he said in 1864, 'not to have controlled events, but confess plainly that events have controlled me. Now, at the end of three years struggle the nation's condition is not what either party, or any man devised or expected. . . .'[2] Lincoln was not a fatalist; he was a wise man who knew that the margin of freedom of action for man is often small. His words do, in fact, echo what has been said right down the ages. Thousands of years earlier, Euripides had put it this way:

> There be many shapes of mystery.
> And many things God makes to be,
> Past hope or fear.
> And the end man looked for cometh not,
> And a path is there where no man thought.
> So hath it fallen here.[3]

To say these things to a European or an Asian is to leave him undisturbed. He knows that this is the way life is; that both optimism and pessimism are biased views; that the story does not have to have a happy ending. He finds nothing incongruous in the fact that dreams go unfulfilled; that what happens often falls far short of what was intended; that life is not an ideal; it is history. But to say these things to an American is to disappoint him; it leaves him uncomfortable; things ought not to be this way. For those who began life as a nation with an appeal to virtue and reason, as well as with an unbounded faith in the power of man to control his fate, the idea that there are limits to human endeavour is difficult to stomach. Other than that he expects things to get better every day, the American has never really asked himself what he has the right to expect of life. Hence, partly, his present disillusionment with so much of it.

Fortunately the present mood in America is not only one of disillusionment; it is also one of re-assessment. At no previous period in their history have the Americans been more concerned with the quality and significance of their lives.

What the outcome of America's present mood will be, no one knows; nothing in life is entirely predictable or inevitable. It could be the end of the comet's flight, or it could equally well be the beginning of an American golden age. Other people's history has been starred with desperate occasions when disintegration seemed certain. Moreover there are few obstacles facing the Americans today over which they have not already triumphed. They have already endured treason, war, insurrection, secession and bankruptcy. (The significant exception, of course, is that most of them have never been conquered.) Time and again domestic and foreign prophets of gloom have predicted their collapse; instead of which, they have not only survived but constantly renewed themselves.

Yet if there is to be any meaningful outcome of the present desire to find a changed and better future certain things will have to be abandoned. The Americans will have to abandon their grandiose schemes to change the world. For a while, at least, the age of the American crusades – the last of the European crusades – is over. They will have to abandon the point of view that sees their way as the only way and the only truth. They will have to abandon the search for perfection; they will have to settle for something less than Utopia, something less than universal plenty. They will have to stop comparing their efforts with some ideal goal that no man can ever reach. They will have to realise that talk of 'conquering' outer space is talk of conquering infinity. It makes all the more urgent the need to define the purpose of life on this earth and what we have the right to expect as mortal, human beings. They will have to realise that an ever-improving science and technology, which are their special pride, are inseparable from the spiritual foundations from which they sprang; that, paradoxically, beyond a certain point, one cannot have a rising Gross National Product if a rising Gross National Product is one's only goal. They will have to realise that the troubles and difficulties of this world are not to be understood in a purely economic context – nor, for that matter, in a purely political or social or intellectual context. The forces that are crucial in the world today are emotional forces, notwithstanding the Supreme Court's 'Rule of Reason'. They will have to appreciate that there are some problems that do not have solutions, some problems that cannot be solved by dollars, some problems that cannot be fathomed, some situations in life that are and will remain completely irrational and grossly unfair. They will have to understand that authority and freedom are inseparable; and that, if liberty degenerates into license, democracy will most certainly degenerate into anarchy. The highly sophisticated civilisation that their forebears have created demands a degree of discipline as no other civilisation has ever done. Increasingly the issue is not between more or less affluence but between order or chaos.

Nor can the American people go on confusing wealth with weal, money with happiness, quality with quantity, riches with culture, progress with production, tools with civilisation, education with virtue, words with deeds, noise with significance, motion with meaning, publicity with worth, popularity with quality, cleverness with character, anarchy with freedom, counting with causation, the useful with the good, and science with God. To use man as the means, and science as the end, is to stand the American tradition on its head.

The same confusion regarding ends and means is also apparent among the economic scientists, most of whom have long since forgotten that the American Economic Association was founded in 1885 to foster the study of economics as a 'Moral science'. Indeed American economists have become so concerned with economic efficiency and production as ends in themselves that they are no longer conscious of the human context of economic activity or of the relation of economics to the whole. If that which cannot be counted does not exist then the human element does not exist. Thus have we lost sight of the vital significance in domestic and world economics of trust and confidence.

It is not science and technology, not magic formulas for nations to grow rich, not computerised predictions of doomsday,[4] not new laws, however well conceived and wisely framed, that will eventually determine America's destiny in the world. It is man. 'It is man that can make truth great', said Confucius, long before Christ was born. 'In all my lectures', said Emerson, 'I have taught one doctrine, namely, the infinitude of the private man'.[5] Under this 'steadfast star' did the American odyssey begin. A new vision of man, a new summons to freedom, was the tide on which the American ship rose. Wherever it has sailed, whatever it has achieved, it has done so through the uniqueness and the freedom of human life. Ultimately, if the Americans are to be true to their origins and to their traditions, it is to this mooring that they must return.

Notes

CHAPTER I: PROLOGUE: ORIGINS

[1] 'A Modell of Christian Charity', *Collections of the Mass. Hist. Soc.*, 3rd series, VII, 47 (1838).

[2] P. H. Smith, 'The American Loyalists: Notes on Their Organization and Strength', *William and Mary Quarterly*, 3rd series, XXV (April 1968) 259–77.

[3] Benjamin Franklin, 'Information to Those Who Would Remove to America' (1782), in *The Complete Works of Benjamin Franklin*, ed. John Bigelow (New York, 1887–8) VIII 173, 175.

[4] Alexis de Tocqueville, *Democracy in America*, translated by Henry Reeve (New York, 1945) I 53.

[5] Herbert Lüthy, 'Colonization and the Making of Mankind', *J. Econ. Hist.*, XXI (Dec 1961) 483–95.

[6] Francisco López de Gómara, *Primera Parte de la Historia General de Las Indias*, Biblioteca de Autores Españoles, xxii (Madrid, 1852) p. 156.

[7] Friedrich von Gentz, 'On the Influence of the Discovery of America on the Prosperity and Culture of the Human Race', translated and quoted in H. S. Commager and Elmo Giordanetti, *Was America a Mistake?: An Eighteenth Century Controversy* (New York, 1967) p. 219.

[8] Ibid., p. 44.

[9] Ibid.

[10] Ibid., p. 188.

[11] G. Chinard, 'Notes on the American Origins of the Declaration des Droits de l'Homme et du Citoyen', *Proc. Am. Phil. Soc.*, XCIII (1954) 383–96.

[12] E. Rosenthal, *Stars and Stripes in Africa* (Cape Town, 1968) p. 20.

[13] Ibid., 129. Ironically certain Americans took a leading part in the Jameson Raid of 1895 aimed at overthrowing the Republic of the Transvaal.

[14] Abbé Roubaud, *The General History of Asia, Africa, and America*, translated and quoted in Commager and Giordanetti, *Was America a Mistake?* p. 164.

[15] Ibid., p. 161.

[16] Ibid.

[17] Ibid., p. 93.

[18] Joseph Mandrillon, 'Philosophical Investigations on the Discovery of America'. Ibid., p. 176.

[19] C. D. Bowen, *Miracle at Philadelphia* (Boston, 1966) p. 44.
[20] J. C. Fitzpatrick (ed.), *The Writings of George Washington* (Washington D.C., 1931–44) XXIX 51.

CHAPTER II: AMERICA'S EMPIRE

[1] H. M. Jones, *O Strange New World* (New York, 1964) p. 295.
[2] R. R. Hill (ed.), *Journal of the Continental Congress. 1774, 1789* (Washington D.C., 1936) XXXII 340–1.
[3] Thomas Jefferson's letter of 18 April 1802, to Robert R. Livingston; A. A. Lipscomb and A. E. Bergh (eds.), *The Writings of Thomas Jefferson* (Washington D.C., 1903) X 313, III 378.
[4] P. C. Brooks, 'Spain's Farewell to Louisiana, 1803–1821', *Miss. Valley Hist. Rev.*, XXVII (June 1940) 29–42.
[5] Reginald Horsman, *Expansion and American Indian Policy, 1783–1812* (East Lansing, Mich., 1967) p. 113.
[6] R. M. Johnson, *Annals of Congress*, 12th Cong., 1st Sess., XXIII 458, (11 Dec 1811).
[7] The most prominent 'war hawks' were Henry Clay (Kentucky), Richard M. Johnson (Kentucky), Joseph Desha (Kentucky), Felix Grundy (Tennessee), John C. Calhoun (South Carolina), William Lowndes (South Carolina), Langdon Cheves (South Carolina), Peter B. Porter (New York), and John A. Harper (New Hampshire).
[8] *Annals of Congress*, ibid., XXIV 1399 (6 May 1812).
[9] Madison's Special Message to Congress of 1 June 1812. H. S. Commager (ed.), *Documents of American History*, 8th ed. (New York, 1968) pp. 207–9.
[10] C. F. Klinck (ed.), *Tecumseh: Fact and Fiction in Early Records* (Englewood Cliffs, N. J., 1961) p. 64.
[11] Ibid., 70–1.
[12] In reasserting the Monroe Doctrine in 1845, President Polk stated that 'the American system of government is entirely different from that of Europe', and consequently the United States could not tolerate any European objection or interference to territories on the North American continent joining the United States if they 'chose' to do so.
[13] Polk's Message to Congress (11 May 1846). Commager, *Documents of American History*, p. 311.
[14] G. W. Price, *Origins of the War with Mexico: The Polk-Stockton Intrigue* (Austin, Tex., 1967) p. 4. An ironical comment in view of Napoleon III's effort to seize Mexico two decades later.
[15] Many Americans – among them, Jefferson and John Quincy Adams – had long thought of the Oregon territory as the American 'window on the Pacific' and a direct route to the trade of Asia. Only six years after the United States and Britain settled their territorial claims in the area, Commodore Matthew C. Perry set out to 'open' Japan with the words, 'The world has assigned this duty to us.' R. W. Van Alstyne, *The Rising American Empire* (Oxford, 1960) p. 173.

[16] W. B. Munro, *American Influences on Canadian Government* (Toronto, 1929) p. 8; E. A. Golder, 'The Purchase of Alaska', *Am. Hist. Rev.* XXV 424 (April 1920).

[17] 'If slavery is not wrong, nothing is wrong. I cannot remember when I did not so think and feel, and yet I have never understood that the presidency conferred upon me an unrestricted right to act officially upon this judgment and feeling.' From a letter to A. G. Hodges, 4 April 1864. J. P. Madden and D. E. Brewster (eds.), *A Philosopher Among Economists* (Philadelphia, 1970) p. 94.

[18] Lincoln's letter of August 1862 to Horace Greeley. Commager, *Documents of American History* I 418. Wrote Alexander Stephens at the time: 'The Union with him, in sentiment, rose to the sublimity of religious mysticism'. Herbert Agar, *The Price of Union* (Boston, 1950) p. 434.

[19] R. A. Arnold, *The History of the Cotton Famine* (London, 1864).

[20] Gladstone's Newcastle speech (7 Oct 1862). B. B. Sideman and Lillian Friedman (eds.), *Europe Looks at the Civil War* (New York, 1960) p. 186.

[21] Lord Russell's letter to Messrs Mason, Slidell and Mann (13 Feb 1865). Sideman and Friedman, ibid., p. 270.

[22] F. A. Golder, 'The Russian Fleet and the Civil War', *Am. Hist. Rev.*, XX (July 1915) 801–12.

[23] Bright's speech to the trade unions of London (Mar 1863). Sideman and Friedman, *Europe Looks at the Civil War*, pp. 230–1.

[24] Address to President Lincoln by the working men of Manchester, England (31 Dec 1862), Frank Moore (ed.), *The Rebellion Record* (New York, 1861–3) VI 344.

[25] Sideman and Friedman, *Europe Looks at the Civil War*, p. 213; also E. D. Seeber, *Anti-Slavery Opinion in France During the Second Half of the Eighteenth Century* (Baltimore, 1937).

[26] Baron de Stoeckl's letter to Prince Gortchakov (1865). Sideman and Friedman, *Europe Looks at the Civil War*, p. 267; also E. A. Golder, 'The American Civil War Through the Eyes of a Russian Diplomat', *Am. Hist. Rev.*, XXVI (April 1921) pp. 454–63.

[27] 'Civil War, Reconstruction, and Great Britain', in *Heard Round the World: The Impact Abroad of the Civil War*, ed. Harold Hyman (New York, 1969) p. 35.

[28] Francis Parkman, *The Oregon Trail: Sketches of Prairie and Rocky-Mountain Life* (Boston, 1910) p. 48.

[29] J. G. Whittier, 'The Kansa Emigrants, in *The Poetical Works of John Greenleaf Whittier*, (Boston, 1892) III p. 176.

[30] B. A. Botkin (ed.), *A Treasury of American Folklore: Stories, Ballads, and Traditions of the People* (New York, 1944) p. 279.

[31] A. K. Hamilton Jenkin, *The Cornish Miner* (London, 1927); A. L. Rowse, *The Cornish in America* (London, 1969).

[32] 'I made out an estimate of the cost of our house', wrote a newcomer to the plains on 10 April 1877. 'This does not include what was paid for in work: Ridgepole and hauling (including two loads of firewood) $1.50; rafters and straw, 50c; 2 lb. nails, 15c; hinges 20c; window 75c; total cash paid, $4.05. Then there was $4 worth of lumber, which was paid for in

work, and $1.50 for hauling it over, which, together with hauling the firewood, 50c, makes $10.05 for a place to live in and firewood enough to last all summer.' Howard Ruede, *Sod-House Days: Letters from a Kansas Homesteader, 1877–78*, ed. John Ise (New York, 1937) p. 43.

[33] An area extending 1300 miles from Canada to Texas, varying in width from 200 to 700 miles across, bound in the west by the Rockies and the east by the 100th meridian.

[34] W. W. Howard, 'The Rush to Oklahoma', *Harper's* (18 May 1889) pp. 391–2.

[35] *Compendium of the Eleventh Census: 1890, Part I, Population* (Washington, D.C., 1892–7) I xxxiv.

[36] Botkin, *Treasury of American Folklore*, p. 314.

[37] G. C. Fite, *The Farmers' Frontier, 1865–1900* (New York, 1966) p. 129.

[38] W. A. Peffer, *The Farmer's Side: His Troubles and Their Remedy* (New York, 1891) p. 73.

[39] 'The Indian nations had always been considered as distinct, independent political communities, retaining their original natural rights, as the undisputed possessors of the soil, from time immemorial . . . the settled doctrine of the law of nations is, that a weaker power does not surrender its independence – its right to self–government, by associating with a stronger, and taking its protection. A weak state, in order to provide for its safety, may place itself under the protection of one more powerful, without stripping itself of the right of government and ceasing to be a state.' – John Marshall, *Worcester vs. The State of Georgia* in Louis Filler and Allen Guttmann (eds.), *The Removal of the Cherokee Nation: Manifest Destiny or National Dishonour?* (Boston, 1962) pp. 75–6.

[40] J. G. Neihardt, *Black Elk Speaks, Being the Life Story of a Holy Man of the Oglala Sioux* (Lincoln, Neb., 1961) pp. 8–9, 217.

[41] The famous Buffalo Bill Cody killed 4280 in one year. On their slaughter, see Peter Mathiessen, *Wild Life in America* (New York, 1959) pp. 147, 149, 151.

[42] *The Reports of the Committees of the Senate of the United States*, 38th Cong., 2nd Sess., Report No. 1214, 27; 39th Cong., 2nd Sess., Report No. 156 (Washington D.C., 1867).

[43] S. L. A. Marshall, *Crimsoned Prairie* (New York, 1973).

[44] Neihardt, *Black Elk Speaks*, pp. 265, 268, 276.

[45] M. D. Beal, *'I Will Fight No More Forever': Chief Joseph and the Nez Percé War* (Seattle, Wash., 1966) p. 229; M. H. Brown, *The Flight of the Nez Percé* (New York, 1967).

[46] There is no agreement on the number of Indians living within the present boundaries of the United States in 1492, but estimates range up to 2,500,000. In 1860, there remained only 340,000; and by 1910 this number had dropped to 220,000. A. M. Josephy, Jr, *The Indian Heritage of America* (New York, 1969) p. 53.

[47] In 1924, the Snyder Act conferred citizenship on all Indians.

[48] Walter Colton, *Three Years in California* (1850; reprinted Stanford 1949) p. 314.

[49] The need to explore other lands had been expressed by Jeremiah N. Reynolds and others from the 1820s onwards. In 1838 Charles Wilkes led an expedition from Norfolk into the South Seas. The expedition returned in 1842; their *Narrative* was published thirty years later. In 1850 Elisha Kent Kane led an expedition between Greenland and Ellesmere Island, reaching farther north than other white men had been before. Kane was followed later by Robert Edwin Peary, who, in 1909, on his sixth expedition reached the North Pole.

[50] Senator A. J. Beveridge, *Congressional Record*, 56th Cong., 1st Sess., 711.

[51] E. M. Burns, *The American Idea of Mission: Concepts of National Purpose and Destiny* (New Brunswick, N.J., 1957) p. 1.

[52] Josiah Strong, *Our Country: Its Possible Future and Its Present Crisis* (New York, 1885) p. 175.

[53] Charles Darwin, *The Descent of Man* (London, 1871) I 172.

[54] U.S. Dep. of State, *Foreign Relations of the U.S.*, 1894, Appdx., II 463–4.

[55] T. N. Bonner, *Our Recent Past: American Civilization in the Twentieth Century* (Englewood Cliffs, N.J., 1963) pp. 82–3.

[56] C. S. Olcott, *The Life of William McKinley* (Boston, 1916) II 111.

[57] Bonner, *Our Recent Past*, p. 86.

[58] Eisenhower wrote in *Crusade in Europe* (New York, 1948) p. 457: 'The past relations between America and Russia were no cause to regard the future with pessimism. Historically the two nations preserved an unbroken friendship since the birth of the United States as an independent republic. . . . Both were free of the stigma of empire building by force.'

[59] Harry Magdoff. *The Age of Imperialism* (New York, 1969); Earl Browder in *Marx and America* (New York, 1958) explains why Marxian predictions have not come true.

CHAPTER III: AMERICANS IN A WORLD CONTEXT

[1] William Woodruff, *Impact of Western Man* (London, 1966) chapter III.

[2] Woodruff, ibid.; also W. S. Woytinsky and E. S. Woytinsky, *World Population and Production: Trends and Outlook* (New York, 1953) pp. 72, 77, 80; and Imre Ferenczi, 'Migrations: Modern', in *Encyclopaedia of the Social Sciences*, ed. E. R. Seligman (New York, 1967) X 435.

[3] According to U.S. Census reports, the rounded figures were:
(in millions)

1790	4	1830	13	1870	40	1910	92	1950	151
1800	5	1840	17	1880	50	1920	106	1960	179
1810	7	1850	23	1890	63	1930	123	1970	200
1820	10	1860	31	1900	76	1940	132		

[4] J. V. Grauman, 'Population: Population Growth', in *International Encyclopedia of the Social Sciences*, ed. D. L. Sills (New York, 1968) XXII 379.

[5] G. R. Gilkey, 'The United States and Italy: Migration and Repatriation', *The Journal of Developing Areas*, II (Oct 1967) 28.

[6] Antonio Mangano, 'The Effect of Emigration on Italy', *Charities and the Commons*, XIX (4 Jan 1908) 1337.

[7] Gilkey, *Journal of Developing Areas*, II 28.

[8] B. J. Hovde, 'Notes on the Effects of Emigration upon Scandinavia', *J. Mod. Hist.*, VI (Sept 1934) 258.

[9] Between 1865 and 1882, bills were introduced in the Swedish parliament with the purpose of placing restrictions on emigration, but not one was adopted. Hovde, ibid., p. 257; F. D. Scott, 'The Study of the Effects of Emigration', *Scand. Econ. Hist. Rev.*, VIII, No. 2 (1960) 163; also by Scott, 'Sweden's Constructive Opposition to Emigration', *J. Mod. Hist.*, XXXVII (Sep 1965) 307.

[10] J. N. Paden and E. W. Soja, *The African Experience*, (Evanston, Ill., 1970) II 106.

[11] Basil Davidson, *Black Mother: The Years of the African Slave Trade* (Boston, 1961) p. 46.

[12] Only after the Civil War and the abolition of slavery in Cuba and Brazil in the 1880s, did the Atlantic trade in African slaves end.

[13] Noel Deerr, *The History of Sugar*, 2 vols. (London, 1949–50) p. 284, gives 20 million; D. A. Farnie, 'The Commercial Empire of the Atlantic, 1607–1783', *Econ. Hist. Rev.*, XV (Dec 1962) 211, gives a figure of 3,400,000 slaves landed in the English colonies between 1619 and 1776; P. D. Curtin, *The Atlantic Slave Trade: A Census* (Madison, Wis., 1969). It is Curtin who suggests (in contrast to the 50 millions of Basil Davidson and others) that not more than 9 million slaves were brought across the ocean in the 400 years of slavery.

[14] J. P. Davis (ed.), *The American Negro Reference Book* (Englewood Cliffs, N.J., 1966) p. 100.

[15] Basil Davidson, *Africa in History: Themes and Outlines* (London, 1968) p. 194.

[16] J. C. Anene and G. N. Brown, *Africa in the Nineteenth and Twentieth Centuries: A Handbook for Teachers and Students* (Ibadan, 1966) p. 107.

[17] Rose Hum Lee, *The Chinese in the United States of America* (Hong Kong, 1960) p. 9; Y. C. Young, *Chinese Intellectuals and the West, 1872–1949* (Chapel Hill, 1966).

[18] Walter Adams (ed.), *The Brain Drain* (New York, 1968).

[19] Theodore Saloutos, *They Remember America: The Story of the Repatriated Greek-Americans* (Berkeley, 1956) p. 50.

[20] Gilkey, *Journal of Developing Areas*, II 28.

[21] Between 1910 and 1916, the Swedish National Association Against Emigration had aided 13,762 repatriated Swedes. Hovde, *J. Mod. Hist.*, VI (Sept 1934) p. 279.

[22] Saloutos, *They Remember America*, p. 63.

[23] F. D. Scott, 'American Influences in Norway and Sweden', *J. Mod. Hist.*, XVIII (Mar 1946) pp. 34–47; also A. B. Benson, 'Cultural Relations Between Sweden and America to 1830', *Germanic Review*, XIII (April 1938) 83–101.

[24] 'The realization of the repatriates' age-old dream for land ownership sent prices spiralling upward in some areas. Choice bottom lands tripled in

value within a very short time, as in the Abruzzi where prices rose to $2100 an acre, and in Calabria where they went up to $920 an acre. Near Caserta, returnees paid up to $1650 an acre for irrigated lands. In the southern provinces, whole sections of mountain lands were purchased by *Americani*. In those regions less desirable plots brought as low as $20 or $25 an acre.' Gilkey, *Journal of Developing Areas*, II 30.

[25] Ibid., pp. 25–6.

[26] E. G. Ingham, *Sierra Leone after a Hundred Years* (London, 1894) pp. 8–10; and Christopher Fyfe, *A History of Sierra Leone* (London, 1962) pp. 31–5.

[27] E. Rubin, 'A Statistical Overview of Americans Abroad', *The Annals of the American Academy of Political and Social Science*, Vol. 368 (Nov 1966) 2; *Summary of U.S. Census of Population* (various).

[28] D. H. Finnie, *Pioneers East: The Early American Experience in the Middle East* (Camb., Mass., 1967) p. 3.

[29] Mira Wilkins, 'The Business Man Abroad', *The Annals*, pp. 83–94.

[30] J. J. Servan-Schreiber, *The American Challenge*, translated by Ronald Steel (New York, 1968) pp. 3, 29, xiii.

[31] K. S. Latourette, 'Missionaries Abroad', *The Annals*, pp. 21–30.

[32] W. E. Strong, *The Story of the American Board* (Boston, 1910); republished (New York, 1969).

[33] J. W. Gould, *Americans in Sumatra* (The Hague, 1961) chapter IV.

[34] L. C. Howard, 'American Involvement in Africa South of the Sahara, 1800–1860', unpublished Ph.D. dissertation, Harvard University, 1956, pp. 98–100.

[35] The 1925 figures have been drawn from the *World Missionary Atlas* for that year. The 1969 figures are from the Missions Advanced Research and Communications Center publication, *North American Protestant Ministries Overseas* (Monrovia, Calif., 1970) pp. 2–6.

[36] F. A. Foy (ed.), *1971 Catholic Almanac* (Garden City, N.Y., 1971) p. 571.

[37] J. N. Parmer (ed.) 'The Peace Corps', *The Annals*, vol. 365 (May 1966).

[38] *Congressional Record*, 87th Cong., 1st Sess., vol. 107, pt. 3, 2937.

[39] J. N. Parmer (ed.), *The Annals*, vol. 365 (May 1966).

[40] Ibid.

[41] B. H. Fisher, 'The Foreign Service Officer', *The Annals*, vol. 368 (Nov 1966) pp. 71–82.

[42] E. W. Kemmerer, 'Economic Advisory Work for Governments', *Am. Econ. Rev.*, XVII (Mar 1927) 1–12; R. N. Seidel, 'American Reformers Abroad: The Kemmerer Missions in South America, 1923–31', *J. Econ. Hist.*, XXXII (June 1972) 520–45; A. C. Milspaugh, *Americans in Persia* (Washington D.C., 1946).

[43] S. R. Waters, 'The American Tourist', *The Annals*, vol. 368 (Nov 1966) 109–18.

[44] D. W. Tarr, 'The Military Abroad', *The Annals*, ibid., 31–42.

[45] Secretary of State Rusk, Department of State *Bulletin* (10 May 1965) p. 695.

CHAPTER IV: AMERICA'S INFLUENCE ON WORLD FINANCE

[1] At a price, of course. Although all civilisations have shared a common revulsion at the social evils of usury; the rise of capitalism caused the Christian church to distinguish between loans made for productive purposes (on which interest might justifiably be charged) and loans made to help one's fellow men meet the needs of basic subsistence (on which interest charged would be morally reprehensible). Thomas Divine, *Interest* (Milwaukee, Wis., 1959).

[2] International capital movements – at least so far as the official statistics showing the amount of funds go – do not necessarily mean a movement of capital goods. They could mean a transfer of paper assets of purchasing power. Moreover, capital, on arrival in a country, can be consumed rather than be placed in productive investment. However, when economists talk about capital transfer, they are usually talking about changes in a country's instruments of production rather than changes in money supply and income. S. K. Cairncross, *Home and Foreign Investment, 1870–1913* (Camb., Eng., 1953) p. 37.

[3] In contrast to short-term investments which mature in less than one year.

[4] R. W. Hidy, *The House of Baring in American Trade and Finance, English Merchant Bankers at Work, 1763–1861* (Camb., Mass., 1949). Established in London in 1763, in 1832 a branch was opened in Liverpool to compete directly with the U.S.-based Brown Brothers. Earlier, in 1818, the Duc de Richelieu, France's chief minister, had named the Six Great Powers in Europe as: 'Great Britain, France, Russia, Austria, Prussia and Baring Brothers.'

[5] H. J. Habakkuk, 'Fluctuations in House-Building in Britain and the United States in the Nineteenth Century', in *The Export of Capital from Britain, 1870–1914*, ed. A. R. Hall (London, 1968); also E. W. Cooney, 'Capital Exports, and Investment in Building in Britain and the U.S.A., 1856–1914', *Economica*, XVI (Nov 1949) 347–54.

[6] W. Isard, 'Transport Development and Building Cycles', *Qtly. J. Econ.*, XVII (Nov 1942) 90–112.

[7] A. G. Ford, 'Overseas Lending and Internal Fluctuations; 1870–1914', *Yorkshire Bulletin of Econ. and Soc. Res.*, XVII (May 1965) 19–31.

[8] 'Direct' investments (unlike other private 'portfolio' investments in foreign securities) are of a private business nature involving control of the foreign undertaking. The United States Department of Commerce defines 'controlling interest' to involve ownership of at least 10 per cent of the equity of the foreign concern. However, for an investment to be categorised 'direct' within the United States, the foreign investor must own at least 25 per cent of the American company's equity. 'Portfolio' investments include stocks and bond issues, and short- and long-term bank lending.

[9] A study of the military casualities of the First World War helps to explain the different psychological attitudes to war existing after 1919. The total casualties in per cent of the total number mobilised was 8 for the United States; Russia, 76; France, 73; Germany, 65; Britain, 36. The cost

to the United States in killed was 126,000, out of a total of 9,000,000 military personnel.

[10] Arthur Salter, quoted in *The Problem of International Investment, R.I.I.A.*, 1937, reprint ed. (New York, 1965) p. 11. For the allegations levelled against American issue houses, see the *United States Senate Inquiry into the Sale of Foreign Bonds* (Washington, D.C., 1932).

[11] Whereas between 1860 and 1920 British external trade was between 50–60 per cent of national income, American external trade was 15–20 per cent from 1819 to 1839 and 10–15 per cent from 1859–1909. K. W. Deutsch and A. Eckstein, 'National Industrialization and the Declining Share of the International Economic Sector, 1890–1959', *World Politics*, XIII (Jan 1961) 267–99.

[12] Juvenal Angel, *Directory of American Firms Operating in Foreign Countries* (New York, 1966).

[13] *Survey of Current Business* (various issues).

[14] Ernest Mandel, *Europe vs. America* (New York, 1970) pp. 30–43; also J. S. Bain, *International Differences in Industrial Structure* (New Haven, 1966).

[15] Gunter Duffey, *The Eurobond Market* (Seattle, 1969) p. 85ff.

[16] If anybody thinks it is as simple as that, he should read the article by P. B. Kenen in *Lloyds Bank Review*, no. 69 (July 1963) 15–30: 'But the perpetual dollar glut grows clever as it ages. One year, it appears in the U.S. trade statistics. The next year, it peers out from long-term borrowing or lurks among the short-term money flows. At times, it even breaks the rules of the game, popping up in errors and omissions. The dollar glut is also an accomplished traveller. At first, it showed up as a German payments surplus, then it moved to France and Italy. At the moment, no one quite knows its address, though some wise surplus hunters hope to find it in Japan and Canada.'

[17] R. N. Cooper, *The Economics of Interdependence* (New York, 1968) p. 117.

[18] The relative importance of each centre in 1967 is given by *The Economist*, 8 July 1967: 'The Decade of the Euro-dollar', p. 179.

[19] They probably were already being met from foreign sources. While we cannot be specific, local borrowings, retained earnings, and depreciation make up a considerable part – if not most – of the direct capital investments made by Americans in the industrial western world.

[20] C. A. Ellis and J. S. Wadsworth, Jr, 'United States Corporations and the International Capital Market Abroad', *Financial Analysts Journal*, XXII (May–June 1966) pp. 169–275: also Judd Polk, et al., *U.S. Production Abroad and the Balance of Payments* (New York, 1966).

[21] Euro-bonds issued in Europe grew from $627 million in 1965 to $1200 million in 1966. Duffy, *The Eurobond Market*; also David Williams, 'Foreign Currency Issues in European Security Markets', *IMF Staff Papers* (May 1967) p. 54.

[22] Gold reserves have declined dramatically since 1945, when the U.S. had roughly 75 per cent of the world's reserves. By 1950 the proportion had fallen to 50 per cent ($23 billion), Table X.

[23] *The Economist* (29 Mar 1969) pp. 59–60. 'Euro-dollars are Forever', and (30 Aug 1969) pp. 40-1, 'Euro-dollars Go Home'.

[24] *Report of the Deutsche Bundesbank* (1960).

[25] *IMF Staff Papers* (July 1964), 329.

[26] Kenen, *Lloyds Bank Review*, no. 69, pp. 19, 25.

[27] Merle Curti, *American Philanthropy Abroad* (New Jersey, 1963).

[28] Hovde, *J. Mod. Hist.*, VI 259.

[29] Ibid.

[30] Gilkey, *Journal of Developing Areas*, II 29.

[31] In 1825, the cheapest cabin passage from Europe to America was about $100. By 1880, the rate from continental ports to New York had dropped to between $25 and $40, and from London to $20. Steerage passage from Liverpool from the 1830s onwards was in the region of $10.

[32] George Liska, *The New Statecraft* (Chicago, 1960), especially chapter II, 'A Short History of "Foreign Aid".'

[33] Niccoló Machiavelli, Chap. 17, translated by Allan Gilbert, *Machiavelli: The Chief Works and Others* (Durham, N.C., 1965) I 62.

[34] H. B. Price, *The Marshall Plan and Its Meaning* (New York, 1955).

[35] Agency for International Development, *U.S. Overseas Loans and Grants and Assistance from International Organizations* (Washington, D.C.: Department of State, 18 Mar 1966) p. 19.

[36] Committee for Economic Development, *Assisting Development in Low Income Countries* (New York, 1969) p. 41.

[37] Organization for Economic Cooperation and Development, *Development Assistance, Efforts, and Policies, Review* (Paris, 1966) p. 118.

[38] Gunnar Myrdal, *The Challenge of World Poverty* (New York, 1970) pp. 227–41; also, E. A. J. Johnson, *American Imperialism* (Minn., 1971).

[39] David Ogg, *England in the Reigns of James II and William III* (Oxford, 1955) pp. 477–8.

[40] To be able to lend or give away $150 billion in foreign aid Congress had to create a new vast administrative organisation which seems to have swallowed another $100 billion, i.e. it took about 50–60 cents for Congress to be able to give away a dollar. See *Hearings before the Subcommittee on International Trade of the Committee on Finance, United States Senate*, 93rd Cong., 1st Sess., Feb and Mar 1973, p. 405.

[41] *The Effects of United States and Other Foreign Investment in Latin America*, by The Council for Latin America (New York, 1969).

[42] A. O. Hirschman, 'How to Divest in Latin America and Why', *Essays in International Finance* (Princeton, 1969); Raul Prebisch, 'The Role of Foreign Private Investment in the Development of Latin America', *Sixth Annual Meeting of the IA-Ecosoc.* (June 1969).

CHAPTER V: THE IMPACT OF AMERICAN TECHNOLOGY

[1] Derived from the Greek word 'téchnē', meaning 'art' or 'skill'. I am using the word broadly to describe changes taking place in tools, machines and processes devised by man to help improve (or impair) his material environment. Where I use the word 'science', I mean 'knowledge' (from the

Latin word 'scientia'), related preponderantly to a basic understanding of the natural sciences. Broadly, technology is directed toward use; science, toward understanding. Singer, Holmyard, Hall and Williams, *A History of Technology* (Oxford, 1954–65) I 38.

[2] H. A. Meier, 'American Technology and the Nineteenth Century World', *American Quarterly*, X (Summer 1958) 117; also A. T. Bining, *British Regulations of the Colonial Iron Industry* (Phila., 1933) pp. 3, 122.

[3] Conversely, G. S. Gibb in his study of textile machinery, *The Saco-Lowell Shops* (Camb., Mass., 1950) pp. 10–11, tells us that by 1813 there were few basic skills with which American mechanics were not already familiar. The problem was not ignorance of skills or mechanical principles, but the shortage (sometimes general but more often particular) of skilled mechanics; T. R. Navin, *The Whitin Machine Works Since 1831* (Camb., Mass., 1950); also H. J. Habakkuk, *American and British Technology in the Nineteenth Century* (Camb., Eng., 1962).

[4] Roger Burlingame, *March of the Iron Men* (New York, 1938) and *Engines of Democracy* (New York, 1940).

[5] Prometheus, in H. W. Smyth, trans., *Aeschylus*, Loeb Classical Library (London, 1922), vols. I and II.

[6] Robert Fulton to Albert Gallatin, 8 Dec 1807, in Report of Albert Gallatin, Secretary of the Treasury, to the Senate, 4 Apr 1808. *American State Papers, Naval Affairs* (Washington, D.C., 1834) I 226.

[7] H. F. Williamson, *Winchester, the Gun that Won the West* (Washington, D.C., 1952).

[8] A. A. Lipscomb and A. E. Bergh (eds.), *The Writings of Thomas Jefferson* (Washington, D.C., 1903) XIII 176–7.

[9] Jacob Bigelow, *Inaugural Address, Delivered in the Chapel of the University at Cambridge*, 11 December 1816 (Boston, 1817) pp. 14–16. Bigelow, who published his *Elements of Technology* in 1829, popularised the word 'technology'.

[10] 'New York Industrial Exhibition: Special Report of Mr Joseph Whitworth', *British Sessional Papers: House of Commons* (London, 1854) XXXVI 145–6.

[11] 'Workingman's Celebration', *New York Sentinel and Working Man's Advocate* (14 July 1830).

[12] de Tocqueville, *Democracy in America*, II 45.

[13] C. S. Gilfillan, *Supplement to the Sociology of Invention* (San Francisco, 1971) pp. 154–6.

[14] Brook Hindle, *The Pursuit of Science in Revolutionary America, 1735–1789* (Chapel Hill, N.C., 1956) p. 255.

[15] Ibid.

[16] W. J. Bell, *Early American Science* (Williamsburg, 1955) p. 30.

[17] G. H. Daniels, *American Science in the Age of Jackson* (New York, 1968). In its first issue in 1817 (I 1–2), the *Journal of the Academy of National Science* laid down its policy to '. . . exclude entirely all papers of mere theory – to confine their communications as much as possible to facts. . . .'

[18] No list of early American scientists could find general agreement. See R. P. Stearns, *Science in the British Colonies of America* (Urbana, Ill., 1970), especially pp. 679–80; also the Selected Bibliographies of Fifty Early Scientists given by Bell, *Early American Science.*

[19] Punch XXI (6 Sept 1851) 117.

[20] W. B. Edwards, *The Story of Colt's Revolver* (Harrisburg, Pa., 1953).

[21] *Brother Jonathan's Epistle*, etc. (Boston, 1852) pp. 4–6, in Hugo Meïer, 'American Technology and the Nineteenth Century World', *American Quarterly*, X (Summer 1958) 116–30.

[22] New York (1853), Paris (1855), London (1862), Paris (1867), Vienna (1873), Philadelphia (1876), Paris (1878), Sydney (1879), Melbourne (1880), Paris (1889), Chicago (1893) and Paris (1900).

[23] *Visite a l'Exposition universelle de Paris en 1855. Sous la direction de M. Tresca* (Paris, 1855) p. 5.

[24] Charles Goodyear, *Gum Elastic* (New Haven, 1855); Thomas Hancock, *Personal Narrative* (London, 1857); William Woodruff, *The Rise of the British Rubber Industry* (Liverpool, 1958).

[25] *Congressional Globe*, 39th Cong., 1st Sess., 1371ff. (13 Mar 1866), in Merle Curti, *Probing Our Past* (Gloucester, Mass., 1962), pp. 248–9.

[26] Ibid., p. 249.

[27] *Congressional Record*, 50th Cong., 1st Sess., XIX 1651 (1 Mar 1888).

[28] S. L. Engerman, 'The Economic Impact of the Civil War', *Explorations in Entrepreneurial History*, III (1966) 176–99.

[29] C. F. Adams, *Report on the Vienna Exhibition* (Boston, 1874) p. 15.

[30] W. D. Howells, 'A Sennight of the Centennial', *The Atlantic Monthly*, XXXVIII (July 1876) 96.

[31] Ibid.

[32] Ibid.

[33] P. J. Marlin, *La Belgique et les Etats Unis* (Brussels, 1876) pp. 57, 102.

[34] Nathan Rosenberg, 'Technical Changes in the Machine Tool Industry, 1840–1910', *J. Econ. Hist.*, XXIII (Dec 1963) pp. 414–43.

[35] C. H. Fitch, *Report on Manufacturing of Interchangeable Mechanisms* (Washington, D.C., 1883).

[36] R. S. Woodbury, *The Legend of Eli Whitney and Interchangeable Parts* (Camb., Mass., 1964).

[37] *The American System of Manufactures: The Report of the Committee on the Machinery of the United States 1855, and the Special Reports of George Wallis and Joseph Whitworth 1854*, ed. Nathan Rosenberg (Edinburgh, 1969).

[38] After 1961 fairs were held at Seattle (1962), New York (1964–5), Montreal (1967), and Osaka, Japan (1970), the only one held outside the western world.

[39] Mira Wilkins, *The Emergence of Multinational Enterprise: American Business Abroad from the Colonial Era to 1914* (Camb., Mass., 1970). The information given on p. 30 conflicts with that given in my 'The American Origins of a Scottish Industry', *Scottish J. Pol. Econ.*, II (Feb 1955) pp. 17–31.

[40] United States, 48th Cong., 2nd Sess., 1884–5, *H.R. Misc. Docs.*, vol. 10 (Dec 1884); also 49th Cong., 2nd Sess., 1886–7, *H.R. Misc. Docs.*, vol. 4 (Aug 1886).

[41] Woodruff, *The Rise of the British Rubber Industry*, pp. 143, 154, 209–15.

[42] R. A. Church, 'The Effect of the American Export Invasion on the British Boot and Shoe Industry, 1885–1914', *J. Econ. Hist.*, XXVIII (June 1968) 223–54.

[43] Rosenthal, *Stars and Stripes in Africa*, p. 121.

[44] Ibid., p. 124.

[45] Ibid., p. 141ff.

[46] L. G. Churchward, 'The American Contribution to the Victorian Goldrush', *The Victorian Hist. Mag.*, XIX (June 1942), 85–95; also Geoffrey Blainey, *The Rush That Never Ended* (Melbourne, 1963).

[47] Rosenthal, *Stars and Stripes in Africa*, pp. 196–7; D. D. Brand, 'The Origin and Early Distribution of New World Cultivated Plants', *Agricultural History*. XIII (April 1939) pp. 109–17; Ping-ti Ho, 'The Introduction of American Food Plants into China', *American Anthropologist*, LVII (1955) 191–201.

[48] *Historical Statistics of the United States, Colonial Times to 1957* (Washington, D.C., 1960) pp. 546–7.

[49] Geoffrey Crowther and W. T. Layton, *An Introduction to the Study of Prices* (London, 1938), appd. D, table VI.

[50] Woytinsky and Woytinsky, *World Population and Production*, p. 1117.

[51] Crowther and Layton, *Study of Prices*, table VIII.

[52] Woytinsky and Woytinsky, *World Population and Production*, p. 797.

[53] Ibid.

[54] J. A. Kouwenhoven, *Made in America: The Arts in Modern Civilization* (Garden City, N.Y., 1949) p. 224.

[55] Ibid., 224–5. Yet Taylor's efforts to reorganise the American Bethlehem Steel Company according to his scientific principles were eventually resisted by the management and disowned.

[56] In the period 1907–17 the Russians looked to the United states as a model of industrialisation. M. M. Laserson, *The American Impact on Russian Diplomacy and Ideology, 1784–1917* (New York, 1950).

[57] E. S. Ferguson, 'On the Origin and Development of American Mechanical "Know-How"', *Midcontinent American Studies Journal*, III (Fall 1962) 3–16; also John B. Rae's 'The "Know-How" Tradition: Technology in American History', *Technology and Culture*, I (Spring 1960) 139–50.

[58] Bureau of Labor Statistics, *Employment and Earnings*, XIX (Sept 1972) 20, 49.

[59] *Statistical Abstract of the United States*, 1972, p. 584.

[60] Service industries usually include commerce, transportation and communications, finance, professional and personal services, public administration, and the armed forces. See V. W. Fuchs, *The Growing Importance of the Service Industries*, Occasional Paper No. 96 (National Bureau of Economic Research) (New York, 1965).

[61] Bureau of Labor Statistics, *Employment and Earnings* (Dec 1973).

[62] J. H. Dunning, *United States Industry in Britain* (London, 1973) p. 4.

[63] *Business Monitor M4 – Overseas Transactions* (April 1973) Table 12, p. 11.

[64] F. A. MacKenzie, *The American Invaders* (London, 1901); W. T. Stead, *The Americanization of the World* (London, 1901); B. H. Thwaite, *The American Invasion* (London, 1902); Denny Ludwell, *America Conquers Britain* (London, 1930); F. A. Southard, *American Industry in Europe* (Boston, 1931); R. H. Heindel, *The American Impact on Great Britain, 1898–1914* (Phila., 1940); Francis Williams, *The American Invasion* (New York, 1962); and E. A. McCreary, *The Americanization of Europe* (New York, 1964).

CHAPTER VI: AMERICA'S CONTRIBUTION TO THE CONQUEST OF DISTANCE

[1] C. F. Adams (ed.), *Memoirs of John Quincy Adams* (Phila., 1874) II 186. In 1787, the American naval officer John Paul Jones accepted an invitation from Catherine II to enter the Russian navy. Laserson, *American Impact on Russian Diplomacy*, p. 21.

[2] A. B. C. Whipple, *Yankee Whalers in the South Seas* (New York, 1954).

[3] W. B. Weeden, *Economic and Social History of New England, 1620–1789* (New York, 1891) I 254.

[4] Richard Champion, *Considerations on the Present Situation of Great Britain and the U.S. of America* (London, 1784) p. 20; also W. L. Marvin, *The American Merchant Marine* (New York, 1902); and Bernard and Lotte Bailyn, *Massachusetts Shipping, 1697–1714: A Statistical Study* (Camb., Mass., 1959).

[5] E. S. Maclay, *A History of American Privateers* (New York, 1899) p. 113; also McPherson Anderson, *Annals of Commerce* (London, 1805) IV 203.

[6] Marvin, *The American Merchant Marine*, p. 39.

[7] Holden Furber, 'The Beginnings of American Trade with India, 1784–1812', *New England Quarterly* XI (June 1938) 241–2.

[8] The general conditions of the 1770s were not fully restored until the second or third decade of the nineteenth century. G. R. Taylor, 'American Economic Growth Before 1840: An Exploratory Essay', *J. Econ. Hist.*, XXIV (Dec 1964) 427–44.

[9] R. G. Albion and J. B. Pope, *Sea Lanes in Wartime: The American Experience, 1775–1942* (New York, 1942) p. 70.

[10] Jefferson to Mr Leiper, 21 January 1809, in *The Writings of Thomas Jefferson*, ed. H. A. Washington (New York, 1853–7) V 417–18.

[11] John Lambert, *Travels Through Lower Canada and the United States of North America in the Years 1806, 1807, and 1808* (London, 1810) II 65.

[12] Albion and Pope, *Sea Lanes in Wartime*.

[13] C. C. Cutler, *Greyhounds of the Sea* (New York, 1930), and A. H. Clark, *The Clipper Ship Era, 1843–1849* (New York, 1910); also A. B.

Lubbock, *The China Clippers* (Glasgow, 1916), and *The Opium Clippers* (Boston, 1933).

[14] 'The clippers were an evolutionary, rather than a revolutionary development, in which the ideas and experiments of Captain Nathaniel B. Palmer, the inspiration of John W. Griffiths, the architecture of Samuel A. Pook and William H. Webb, the imaginative craftsmanship of Donald McKay, and the contributions of countless others were combined with the commercial demands of the times to produce the best in sail.' R. A. Rydell, 'The California Clippers', *Pacific Hist. Rev.*, XVIII (Feb 1949) 70–83.

[15] Rydell, ibid., p. 74.

[16] Clark, *The Clipper Ship Era*, p. 96–8.

[17] Gould, *Americans in Sumatra*, p. 13.

[18] Full title: *An Explanation for Keeping a Ship's Traverse at Sea, by the Columbia Ready Reckoner.*

[19] C. L. Lewis, *Matthew Fontaine Maury, the Pathfinder of the Seas* (Annapolis, Mdd., 1927).

[20] H. W. Dickinson, *Robert Fulton, Engineer and Artist: His Life and Works* (London, 1913).

[21] On the competing claims of western river steamboat pioneers, see L. C. Hunter, 'The Invention of the Western Steamboat', *J. Econ. Hist.* (Nov 1943), 201–20; also by Hunter, *Steamboats on the Western Rivers* (Camb., Mass., 1959). In addition, H. M. Chittenden, *History of the Early Steamboat Navigation on the Missouri River* (New York, 1903), and W. J. Petersen, *Steamboating on the Upper Mississippi* (Iowa City, Ia., 1937).

[22] Henry Fry, *History of North Atlantic Steam Navigation* (New York, 1896) pp. 33–4; also A. J. Maginnis, *The Atlantic Ferry* (London, 1900) p. 6.

[23] Felix Rivet, 'American Technique and Steam Navigation on the Saône and the Rhône, 1827–1850', *J. Econ. Hist.*, XVI (Mar 1956), 18–33; the articles by E. K. Haviland, which appeared in the *American Neptune* between July 1956, and July 1966; and K. C. Liu, *Anglo-American Steamship Rivalry in China, 1862–1874* (Camb., Mass., 1962).

[24] Between 1845 and 1859, about $14·5 million was given in subsidies to the American mercantile marine (it worked out to about a dollar a ton less than the British government gave Cunard for every ton of shipping crossing the Atlantic). In the latter year, President Pierce removed all government support from the ocean-going mercantile marine. J. G. B. Hutchins, *The American Maritime Industries and Public Policy, 1789–1914: An Economic History* (Camb., Mass., 1941). Cunard's story is told by H. K. Grant, *Samuel Cunard, Pioneer of the Atlantic Steamship* (London, 1967).

[25] Arnold Schrier, *Ireland and the American Emigration, 1850–1900* (Minneapolis, 1958) p. 151.

[26] W. A. Radius, *United States Shipping in Transpacific Trade, 1922–1938* (London, 1944).

[27] Woodruff, *Impact*, pp. 258–9; also D. C. North, 'Ocean Freight Rates and Economic Development, 1750–1913', *J. Econ. Hist.*, XVIII (Dec 1958) 537–55.

200   *America's Impact on the World*

[28] S. B. Okun, *The Russian–American Companies* (Camb., Mass., 1951) p. 249.

[29] *The Report of the Commissioner of Navigation, 1891 and 1892*, p. 8, gives northern losses (the south had few ships) as 239 vessels, aggregating 104,605 tons.

[30] Cutler, *Greyhounds of the Sea*, p. 309.

[31] J. G. B. Hutchins, 'The Declining American Maritime Industries: An Unsolved Problem, 1860–1940', *J. Econ. Hist.*, Suppl. 6 (1946) 103–22.

[32] L. F. L. Oppenheim, *The Panama Canal Conflict Between Great Britain and the United States of America: A Study* (Camb., Eng., 1913).

[33] W. R. Willoughby, *The St. Lawrence Waterway: A Study in Politics and Diplomacy* (Madison, Wis., 1961).

[34] O. O. Winther, *The Transportation Frontier, Trans-Mississippi West, 1865–1890* (New York, 1964) pp. 114–5.

[35] Doubtless, much that was done with the aid of railways (and this applies to other forms of transport) could have been done without them; transport, after all, whatever form it takes, is no more than a facilitating factor dependent upon other forces; no one kind is indispensable. K. T. Healy, 'Transportation as a Factor in Economic Growth', *J. Econ. Hist.*, Suppl. VII (1947) 72–88; also Robert Fogel, *Railroads and American Economic History* (Baltimore, 1964); Fritz Redlich, 'New and Traditional Approaches to Economic History and Their Interdependence', *J. Econ. Hist.*, XXV (Dec 1965) 480–95; L. M. Hacker, 'The New Revolution in Economic History', *Explorations in Entrepreneurial History*, Second Series, III (Spring 1966) pp. 159–75; Peter McClelland, 'Railroads, American Growth, and Economic History: A Critique'. *J. Econ. Hist.*, XXVIII (Mar 1968) pp. 102–23. While it saves us from a credulous acceptance of what has happened, to compare what was with what might have been *in the absence of history* is hardly history.

[36] Between 1870 and 1890, Kansas, Nebraska and the Dakotas increased their numbers sixfold; Utah and Colorado, threefold; Oklahoma, that had almost no whites in 1880, had two million by 1960; Texas, that in 1880 had a white population of one and a half million, had by 1900 increased its numbers to three million, and by 1960 to ten million; the Oregon Territory – which later was divided into Oregon, Washington, and Idaho – had a white population of 282,000 in 1880, 2 million in 1910, and 5·3 million in 1960; California, which had a white population of one-half million in 1869, had increased to almost 16 million in 1960.

[37] In 1970 the railroad mileage of the United States was 209,000, compared to U.S.S.R. 81,000, Canada 44,000, France 23,000, Germany 18,000, Mexico 15,000 and United Kingdom 12,000. These figures are taken from the *Railway Directory and Yearbook* (London, 1972) pp. 634–6. (For earlier figures see my *Impact of Western Man*.)

[38] Including the contributions of John Stevens (who in 1826 improved the multi-tubular boiler, the first patent for which went to John Howard in 1830); Robert (son of John) Stevens (who in 1830 introduced the balance valve for steam engines and the T-rail); various American inventors (whose joint efforts resulted in the introduction of the pilot truck and bogie and

double-slide cutoff for locomotives); Peter Cooper (who in 1830 designed and constructed for the Baltimore and Ohio Railroad the first American steam locomotive, popularly known as 'Tom Thumb'); John Jervis (who in 1831 devised the swivel truck for locomotives); and Joseph Harrison (who in 1837 invented the equalising lever).

[39] E. E. Ferguson, 'On the Origin and Development of American Mechanical "Know-How"', *Midcontinent Studies Journal*, III (Fall 1962) and 'Steam Transportation' in Vol. I of Kranzberg, *Technology in Western Civilization, op. cit.*; also E. P. Alexander, *Iron Horses: American Locomotives, 1829–1900* (New York, 1941); and J. H. White, *American Locomotives* (Baltimore, 1968).

[40] F. W. Powell, *The Railroads of Mexico* (Boston, 1921); also D. M. Pletcher, *Rails, Mines, and Progress: Seven American Promoters in Mexico, 1867–1911* (New York, 1958).

[41] Rosenthal, *Stars and Stripes in Africa*, p. 137ff.

[42] F. M. Halsey, *Railway Expansion in Latin America* (New York, 1916).

[43] P. A. Varg, *The Making of a Myth: The United States and China, 1897–1912* (East Lansing, 1968) p. 53. The rebuilding of the South Manchuria Railway after the Russo-Japanese War was done largely with American-made rails and locomotives. R. S. Greene, U.S. Consul in Dalny, *Commercial Relations of the U.S. with Foreign Countries During the Year 1907* (Washington, D.C., 1908) I 360; also U.S. Department of Commerce and Labor, *The Foreign Commerce and Navigation of the U.S. for the Year Ending June 30, 1910* (Washington, D.C., 1910) p. 627.

[44] On the use of mass media by the Americans in the world, see the relevant parts of Vol. 6 of UNESCO's *History of Mankind: The Twentieth Century* (New York, 1966), especially Part Four: 'Expression'.

[45] A. D. Chandler (ed.), 'Giant Enterprise: Ford, General Motors, and the Automobile Industry', *Sources and Readings* (New York, 1964); also Mira Wilkins and F. E. Hill, *American Business Abroad: Ford on Six Continents* (Detroit, 1964).

[46] *History of Standard Oil Company* (New York, 1955–71): *Pioneering in Big Business, 1822–1911*, by R. W. and M. E. Hidy; *The Resurgent Years, 1911–1927*, by G. S. Gibb and E. H. Knowlton (especially chap. 4, 'Looking Abroad for Oil, 1912–1917', and chap. 11, 'The Quest for Crude Oil in the Middle East, 1919–1928'); and H. M. Larson, Evelyn Knowlton, and Sterling Popple, *New Horizons, 1927–1950*.

[47] The unusual turn in these events was the decision made by Congress in 1971 to end its financial support of the S.S.T. (supersonic aircraft) programme. Meanwhile the British and the French continued their joint effort which resulted in the supersonic *Concorde*.

[48] Wernher von Braun and F. I. Ordway, *History of Rocketry and Space Travel*, rev. ed. (New York, 1969); Willy Ley, *Rockets, Missiles, and Men in Space*, (New York, 1968).

CHAPTER VII: AMERICA AND WORLD COMMERCE

[1] To protect its early manufactures, as well as to provide revenue for the new State, tariffs were introduced in 1789. Government intervention with

202 *America's Impact on the World*

market forces is also reflected in the history of slavery, railways, interstate commerce, antitrust legislation, conservation of natural resources, labour laws, social security, and welfare.

[2] By 1770 the value of the fish exports from the British continental colonies had become five times greater than that of New England's earlier staple, furs. Timothy Pitkin, *A Statistical View of the Commerce of the United States of America* (Hartford, Conn., 1816) pp. 19–23.

[3] E. R. Johnson, et al., *History of the Domestic and Foreign Commerce of the United States* (Washington, D.C., 1915); H. J. Carman, *American Husbandry* (New York, 1939); David Macpherson, *Annals of Commerce, Manufactures, Fisheries, and Navigation* (London, 1805).

[4] In 1775, in addition to its imports of tobacco, rice, indigo, and West Indian goods, Russia bought more than 50,000 beaver and other skins. A. W. Crosby, *America, Russia, Hemp, and Napoleon* (Columbus, Oh., 1965); also E. E. Rich, 'Russia and the Colonial Fur Trade', *Econ. Hist. Rev.*, 2nd series, VII (April 1955) 307–28.

[5] There are two kinds of cod: 'merchantable' and 'refuse'. A great deal of the 'refuse' found a ready market among the growing slave population of the West Indies. See the James Ford Bell Lecture, No. 3, by Herbert Heaton: 'The Economics of Empire', 1966, p. 22.

[6] J. R. Spears, *The American Slave Trade* (New York, 1900) pp. 42–3; also E. D. Moore, *Ivory, Scourge of Africa* (New York, 1931).

[7] U.S. Congress, *Ex. Docs.*, 26th Cong., 1st Sess. II, 1839–40, H. Doc. No. 57, 10.

[8] G. C. Bjork, 'The Weaning of the American Economy: Independence, Market Changes, and Economic Development', *J. Econ. Hist.*, XXIV (Dec 1964) 541–60.

[9] W. A. Cole, 'Trends in Eighteenth-Century Smuggling', *Econ. Hist. Rev.*, 2nd series, X (1958) 395–409.

[10] J. B. Hedges, *The Browns of Providence Plantations: Colonial Years* (Camb., Mass., 1952) p. 43.

[11] Chapter VIII, 'Fraudulent Trading', of Crosby, *America, Russia, Hemp, and Napoleon*; G. E. Brooks, *Yankee Traders, Gold Coasters, and African Middlemen* (Boston, 1970).

[12] Crosby, *America, Russia, Hemp, and Napoleon*, p. 46.

[13] J. A. Carr, 'John Adams and the Barbary Problem', *American Neptune*, XXVI (Oct 1966) 231–57. The Caribbean, which had been dangerous to merchantmen since the early seventeenth century, was finally cleared of pirates by the United States Navy in the early part of the nineteenth century.

[14] On the benefits and burdens of British mercantilist policy see Lawrence Harper, 'The Effect of the Navigation Acts on the Thirteen Colonies', in R. B. Morris (ed.), *The Era of the American Revolution* (New York, 1939) pp. 3–39; C. P. Nettels, 'British Mercantilism and the Economic Development of the Thirteen Colonies', *J. Econ. Hist.*, XII (Spring 1952) pp. 105–14; D. North, *J. Econ. Hist.* XVIII (Dec 1958)45–9; G. L. Beer, *The Old Colonial System*, 2 vols. (New York, 1912). Recent debate is continued in several articles of the *Journal of Economic History* by

Notes

R. P. Thomas (Dec 1965), R. L. Ransom (Sept 1968), and G. M. Walton (Sept 1968), and *Econ. Hist. Rev.* (Nov 1971).

[15] Bjork, *J. Econ. Hist.*, XXIV (Dec 1964) 541–60; also North, *J. Econ. Hist.*, XVIII (Dec 1958) 57–64.

[16] A. C. Clouder, *American Commerce as affected by the Wars of the French Revolution and Napoleon, 1793–1812* (Phila., 1932).

[17] Wrote American merchant Robert Morris to John Jay in 1783: 'I am sending some ships to China in order to encourage in others the adventurous pursuit of commerce.' Sydney and Marjorie Greenbie, *Gold of Ophir*, (Garden City, N.Y., 1925) p. 29. Vessels from Newport, Salem and Philadelphia either proceeded or accompanied Morris's *Empress of China* in its exploratory voyage to the east.

[18] Joshua Rowntree, *The Imperial Drug Trade* (London, 1908).

[19] S. E. Morison, *The Maritime History of Massachusetts, 1783–1860* (Boston, 1930) pp. 294–5. In 1811 Russia took 10 per cent of United States exports, a figure not to be reached again until the Second World War.

[20] J. H. Franklin, *From Slavery to Freedom: A History of American Negroes*, 2nd ed. (New York, 1956) p. 182. The slave trade was forbidden to British subjects in 1807 and to American citizens in 1808. The former enactment was enforced by the greatest navy in the world; the latter remained largely ineffective.

[21] Rosenthal, *Stars and Stripes in Africa*, p. 42; Brooks, *Yankee Traders, Gold Coaster, and African Middlemen* and Part I of 'American Traders' in *Americans in Black Africa* by C. C. Clendenen and Peter Duignan (Stanford, 1964). Although much fostered by the American authorities, it is doubtful if legitimate U.S. commerce with Africa, south of the Sahara, made up more than 1–2 per cent of the total U.S. foreign trade.

[22] Richard H. McKey, 'Elias Hasket Derby and the Founding of the Eastern Trade', *Essex Institute Historical Collections*, XCVIII (1962) 24.

[23] Dudley Dillard, *Economic Development of the North Atlantic Community; Historical Introduction to Modern Economics* (Englewood Cliffs, N.J., 1967) pp. 345–6; also Robert Albion, *The Rise of New York Port, 1815–1860* (New York, 1939), Chap. VI.

[24] T. C. Cochran, 'Did the Civil War Retard Industrialization?' *Miss. Valley Hist. Rev.*, XLVIII (Sept 1961) 197–210; Stephen Salsbury, 'The Effect of the Civil War on American Industrial Development', *The Economic Impact of the American Civil War*, ed. Ralph Andreano (Camb., Mass., 1962) pp. 161–8; Pershing Vartanian, 'The Cochran Thesis: A Critique in Statistical Analysis', *J. Am. Hist.*, LI (June 1964) 77–89; and H. N. Scheiber, 'Economic Change in the Civil War Era: An Analysis of Recent Studies', *Civil War History*, XI (Dec 1965), 396–411. A review of the various arguments can be found in S. L. Engerman, 'The Effects of Slavery upon the Southern Economy: A Review of the Recent Debate', *Explorations in Entrepreneurial History*, 2nd series, IV (Winter 1967) 71–97.

[25] If we take a purely political criterion of trade, and measure (which is how western trade figures are calculated) merely the trade entering and leaving American ports, then, in 1913, with the United Kingdom and

Germany, the United States was the third leading trading nation in the world. If, however, we add the internal trade done between the different American States (say, that done between the State of New York and the State of California) to America's intercontinental trade (as we do in calculating continental Europe's share of world trade), then, in 1913, the United States was probably the greatest trading nation on earth. The region in which United States internal trade is done is roughly the geographical equivalent of the European area. William and Helga Woodruff, *Technology and the Changing Trade Pattern of the United States*, (Gainesville, Fla, 1968).

[26] 'Role of Foreign Trade in the United States Economy', *World Trade Information Service: Statistical Reports*, part 3, no. 57–8, U.S. Department of Commerce (Nov 1957). Foreign trade declined from one-ninth of domestic trade in 1908 to one-eighteenth in 1939. Not since 1865 has it been more than 8 per cent of the National Income.

[27] Indeed, from 1876 until 1970, with the exception of four years, America consistently sold more goods than it bought. The ratio of imports to the American G.N.P. had continued to fall from the 1870s (when it was about 7 per cent) to the 1970s (when it was about 2–3 per cent).

[28] J. H. Williams, *Economic Stability in a Changing World: Essays in Economic Theory and Policy* (New York, 1953).

[29] It is estimated that of this $12 billion, $5·5 billion was used for industrial products, $5·2 billion for food and other agricultural commodities, and $800 million for freight costs. The Europeans contributed $9 billion to the recovery programme.

[30] R. N. Cooper, *The Economics of Interdependence* chap. 2.

[31] In 1970 the United States percentage of world trade was 13, compared to 55 for Europe (including Russia), 10 for the German Federal Republic, 6 each for France and the United Kingdom. These figures are taken from the *U.N. Statistical Yearbook* (New York, 1971) pp. 382–5. (For earlier figures see my *Impact of Western Man*.)

[32] Net imports increased from $52 million in 1920–9 to $2502 million in 1961; from 0·7 per cent to 14 per cent of domestic consumption. *U.S. Bureau of the Census, Working Paper No. 6*, 'Raw Materials in the United States Economy, 1900–1961' (Washington, D.C. 1963).

[33] Source: Calculated from the *Statistical Abstract of the United States* (Washington, D.C., various), and *Minerals Yearbook, 1971* (Washington, D.C., 1973).

[34] *Staff Papers Presented to the Commission* (Washington, D.C., Feb 1954), 224.

[35] Pierre Jalée, *The Third World in World Economy* (New York, 1969) p. 72ff.

[36] C. D. Hyson and A. M. Strout, see table XXVII.

[37] Myrdal, *The Challenge of World Poverty*, 291; Jaleé, *The Third World in World Economy*. There is still no coherent theory applicable to the different trade situations with which America and the world must deal. The more recent failure of the UNCTAD conference in Chile in 1972 is evidence of this.

[38] Arthur Neef, 'Unit Labor Costs in Eleven Countries', U.S. Bureau of Lab. Statistics, *Monthly Labor Review*, 94 (Aug 1971) 3–12.

CHAPTER VIII: EPILOGUE

[1] Carl Bridenbaugh, 'The Great Mutation', *Am. Hist. Rev.*, LXVIII (Jan 1963) 315–31.

[2] Lincoln's letter of 4 April 1864 to Albert G. Hodges; R. P. Basler (ed.), *The Collected Works of Abraham Lincoln* (New Brunswick, N.J., 1953) VII 282.

[3] *The Bacchae*, translated by Gilbert Murray (London, 1920) p. 82.

[4] Denis Meadows *et al.*, *The Limits to Growth* (New York, 1972).

[5] E. W. Emerson and W. E. Forbes, *Journals of Ralph Waldo Emerson* (Boston, 1909–14) V 380.

Bibliography

References given elsewhere in this book do not appear here.

GENERAL

Adams, J. T., *The Epic of America*, Boston, 1931.
Barraclough, Geoffrey, *An Introduction to Contemporary History*, Harmondsworth, Eng., 1967.
Beard, C. A., *The Making of American Civilization*, New York, 1939.
Beard, Miriam, *A History of the Business Man*, New York, 1938.
Blum, J. M., *The Promise of America: An Historical Inquiry*, Boston, Mass., 1965.
Boorstin, D. J., *The Americans: The National Experience*, New York, 1965.
Clough, S. B. *et al.*, *A History of the Western World*, Boston, Mass., 1964.
Commager, H. S., and Morison, S. E., *The Growth of the American Republic*, 2 vols., New York, 1950.
Curti, Merle, *The Growth of American Thought*, New York, 1943.
—— *et al.*, *A History of American Civilization*, New York, 1958.
David, Henry (ed.), *et al.*, *The Economic History of the United States*, 9 vols., New York, 1945.
Dorfman, Joseph, *The Economic Mind in American Civilization*, 5 vols, New York, 1946–59.
Gabriel, R. H., *The Course of American Democratic Thought*, New York, 1956.
Hacker, L. M., *The Shaping of the American Tradition*, 2 vols, New York, 1947.
——, *The Triumph of American Capitalism*, New York, 1940.
Jones, P. d'A., *The Consumer Society: A History of American Capitalism*, Baltimore, 1965.
Lerner, Max., *America as a Civilization: Life and Thought in the United States Today*, New York, 1957.
Morison, S. E., *The Oxford History of the American People*, New York, 1965.
Morris, Charles, *The Pragmatic Movement in American Philosophy*, New York, 1970.
Parkes, H. B., *The American Experience*, New York, 1947.
Parrington, V. L., *Main Currents in American Thought*, 3 vols, New York, 1958
Polanyi, Karl, *The Great Transformation*, New York, 1944.

Stavrianos, L. S., *The World Since 1500*, Englewood Cliffs, N.J., 1966.
Thistlethwaite, Frank, *The Great Experiment: An Introduction to the History of the American People*, Cambridge, 1955.
Thomson, David, *World History from 1914 to 1968*, London, 1969.
Vann Woodward, C. (ed.), *The Comparative Approach to American History*, New York, 1968.

CHAPTER I: PROLOGUE: ORIGINS

The World Conflict for North America
Bird, Harrison, *Battle for a Continent*, New York, 1965.
Graham, G. S., *Empire of the North Atlantic: The Maritime Struggle for North America*, Toronto, 1950.
Parkman, Francis, *A Half-Century of Conflict: France and England in North America*, 2 vols, Boston, Mass., 1903.
Peckham, H. H., *The Colonial Wars, 1689–1762*, Chicago, 1964.
Wright, J. L., Jr, *Anglo-Spanish Rivalry in North America*, Athens, Ga., 1971.

The Making of a New Society and Its Early Impact Abroad
Adams, Henry, *The Education of Henry Adams*, Boston, Mass., 1918.
Adams, J. T., *The American: The Making of a New Man*, New York, 1943.
——, *Revolutionary New England, 1691 – 1776*, Boston, Mass., 1923.
Andrews, C. M., *Colonial Self-Government, 1652–1689*, London, 1904.
Bailyn, Bernard, *The Ideological Origins of the American Revolution*, Camb., Mass., 1967.
——, 'Political Experience and Enlightenment Ideas in Eighteenth-Century America', *Am. Hist. Rev.* LXVII (Jan 1962) 339–51.
Barlow, Joel, *Advice to the Privileged Orders in the Several States of Europe*, London, 1792–3; Ithaca, N.Y., 1956.
Beard, C. A., *An Economic Interpretation of the Constitution of the United States*, New York, 1936.
Becker, Carl, *The Declaration of Independence*, New York, 1942.
Boorstin, D. J., *America and the Image of Europe: Reflections on American Thought*, Cleveland, 1960.
——, *The Americans: The Colonial Experience*, New York, 1958.
Botsford, J. B., *English Society in the Eighteenth Century as Influenced from Oversea*, New York, 1924.
Bridenbaugh, Carl, *Mitre and Sceptre: Transatlantic Faiths, Ideas, Personalities, and Politics, 1689–1775*, New York, 1962.
——, *Vexed and Troubled Englishmen, 1590–1642*, New York, 1968.
Brooks, Van Wyck, *The Wine of the Puritans*, New York, 1909.
Brown, S. G., *The First Republicans*, Syracuse, 1954.
Brumm, Ursula, *Puritanismus und Literatur in Amerika*, Darmstadt, 1973.
Bury, J. B., *The Idea of Progress*, New York, 1932.
Carroll, P. N., *Puritanism and the Wilderness: The Intellectual Significance of the New England Frontier, 1629–1700*, New York, 1969.
Chinard, G., 'Eighteenth Century Themes on America as a Human Habitat', *Proc. Am. Phil. Soc.*, XCI (1947) 25–57.

Clark, D. M., *British Opinion and the American Revolution*, New York, 1966.

Cunliffe, Marcus, 'The American Character', in *The Nation Takes Shape, 1789–1837*, Chicago, 1959.

Curti, M. E., 'Human Nature in American Thought: The Age of Reason and Morality, 1750–1860', *Political Science Quarterly*, LXVIII (Sep 1953) 354–75.

——, 'The Reputation of America Overseas, 1776–1860', in *Probing Our Past*, Gloucester, Mass., 1962.

Echeverria, Durand, 'Roubaud and the Theory of American Degeneration', *French American Review*, III (Jan–Mar 1950) 24–33.

Ekirch, A. A., *The Idea of Progress in America, 1815–1860*, New York, 1944.

Elliott, J. H., *The Old World and the New, 1492–1650*, Cambridge, Eng., 1970.

Fairchild, H. N., *The Noble Savage: A Study in Romantic Naturalism*, New York, 1928.

Fay, Bernard, *The Revolutionary Spirit in France and America at the End of the Eighteenth Century*, translated by Ramon Guthrie, New York, 1927.

Fess, G. M., *The American Revolution in Creative French Literature (1775–1937)*, University of Missouri Studies, XVI, no. 2, 1941.

Foster, Stephen, *Their Solitary Way: The Puritan Social Ethic in the First Century of Settlement in New England*, New Haven, 1971.

French, Allen, *Charles I and the Puritan Upheaval: A Study of the Causes of the Great Migration*, Boston, Mass., 1955.

Gottschalk, Louis, 'The Place of the American Revolution in the Causal Pattern of the French Revolution', in *Causes and Consequences of the American Revolution*, ed. Esmond Wright, Chicago, 1966.

Griffin, C. C., *The United States and the Disruption of the Spanish Empire, 1810–1822*, New York, 1937.

Haraszti, Zoltán, *John Adams and the Prophets of Progress*, Camb., Mass., 1952.

Heilman, R. B., *America in English Fiction, 1760–1800: The Influences of the American Revolution*, Baton Rouge, La., 1937.

Hill, Christopher, *The Century of Revolution, 1603–1714*, Edinburgh, 1961.

Jameson, J. F., *The American Revolution Considered as a Social Movement*, Boston, Mass., 1956.

Jensen, Merrill, *The Founding of a Nation: A History of the American Revolution, 1763–1776*, New York, 1968.

Johnson, E. A. J., *American Economic Thought in the Seventeenth Century*, London, 1932.

Kammen, M. G., *A Rope of Sand: The Colonial Agents, British Politics, and the American Revolution*, Ithaca, N.Y., 1968.

Koch, Adrienne, *Power, Morals, and the Founding Fathers*, Ithaca, N.Y., 1961.

Koht, Halvdan, *The American Spirit in Europe: A Survey of Transatlantic Influences*, Philadelphia, 1949.

Kraus, Michael, *The Atlantic Civilization: Eighteenth-Century Origins*, Ithaca, N.Y., 1949.

——, 'Scientific Relations Between Europe and America In the Eighteenth Century', *Scientific Monthly*, LV (Sept 1942) 259–72.

Leder, L. H. (ed.), *The Meaning of the American Revolution*, Chicago, 1969.

Lingelbach, W. E., 'American Democracy and European Interpreters', *Pennsylvania Magazine of History and Biography*, LXI (Jan 1937) 1–25.

May, J. M., *Atlas of the Distribution of Disease*, New York, 1944.

Miller, Perry, *Errand into the Wilderness*, Camb., Mass., 1956.

——, *Roger Williams: His Contribution to the American Tradition*, New York, 1962.

Morgan, E. S., 'The Puritan Ethic and the American Revolution', *William and Mary Quarterly*, XXIV (Jan 1967), 3–43.

Morgan, E. S., and Morgan, H. M., *The Stamp Act Crisis: Prologue to Revolution*, Chapel Hill, N.C., 1953.

Morison, S. E. (ed.), *Sources and Documents Illustrating the American Revolution, 1764–1788, and the Formation of the Federal Constitution*, New York, 1965.

Morris, R. B., *The Peacemakers: The Great Powers and American Independence*, New York, 1965.

Munro, W. B., *American Influences on Canadian Government*, Toronto, 1929.

Nash, Roderick, *Wilderness and the American Mind*, New Haven, 1967.

Nettels, C. P., *The Roots of American Civilization: A History of American Colonial Life*, New York, 1938.

Nye, R. B., *This Almost Chosen People*, East Lansing, Mich., 1966.

O'Gorman, Edmundo, *The Invention of America*, Bloomington, Ind., 1961.

Palmer, R. R., *The Age of the Democratic Revolution: A Political History of Europe and America, 1760–1800*, 2 vols, Princeton, 1959–64.

Parry, J. H., *The Age of Reconnaissance*, Cleveland, 1963.

Potter, D. M., 'The Quest for the National Character', in *The Reconstruction of American History*, ed. John Higham, New York, 1962.

Rahv, Philip (ed.), *Discovery of Europe*, Boston, Mass., 1947.

Rankin, H. F., *The American Revolution*, New York, 1964.

Rosenthal, Lewis, *America and France: The Influence of the United States on France in the XVIIIth Century*, New York, 1882.

Rodenwaldt, E., *World-Atlas of Epidemic Diseases*, Hamburg, 1952.

Rossiter, C. L., *The First American Revolution: The American Colonies on the Eve of Independence*, New York, 1956.

Rourke, Constance, *The Roots of American Culture*, New York, 1942.

Rowse, A. L., *The Elizabethans and America*, New York, 1959.

——, *The Expansion of Elizabethan England*, London, 1955.

Rowland, K. M., *The Life of George Mason, 1725–1792*, New York, 1892.

Russell, Bertrand *et al.*, *The Impact of America on European Culture*, Boston, Mass., 1951.

Sanford, C. L., *The Quest for Paradise: Europe and the American Moral Imagination*, Urbana, Ill., 1961.

Savelle, Max., *Seeds of Liberty: The Genesis of the American Mind*, Seattle, 1965.

Schlesinger, A. M., Sr., 'The American Revolution Reconsidered', *Political Science Quarterly*, XXXIV (Mar 1919) 61–78.

——, *The Colonial Merchants and the American Revolution, 1763–1776*, New York, 1918.

Schneider, H. W., *The Puritan Mind*, Ann Arbor, Mich., 1958.

Shepherd, W. R., 'The Expansion of Europe', *Political Science Quarterly*, XXXIV (Mar, June, Sep 1919) 43–60, 210–25, 392–412.

Shipton, C. K., 'The Hebraic Background of Puritanism', *Publications of the American Jewish Historical Society*, XLVII, (Mar 1958) 140–53.

Simpson, Alan, *Puritanism in Old and New England*, Chicago, 1955.

Skard, Sigmund, *The American Myth and the European Mind: American Studies in Europe, 1776–1960*, Philadelphia, 1961.

Smith, T. V., *The American Philosophy of Equality*, Chicago, 1927.

——, *The Democratic Tradition in America*, New York, 1941.

Strout, Cushing, *The American Image of the Old World*, New York, 1963.

Taylor, W. R., *Cavalier and Yankee: The Old South and the American National Character*, New York, 1961.

Tuveson, E. L., *Millennium and Utopia, a Study of the Background of the Idea of Progress*, Berkeley, 1949.

Van Alstyne, Richard, *Empire and Independence: The International History of the American Revolution*, New York, 1965.

Van Tyne, C. H., *The Loyalists in the American Revolution*, New York, 1929.

Varg, P. A., *Foreign Policies of the Founding Fathers*, East Lansing, Mich., 1963.

von Gentz, Friedrich, *The French and American Revolutions Compared*, translated by John Quincy Adams, Chicago. 1955, (1800).

Walzer, Michael, *The Revolution of the Saints: A Study in the Origins of Radical Politics*, Camb., Mass., 1965.

Weber, Max, *The Protestant Ethic and the Spirit of Capitalism*, translated by Talcott Parsons, London, 1930.

Wertenbaker, T. J., *The First Americans, 1607–1690*, New York, 1927.

——, *The Puritan Oligarchy: The Founding of American Civilization*, New York, 1947.

Whitaker, A. P., *The United States and the Independence of Latin America, 1800–1830*, Baltimore, 1941.

White, E. A., *Science and Religion In American Thought*, Stanford, 1952.

Wright, L. B., *The Atlantic Frontier: Colonial American Civilisation, 1607–1763*, Ithaca, N.Y., 1959.

CHAPTER II: AMERICA'S EMPIRE

General
Adams, J. T. (ed.), *Atlas of American History*, New York, 1943.

Debenham, Frank, *Discovery and Exploration: An Atlas-History of Man's Wanderings*, New York, 1960.

Fieldhouse, D. K., *The Colonial Empires: A Comparative Survey from the Eighteenth Century*, New York, 1967.

Healy, David, 'Modern Imperialism: Changing Styles in Historical Interpretation', *Am. Hist. Assoc.*, no. 69, 1967.

Kohn, Hans, *American Nationalism*, New York, 1957.

Niebuhr, Reinhold, *The Structure of Nations and Empires*, New York, 1959.

Perkins, Dexter, 'Is There an American Imperialism?', in *The American Approach to Foreign Policy*, Camb., Mass., 1952.

Snyder, L. L. (ed.), *The Imperialism Reader: Documents and Readings on Modern Expansionism*, Princeton, 1962.

Strausz-Hupé, Robert, and Hazard, H. W. (eds.), *The Idea of Colonialism*, New York, 1958.

Winks, R. W., 'Imperialism', in *The Comparative Approach to American History*, ed. C. Vann Woodward, New York, 1968.

Winslow, E. M., *The Pattern of Imperialism: A Study in the Theories of Power*, New York, 1948.

Wolfe, Martin (ed.), *The Economic Causes of Imperialism*, New York, 1972.

The Course and Implications of Empire: The American Continent
The United States and Canada

Callahan, J. M., *American Foreign Policy in Canadian Relations*, New York, 1937.

Corbett, P. E., *The Settlement of Canadian-American Disputes: A Critical Study of Methods and Results*, New Haven, 1937.

Horsman, Reginald, *The War of 1812*, New York, 1969.

Mahon, John, *The War of 1812*, Gainesville, Fla., 1972.

Perkins, Bradford, *Prologue to War: England and the United States, 1805–1812*, Berkeley, 1961.

Pratt, J. W., *Expansionists of 1812*, New York, 1925.

Warner, D. F., *The Idea of Continental Union: Agitation for the Annexation of Canada to the United States, 1849–1893*, Lexington, Ky., 1960.

White, P. C. T., *A Nation on Trial: America and the War of 1812*, New York, 1965.

The Westward Movement

Anderson, P. S., *Westward is the Course of Empires*, Oslo, 1956.

Billington, R. A., *America's Frontier Heritage*, New York, 1966.

Burt, A. L., *The United States, Great Britain, and British North America from the Revolution to the Establishment of Peace After the War of 1812*, New Haven, 1940.

Carter, C. E., 'Colonialism in Continental United States', *South Atlantic Quarterly*, XLVII (Jan 1948) 17–28.

Coman, Katherine, *Economic Beginnings of the Far West*, New York, 1925.

DeVoto, B. A., *The Course of Empire*, Boston, Mass., 1962.

Gabriel, R. H., *The Lure of the Frontier*, New Haven, 1929.

Graebner, N. A., *Empire on the Pacific: A Study in American Continental Expansion*, New York, 1955.

LaFeber, Walter, *The New Empire: An Interpretation of American Expansion, 1860–1898*, Ithaca, N.Y., 1963.

Paul, R. W., *Mining Frontiers of the Far West, 1848–1880*, New York, 1963.

Price, A. G., *The Western Invasions of the Pacific and its Continents: A Study of Moving Frontiers and Changing Landscapes, 1513–1958*, Oxford, 1963.

Turner, F. J., *The Frontier in American History*, New York, 1920.

Webb, W. P., *The Great Frontier*, Boston, 1952.

Winther, O. O., *The Transportation Frontier*, New York, 1964.

The United States and Mexico

Callahan, J. M., *American Foreign Policy in Mexican Relations*, New York, 1932.

Castaneda, C. E. (ed.), *The Mexican Side of the Texas Revolution, 1836*, Dallas, Tex., 1928.

Ramíriz, J. F., *Mexico During the War with the United States*, edited by W. V. Scholes; translated by E. B. Scherr, Columbia, Mo., 1950.

Rippy, J. F., *The United States and Mexico*, New York, 1931.

Rives, G. L., *The United States and Mexico, 1821–1848*, 2 vols, New York, 1913.

Ruiz, R. E., *The Mexican War: Was It Manifest Destiny?* New York, 1963.

Singletary, O. A., *The Mexican War*, Chicago, 1960.

The Indians

Armstrong, V. I. (ed.), *I Have Spoken*, New York, 1971.

Brown, Dee, *Bury My Heart at Wounded Knee: An Indian History of the American West*, New York, 1971.

Chamberlain, A. F., 'The Contribution of the American Indian to Civilization', *Proceedings of the American Antiquarian Society*, N.S. 16 (1905) 91–126.

Dunn, J. P., *Massacres of the Mountains: A History of the Indian Wars of the Far West, 1815–1875*, New York, 1958.

Forbes, J. D. (ed.), *The Indian in America's Past*, Englewood Cliffs, N.J., 1964.

Foreman, Grant, *Indian Removal: The Emigration of the Five Civilized Tribes of Indians*, Norman, Okla, 1953.

Jackson, H. H., *A Century of Dishonour*, New York, 1881.

Jennison, Keith, and Tebbel, John, *The American Indian Wars*, New York, 1960.

MacLeod, W. C., *The American Indian Frontier*, New York, 1928.

Mails, T. E., *The Mystic Warriors of the Plains*, New York, 1972.

Malin, J. C., *Indian Policy and Westward Expansion*, Lawrence, Kan., 1921.

Pearce, R. H., *Savagism and Civilization: A Study of the Indian and the American Mind*, Baltimore, 1967.

Prucha, F. P., *American Indian Policy in the Formative Years*, Camb., Mass., 1962.

U.S. Commissioners of Indian Affairs, *Annual Report* (various).

The American Civil War as Seen from Abroad

Adamov, E. A., 'Russia and the United States at the Time of the Civil War', *J. Mod. Hist.*, II (Dec 1930), 586–602.

Adams, E. D., *Great Britain and the American Civil War*, 2 vols, New York, 1925.

Beloff, Max, 'Great Britain and the American Civil War', *History*, XXXVII (Feb 1952) 40–8.

Blumenthal, Henry, 'Confederate Diplomacy: Popular Notions and International Realities', *Journal of Southern History*, XXXII (May 1966) 151–71.

Case, L. M. and Spencer, W. F., *The United States and France: Civil War Diplomacy*, Philadelphia, 1970.

Gavronsky, Serge, *The French Liberal Opposition and the American Civil War*, New York, 1968.

Harrison, Royden, 'British Labour and the Confederacy', *International Rev. Soc. Hist.*, II (1957) 78–105.

Jordan, Donaldson, and Pratt, Edwin, *Europe and the American Civil War*, Boston, Mass., 1931.

Luvaas, Jay, *The Military Legacy of the Civil War*, vol. I. Chicago, 1959.

MacDonald, H. G., *Canadian Public Opinion on the American Civil War*, New York, 1926.

Vann Woodward, C., *Origins of the New South, 1877–1913*, Baton Rouge, 1951.

West, W. R., *Contemporary French Opinion on the American Civil War*, Baltimore, 1924.

Winks, R. W., *Canada and the United States: The Civil War Years*, Baltimore, 1960.

Woldman, A. A., *Lincoln and the Russians*, New York, 1961.

The Course and Implications of Empire:
Asia and the Pacific

Bailey, T. A., 'Japan's Protest Against the Annexation of Hawaii', *J. Mod. Hist.*, III (Mar 1931) 46–61.

Battistini, L. H., *The Rise of American Influence in Asia and the Pacific*, East Lansing, Mich., 1960.

Callahan, J. M., *American Relations in the Pacific and the Far East, 1784–1900*, Baltimore, 1901.

Campbell, C. S., *Special Business Interests and the Open Door Policy*, New Haven, 1951.

Clyde, P. H., *The Far East: A History of the Impact of the West on Eastern Asia*, Englewood Cliffs, N.J., 1958.

Cohen, W. I., *America's Response to China*, New York, 1971.

Danton, G. H., *The Culture Contacts of the United States and China: The Earliest Sino-American Culture Contacts, 1784–1844*, New York, 1931.

Dulles, F. R., *America in the Pacific: A Century of Expansion*, Boston and New York, 1932.

Dulles, F. R., *China and America: The Story of Their Relations Since 1784*, Princeton, 1946.

Fairbank, J. K., *The United States and China*, Camb., Mass., 1958.

Fairbank, J. K. and Ssu-yü Teng, *China's Response to the West*, Camb., Mass., 1954.

Griswold, A. W., *The Far Eastern Policy of the United States*, New York, 1938.

Hayden, J. R. and Worcester, D. C., *The Phillippines, Past and Present*, New York, 1930.

Latourétte, K. S., *The American Record in the Far East*, 1945–1951, New York, 1952.

——, *The History of Early Relations Between the United States and China, 1784–1844*, New Haven, 1917.

Lieu, Kwang-ching, *Americans and Chinese*, Cambridge, Mass., 1963.

McCormick, T. J., *China Market: America's Quest for Informal Empire, 1893–1901*, Chicago, 1967.

Morgan, Theodore, *Hawaii: A Century of Economic Change, 1778–1876*, Camb., Mass., 1948.

Sakamaki, Shunzo, 'Japan and the United States, 1790–1853', *Trans. Asiatic Soc. Japan*, 2nd series, XVIII (Dec 1939).

Stevens, S. K., *American Expansion in Hawaii, 1842–1898*, Harrisburg, Pa., 1945.

Swisher, Earl (ed.), *China's Management of the American Barbarians: A Study of Sino-American Relations, 1841–1861, with Documents*, New Haven, 1953.

Thomas, L. V. and Frye, R. N., *The United States and Turkey and Iran*, Cambridge, Mass., 1962.

Latin America

Bemis, S. F., 'The Myth of Economic Imperialism', in *The Latin American Policy of the United States: An Historical Interpretation*. New York, 1943.

Callcott, W. H., *The Caribbean Policy of the United States, 1890–1920*, Baltimore, 1942.

Cox, I. J., *Nicaragua and the United States, 1909–1927*, Boston, Mass., 1927.

Fitzgibbon, R. H., *Cuba and the United States, 1900–1935*, Monasha, Wis., 1935.

Freidel, Frank, *The Splendid Little War*, Boston, Mass., 1958.

Healy, David, *U.S. Expansionism: The Imperialist Urge in the 1890s*, Madison, Wis., 1970.

Jenks, L. H., *Our Cuban Colony*, New York, 1928.

Knight, Melvin, *The Americans in Santo Domingo*, New York, 1928.

Merk, Frederick, *The Monroe Doctrine and American Expansionism, 1843–1849*, New York, 1966.

Munro, D. G., *Intervention and Dollar Diplomacy in the Caribbean, 1900–1921*, Princeton, 1964.

——, *The United States and the Caribbean Area*, Boston, Mass., 1934.

Perkins, Dexter, *The Monroe Doctrine, 1823–1826*, Camb., Mass., 1932.

——, *The Monroe Doctrine, 1826–1867*, Baltimore, 1933.

——, *The Monroe Doctrine, 1867–1907*, Baltimore, 1937.

Robinson, A. G., *Cuba and the Intervention*, New York, 1905.

Ruiz, R. E., *Cuba: The Making of a Revolution*, Amherst, Mass., 1968.

Willoch, Roger, 'Gunboat Diplomacy, Operations of the North American and West Indies Squadron, 1875–1915', *American Neptune*, XXVIII, part I (Jan 1968) 5–30; part II (Apr 1968) 85–112.

Woods, K. F., 'Imperialistic America': A Landmark in the Development of U.S. Policy toward Latin America', *Inter-American Economic Affairs*, XXI (winter 1967) 55–72.

Woodruff, William and Helga, 'The Illusions about the Role of Integration in Latin America's Future', in *Latin America and the United States in the 1970s*, R. B. Gray (ed.), Itaska, Ill., 1971.

Global

Adams, Brooks, *America's Economic Supremacy*, London, 1900.

Allen, F. L., *The Lords of Creation*, London, 1935.

Ambrose, S. E., *Rise to Globalism*, London, 1971.

Bailey, T. A., *America Faces Russia*, Ithaca, N.Y., 1950.

——, *A Diplomatic History of the American People*, New York, 1958.

Bemis, S. F., *A Diplomatic History of the United States*, New York, 1955.

Blumenthal, Henry, *A Reappraisal of Franco-American Relations, 1830–1871*, Chapel Hill, N.C., 1959.

Bowles, Chester, *Africa's Challenge to America*, Berkeley, 1956.

——, *American Politics in a Revolutionary World*, Camb., Mass., 1956.

Brown, R. H., 'American World Mission', in *America: Purpose and Power*, ed. G. M. Lyons, Chicago, 1965.

Carleton, W. G., *The Revolution in American Foreign Policy: Its Global Range*, New York, 1964.

Chomsky, Noam, *American Power and the New Mandarins*, New York, 1969.

Conant, C. A., 'The Economic Basis of Imperialism', *N. Am. Rev.*, (Sep 1898) 326–40.

de Riencourt, Amaury, *The Coming Caesars*, New York, 1957.

——, *The American Empire*, New York, 1968.

Dulles, F. R., *America's Rise to World Power, 1898–1954*, New York, 1955.

Foreman, Joseph, and Nearing, Scott, *Dollar Diplomacy: A Study in American Imperialism*, New York, 1925.

Graebner, N. A., *Cold War Diplomacy*, Princeton, 1962.

Greene, T. P. (ed.), *American Imperialism in 1898*, Boston, Mass., 1955.

Halle, L. J., *Civilization and Foreign Policy*, New York, 1955.

Kennan, G. F., *American Diplomacy, 1900–1950*, New York, 1952.

——, *Realities of American Foreign Policy*, Princeton, 1954.

Lashley, W. L., *The Debate over Imperialism in the United States, 1898–1900*, Ann Arbor, Mich., 1966.

Mahan, A. T., 'The United States Looking Outward', *Atlantic Monthly*, LXVI (Dec 1890) 816–24.

May, E. R., *Imperial Democracy: The Emergence of America as a Great Power*, New York, 1961.

Merk, Frederick, *Manifest Destiny and Mission in American History: A Reinterpretation*, New York, 1963.

Morgan, H. W., *America's Road to Empire: The War with Spain and Overseas Expansion*, New York, 1965.

Neale, R. G., *Great Britain and United States Expansion: 1898–1900*, East Lansing, Mich., 1966.

Perkins, W. T., *Denial of Empire: The United States and Its Dependencies*, Leyden, 1962.

Plesur, Milton, 'Rumblings Beneath the Surface: America's Outward Thrust, 1865–1890', in *The Gilded Age: A Reappraisal*, ed. H. W. Morgan, Syracuse, N.Y., 1963.

Pratt, J. W., *America's Colonial Experiment: How the United States Gained, Governed, and in Part Gave Away a Colonial Empire*, New York, 1950.

——, *Expansionists of 1898: The Acquisition of Hawaii and the Spanish Islands*, New York, 1951.

——, *A History of United States Foreign Policy*, New York, 1955.

Rostow, W. W., *The United States in the World Arena*, New York, 1960.

Seton-Watson, Hugh, *Neither War Nor Peace: The Struggle for Power in the Postwar World*, New York, 1960.

Tompkins, E. B., *Anti-Imperialism in the United States: The Great Debate, 1890–1920*, Philadelphia, 1970.

Van Alstyne, R. W., *The American Empire: Its Historical Pattern and Evolution*, London, 1960.

Weinberg, A. K., *Manifest Destiny: A Study in Nationalist Expansionism*, Baltimore, 1935.

Williams, W. A., *The Roots of the Modern American Empire*, New York, 1969.

zu Stolberg-Wernigerode, Otto, *Germany and the United States of America During the Era of Bismarck*, Reading, Pa, 1937.

CHAPTER III: AMERICANS IN A WORLD CONTEXT

Migration to the United States and Its Effects Upon the World

Allen, H. C., *Great Britain and the United States*, London, 1954.

Barth, Gunther, *Bitter Strength; A History of the Chinese in the United States, 1850–1870*, Camb., Mass., 1964.

Benson, A. B. and Hedin, Naboth, *Americans from Sweden*, Philadelphia, 1950.

Berthoff, R. T., *British Immigrants in Industrial America, 1790–1950*, Camb., Mass., 1953.

Blegen, T. C. (ed.), *Land of Their Choice: The Immigrants Write Home*, Minneapolis, 1955.

——, *Norwegian Migration to America*, Northfield, Minn., 1931.

Curti, Merle and Birr, Hendall, 'The Immigrant and the American Image in Europe, 1860–1915', *Miss. Valley Hist. Rev.*, XXXVII (Sep 1950) 203–30.

Davis, Jerome, *The Russian Immigrant*, New York, 1922.
Fairchild, H. P., *Immigration: A World Movement and Its American Significance*, New York, 1933.
Govorchin, G. G., *Americans from Yugoslavia*, Gainesville, Fla, 1961.
Haiman, Miecislaus, *Polish Past in America, 1608–1865*, Chicago, 1939.
Handlin, Oscar (ed.), *Immigration as a Factor in American History*, Englewood Cliffs, N.J., 1961.
Hansen, M. L., *The Atlantic Migration, 1607–1860*, Camb., Mass., 1940.
——, *The Immigrant in American History*, Camb., Mass., 1940.
Hansen, N. L. and Brebner, J. B., *The Mingling of the Canadian and American Peoples*, New Haven, 1940.
Hoglund, A. W., *Finnish Immigrants in America, 1880–1920*, Madison, Wis., 1960.
Issac, Julius, *The Effect of European Migration on the Economy of Sending and Receiving Countries*, The Hague, 1953.
Lengyel, Emil, *Americans from Hungary*, Philadelphia, 1948.
Saloutos, Theodore, *The Greeks in the United States*, Camb., Mass., 1964.
Smith, Bradford, *Americans from Japan*, Philadelphia, 1948.
Thomas, Brinley, *Migration and Economic Growth: A Study of Great Britain and the Atlantic Economy*, Camb., 1954.
U.S. House of Representatives, Staff Study, *The Brain Drain into the U.S. etc.*, July 1967.
Wabeke, B. H., *Dutch Emigration to North America, 1624–1860: A Short History*, New York, 1944.
Walker, Mack, *Germany and the Emigration, 1816–1885*, Camb., Mass., 1964.

The Forced Migration of Africans to America
Bontemps, Arna (ed.), *Great Slave Narratives*, Boston, Mass., 1969.
Clendenen, C. C. and Duignan, Peter, *The United States and the African Slave Trade, 1619–1862*, Stanford, 1963.
Curtin, P. D., *African History*, New York, 1964.
Curtin, P. D., and Vansina, Jan, 'Sources of the Nineteenth Century Atlantic Slave Trade', *Journal of African History*, v (1964) 185–208.
Daaku, K. Y., 'The Slave Trade and African Society', *Emerging Themes of African History*, ed. T. O. Ranger, Nairobi, Kenya, 1968.
Davidson, Basil with Buah, F. K. and Ajayi, J. F. A., *The Growth of African Civilisation: West Africa, 1000–1800*, London, 1965.
de Graft-Johnson, J. C., *African Glory: The Story of Vanished Negro Civilisations*, New York, 1955.
Donnan, Elizabeth (ed.), *Documents Illustrative of the History of the Slave Trade to America*, 4 vols., Washington, D. C., 1935; reprinted New York, 1965.
du Bois, W. E. B., *The World and Africa*, New York, 1947.
Fage, J. D., 'Slavery and the Slave Trade in the Context of West African History', *J. Afr. Hist.*, x (1969) 393–404.
Gann, L. H. and Duignan, Peter, *Africa and the World*, San Francisco, 1972.

Mannix, D. P., *Black Cargoes: A History of the Atlantic Slave Trade, 1518–1865*, New York, 1962.

Myrdal, Gunnar, *An American Dilemma*, New York, 1944.

Pope-Hennessy, James, *Sins of the Fathers: A Study of the Atlantic Slave Traders, 1441-1807*, New York, 1968.

Redding, J. S., *They Came in Chains: Americans from Africa*, Philadelphia, 1950.

Rodney, Walter, 'African Slavery and Other Forms of Social Oppression on the Upper Guinea Coast in the Context of the Atlantic Slave-Trade', *J. Afr. Hist.*, VII (1966) 431–43.

Williams, Eric, *Capitalism and Slavery*, Chapel Hill, N.C., 1944.

The Reverse Flow: The Impact of Americans Abroad

Aitkin, Thomas, *A Foreign Policy for American Business*, New York, 1962.

Babey, A. M., *Americans in Russia, 1776–1917*, New York, 1938.

Baker, P. R., *The Fortunate Pilgrims: Americans in Italy, 1800–1860*, Camb., Mass., 1964.

Brown, G. W., *The Economic History of Liberia*, Washington, D.C., 1941.

Chisholm, L. W., *The Far East and American Culture*, New Haven and London, 1963.

Crabitès, Pierre, *Americans in the Egyptian Army*, London, 1938.

Cleveland, Harlan; Mangone, G. J.; and Adams, J. C., *The Overseas Americans*, New York, 1960.

Dennett, Tyler, *Americans in Eastern Asia: A Critical Study of the Policy of the United States with Reference to China, Japan and Korea in the 19th Century*, New York, 1922.

Field, J. A., Jr., *America and the Mediterranean World, 1776–1882*, Princeton, 1969.

Foreman, C. T., *Indians Abroad, 1493–1938*, Norman, Okla, 1943.

Griggs, D. T., *Americans in China: Some Chinese Views*, Washington, D.C., 1948.

Handlin, Oscar, 'Immigrants Who Go Back', *Atlantic Monthly*, CXCVIII (July 1956) 70–4.

Haven, Gilbert, 'America in Africa', *N. Am. Rev.*, CXXV (July 1877) 147–58; (Nov 1877) 517–28.

Johnston, Harry, *Liberia*, 2 vols., London, 1906.

Lambert, R. D. (ed.), 'Americans Abroad', *The Annals*, CCCLXVIII (Nov 1966) entire issue.

Larrabee, S. A., *Hellas Observed: The American Experience of Greece,* *1775–1865*, New York, 1957.

Neago, Peter, *Americans Abroad*, The Hague, 1932.

Price, A. G., *Island Continent: Aspects of the Historical Geography of Australia and its Territories*, Sydney, 1972.

Sachse, W. L., *The Colonial American in Britain*, Madison, Wis., 1956.

——, 'The Migration of New Englanders to England, 1640-1660', *Am. Hist. Rev.*, LIII (Jan 1948) 251–78.

Shepperson, George, 'Notes on Negro American Influences on the Emergence of African Nationality', *Journal of African History*, I (1960) 299–312.

Shepperson, Wilbur S., *Emigration and Disenchantment*, Norman, Okla, 1965.

Steiner, E. A., 'How Returning Emigrants are Americanizing Europe', *Am. Rev. of Rev.*, XXXIX (June 1909) 701–3.

Strauss, W. P., *Americans in Polynesia, 1783–1842*, East Lansing, Mich., 1964.

Tibawi, A. L., *American Interests in Syria, 1800–1901*, Oxford, 1966.

The Reverse Flow: The Missions

Bascom, W. R., 'African Culture and the Missionary', *Civilisations*, III (1953) 491–502.

Clendenen, C. C. and Duignan, Peter, 'Missionaries and Colonization Societies', in *Americans in Black Africa up to 1865*, Stanford, 1964.

Collins, R. O. and Duignan, Peter, *Americans in Africa: A Preliminary Guide to American Missionary Archives and Library Manuscript Collections on Africa*, Stanford, 1963.

Earle, E. M., 'American Missions in the Near East', *Foreign Affairs*, VII (Apr 1929) 398–417.

Elsbree, O. W., *The Rise of the Missionary Spirit in America, 1790–1815*, Williamsport, Pa, 1928.

International Missionary Council, *Interpretative Statistical Survey of the World Mission of the Christian Church*, New York, 1938.

Latourette, K. S., *A History of the Expansion of Christianity*, 7 vols, London, 1937–45, vol. 6: *The Great Century in Northern Africa and Asia, A.D. 1800–1914*.

Neill, Stephen, *A History of Christian Missions*, London, 1965.

Rowbotham, A. H., *Missionary and Mandarin*, Berkeley, 1942.

Thomas, W. T., *Protestant Beginnings in Japan: The First Three Decades, 1859–1889*, Tokyo, 1959.

Tibawi, A. L., 'The American Missionaries in Beirut and Butrus al-Bustani', *St. Antony's Papers*, VI, Middle Eastern Affairs, no. 4 (London, 1963).

Van Leeuwen, A. T., *Christianity in World History*, London, 1964.

Wu, Chao-Kwang, *The International Aspect of the Missionary Movement in China*, Baltimore, 1930.

CHAPTER IV: AMERICA'S INFLUENCE ON WORLD FINANCE

America's Impact as Borrower and Lender

Aliber, R. Z., *The International Money Game*, New York, 1973.

Aubrey, H. G., *The Dollar in World Affairs: An Essay in International Financial Policy*, New York, 1964.

Bacon, Nathaniel T., 'American International Indebtedness', *Yale Review*, IX (Nov 1900) 265–85.

Clendenning, E. W., *The Euro-dollar Market*, Oxford, 1970.

Committee for Economic Development, *The Dollar and the World Monetary System*, New York, 1966.

Corey, Lewis, *The House of Morgan: A Social Biography of the Masters of Money*, New York, 1930.

Dunning, J. H., 'Capital Movements in the 20th Century', *Lloyds Bank Review*, LXXI (Apr 1964) 17–42.

220   *America's Impact on the World*

Dunning, J. H., *Studies in International Investment*, London, 1970.
Einzig, Paul, *Foreign Dollar Loans in Europe*, New York, 1965.
Feis, Herbert, *The Diplomacy of the Dollar: First Era, 1919–1932*, Baltimore, 1950.
Friedrich, Klaus, *The Euro-Dollar System*, Ann Arbor, Mich., 1968.
Hidy, R. W., 'The Origin and Functions of Anglo-American Merchant-Bankers, 1815–1860', *J. Econ. Hist.*, I (Supplement, Dec 1941) 53–66.
Jolliffe, M. F., *The United States as a Financial Centre, 1919–1933, with Reference to Imports and Exports of Capital*, Cardiff, Wales, 1935.
Kindleberger, C. P., *Power and Money: The Economics of Inernational Politics and the Politics of International Economics*, New York, 1970.
Kouwenhoven, J. A., *Partners in Banking: An Historical Portrait of a Great Private Bank, Brown Brothers, Harriman & Co., 1818–1968*, Garden City, N.Y., 1968.
Lary, H. B., *Problems of the United States as World Trader and Banker*, New York, 1963.
Madden, J. T., Nadler, M. and Sauvain, H. C., *America's Experience as a Creditor Nation*, New York, 1937.
Mikesell, R. F. (ed.), *U.S. Private and Government Investment Abroad*, Eugene, Ore., 1962.
Model, Leo, 'The Politics of Private Foreign Investment', *Foreign Affairs*, XLV (July 1967) 639–51.
Rothschild, Jacob and Leach, Rodney, 'Recent Developments in the International Capital Markets', *The Banker*, CXVII (Apr 1967) 297–307.
Tew, Brian, *International Monetary Cooperation, 1945–1963*, London, 1963.
Triffin, Robert, *The World Money Maze*, New Haven, 1966.
U.N. Dept. of Economic Affairs, *International Capital Movements During the Inter-War Period*, Lake Success, 1949.

United States Foreign Business Investments
Aitkin, H. G. J., *American Capital and Canadian Resources*, Camb., Mass., 1961.
Australia, Dept. of Trade and Industry, *Directory of Overseas Investment in Australian Manufacturing Industry*, Canberra, 1966.
Brash, D. T., *American Investment in Australian Industry*, Camb., Mass., 1966.
Caves, R. E., 'International Corporations: The Industrial Economics of Foreign Investment', *Economica*, XXXVIII (Feb 1971) 1–27.
Dickens, P. D., *American Direct Investments in Foreign Countries*, Washington, D.C., 1930.
——, *American Direct Investments in Foreign Countries—1936*, Washington, D.C., 1938.
Dunning, John, *American Investment in British Manufacturing Industry*, London, 1958.
Hou, Chi-ming, *Foreign Investment and Economic Development in China, 1840–1937*, Camb., Mass., 1965.
Kidron, Michael, *Foreign Investments in India*, London, 1965.
Kindleberger, C. P., *American Business Abroad*, New Haven, 1969.

Layton, Christopher, 'Trans-Atlantic Investments', *Atlantic Community Quarterly*, IV (summer 1966) 263-7.

Marjolin, Robert, *Europe and the United States in the World Economy*, Durham, N.C., 1953.

Marshall, H., Southard, F. A., Jr and Taylor, K. W., *Canadian-American Industry: A Study in International Investment*, New Haven, 1936.

McMillan, James and Harris, Bernard, *The American Take-Over of Britain*, New York, 1968.

Rolfe, S. E., *Capital Markets in the Atlantic Economic Relationships*, Boulogne-sur-Seine, 1967.

Safarian, A. E., *Foreign Ownership of Canadian Industry*, Toronto, 1966.

Southard, F. A., Jr, *American Industry in Europe*, Boston, Mass., 1931.

U.S. Dept. of Commerce, *United States Business Investments in Foreign Countries*, Washington, D.C., various years.

———, *U.S. Direct Investments Abroad 1966*, Part I: Balance of Payments Data, Washington, D.C., 1970.

Vernon, Raymond, *Sovereignty at Bay*, New York, 1971.

United States Foreign Aid and Development

Baldwin, D. A., *Foreign Aid and American Foreign Policy: A Documentary Analysis*, New York, 1966.

Banfield, E. C., *American Foreign Aid Doctrines*, Washington, D.C., 1963.

Bettelheim, Charles, *Planification et Croissance accélérée*, Paris, 1967.

Bingham, J. B., *Shirt-Sleeve Diplomacy: Point 4 in Action*, New York, 1954.

Bremner, R. H., *American Philanthropy*, Chicago, 1960.

Curti, Merle and Birr, Kendall, *Prelude to Point Four: American Technical Missions Overseas, 1838-1938*, Madison, Wis., 1954.

Feis, Herbert, *Foreign Aid and Foreign Policy*, New York, 1964.

Gollin, A. E., *Education for National Development: Effects of U.S. Technical Training Programs*, New York, 1969.

Heilbroner, Richard, *The Great Ascent: The Struggle for Economic Development in Our Time*, New York, 1963.

Kaplan, J. J., *The Challenge of Foreign Aid*, New York, 1967.

Loeber, T. S., *Foreign Aid: Our Tragic Experiment*, New York, 1961.

Mason, E. S., *The Diplomacy of Economic Assistance: Aid with or without 'Strings'*, Middlebury, Vt, 1966.

Mikesell, R. F., *The Economics of Foreign Aid*, Chicago, 1968.

Montgomery, J. D., *Foreign·Aid in International Politics*, Englewood Cliffs, N.J., 1967.

Myrdal, Gunnar, *Rich Lands and Poor—The Road to World Prosperity*, New York, 1957.

———, *Challenge to Affluence*, New York, 1963.

Nelson, J. M., *Aid, Influence and Foreign Policy*, New York, 1968.

Pinous, John, *Trade, Aid and Development: The Rich and Poor Nations*, New York, 1967.

Robinson, Joan, 'The Third World', in *Economics: Mainstream Readings and Radical Critiques*, ed. David Mermelstein, New York, 1972.

Rubin, S. J., *The Conscience of the Rich Nations: The Development Assistance Committee and the Common Aid Effort*, New York, 1966.

'U.S. Aid in a World Setting', *Current History*, LI (Aug 1966) entire issue.

Ward, Barbara, *Rich Nations and Poor Nations*, London, 1962.

Ward, Barbara, d'Anjou, Lenore and Runnalls, J. D.(eds.), *The Widening Gap: Development in the 1970's*, New York, 1971.

Zimmerman, L. J., *Poor Lands, Rich Lands: The Widening Gap*, New York, 1965.

CHAPTER V: THE IMPACT OF AMERICAN TECHNOLOGY

General

Clough, S. B., 'The Diffusion of Industry in the Last Century and a Half', *Studi in Onore di Armando Sapori*, Milan, 1957.

Clough, S. B. and Marburg, T. F., *The Economic Basis of American Civilization*, New York, 1968.

Elton, C. S., *The Ecology of Invasions by Animals and Plants*, London, 1958.

Ferguson, E. S., *Bibliography of the History of Technology*, Camb., Mass., 1968.

Giedion, Sigfried, *Mechanization Takes Command: A Contribution to Anonymous History*, New York, 1948.

Hacker, L. M., *The Course of American Economic Growth and Development*, New York, 1970.

Jewkes, John, 'The Growth of World Industry', *Oxford Economic Papers*, new series, III (Feb 1951) 1–15.

Kranzberg, Melvin and Pursell, C. W., Jr, *Technology in Western Civilization*, 2 vols, New York, 1967.

Kuznets, Simon, *Economic Growth of Nations*, Camb., Mass., 1971.

Maddison, Angus, *Economic Growth in the West: Comparative Experience in Europe and North America*, New York, 1964.

North, D. C., *The Economic Growth of the United States, 1790–1860*, Englewood Cliffs, N.J., 1961.

Rolt, L. T. C., *A Short History of Machine Tools*, Camb., Mass., 1965.

Rosenberg, Nathan, *Technology and American Economic Growth*, New York, 1972.

Rostow, W. W., *The Stages of Economic Growth*, Camb., Mass., 1959.

Sarton, George, *A History of Science*, Camb., Mass., 1952.

Schmookler, Jacob, *Invention and Economic Growth*, Camb., Mass., 1966.

Singer, C. J., *A Short History of Scientific Ideas to 1900*, Oxford, 1959.

Smith, C. S. (ed.), *The Sorby Centennial Symposium on the History of Metallurgy, Proceedings*, New York, 1965.

Thomas, W. L. et al., *Man's Role in Changing the Face of the Earth*, Chicago, 1956.

Usher, A. P., *A History of Mechanical Inventions*, Boston, Mass., 1959.

Science and Technology in America

Browne, C. A., *Thomas Jefferson and the Scientific Trends of His Time*, Waltham, Mass., 1944.

Burlingame, Roger, *Backgrounds of Power: The Human Story of Mass Production*, New York, 1949.
——, *Machines That Built America*, New York, 1953.
Copley, F. B., *Frederick W. Taylor, Father of Scientific Management*, 2 vols, New York, 1923.
Danhof, C. H., *Change in Agriculture: The Northern United States, 1820–1870*, Camb., Mass., 1969.
Daniels, G. H., 'The Big Questions in the History of American Technology', *Technology and Culture*, XI (Jan 1970) 1–21.
de Camp, L. S., *The Heroic Age of American Invention*, Garden City, N.Y., 1961.
Dupree, A. H., 'Science in America – A Historian's View', *Cahiers d'Histoire Mondiale*, VIII (1964–5) 613–19.
Gilfillan, S. C., *Invention and the Patent System*, Washington, D.C., 1964.
——, 'Invention as a Factor in Economic History', *Journal of Economic History*, supplement 5 (Dec 1945) 66–85.
——, *The Sociology of Invention*, Chicago, 1935.
Gray, L. C., *History of Agriculture in the Southern United States to 1860*, Washington, D.C., 1933.
Haber, L. F., *The Chemical Industry During the Nineteenth Century: A Study of the Economic Aspect of Applied Chemistry in Europe and North America*, Oxford, 1958.
Hacker, L. M., *The World of Andrew Carnegie: 1865–1901*, Philadelphia, 1968.
Jaffe, Bernard, *Men of Science in America*, New York, 1958.
Jewkes, John, Sawyers, David and Stillerman, Richard, *The Sources of Invention*, London, 1958.
MacLaren, Malcolm, *The Rise of the Electrical Industry During the Nineteenth Century*, Princeton, 1943.
McCormick, C. H., *The Century of the Reaper*, Boston, Mass., 1931.
Mirsky, Jeanette and Nevins, Allan, *The World of Eli Whitney*, New York, 1952.
Nevins, Allan, *John D. Rockefeller: The Heroic Age of American Enterprise*, 2 vols, New York, 1940.
Nordenskiöld, Erland, 'The American Indian as an Inventor', *J. Roy. Anthropolog. Inst.*, LIX (1929) 273–309.
North, D. C., 'Industrialization in the United States'. *Cambridge Economic History of Europe*, ed. H. J. Habakkuk and M. Postan, vol. VI, Cambridge, 1966.
Rasmussen, W. D., 'The Impact of Technological Change on American Agriculture, 1862–1962', *J. Econ. Hist.*, XXII (Dec 1962) 578–91.
Rezneck, Samuel, 'The Rise and Early Development of Industrial Consciousness in the United States, 1750–1830', *J. Econ. and Bus. Hist.*, IV (supplement, Aug 1932) 784–811.
Roe, J. W., *English and American Tool Builders*, New Haven, 1916.
——, 'Interchangeable Manufacture', *Newcomen Society Transactions*, XVII (1936–7) 165–74.
Rothbarth, Erwin, 'Causes of the Superior Efficiency of U.S.A. Industry as Compared with British Industry', *Econ. Journal*, LVI (Sep 1946) 383–90.

224   *America's Impact on the World*

Saul, S. B. (ed.), *Technological Change: The United States and Britain in the Nineteenth Century*, London, 1970.
Sawyer, J. E., 'The Social Basis of the American System of Manufacturing', *J. Econ. Hist.*, XIV (Fall 1954) 361–79.
Strassmann, W. P., *Risk and Technological Innovation: American Manufacturing Methods During the Nineteenth Century*, Ithaca, N.Y., 1959.
Temin, Peter, 'Labour Scarcity and the Problem of American Industrial Efficiency in the 1850's', *J. Econ. Hist.*, XXVI (Sep 1966) 277.–98; Drummond, I. A., 'A Comment', (on Temin's article) XXVII (Sep 1967) 383–90; Temin, Peter, 'A Reply', (to Drummond's 'Comment') XXVIII (Mar 1968) 124–5.
Wall, J. F., *Andrew Carnegie*, New York, 1970.
White, Morton, *Science and Sentiment in America: Philosophical Thought from Jonathan Edwards to John Dewey*, New York, 1972.
Williamson, H. F., 'Mass Production, Mass Consumption and American Industrial Development', *Contributions and Communications of the First International Conference of Economic History* (Stockholm, 1960) I 137–47.
Woodbury, R. S., *History of the Gear-Cutting Machine: A Historical Study in Geometry and Machines*, Camb., Mass., 1958.
——, *History of the Grinding Machine: A Historical Study in Tools and Precision Production*, Camb., Mass., 1959.
——, *History of the Lathe to 1850: A Study in the Growth of a Technical Element of an Industrial Economy*, Cleveland, 1961.
——, *History of the Milling Machine: A Study in Technical Development*, Camb., Mass., 1960.

The Diffusion of American Technology
Aitkin, Hugh *et al.*, *The American Economic Impact on Canada*, Durham, N.C., 1959.
Cohen, Bernard, 'The New World as a Source of Science for Europe', *Actes du IXe Congres International d'Histoire des Sciences*, (Barcelona 1959) 95–130.
Merrill, E. D., 'Plants and Civilization', in *Independence, Convergence and Borrowing in Institutions, Thought, and Art*, Camb., Mass., 1937.
Woodruff, William, 'Growth of the Rubber Industry of Great Britain and the United States', *J. Econ. Hist.*, XV (Dec 1955) 376–91.
——, 'An Inquiry into the Origins of Invention and the Intercontinental Diffusion of Techniques of Production in the Rubber Industry', *Econ. Record*, XXXVIII (Dec 1962) 479–97.
——, 'Origins of an Early English Rubber Manufactory', *Bus. Hist. Rev.*, XXV (Mar 1951) 31–51.

Science, Technology and Civilization
Ayres, C. E., *Science, the False Messiah*, Indianapolis, 1927.
Clough, S. B., *Basic Values of Western Civilization*, New York, 1960.
Dorfman, Joseph, *Thorstein Veblen and His America*, New York, 1961.
Ellul, Jacques, *The Technological Society*, translated by John Wilkinson, New York, 1964.

Jünger, F. G., *The Failure of Technology*, Hinsdale, Ill., 1949.

Lombroso-Ferrero, Gina, *The Tragedies of Progress*, New York, 1931.

Marx, W. J., *Mechanization and Culture*, St Louis, 1941.

McHale, John, 'Science, Technology and Change', *The Annals*, CCCLXXIII (Sep 1967) 120–40.

Mesthene, E. G., 'Some General Implications of the Research of the Harvard University Program on Technology and Society', *Technology and Culture*, X (Oct 1969) 489–513 and 535–6.

Mumford, Lewis, *The Myth of the Machine: Technics and Human Development*, New York, 1967.

——, *Technics and Civilization*, New York, 1963.

Reuleaux, Franz, 'Technology and Civilization', *Smithsonian Institution Annual Report, 1890*, Washington, D.C., 1891, 705–19.

Rhee, H. A., *Office Automation in Social Perspective: The Progress and Social Implications of Electronic Data Processing*, Oxford, 1968.

Veblen, Thorstein, *The Place of Science in Modern Civilization and Other Essays*, New York, 1919.

CHAPTER VI: AMERICA'S CONTRIBUTION TO THE CONQUEST OF DISTANCE

General

Chatterton, E. K., *Sailing Ships and Their Story*, London, 1923.

Clarke, Arthur C. (comp.), *The Coming of the Space Age: Famous Accounts of Man's Probing of the Universe*, New York, 1967.

de Latil, Pierre, *Thinking by Machine: A Study of Cybernetics*, translated by Y. M. Golla, Boston, 1956.

Dizard, W. P., *Television: A World View*, Syracuse, N.Y., 1966.

Dunlap, O, E., *Communications in Space: From Wireless to Satellite Relay*, New York, 1962.

Emme, E. M. (ed.), *The Impact of Air Power: National Security and World Politics*, Princeton, 1959.

Ley, Willy, *Rockets, Missiles and Men in Space*, New York, 1968.

Locklin, D. P., *Economics of Transportation*, Homewood, Ill., 1972, 7th edition.

North, D. C., 'Ships, Railroads and Economic Growth', *Growth and Welfare in the American Past: A New Economic History*, Englewood Cliffs, N.J., 1966.

Page, R. M., *The Origin of Radar*, Garden City, N.Y., 1962.

Taylor, George R., *The Transportation Revolution, 1815–1860*, New York, 1951.

Tyler, D. B., *Steam Conquers the Atlantic*, New York, 1939.

Space and Time

Giedion, Sigfried, *Space, Time and Architecture*, Camb., mass., 1962.

Innis, H. A., *Changing Concepts of Time*, Toronto, 1952.

Lewis, Wyndham, *Time and Western Man*, New York, 1928.

Mead, S. E., 'The American People: Their Space, Time and Religion', *J. Religion*, XXXIV (Oct 1954) 244–55.

Moore, W. E., *Man, Time and Society*, New York, 1963.

Water Transport

Albion, R. G., *Square-Riggers on Schedule*, Princeton, 1938.

Alexandersson, Gunnar and Noström, Göran, *World Shipping: An Economic Geography of Ports and Seaborne Trade*, New York, 1963.

Ashley, C. W., *The Yankee Whaler*, Boston, Mass., 1938.

Barrows, E. M., *The Great Commodore: The Exploits of Matthew Calbraith Perry*, New York, 1935.

Carse, Robert, *The Moonrakers: The Story of the Clipper Ship Men*, New York, 1961.

Davis, Forrest, *The Atlantic System: The Story of Anglo-American Control of the Seas*, New York, 1941.

Dunmore, W. T., *Ship Subsidies*, New York, 1907.

Flexner, J. T., *Steamboats Come True: American Inventors in Action*, New York, 1944.

Frederickson, J. W., 'American Shipping in the Trade with Northern Europe, 1783–1880', *Scand. Econ. Hist. Rev.*, IV (1956).

Goodrich, Carter, *Canals and American Economic Development*, New York, 1961.

Hart, R. A. *et al.*, *The Great White Fleet: Its Voyage Around the World, 1907–1909*, Boston, Mass., 1965.

Hatcher, H. H., *The Great Lakes*, London, 1944.

Henderson, Daniel, *The Hidden Coasts: A Biography of Admiral Charles Wilkes*, New York, 1953.

Hohman, E. P., *The American Whaleman*, New York, 1928.

Keiler, Hans, *American Shipping*, Jena, 1913.

Kirker, James, *Adventures to China: Americans in the Southern Oceans, 1792–1812*, New York, 1970.

Latourette, K. S., *Voyages of American Ships to China, 1784–1844*, New Haven, 1927.

Lawrence, S. A., *United States Merchant Shipping Policies and Practices*, Washington, D.C., 1966.

Liu, Kwang-Ching, 'Steamship Enterprise in Nineteenth-Century China', *J. Asian Studies*, XVIII, (Aug 1959) 435–55.

Morrison, J. H., *History of American Steam Navigation*, New York, 1958.

Sprout, Harold and Sprout, Margaret, *The Rise of American Naval Power, 1776–1918*, Princeton, 1967.

——, *Toward a New Order of Sea Power: American Naval Policy and the World Scene, 1918–1922*, Princeton, 1940.

Stackpole, E. A., *Whales and Destiny; the Rivalry between America, France and Britain for Control of the Southern Whale Fishery, 1785–1825*, Amherst, Mass., 1972.

Tate, E. M., 'American Merchant and Naval Contacts with China, 1784–1850', *American Neptune*, XXXI (July 1971) 177–91.

U.S. House of Representatives, Committee on Merchant Marine and Fisheries, *American Merchant Marine in Foreign Trade and the National Defense: Report*, Washington, D.C., 1910.

Ver Steeg, C. L., 'Financing and Outfitting the First United States Ship to China', *Pacific Hist. Rev.*, XXII, (Feb 1953) 1–12.

Zeis, P. M., *American Shipping Policy*, Princeton, 1938.

Land Transport

Crabb, A. R., *Birth of a Giant: The Men and Incidents that Gave America the Motorcar*, Philadelphia, 1969.

Douglass, P. F., *Six Upon the World: Toward an American Culture for an Industrial Age*, Boston, Mass., 1954.

Ford, Henry, *My Life and Work*, Garden City, N.Y., 1922.

Gates, P. W., *The Illinois Central Railroad and Its Colonization Work*, Harvard Economic Studies, XLII, Camb., Mass., 1934.

Jenks, L. H., 'Britain and American Railway Development', *J. Econ. Hist.*, XI (Fall 1951) 375–88.

Nevins, Allan, with collaboration of Hill, F. E., *Ford*, 3 vols, New York, 1954–63.

Overton, Richard, *Burlington Route*, New York, 1965.

Pletcher, David M., 'The Building of the Mexican Railway', *Hisp. Am. Hist. Rev.*, XXX (Feb 1950) 26–62.

Rae, J. B., *American Automobile Manufacturers: The First Forty Years*, Philadelphia, 1959.

Riegel, R. E., 'Trans-Mississippi Railroads During the Fifties', *Miss. Valley Hist. Rev.*, X (Sep 1923) 153–72.

Rippy, J. F., 'The Inter-American Highway', *Pacific Hist. Rev.*, XXIV (Aug 1955) 287–98.

Stover, J. F., *The Life and Decline of the American Railroad*, New York, 1970.

Wilgus, W. J., *The Railway Interrelations of the United States and Canada*, New Haven, 1937.

Winther, O. O., *Express and Stagecoach Days in California, from the Gold Rush to the Civil War*, Stanford, 1936.

——, *Via Western Express and Stagecoach*, Stanford, 1945.

Air Transport

Kelly, F. C., *The Wright Brothers*, New York, 1951.

Mansfield, Harold, *Vision: The Story of Boeing, a Saga of the Sky and the New Horizons of Space*, New York, 1966.

Rae, J. B., *Climb to Greatness: The American Aircraft Industry, 1920–1960*, Camb., Mass., 1968.

Smith, H. L., *Airways Abroad*, Madison, Wis., 1950.

Communications

De Forest, Lee, *Father of Radio: The Autobiography of Lee De Forest*, Chicago, 1950.

Field, H. M., *History of the Atlantic Telegraph*, New York, 1867.

Harley, J. E., *World-Wide Influence of the Cinema*, Los Angeles, 1940.

Klapper, J. T., *The Effects of Mass Communication*, Glencoe, Ill., 1960.

Mott, F. L., *American Journalism: A History, 1690–1960*, New York, 1962.

Thompson, R. L., *Wiring a Continent*, Princeton, 1947.

228 *America's Impact on the World*

CHAPTER VII: AMERICA AND WORLD COMMERCE
General
Ashworth, William, *A Short History of the International Economy Since 1850*, London, 1962.
Bruchey, S. W., *The Roots of American Economic Growth, 1607–1861*, New York, 1965.
Condliffe, J. B., *The Commerce of Nations*, London, 1951.
Dietrich, E. B., *World Trade*, New York, 1939.
——, *Far Eastern Trade of the United States*, New York, 1940.
Haberler, Gottfried, 'Integration and Growth of the World Economy', *Am. Econ. Rev.*, LIV (Mar 1964) 1–21.
Hilgerdt, Folke, *Industrialization and Foreign Trade*, Geneva, 1945.
Horn, P. V., *International Trade*, New York, 1945.
Kilduff, V. R., 'Economic Factors in the Development of Canadian-American Trade', *Southern Econ. Journal*, VIII (Oct 1941) 201–17.
Myrdal, Gunnar, *An International Economy*, New York, 1956.
Walton, S. D., *American Business and Its Environment*, New York, 1966.
Woodruff, William, *The Emergence of an International Economy, 1700–1914*, (London 1971).

Theoretical
Berrill, K., 'International Trade and the Rate of Economic Growth', *Econ. Hist. Rev.*, XII (Apr 1960) 351–9.
Cairncross, A. K., 'International Trade and Economic Development', *Kyklos*, XIII (1960) 545–58.
Hamberg, Daniel, *Principles of a Growing Economy*, New York, 1961.
Harrod, Roy and Hague, Douglas (eds.), *International Trade Theory in a Developing World*, London, 1963.
Kenen, P. B., *International Economics*, Englewood Cliffs, N.J., 1964.
Kindleberger, C. P., *Foreign Trade and the National Economy*, New Haven, 1962.
——, *International Economics*, Homewood, Ill., 1963.
——, *The Terms of Trade*, Camb., Mass., 1956.
Nurkse, Ragnar, *Patterns of Trade and Development*, Stockholm, 1959.
Viner, Jacob, *International Trade and Economic Development*, Glencoe, Ill., 1952.

American Foreign Trade
The Colonial Period
Andrews, C. M., 'Colonial Commerce', *Am. Hist. Rev.*, XX (Oct 1914) 43–63.
Bailyn, Bernard, 'Communications and Trade: The Atlantic in the Seventeenth Century', *J. Econ. Hist.*, XIII (Fall 1953) 378–87.
——, *The New England Merchants in the Seventeenth Century*, Camb., Mass., 1955.
Barrow, T. C., *Trade and Empire: The British Customs Service in Colonial America, 1660–1775*, Camb., Mass., 1967.
Bhagat, G., 'America's First Contacts with India, 1784–1785', *Am. Neptune*, XXXI (Jan 1971) 38–48.

Biddulph, John, *The Pirates of Malabar*, London, 1907.

Bradlee, F. B. C., *Piracy in the West Indies and Its Suppression*, Salem, 1923.

Bruce, P. A., *Economic History of Virginia in the Seventeenth Century*, 2 vols, New York, 1895.

Dulles, F. R., *The Old China Trade*, Boston, 1930.

Haring, C. H., *The Buccaneers to the West Indies in the XVII Century*, New York, 1910.

Harrington, V. D., *The New York Merchant on the Eve of the Revolution*, New York, 1935.

Jameson, J. F. (ed.), *Privateering and Piracy in the Colonial Period*, New York, 1923.

Kammen, M. G., *Empire and Interest: The American Colonies and the Politics of Mercantilism*, Philadephia, 1970.

Pares, Richard, *Yankees and Creoles: The Trade between North America and the West Indies Before the American Revolution*, Camb., Mass., 1956.

Parry, J. H., *The Establishment of the European Hegemony, 1415–1715: Trade and Exploration in the Age of the Renaissance*, New York, 1961.

Williamson, J. G., 'International Trade and United States Economic Development, 1827–1843, *J. Econ. Hist.*, xxi (Sep 1961) 372–83.

1789–1860

Bennett, N. R. and Brooks, G. E., Jr (eds.), *New England Merchants in Africa, A History Through Documents, 1802 to 1865*, Brookline, Mass., 1965.

Carnes, J. A., *Journal . . .*, Boston, 1852.

Crosby, A. W., *America, Russia, Hemp and Napoleon*, Columbus, Ohio, 1965.

Dart, M. S., *Yankee Traders at Sea and Ashore*, New York, 1964.

Evans, C. H., 'Exports, Domestic, from the United States to All Countries from 1789 to 1883, Inclusive', *House Miscellaneous Document*, no. 49, part 2, 48th Cong., 1st Sess., 1884, 1–266.

Fairbank, J. K., *Trade and Diplomacy on the China Coast: The Opening of the Treaty Ports, 1842–1854*, 2 vols, Camb., Mass., 1953.

Furber, Holden, 'The Beginnings of American Trade with India, 1784–1812', *New England Quarterly*, xi (June 1938) 235–65.

Kimball, G. S., *The East-India Trade of Providence from 1787–1807*, Providence, R. I., 1896.

White, P. L., *The Beckmans of New York in Politics and Commerce, 1647–1877*, New York, 1956.

1860–1914

Beu, M. J., *The Open Door Doctrine*, New York, 1923.

Campbell, C. S., *Special Business Interests and the Open Door Policy*, New Haven, 1951.

Rothstein, Morton, 'America in the International Rivalry for the British Wheat Market, 1860–1914', *Miss. Valley Hist. Rev.*, xlvii (Dec 1960) 401–18.

Simon, Matthew and Novak, David, 'Some Dimensions of the American Commercial Invasion of Europe, 1871–1914: An Introductory Essay', *J. Econ. Hist.*, XXIV (Dec 1964) 591–608.
Varg, Paul A., 'The Myth of the China Market, 1890–1914', *Am. Hist. Rev.*, LXXIII (Feb 1968) 742–58.

Post-First World War
Brown, W. A., Jr, *The United States and the Restoration of World Trade*, Washington, D.C., 1950.
Dowd, D. F. (ed.), *America's Role in the World Economy: The Challenge to Orthodoxy*, Boston, Mass., 1966.
Hinshaw, R. W., *The European Community and American Trade*, New York, 1964.
Humphrey, D. D., *American Imports*, New York, 1955.
——, *The United States and the Common Market*, New York, 1962.
Hunsberger, W. S., *Japan and the United States in World Trade*, New York, 1964.
Krause, L. B., 'European Economic Integration and the United States', *Am. Econ. Rev.*, XIII (May 1963) 185–96.
Maddison, Angus, 'Growth and Fluctuation in the World Economy, 1870–1960', *Banca Nazionale del Lavoro Quarterly Review*, XV (June 1962) 127–95.

Tariff History
Taussig, F. W., *The Tariff History of the United States*, New York, 1931.
Towle, L. W., *International Trade and Commercial Policy*, New York, 1956, *U.S. Tariff Commission Report*, 'Implications of Multinational Firms for World Trade and Investment and for U.S. Trade and Labor', Washington, D.C., Feb 1973.

CHAPTER VIII: EPILOGUE

Adams, Henry, *The Degradation of the Democratic Dogma*, New York, 1919.
Adams, J. T., *Our Business Civilization: Some Aspects of American Culture*, New York, 1929.
Baldwin, L. D., *The Meaning of America: Essays Toward an Understanding of the American Spirit*, Pittsburgh, 1955.
Barghoorn, F. C., *The Soviet Image of the United States*, New York, 1950.
Barzini, Luigi, *Americans Are Alone in the World*, New York, 1953.
Beard, Charles and Beard, Mary, *The American Spirit: A Study of the Idea of Civilization in the United States*, New York, 1942.
Belloc, Hilaire, *The Contrast*, London, 1923.
Boorstein, D. J., *The Image: or, What Happened to the American Dream*, New York, 1962.
Boulding, Kenneth, *The Meaning of the Twentieth Century*, New York, 1964.

Bradshaw, George (ed.), *A Collection of Travel in America by Various Hands*, New York, 1948.

Brogan, Denis, *America in the Modern World*, New Brunswick, N.J., 1960.

——, *The American Character*, New York, 1944.

Bruckberger, Raymond, *Image of America*, translated by C. G. Paulding and V. Peterson, New York, 1959.

Bryce, J. B., *The American Commonwealth*, 2 vols, New York, 1888, 1931–3.

Chester, E. W., *Europe Views America*, Washington, D.C., 1962.

Commager, H. S. (ed.), *America in Perspective: The United States Through Foreign Eyes*, New York, 1947.

——, *The American Mind: An Interpretation of American Thought and Character Since the 1880's*, New Haven, 1950.

Curti, M. E., *American Paradox: The Conflict of Thought and Action*, New Brunswick, N.J., 1956.

Fulbright, J. W., *The Arrogance of Power*, New York, 1966.

Galantiere, Louis (ed.), *America and the Mind of Europe*, New York, 1952.

Hartshorne, T. L., *The Distorted Image: Changing Conceptions of the American Character Since Turner*, Cleveland, 1968.

Jones, H. M., *The Pursuit of Happiness*, Camb., Mass., 1953.

Joseph, F. M. (ed.), *As Others See Us: The United States Through Foreign Eyes*, Princeton, 1959.

Kahler, Erich, *Man the Measure*, New York, 1943.

Kaufman, B. I. (ed.), *Washington's Farewell Address: The View From the 20th Century*, Chicago, 1969.

Laski, H. J., *The American Democracy*, New York, 1948.

Lillibridge, G. D. (ed.), *The American Image, Past and Present*, Lexington, Mass., 1968.

Madariaga, Salvador de, *Americans*, London, 1930.

Mead, R. O., *The Atlantic Legacy*, New York, 1969.

Maritain, Jacques, *Reflections on America*, New York, 1958.

Mosier, R. D., *The American Temper: Patterns of Our Intellectual Heritage*, Berkeley, 1952.

Nef, J. U., *The United States and Civilization*, Chicago, 1942.

Nevins, Allan, *America in World Affairs*, New York, 1942.

—— (ed.), *America Through British Eyes*, New York, 1948.

Niebuhr, Reinhold, *The Irony of American History*, New York, 1952.

Niebuhr, Reinhold and Heimert, Alan, *A Nation So Conceived*, New York, 1963.

Osgood, Robert E., *Ideals and Self-Interest in America's Foreign Relations: The Great Transformation of the Twentieth Century*, Chicago, 1953.

Potter, D. M., *People of Plenty: Economic Abundance and the American Character*, Chicago, 1954.

Schlesinger, A. M., 'What Then is the American, This New Man?' in *Paths to the Present*, New York, 1949.

Toynbee, A. J., *America and the World Revolutions*, New York, 1962.

von Keyserling, H. A., *America Set Free*, New York, 1929.

Wedge, Bryant, *Visitors to the United States and How They See Us*, Princeton, 1965.

Tables

TABLE I

The Distribution and Employment of Peace Corps Volunteers, 1961–71

AFRICA	1961	1962	1963	1964	1965	1966	1967	1968	1969	1970	Est. 1971	Est. 1972
Ghana	51	114	140	128	109	130	252	207	212	285	240	245
Nigeria	104	189	473	559	621	742	328	111	66	...	..	..
Sierra Leone	37	125	130	148	198	219	289	285	286	211	140	145
Tanzania/Tanganyika	35	62	97	292	335	330	166	41	..	..	..	..
Cameroon		40	90	105	101	84	55	45	50	64	55	60
Ethiopia		276	415	434	587	465	420	458	318	156	170	175
Ivory Coast		31	56	56	60	75	82	98	110	108	95	100
Liberia		89	283	350	347	295	222	261	256	147	145	150
Niger		7	14	43	81	114	122	84	71	71	50	55
Senegal		5	66	68	78	91	121	129	95	93	75	80
Somali Republic		44	29	58	86	99	96	74	42	..	..	..
Togo		46	37	63	75	77	104	89	77	88	55	60
Gabon		72	36	52	62	57	..	..	..	..	..	..
Malawi/Nyasaland		43	205	254	218	117	138	140	50	25	25	
Guinea		54	70	66	..	..	19	22	..	..		
Kenya				75	123	197	225	198	243	295	200	205
Uganda				38	35	33	114	91	72	70	95	95
Botswana						58	54	74	53	60	60	65
Chad						33	30	41	52	45	30	35
Mauritania						12	..	..	..	..	..	..
Gambia							17	14	18	39	50	50
Upper Volta							47	44	56	49	45	60
Lesotho							71	59	50	27	30	30
Dahomey								26	32	43	30	35
Swaziland								30	41	24	30	35
Mali										1	25	25
Mauritius										23	20	20
Republic of the Congo										9	50	50
Totals	227	1028	1999	2728	3208	3334	2989	2597	2359	1980	1715	1800

LATIN AMERICA	1961	1962	1963	1964	1965	1966	1967	1968	1969	1970	Est. 1971	Est. 1972
Chile	45	100	107	268	383	389	317	236	201	109	90	90
Colombia	62	166	429	610	512	636	687	632	276	132	210	225
Eastern Caribbean	15	15	17	15	47	41	133	163	163	168	155	160
Brazil		145	214	489	652	664	616	538	405	334	215	225
El Salvador		23	44	45	60	132	124	104	58	67	60	65
Jamaica		34	38	50	85	109	128	121	159	199	160	165
Venezuela		91	99	250	326	334	359	195	164	129	165	175
Bolivia		70	121	237	306	308	278	236	133	130	..	..
British Honduras		33	27	28	48	45	46	40	28	42	45	50
Dominican Republic		62	173	114	105	157	151	161	68	40	50	50
Ecuador		167	236	308	258	243	297	267	112	114	120	135
Honduras		25	61	106	118	128	179	152	106	117	100	110
Peru		202	366	404	417	391	329	194	101	220	190	200
Costa Rica			68	54	85	171	134	86	57	102	110	115
Guatemala			112	113	70	98	110	111	75	77	100	105
Panama			57	155	140	131	186	154	84	107	..	..
Uruguay			18	19	51	66	23	4	22	14	15	15
Guyana						43	53	44	55	24	..	..
Paraguay						1	34	51	66	70	50	50
Nicaragua								9	28	50	60	65
Totals	122	1133	2187	3265	3663	4087	4184	3498	2361	2245	1895	2000

TABLE I—*continued*

EAST ASIA AND THE PACIFIC	1961	1962	1963	1964	1965	1966	1967	1968	1969	1970	Est. 1971	Est. 1972
Philippines	182	573	548	335	569	706	758	730	410	347	275	320
Malaysia				119	466	549	588	519	313	403	310	335
Malaya		114	143	171	46	..	..	..	..	..	..	..
Sabah/Sarawak		62	85	114	57	6	..	..	..	..	..	..
Thailand		99	243	278	311	422	308	253	231	216	200	215
Indonesia			17	45	..	..	..	..	..	..	..	..
Korea											110	120
Micronesia						96	266	196	118	174	295	320
Western Samoa						316	663	546	390	286	270	225
Tonga							76	117	35	46	70	85
Fiji							41	103	31	40	65	80
Solomon Islands								48	109	98	9	20
Totals	182	848	1036	1062	1449	2095	2700	2512	1637	1610	1604	1720

NORTH AFRICA, NEAR EAST, SOUTH ASIA	1961	1962	1963	1964	1965	1966	1967	1968	1969	1970	Est. 1971	Est. 1972
India	26	74	123	275	590	1264	977	561	452	433	390	425
Pakistan	57	120	195	179	47	13	..	..	..	..	..	..
Tunisia		64	92	165	218	238	239	201	136	84	100	110
Afghanistan		9	35	112	186	176	197	205	137	112	135	150
Ceylon		39	34	..	..	..	58	39	14	..	..	..
Cyprus		22	22	..	..	..	..	..	..	..	..	..
Iran		43	45	160	255	331	328	245	200	153	155	165
Nepal		69	101	118	134	201	239	188	126	143	160	175
Turkey		39	142	319	527	447	220	236	164	1	1	5
Morocco			103	104	103	109	84	101	106	132	135	150
Libya						18	13	177	..	..	..	..
Malta										7	9	10
Totals	83	479	892	1432	2060	2797	2355	1953	1335	1065	1085	1190

Regional Capacities of Volunteers in 1971

	Africa		Latin America		East Asia and the Pacific		North Africa Near East, S. Asia	
Number of volunteers in:								
Agriculture	303	(17%)	609	(32%)	176	(11%)	297	(35%)
Education	920	(52%)	391	(21%)	1031	(66%)	336	(40%)
Community Development	105	(6%)	229	(12%)	23	(2%)	6	(1%)
Health	158	(9%)	145	(8%)	179	(11%)	25	(3%)
Other	295	(16%)	507	(27%)	163	(10%)	176	(21%)
Total	1781*	(100%)	1881*	(100%)	1572*	(100%)	840*	(100%)

* Figures do not include 1971 trainees.

Note: The actual number of Volunteers in each country may vary from these projections as Volunteer allocations for each country are made at a later date on the basis of firm host country requests and worldwide comparisons of programmes.

Source: Director of Action, *Peace Corps Tenth Annual Report* (Washington, D.C., 1971) pp. 17–23.

TABLE II

Geographical Distribution of Total Private United States Foreign Investments compared with those of the United Kingdom, France and Germany for Selected Years
(in millions of U.S. dollars to the nearest $50 million)

Area of investment	1913					1938					1960				1970			
	U.S.	U.K.	Fr.	Ger.	World	U.S.	U.K.	Fr.	Ger.	World	U.S.	U.K. (1957)	West Ger. (1962)	World	U.S.	U.K.	West Ger.	World
North America																		
U.S.A.	..	4,250	400	950	7,100	..	2,750	400	100	7,000	..	..	100	18,400	..	..	..	48,800
Canada	900	2,800	100	200	3,800	3,725	2,700	50	..	6,650	16,600	..	150	22,200	35,000	..	..	..
Total (Vertical %)	900 (26%)	7,050 (36%)	500 (5%)	1,150 (20%)	11,100	3,725 (34%)	5,450 (24%)	450 (12%)	100 (15%)	13,650	16,600 (37%)	..	250 (20%)	40,600	35,000 (34%)	..	..	..
Other Western Hemisphere																		
Mexico	850	500	400	n.a.	2,200	675	900	100	n.	1,800								
Argentina	n.	1,550	400	200	2,950	600	1,950	150	50	3,200								
Brazil	n.	700	700	500	2,200	550	800	50	n.	2,000								
Chile	n.	300	50	n.	1,550	600	400	100	n.	1,300								
Unclassified	800	650	50	200	..	800	850	100	100	3,000								
Total (Vertical %)	1,650 (47%)	3,700 (19%)	1,600 (18%)	900 (15%)	8,900	3,225 (29%)	4,900 (21%)	400 (11%)	150 (23%)	11,300	9,900 (22%)	..	350 (28%)	..	18,100 (17%)	..	..	..
Europe (Vertical %)	700 (20%)	1,050 (5%)	4,700 (52%)	2,550 (44%)	12,000	2,325 (21%)	1,750 (8%)	1,050 (27%)	250 (39%)	10,300	10,000 (22%)	..	500 (40%)	..	29,600 (28%)	..	..	..
Oceania (Vertical %)	20 (n.%)	2,000 (10%)	100 (1%)	..	2,200	225 (2%)	3,350 (15%)	n.a.	n.a.	4,450	c. 1,000 (2%)	..	30 (2%)	..	..	..	..	..
Asia (Vertical %)	250 (7%)	3,550 (18%)	1,250 (14%)	700 (12%)	7,100	600 (5%)	5,230 (23%)	900 (23%)	150 (23%)	11,200	c. 2,200 (5%)	..	50 (4%)	..	..	..	..	..
Africa (Vertical %)	10 (n.%)	2,450 (12%)	900 (10%)	500 (9%)	4,050	100 (1%)	2,150 (9%)	1,050 (27%)	..	4,050	c. 900 (2%)	..	80 (6%)	..	..	..	..	..
Unallocated (Vertical %)	..	..	..	..	..	875 (8%)	..	..	..	..	c. 4,800 (10%)	26,400 (100%)	..	..	22,000 (21%)	..	..	..

TABLE III
Private International Long-term Investments of the United States, 1869–1970 (in billions of dollars)

Year	Direct	Portfolio	Total	Direct as a percentage of total
1869	n.	0·1	0·1	0
1897	0·6	0·1	0·7	86
1908	1·6	0·9	2·5	64
1914	2·7	0·8	3·5	78
1919	3·9	2·6	6·5	60
1924	5·4	4·6	10·0	54
1930	8·0	7·2	15·2	53
1935	7·8	4·8	12·6	62
1940	7·3	4·0	11·3	65
1945	8·4	5·3	13·7	61
1950	11·8	5·7	17·5	68
1957	25·3	8·3	33·6	75
1964	44·4	20·5	64·9	68
1970	78·1	26·6	104·7	75

Sources:

Historical Statistics of the United States from Colonial Times to 1957, Series U193–206, 565.

Investments of the United States (Washington, D.C., U.S. Government Printing Office, 1953).

National Industrial Conference Board, *Economic Almanac for 1967–68*, 483–4.

U.S. Dept. of Commerce, *Survey of Current Business* (various).

Footnotes to Table II

* This figure differs slightly from the estimate of $1·4 billion made by the Deutsche Bundesbank whose *Monthly Reports* I have used.

†Guesses made by Sir Alec Cairncross in *Control of International Capital Movements* (Washington, D.C., 1973) 15.

n. = negligible; n.a. = not available.

Sources: Considerable variation exists concerning the amount of private foreign investment. In addition to the data contained in my earlier *Impact of Western Man*, I have drawn upon the *Historical Statistics* of both the United States and Canada. I have also used the various *Trade Information Bulletin* and *Survey of Current Business* issued by the United States government; also, the statistical appendix of the reports of the U.S. National Advisory Council on International Monetary and Financial Policies, as well as the various United Nation's publications, such as the *International Capital Movements during the Inter-War Period, 1949*, and *The International Flow of Private Capital* for various years. British figures, apart from secondary sources given in the bibliography, I have drawn from British Government papers, including copies of the *Board of Trade Journal* and the *Bank of England, Quarterly Bulletin*, and *Business Monitor M4 – Overseas Transactions*, U.K. Department of Trade and Industry, London, April 1973.

TABLE IV

The Geographical Distribution and Employment of United States Priva Foreign Business Investments, 1914–70

PART A – 1914

Country or area	Total investment in country m$	Distribution of U.S. Funds by country %	Total investment in industry m$	Manufacturing Distribution by World Industry Group %	Employment of U.S. Funds within country %	Total investment in industry m$	Mining Distribution by World Industry Group %	Employment of U.S. Funds within country %	Total investment in industry m$	Petroleum Distribution by World Industry Group %	Employment of U.S. Funds %
Canada	618	23·3	221	46·2	35·8	159	22·1	25·7	25	7·3	4
Latin America	1281	48·3	37	7·7	2·9	549	76·2	42·8	133	38·8	10
Mexico	587	22·1	10	2·1	1·7	302	41·9	51·4	85	24·8	14
Panama	..	..	..	..	..	..	..	..	..	..	
Other Central Amer.	..	..	..	..	..	..	..	..	..	..	
Argentina	..	..	..	..	..	..	..	..	..	..	
Brazil	..	..	..	..	..	..	..	..	..	..	
Chile	..	..	..	..	..	..	..	..	..	..	
Columbia	..	..	..	..	..	..	..	..	..	..	
Peru	..	..	..	..	..	..	..	..	..	..	
Venezuela	..	..	..	..	..	..	..	..	..	..	
Other Western Hem.	..	..	..	..	..	..	..	..	..	..	
Europe	593‡	21·6	200	41·8	34·9	5	0·7	0·9	138	40·2	24
Belgium and Luxembourg	..	..	..	..	..	..	..	..	..	..	
France	..	..	..	..	..	..	..	..	..	..	
Germany	..	..	..	..	..	..	..	..	..	..	
Italy	..	..	..	..	..	..	..	..	..	..	
Netherlands	..	..	..	..	..	..	..	..	..	..	
United Kingdom	..	..	..	..	..	..	..	..	..	..	
Denmark	..	..	..	..	..	..	..	..	..	..	
Norway	..	..	..	..	..	..	..	..	..	..	
Spain	..	..	..	..	..	..	..	..	..	..	
Sweden	..	..	..	..	..	..	..	..	..	..	
Switzerland	..	..	..	..	..	..	..	..	..	..	
Other Europe	..	..	..	..	..	..	..	..	..	..	
Africa	13	0·5	..	..	..	4	0·6	30·8	5	1·5	38
Liberia	..	..	..	..	..	..	..	..	..	..	
Libya	..	..	..	..	..	..	..	..	..	..	
South Africa	..	..	..	..	..	..	..	..	..	..	
Other Africa	..	..	..	..	..	..	..	..	..	..	
Asia and Oceania	137	5·2	20	4·2	14·6	3	0·4	2·2	42	12·2	3
Australia	..	..	..	..	..	..	..	..	..	..	
India	..	..	..	..	..	..	..	..	..	..	
Japan	..	..	..	..	..	..	..	..	..	..	
New Zealand	..	..	..	..	..	..	..	..	..	..	
Philippines	..	..	..	..	..	..	..	..	..	..	
Middle East	..	..	..	..	..	..	..	..	..	..	
Other Asia and Oceania	..	..	..	..	..	..	..	..	..	..	
International Unallocated	30	1·1	..	..	..	..	..	..	..	..	
Total all areas	2652‡	100·0	478	100·0	18·0	720	100·0	27·1	343	100·0	1

See p. 243 for Notes and Sources.

TABLE IV—continued

Total Other — Total investment in industry (m$)	Distribution by World Industry Group (%)	Employment of U.S. Funds within country (%)	Agriculture — Total investment in industry (m$)	Distribution of World Industry Group (%)	Employment of U.S. Funds within country (%)	Railroads — Total investment in industry (m$)	Distribution by World Industry Group (%)	Employment of U.S. Funds within country (%)	Trade — Total investment in industry (m$)	Distribution by World Industry Group (%)	Employment of U.S. Funds within country (%)	Utilities — Total investment in industry (m$)	Distribution by World Industry Group (%)	Employment of U.S. Funds within country (%)	Miscellaneous — Total investment in industry (m$)	Distribution by World Industry Group (%)	Employment of U.S. Funds within country (%)
205	21·7	33·2	101	28·4	16·3	69	27·1	11·2	27	15·9	4·4	8	6·0	1·3	..	..	..
551	58·4	43·0	243	68·3	19·0	176	69·0	13·7	34	20·0	2·6	98	73·7	7·7	..	..	..
184	19·5	31·3	37	10·4	6·3	110	43·1	18·7	4	2·3	0·7	33	24·8	5·6	..	..	..
..	..	..	..	..	..	..	..	..	..	..	..	..	..	..	..	..	..
..	..	..	..	..	..	..	..	..	..	..	..	..	..	..	..	..	..
..	..	..	..	..	..	..	..	..	..	..	..	..	..	..	..	..	..
..	..	..	..	..	..	..	..	..	..	..	..	..	..	..	..	..	..
..	..	..	..	..	..	..	..	..	..	..	..	..	..	..	..	..	..
..	..	..	..	..	..	..	..	..	..	..	..	..	..	..	..	..	..
96	10·2	16·8	..	..	..	..	..	..	85	50·0	14·8	11	8·3	1·9	..	..	..
..	..	..	..	..	..	..	..	..	..	..	..	..	..	..	..	..	..
..	..	..	..	..	..	..	..	..	..	..	..	..	..	..	..	..	..
..	..	..	..	..	..	..	..	..	..	..	..	..	..	..	..	..	..
..	..	..	..	..	..	..	..	..	..	..	..	..	..	..	..	..	..
..	..	..	..	..	..	..	..	..	..	..	..	..	..	..	..	..	..
..	..	..	..	..	..	..	..	..	..	..	..	..	..	..	..	..	..
..	..	..	..	..	..	..	..	..	..	..	..	..	..	..	..	..	..
..	..	..	..	..	..	..	..	..	..	..	..	..	..	..	..	..	..
4	0·4	30·8	..	..	..	..	..	..	4	2·3	30·8	..	..	..	..	..	..
..	..	..	..	..	..	..	..	..	..	..	..	..	..	..	..	..	..
..	..	..	..	..	..	..	..	..	..	..	..	..	..	..	..	..	..
..	..	..	..	..	..	..	..	..	..	..	..	..	..	..	..	..	..
58	6·1	42·3	12	3·4	8·8	10	3·9	7·3	20	11·8	14·6	16	12·0	11·7	..	..	..
..	..	..	..	..	..	..	..	..	..	..	..	..	..	..	..	..	..
..	..	..	..	..	..	..	..	..	..	..	..	..	..	..	..	..	..
..	..	..	..	..	..	..	..	..	..	..	..	..	..	..	..	..	..
..	..	..	..	..	..	..	..	..	..	..	..	..	..	..	..	..	..
30	3·2	100·0	..	..	..	..	..	..	..	..	..	..	..	..	30	100·0	..
44	100·0	5·6	356	100·0	13·4	255	100·0	9·6	170	100·0	6·4	133	100·0	5·0	30	100·0	1·1

[Continued overleaf

TABLE IV – *continued*

PART B – 1929

Country or area	Total* Total investment in country m$	Total* Distribution of U.S. Funds by Country %	Manufacturing Total investment in industry m$	Manufacturing Distribution by World Industry Group %	Manufacturing Employment of U.S. Funds within country %	Mining Total investment in industry m$	Mining Distribution by World Industry Group %	Mining Employment of U.S. Funds within country %	Petroleum Total investment in industry m$	Petroleum Distribution by World Industry Group %	Petroleum Employment of U.S. Funds %
Canada	2010	26·7	819	45·2	40·7	400	33·8	19·9	55	4·9	2
Latin America	3519	46·7	231	12·7	6·6	732	61·8	20·8	617	55·2	17
Mexico	682	9·0	..	..	..	..	..	..	..	..	
Panama	29	0·4	..	..	..	..	..	..	..	..	
Other Central Amer.	1208	16·0	..	..	..	..	..	..	..	..	
Argentina	332	4·4	..	..	..·	..	..	..	..	..	
Brazil	194	2·6	..	..	..	..	..	..	..	..	
Chile	423	5·6	..	..	..	..	..	..	..	..	
Columbia	124	1·6	..	..	..	..	..	..	..	..	
Peru	124	1·6	..	..	..	..	..	..	..	..	
Venezuela	233	3·1	..	..	..	..	..	..	..	..	
Other Western Hem.	170	2·2	..	..	..	..	..	..	..	..	
Europe	1353	18·0	629	34·7	46·5	*	..	..	231	20·7	17
Belgium and Luxembourg	64	0·8	..	..	..	..	..	..	..	..	
France	145	1·9	..	..	..	..	..	..	..	..	
Germany	217	2·9	..	..	..	..	..	..	..	..	
Italy	113	1·5	..	..	..	..	..	..	..	..	
Netherlands	43	0·6	..	..	..	..	..	..	..	..	
United Kingdom	485	6·4	..	..	..	..	..	..	..	..	
Denmark	16	0·2	..	..	..	..	..	..	..	..	
Norway	23	0·3	..	..	..	..	..	..	..	..	
Spain	72	1·0	..	..	..	..	..	..	..	..	
Sweden	19	0·2	..	..	..	..	..	..	..	..	
Switzerland	17	0·3	..	..	..	..	..	..	..	..	
Other Europe	139	1·8	..	..	..	..	..	..	..	..	
Africa	102	1·4	7	0·4	6·9	43	3·6	42·2	31	2·8	3
Liberia	5	0·1	..	..	..	..	..	..	..	..	
Libya	*	..	..	..	..	..	..	..	..	..	
South Africa	77	1·0	..	..	..	..	..	..	..	..	
Other Africa	20	0·3	..	..	..	..	..	..	..	..	
Asia and Oceania	544	7·2	126	6·9	23·2	10	0·8	1·8	183	16·4	3
Australia and New Zealand	149	2·0	..	..	..	..	..	..	..	..	
India	33	0·4	..	..	..	..	..	..	..	..	
Japan	61	0·8	..	..	..	..	..	..	..	..	
Philippines	80	1·1	..	..	..	..	..	..	..	..	
Middle East	14	0·2	..	..	..	..	..	..	..	..	
Other Asia and Oceania	207	2·7	..	..	..	..	..	..	..	..	
International, unallocated	..	..	..	..	..	..	..	..	..	..	
Total All Areas	7528	100·0	1813	100·0	24·1	1185	100·0	15·7	1117	100·0	1

See p. 243 for Notes and Sources.

TABLE IV—continued

Total Other***			Agriculture			Trade			Utilities			Miscellaneous		
Total investment in industry	Distribution by World Industry Group	Employment of U.S. Funds within country	Total investment in industry	Distribution by World Industry Group	Employment of U.S. Funds within country	Total investment in industry	Distribution by World Industry Group	Employment of U.S. Funds within country	Total investment in industry	Distribution by World Industry Group	Employment of U.S. Funds within country	Total investment in industry	Distribution by World Industry Group	Employment of U.S. Funds within country
m$	%	%	m$	%	%	m$	%	%	m$	%	%	m$	%	%
737	21·6	36·7	21	2·4	1·0	38	10·3	1·9	542	33·7	27·0	136	24·5	6·8
1939	56·8	55·1	817	92·8	23·2	119	32·3	3·4	887	55·1	25·2	116	20·9	3·3
..	..	..	..	..	..	..	..	..	..	..	..	..	..	..
..	..	..	..	..	..	..	..	..	..	..	..	..	..	..
..	..	..	..	..	..	..	..	..	..	..	..	..	..	..
..	..	..	..	..	..	..	..	..	..	..	..	..	..	..
..	..	..	..	..	..	..	..	..	..	..	..	..	..	..
..	..	..	..	..	..	..	..	..	..	..	..	..	..	..
..	..	..	..	..	..	..	..	..	..	..	..	..	..	..
..	..	..	..	..	..	..	..	..	..	..	..	..	..	..
493	14·4	36·4	—	..	—	139	37·8	10·3	145	9·0	10·7	209	37·6	15·4
..	..	..	..	..	..	..	..	..	..	..	..	..	..	..
..	..	..	..	..	..	..	..	..	..	..	..	..	..	..
..	..	..	..	..	..	..	..	..	..	..	..	..	..	..
..	..	..	..	..	..	..	..	..	..	..	..	..	..	..
..	..	..	..	..	..	..	..	..	..	..	..	..	..	..
..	..	..	..	..	..	..	..	..	..	..	..	..	..	..
..	..	..	..	..	..	..	..	..	..	..	..	..	..	..
..	..	..	..	..	..	..	..	..	..	..	..	..	..	..
21	0·6	20·6	..	..	..	16	4·3	15·7	..	..	..	5	0·9	4·9
..	..	..	..	..	..	..	..	..	..	..	..	..	..	..
..	..	..	..	..	..	..	..	..	..	..	..	..	..	..
..	..	..	..	..	..	..	..	..	..	..	..	..	..	..
225	6·6	41·4	43	4·9	7·9	56	15·2	10·3	36	2·2	6·6	96	16·2	16·5
..	..	..	..	..	..	..	..	..	..	..	..	..	..	..
..	..	..	..	..	..	..	..	..	..	..	..	..	..	..
..	..	..	..	..	..	..	..	..	..	..	..	..	..	..
..	..	..	..	..	..	..	..	..	..	..	..	..	..	..
..	..	..	..	..	..	..	..	..	..	..	..	..	..	..
413	100·0	45·3	880	100·0	11·7	368	100·0	4·9	1610	100·0	21·4	555	100·0	7·4

[Continued overleaf

TABLE IV – *continued*

PART C – 1950

Country or Area	Total investment in country m$	Distribution of U.S. Funds by country %	Total investment in industry m$	Manufacturing Distribution by World Industry Group %	Employment of U.S. Funds within country %	Total investment in industry m$	Mining Distribution by World Industry Group %	Employment of U.S. Funds within country %	Total investment in industry m$	Petroleum Distribution by World Industry Group %	Employment of U.S. Funds %
Canada . . .	3579	30·4	1897	49·5	53·0	334	29·6	9·3	418	12·3	11
Latin America . .	4576	38·8	781	20·4	17·1	666	59·0	14·6	1303	38·4	28
Mexico . . .	415	3·5	133	3·5	32·0	121	10·7	29·2	13	0·4	3
Panama . . .	58	0·5	2	0·0	3·4	..	..	..	6	0·2	10
Other Central Amer..	1015	8·6	†	†	†	†	†	†	†	†	†
Argentina . .	356	3·0	161	4·2	45·2	†	†	†	†	†	†
Brazil . . .	644	5·5	285	7·4	44·2	†	†	†	112	3·3	17
Chile . . .	540	4·6	29	0·8	5·4	351	31·1	65·0	†	†	†
Columbia . .	193	1·6	25	0·6	13·0	†	†	†	112	3·3	58
Peru . . .	145	1·2	16	0·4	11·0	55	4·9	37·9	†	†	†
Venezuela . .	993	8·4	24	0·6	2·4	†	†	†	857	25·3	86
Other Western Hem..	217	1·8	40	1·0	18·4	44	3·9	20·3	76	2·2	35
Europe . . .	1733	14·7	932	24·3	53·8	31	2·7	1·8	426	12·6	24
Belgium and Luxembourg .	69	0·6	38	1·0	55·1	..	..	..	17	0·5	24
France . . .	217	1·8	114	3·0	52·5	3	0·3	1·4	76	2·2	35
Germany . .	204	1·7	123	3·2	60·3	†	†	†	38	1·1	18
Italy . . .	63	0·5	19	0·5	30·2	..	..	..	37	1·1	58
Netherlands . .	84	0·7	23	0·6	24·4	†	†	†	43	1·3	51
United Kingdom .	847	7·2	542	14·1	64·0	3	0·3	0·4	123	3·6	14
Denmark . .	32	0·3	8	0·2	25·0	..	..	..	20	0·6	62
Norway . . .	24	0·2	5	0·1	20·8	†	†	†	6	0·2	25
Spain . . .	31	0·3	15	0·4	48·4	†	†	†	6	0·2	19
Sweden . . .	58	0·5	26	0·7	44·8	..	..	..	25	0·7	43
Switzerland . .	25	0·2	11	0·3	44·0	..	..	..	6	0·2	24
Other Europe . .	79	0·7	9	0·2	11·4	15	1·3	19·0	31	0·9	39
Africa . . .	287	2·4	55	1·4	19·2	64	5·7	22·3	124	3·6	43
Liberia . . .	16	0·1	..	..	..	..	..	..	..	..	
Libya . . .	*	..	..	..	..	..	..	..	..	..	
South Africa . .	140	1·2	44	1·1	31·4	33	2·9	23·6	45	1·3	32
Other Africa . .	131	1·1	..	.	..	..	..	..	..	..	
Asia and Oceania .	1257	10·7	167	4·4	13·3	33	2·9	2·6	879	25·9	69
Australia . . .	201	1·7	98	2·6	48·7	11	1·0	5·5	†	†	†
India . . .	38	0·3	16	0·4	42·1	†	†	†	†	†	†
Japan . . .	19	0·2	5	0·1	26·3	..	..	..	†	†	†
New Zealand . .	25	0·2	9	0·2	36·0	†	†	†	†	†	†
Philippines . .	149	1·3	23	0·6	15·4·	†	†	†	†	†	†
Middle East . .	692	5·9	1	0·0	0·1	10	0·9	1·4	666	19·6	96
Other Asia and Oceania .	133	1·1	..	..	..	..	..	..	..	..	
International, unallocated .	356	3·0	..	..	..	..	..	..	240	7·1	67
Total, All Areas . .	11,788	100·0	3831	100·0	32·5	1129	100·0	9·6	3390	100·0	28

See p. 243 for notes and sources.

TABLE IV—continued

	Total Other***			Agriculture			Trade			Utilities			Miscellaneous		
	Total investment in industry (m$)	Distribution by World Industry Group (%)	Employment of U.S. Funds within country (%)	Total investment in industry (m$)	Distribution by World Industry Group (%)	Employment of U.S. Funds within country (%)	Total investment in industry (m$)	Distribution by World Industry Group (%)	Employment of U.S. Funds within country (%)	Total investment in industry (m$)	Distribution by World Industry Group (%)	Employment of U.S. Funds within country (%)	Total investment in industry (m$)	Distribution of World Industry Group (%)	Employment of U.S. Funds within country (%)
929	27·0	26·0	21	3·6	0·6	240	31·5	6·7	284	19·9	7·9	384	58·0	10·7
1829	53·2	40·0	523	88·8	11·4	245	32·2	5·4	944	66·2	20·6	117	17·7	2·6
148	4·3	35·7	3	0·5	0·7	30	3·9	7·2	107	7·5	25·8	8	1·2	1·9
†	†	†	†	†	..	11	1·4	19·0	18	1·3	31·0	5	0·8	8·6
†	†	†	†	†	†	27	3·5	2·7	394	27·6	38·8	†	†	†
..	..	..	†	†	†	35	4·6	9·8	77	5·4	21·6	16	2·4	4·5
240	7·0	37·3	†	†	†	73	9·6	11·3	138	9·6	21·4	29	4·4	4·5
..	..	..	..	..	..	14	1·8	2·6	†	†	†	3	0·4	0·6
45	1·3	23·3	†	†	†	9	1·2	4·7	29	2·0	15·0	7	1·0	3·6
..	..	..	†	†	†	13	1·7	9·0	†	†	†	1	0·2	0·7
..	..	..	†	†	†	24	3·1	2·4	10	0·7	1·0	20	3·0	2·0
58	1·7	26·7	5	0·8	2·3	11	1·4	5·1	24	1·7	11·0	18	2·7	8·3
343	10·0	19·8	1	0·2	0·1	186	24·4	10·7	27	1·9	1·6	129	19·5	7·4
13	0·4	18·8	..	..	..	11	1·4	15·9	*	..	..	2	0·3	2·9
25	0·7	11·5	..	..	..	5	0·6	2·3	5	0·4	2·5	15	2·3	6·9
44	1·3	21·6	†	†	†	19	2·5	9·3	4	0·3	2·0	21	3·2	10·3
8	0·2	12·7	*	..	..	1	0·1	1·6	1	0·1	1·6	6	0·9	9·5
19	0·6	23·6	†	†	†	13	1·7	15·5	1	0·1	1·2	5	0·8	6·0
179	5·2	21·1	..	..	..	102	13·4	12·0	11	0·8	1·3	66	10·0	7·8
4	0·1	12·5	..	..	..	4	0·5	12·5	†	†	†	*	..	..
..	..	..	..	..	..	1	0·1	4·2	1	0·1	4·2	1	0·2	4·2
7	0·2	22·6	†	†	†	2	0·3	6·5	†	†	†	5	0·8	16·1
7	0·2	12·1	..	..	..	5	0·6	8·6	†	†	†	2	0·3	3·4
9	0·3	36·0	..	..	..	6	0·8	24·0	*	..	..	3	0·5	12·0
24	0·7	30·4	..	..	..	16	2·1	20·2	3	0·2	3·8	5	0·8	6·3
44	1·3	15·3	10	1·7	3·5	24	3·1	8·4	3	0·2	1·0	8	1·2	2·8
..	..	..	..	..	..	..	..	..	..	..	..	..	..	..
16	0·5	11·4	..	..	..	14	1·8	10·0	†	†	†	2	0·3	1·4
..	..	..	..	..	..	..	..	..	..	..	..	..	..	..
177	5·1	14·1	35	5·9	2·8	67	8·8	5·3	52	3·6	4·1	23	3·5	1·8
..	..	..	..	..	..	14	1·8	7·0	†	†	†	8	1·2	4·0
..	..	..	..	..	..	6	0·8	15·8	2	0·1	5·3	1	0·2	2·6
..	..	..	..	..	..	*	..	..	1	0·1	5·3	1	0·2	5·3
..	..	..	..	..	..	4	0·5	16·0	†	†	†	1	0·2	4·0
..	..	..	15	2·5	10·1	30	3·9	20·1	47	3·3	31·5	(−1)	(−)	0·7)
14	0·5	2·3	1	0·2	0·1	3	0·4	0·4	2	0·1	0·3	10	1·5	1·4
116	3·4	32·6	..	..	..	..	..	..	116	8·1	32·6	..	..	..
3438	100·0	29·2	589	100·0	5·0	762	100·0	6·5	1425	100·0	12·1	662	100·0	5·6

[Continued overleaf

TABLE IV – *continued*

PART D – 1970

Country or Area	Total		Manufacturing			Mining		
	Total investment in country m$	Distribution of U.S. Funds by Country %	Total investment in industry m$	Distribution by World Industry Group %	Employment of U.S. Funds within country %	Total investment in industry m$	Distribution by World Industry Group %	Employment of U.S. Funds within country %
Canada . . .	22,801	29·2	10,050	31·2	44·1	3,014	49·1	13·2
Latin America . .	14,683	18·8	4,604	14·3	31·4	2,037	33·2	13·9
Mexico . . .	1,774	2·3	1,191	3·7	67·1	151	2·5	8·5
Panama . . .	1,233	1·6	117	0·4	9·5	19	0·3	1·5
Other Central Amer..	624	0·8	73	0·2	11·7	10	0·2	1·6
Argentina . .	1,288	1·6	777	2·4	60·3	†	†	†
Brazil . .	1,843	2·4	1,247	3·9	67·7	127	2·1	6·9
Chile . .	748	1·0	66	0·2	8·8	455	7·4	60·8
Columbia . .	691	0·9	229	0·7	33·1	†	†	†
Peru . . .	691	0·9	89	0·3	12·9	426	6·9	61·6
Venezuela . .*	2,696	3·4	456	1·4	16·9	†	†	†
Other Western Hem..	3,095	4·0	359	1·1	11·6	698	11·4	22·6
Europe . . .	24,471	31·3	13,703	42·5	56·0	71	1·2	0·3
Belgium and Luxembourg .	1,510	1·9	855	2·6	56·6	*	..	..
France . . .	2,588	3·3	1,867	5·8	72·1	10	0·2	0·4
Germany . .	4,579	5·9	2,812	8·7	61·4	†	†	†
Italy . . .	1,521	1·9	801	2·5	52·7	†	†	†
Netherlands .	1,495	1·9	790	2·4	52·8	*	..	..
United Kingdom .	8,015	10·3	4,988	15·5	62·2	1	0·0	0·0
Denmark . .	361	0·5	65	0·2	18·0	1	0·0	0·3
Norway . . .	269	0·3	68	0·2	25·3	†	†	†
Spain . . .	759	1·0	402	1·2	53·0	†	†	†
Sweden . .	618	0·8	163	0·5	26·4	*	..	..
Switzerland . .	1,766	2·3	463	1·4	26·2	*	..	..
Other Europe . .	991	1·3	428	1·3	43·2	23	0·4	2·3
Africa . . .	3,476	4·4	538	1·7	15·5	440	7·2	12·6
Liberia . .	201	0·2	†	†	†	†	†	†
Libya . . .	1,009	1·3	†	†	†	†	†	†
South Africa .	864	1·1	438	1·4	50·7	90	1·5	10·4
Other Africa .	1,402	1·8	99	0·3	7·1	287	4·7	20·5
Asia and Oceania .	9,096	11·6	3,334	10·3	36·6	576	9·4	6·3
Australia . .	3,305	4·2	1,704	5·3	51·6	478	7·8	14·5
India . . .	305	0·4	157	0·5	51·5	†	†	†
Japan . . .	1,491	1·9	753	2·3	50·5	..	..	..
New Zealand .	180	0·2	99	0·3	55·0	4	0·1	2·2
Philippines . .	710	0·9	267	0·8	37·6	†	†	†
Middle East .	1,645	2·1	86	0·3	5·2	3	0·0	0·2
Other Asia and Oceania	1,460	1·9	267	0·8	18·3	..	..	..
International, unallocated	3,563	4·6	..	..	..	..	..	..
Total All Areas .	78,090	100·0	32,231	100·0	41·3	6,137	100·0	7·8

TABLE IV—*continued*

	Petroleum			Total Other ***		
	Total investment in industry	Distribution by World Industry Group	Employment of U.S. Funds within country	Total investment in industry	Distribution by World Industry Group	Employment of U.S. Funds within country
	m$	%	%	m$	%	%
	4,809	22·1	21·1	4,927	27·5	21·6
	3,929	18·0	26·8	4,115	22·9	28·0
	33	0·2	1·9	399	2·2	22·5
	258	1·2	20·9	839	4·7	68·0
	160	0·7	25·6	381	2·1	61·1
	†	†	†	511	2·8	39·7
	121	0·6	6·6	348	1·9	18·9
	†	†	†	228	1·3	30·5
	334	1·5	48·3	128	0·7	18·5
	†	†	†	176	1·0	25·5
	1,734	8·0	64·3	506	2·8	18·8
	1,007	4·6	32·5	1,034	5·8	33·4
	5,488	25·2	22·4	5,207	29·0	21·3
	65	0·3	4·3	589	3·3	39·0
	320	1·5	12·4	391	2·2	15·1
	1,198	5·5	26·2	569	3·2	12·4
	501	2·3	32·9	219	1·2	14·4
	441	2·0	29·5	264	1·5	17·7
	1,852	8·5	23·1	1,174	6·5	14·6
	238	1·1	65·9	57	0·3	15·8
	136	0·6	50·6	65	0·4	24·2
	142	0·6	18·7	214	1·2	28·2
	322	1·5	52·1	133	0·7	21·5
	(37)	(−)	(2.1)	1,340	7·5	75·9
	311	1·4	31·4	227	1·3	22·9
	2,088	9·6	60·1	408	2·3	11·7
	†	†	†	201	1·1	100·0
	†	†	†	1,009	5·6	100·0
	172	0·8	19·9	163	0·9	18·9
	932	4·3	66·5	87	0·5	6·2
	3,809	17·5	41·9	1,380	7·7	15·2
	†	†	†	1,122	6·3	33·9
	†	†	†	149	0·8	48·8
	540	2·5	36·2	198	1·1	13·3
	†	†	†	77	0·4	42·8
	†	†	†	443	2·5	62·4
	1,466	6·7	89·1	90	0·5	5·5
	†	†	†	1,194	6·6	81·8
	1,667	7·7	46·8	1,896	10·6	53·2
	21,790	100·0	27·9	17,932	160·0	23·0

Notes and Sources to Table IV

  * Less than $500,000.

  † Not separately shown.

  ‡ See Wilkins below.

*** : Total Other includes Agriculture, Railroads, Trade, Utilities and Miscellaneous.

Sources: In addition to the references given elsewhere in this book, I have drawn (for 1914) upon Mira Wilkins, *The Emergence of Multinational Enterprise: American Business Abroad from the Colonial Era to 1914* (Cambridge, Mass., 1970), p. 110. Figures for 1929 and 1950 come from the *United States Business Investments in Foreign Countries* (Washington, D.C., 1960). The data for 1970 come from the *Survey of Current Business*, October 1971.

TABLE V/A

Estimates of United States Share in Certain Industries in France and West Germany, 1963

Industry	U.S. firms (per cent of sales)
France 1963	
Petroleum refining	20
Razor blades and safety razors	87
Cars	13
Tyres	over 30
Carbon black	95
Refrigerators	25
Machine tools	20
Semiconductors	25
Washing machines	27
Lifts and elevators	30
Tractors and agricultural machinery	35
Telegraphic and telephone equipment	42
Electronic and statistical machines (of which computers 75%)	43
Sewing machines	70
Electric razors	60
Accounting machines	75
West Germany	
Petroleum	38
Machinery, vehicles, metal products (of which cars 40%)	15
Food industry	7
Chemicals, rubber, etc.	3
Electrical, optics, toys, musical (of which computers 84%)	10

Source:
Christopher Layton, *Trans-Atlantic Investments*, (Boulogne-sur-Seine, France, The Atlantic Institute, 1966), p. 19.

TABLE V/B

United States Affiliates' Share of Particular Products Produced in the United Kingdom, 1971

It has been possible to compile a list, from a number of sources, of the *approximate* share in 1971 of the total *production* of all British enterprises of various products accounted for by American financed companies. In some cases, their share of the total goods *bought* by British consumers will be less, because of the contribution of imports.

Percentage:

80 or more   Boot and shoe machinery, cameras, photo-copying equipment, carbon black, cash registers, colour films, starch, tinned baby foods, typewriters.

69–79   Aluminium semi-manufactures, breakfast cereals, calculating machines, cigarette lighters, domestic boilers, sewing machines, sparking plugs.

50–59   Cake mixes, commercial vehicles, computers, cosmetics and toilet preparations, crawlers and tractors, dog and cat foods, electric shavers, electric switches, pens and pencils, motor cars, petroleum refinery construction equipment, synethetic detergents, tinned milk, vacuum cleaners.

40–49   Abrasives, agricultural implements, electronic and measuring and testing instruments, ethical proprietaries (drugs sold to National Health Service), locks and keys, printing and typesetting machinery, razor blades and safety razors, refined petroleum products, rubber tyres, safes, locks, latches, etc., watches and clocks.

30–39   Agricultural tractors, commercial vehicles, contractors plant (graders), excavators, dumpers, etc., floor polishers, foundation garments, instant coffee, potato crisps, lifts and escalators, portable electric tools, polystyrene plastics, refrigerators, washing machines.

15–29   Greetings cards, materials handling equipment, medicinal preparations, machine tools, paperback books, petrochemicals, polyethylene plastics, man-made fibres, telephones and telecommunications equipment, tobacco products, toilet tissues.

U.S. firms are also important producers of specialised automatic transmission equipment, copper tubing and nickel alloys, cork products, electric blankets, chocolates and sweets, kitchen apparatus, laundry machinery, ophthalmic products, plastic semi-manufactures, refined platinum, polishes, tinned soup and vegetables, processed cheese products, caravans and trailers, mining machinery, distilled whisky. Outside the manufacturing industry, they are especially strongly represented in advertising, credit and financial reporting, market research and the production and distribution of films. American firms account for more than 15% of the bank deposits in Britain. Three of the leading car rental companies are U.S. owned, as are several publishing companies, hotels and supermarkets.

Source:
J. H. Dunning, *United States Industry in Britain. Op. cit.*

TABLE V/C

Percentage of Total Canadian Industry owned and controlled by United States Residents in 1963

Industry	1963 Ownership	1963 Control
Manufacturing	44	46
Petroleum and natural gas	54	62
Mining and smelting	54	52
Railways	9	2
Other utilities	23	4
Total of above industries and merchandising	28	27

Source:
Task Force on the Structure of Canadian Industry, *Foreign Ownership and the Structure of Canadian Industry* (Ottawa, 1968), p. 422.

TABLE V/D

United States Companies with assets of $A50 million and over operating in Australia in 1970

Company	Assets $ million	U.S. Equity
Mt. Newman	380	25
G.M.H.	322	100
Mt. Isa	274	53
Alcoa	255	51
Qld. Alumina	215	44
Ford	197	100*
Mobil Oil	184	100
Esso	183	100
Comalco	161	45
H.C. Sleigh	129	29
Caltex	119	100
Chrysler	116	97
A.O.R.	81	100
Savage River Mines	76	50
International Harvester	75	100
Amoco	72	100
Goodyear	62	100
Kodak	53	100
Austral Pacific Fertilisers	52	76
Petroleum Refineries	50	100

*via Canada

Source:
The Directory of Overseas Investment in Australian Manufacturing Industry, 1971 (Department of Trade and Industry, Canberra, A.C.T.). See also Gordon McCarthy, *The Great Big Australian Takeover Book* (Angus and Robertson, Sydney, 1973).

TABLE V/E

The Largest 100 United States Manufacturing and Petroleum Affiliates in the United Kingdom 1970–71

Company and rating*	Main activity	Sales		Capital employed £'000
		Total £'000	Exports £'000	
1. Esso Petroleum (11)	Oil industry	611,985	21,599	404,443
2. Ford Motor Co. (12)	Motor vehicle manufacturers	589,100	232,500	264,100
3. Gallaher (16)	Tobacco	436,393	2,382	121,641
4. Vauxhall (59)	Motor vehicle manufacturers	209,912	81,000	121,698
5. Texaco (66)	Distributors of petroleum products	188,000	20,000	105.476
6. Chrysler (U.K.) (72)	Motor vehicle manufacturers	178,829	53,042	73,025
7. Rank Xerox (80)	Xerographic equipment, etc.	153,305	40,114	122,475
8. I.B.M. (U.K.) (96)	Business machines	138,340	38,684	91,433
9. Mobil Oil (101)	Oil industry	132,112	8,635	78,181
10. Standard Telephone & Cables (109)	Telecommunications and electronics	123,362	31,543	89,238
11. Mars (125)	Food products	106,175	3,503	17,349
12. H. J. Heinz (146)	Food manufacturers	83,408	3,142	45,633
13. Goodyear Tyre & Rubber (U.K.) (159)	Tyres and rubber products	75,650	12,180	52,646
14. Kodak (167)	Photographic goods manufacturers	73,200	20,495	55,922
15. Monsanto Textiles (168)	Chemical and plastic products	73,189	22,535	72,529
16. Caltex U.K. (174)	Petroleum distributors	72,253	4,178	50,682
17. National Cash Register (178)	Data processing equipment, accounting machines	70,971	15,600	56,100
18. Hoover (197)	Household appliance manufacturers	67,261	15,726	43,282
19. Procter & Gamble (199)	Detergents and allied products	65,953	7,200	19,735
20. Caterpillar Tractor (239)	Manufacturers of earth moving equipment	50,934	16,887	31,789
21. Burroughs Machines (248)	Computational equipment	48,636	9,055	60,991
22. U.S.M.C. International (251)	Machinery for leather and plastics industry	48,129	11,776	37,827
23. Honeywell (253)	Automation equipment and control systems	47,341	17,964	51,419
24. General Motor (282)	Vehicle components and domestic appliance manufacturers	42,583	7,077	23,456
25. Godfrey Phillips (288)	Tobacco manufacturers	40,343	960	8,201
26. Du Pont (U.K.) (303)	Chemical manufacturers	37,264	8,066	33,388
27. Gulf Oil (G.B.) (312)	Distributors of petroleum products	35,608	6,264	78,586
28. Sperry Rand (313)	Engineering, business machines, etc.	35,598	6,848	26,041
29. Foster Wheeler (314)	Petroleum and chemical engineers	35,515	8,470	8,077
30. Brown & Polson (336)	Food, glucose syrups, starches, etc.	32,531	2,575	19,191
31. International Harvester Co. of G.B. (337)	Agricultural and construction equipment	32,399	19,887	30,424
32. Minnesota Mining & Manf. (349)	Coated materials and related products	30,690	4,454	16,607
33. Firestone Tyre & Rubber Co. (356)	Manufacturers of motor vehicle tyres	30,066	2,568	19,895
34. Union Carbide U.K. (365)	Metals, chemicals, eng., carbon products	29,409	1,731	18,633

[Continued overleaf]

TABLE V/E (continued)
The Largest 100 United States Manufacturing and Petroleum Affiliates in the United Kingdom 1970–71

Company and rating*	Main activity	Sales Total £'000	Exports £'000	Capital employed £'000
35. Kellogg Co. of G.B. (370)	Cereal food manufacturing	29,126	2,803	9,041
36. General Foods (373)	Manufacturers and dealers in food products	28,688	1,110	13,529
37. Kraft Foods (374)	Food manufacturers	28,458	788	9,470
38. Head Wrightson (382)	General engineers	27,520	5,740	9,862
39. Alcoa of Great Britain (390)	Smelters and fabricators of aluminium	26,465	2,090	15,984
40. Borg Warner (397)	Automotive engineers	25,659	9,223	23,391
41. Sterling-Winthrop Group (448)	Pharmaceutical and chemists	21,764	6,061	14,579
42. Britannia Lead Co. (450)	Lead and silver refiners	21,709	7,915	16,173
43. Uniroyal (456)	Rubber products	21,418	5,507	14,822
44. General Motors Scotland (465)	Earthmoving equipment manufacturers	20,905	13,257	16,052
45. Gillette Industries (479)	Razor and blade manufacturers	20,184	11,638	14,691
46. Black & Decker (483)	Power tool manufacturers	19,800	10,112	11,597
47. Swift & Co. (484)	Meat importers	19,687	397	3,657
48. Smiths Food Group (490)	Potato crisp manufacturers	19,540	176	12,159
49. Singer Manufacturing Co. (491)	Manufacturers of sewing machines, etc.	19,463	15,934	15,447
50. Ruston Bucyrus (500)	Manufacturers of excavators and cranes	19,040	8,202	17,710
51. Cummins Engine Co. (510)	Diesel engine and component manufacturers	18,655	12,937	12,561
52. Prestige Group (519)	Domestic houseware manufacturers	18,039	2,065	9,681
53. Merck Sharp & Dohme Holdings (520)	Manufacturing chemists	18,018	4,164	10,048
54. Air Products (522)	Industrial gases and equipment manufacturers	17,934	4,172	19,853
55. Long John International (536)	Distillers wine and spirit manufacturers, etc.	17,365	3,815	16,159
56. Otis Elevator Co. (541)	Manufacturers of heating equipment	17,229	5,682	8,230
57. Kimberley-Clark (548)	Boilers, radiators, heating accessories, etc.	17,019	975	8,303
58. Crane (556)	Boilers, radiators, heating accessories, etc.	16,764	2,520	11,783
59. Ideal Standard (564)	Boilers, radiators, heating accessories, etc.	16,405	1,463	8,821
60. Avon Cosmetics (565)	Manufacturers of cosmetics, etc.	16,374	2,358	4,848
61. Cam Gears (567)	Motor steering gears	16,319	2,760	9,739
62. Libby, McNeill & Libby (571)	Canned food manufacturers	16,176	504	6,082
63. Colgate Palmolive (602)	Toilet and domestic cleaning products	15,361	1,873	4,750
64. Johnson & Johnson (619)	Surgical and baby products manufacturers	14,826	2,680	6,806
65. Singer Sewing Machine Co. (626)	Sewing machines, household and electrical equipment	14,534	353	7,951
66. Chevron Oil (U.K.) (634)	Petroleum distributors	14,378	. .	2,621
67. Clark Equipment (644)	Construction machinery and cargo van carriers	13,910	9,236	7,130
68. Carborundum Co. (653)	Manufacturers of abrasives	13,765	3,148	10,279

The Largest 100 United States Manufacturing and Petroleum Affiliates in the United Kingdom 1970–71

Company and rating*	Main activity	Sales Total £'000	Exports £'000	Capital employed £'000
69. Nabisco (689)	Cereal, biscuit and cake mix manufacturers	12,897	432	5,352
70. Addressograph-Multigraph (695)	Office machinery manufacturers	12,815	951	6,802
71. Associated Octel Co. (698)	Manufacture of antiknock compounds	12,702	nil	24,322
72. Ronson Products (699)	Lighters, razors and domestic appliances	12,680	4,677	6,785
73. Pfizer (703)	Pharmaceuticals	12,617	4,115	16,261
74. Consolidated Pneumatic Tool Co. (710)	Pneumatic tool manufacturers, etc.	12,530	3,161	10,263
75. A. C. Cossor (721)	Radar and V.H.F. communications	12,212	3,164	5,198
76. Quaker Oats (728)	Grocery products	12,000	199	4,628
77. Lilly Industries (756)	Pharmaceuticals, etc.	11,082	4,392	9,431
78. A.M.F. International (759)	Manufacturers of tobacco and other machinery	10,943	8,477	5,596
79. Hercules Powder Co. (790)	Chemical manufacturers	10,474	2,026	4,268
80. Cyanamid of Great Britain (800)	Pharmaceutical products	10,416	4,300	4,695
81. Lennig Chemicals (803)	Chemical manufacturers	10,367	2,424	10,776
82. Armstrong Cork Co. (805)	Thermoplastic flooring manufacturers	10,324	1,123	7,564
83. Cameron Iron Works (824)	Manufacturers of valves and oilfield equipment	9,860	4,279	15,987
84. Vantorex (867)	Pharmaceutical and plastic products	9,157	2,822	6,124
85. Eaton (868)	Engineers	9,146	615	7,127
86. Allis-Chalmers Great Britain (873)	Agricultural and industrial machine manufacturers	9,100	6,051	4,535
87. Ranco (876)	Manufacturers of electric motors, etc.	9,056	4,966	4,912
88. Hewlett-Packard (881)	Electronic apparatus manufacturers	8,953	2,875	4,334
89. Amoco (U.K.) (898)	Petroleum products	8,798	1,234	14,336
90. W. W. Grace (902)	Manufacturers of chemical products	8,658	2,620	3,545
91. Fluor (England) (911)	Constructional engineers	8,578	108	410
92. Eric Technological Products (938)	Manufacturers of electronic components	8,258	1,017	2,868
93. Lummus Co. (965)	Refinery engineers	8,030	744	804
94. William R. Warner & Co. (968)	Manufacturing chemists	7,968	2,738	3,440
95. Champion Sparking Plug Co. (969)	Spark plug manufacturers	7,964	2,443	2,916
96. R.C.A. (974)	Electronic engineers	7,853	68	10,027
97. Leesona (977)	Coil winding and textile machinery	7,844	5,121	3,185
98. Carbor Carbon (985)	Carbon black manufacturers	7,763	2,246	5,386
99. Linotype & Machinery (994)	Makers of composing and printing machinery	7,639	3,642	5,869
100. Creed & Co. (996)	Telegraphic engineers	7,629	427	4,939

* By sales, in leading 1000.

Source: The Times, 1000, 1971/72.

TABLE V/F
The World Scene: Sales and Profits of Multinational Corporations in 1970

Company	Net sales (millions)	Estimated foreign sales (millions)	Per cent total	Net income (millions)	Per cent foreign	Where the profits come from
Standard Oil (New Jersey)	$16,554	$8,277	50	$1,310	52	Worldwide
Ford Motor	14,980	3,900[1]	26	516	24[1]	Germany, Britain, Australia
General Motors	18,752	3,563[1]	19	609	19[1]	Worldwide
Mobil Oil	7,261	3,267	45	483	51	Canada, Middle East
International Business Machines	7,504	2,933	39	1,018	50	Worldwide
International Telephone & Telegraph	6,365	2,673[1]	42	353	35[1]	Canada, Europe, Latin America
Texaco	6,350	2,540	40	822	(²)	Worldwide
Gulf Oil	5,396	2,428	45	550	21[3]	Middle East, South America, Canada
Standard Oil of California	4,188	1,885	45	455	46[3]	Middle East, Indonesia, South America
Chrysler	7,000	1,700[1]	24	7·6[4]	(²)	Worldwide
General Electric	8,727	1,393	16	329	20	South America, Canada, Italy
Caterpillar Tractor	2,128	1,118	53	144	(²)	Export sales, Worldwide
Occidental Petroleum	2,402	1,105[1]	46	175	(²)	Middle East, South America, Africa
F. W. Woolworth	2,528	1,001[5]	35	77	61	Canada, Germany, Britain
Eastman Kodak	2,785	874	31	404	19	Worldwide
Union Carbide	3,026	870	29	157	(²)	Worldwide
Procter & Gamble	3,178	795	25	238	25	Britain, Europe, Latin America
Singer	2,125	775	37	75	(²)	Europe, Latin America
Dow Chemical	1,911	771	40	103	45[6]	Worldwide
C.P.C. International	1,376	692	50	61	51	Worldwide
International Harvester	2,712	680	25	52	(²)	Canada, Europe, Africa
Firestone Tyre & Rubber	2,335	677	29	93	39	Worldwide
Colgate-Palmolive	1,210	670	55	40	(²)	Worldwide
Honeywell	1,921	622	35	58	(²)	Europe, British Commonwealth
National Cash Register	1,421	643	45	30	51[6]	Worldwide

Company						Regions
E. I. du Pont	3,618	634	18	329	[2]	Export sales, Europe
W. R. Grace	1,938	633	33	30	39[1,6]	Latin America
Minnesota Mining & Manufacturing	1,687	605	36	188	[2]	Europe, Canada, Australia
First National City Corp	1,704	600	35	139	40	Worldwide
Englehard Minerals & Chemical	1,474	589	40	36	[2]	Britain, Europe, Japan
Sperry Rand	1,739	589	34	72	[2]	Europe, Japan
Xerox	1,719	518	30	188	38	Britain, Canada, Latin America
American Standard	1,418	511	36	13	33	Europe
Coca-Cola	1,606	498	31	147	[1]	Worldwide
Swift	3,076	492	16	29	[2]	Canada, Britain, Germany
General Foods	2,282	479	21	119	[2]	Canada
American Smelting & Refining	718	467	65	89	55[7]	Australia, Peru, Mexico
Monsanto	1,972	467	24	67	31	Canada, Latin America, Europe
Warner-Lambert	1,257	453	36	98	[2]	Worldwide
General Telephone & Electronics	3,439	441	13	236	7	Canada, Europe, Latin America
H. J. Heinz	990	433	44	38	44	Worldwide
Uniroyal	1,556	420	27	24	75	Canada, Mexico
Pfizer	870	412	47	81	55	Britain, Europe, Latin America
Litton Industries	2,404	409	17	69	[2]	Europe, Latin America
Schlumberger	579	341	59	49	[2]	France, Canada
Otis Elevator	601[3]	301	50	24	35	Worldwide
Gillette	673	289	43	66	50	Worldwide
U.S.M.	440	203	46	10	98	British Commonwealth, Europe, Latin America
Chesebrough-Pond's	261	111	43	21	40	Europe, Canada, Latin America
Black & Decker	255	107	42	20	50	Export sales

[1] Excludes Canada.
[2] Not available.
[3] Contracts completed.
[4] Deficit.
[5] Per cent based on consolidated sales and equity in unconsolidated subsidiary.
[6] Percent based on operating income.
[7] Per cent based on earnings before taxes and extraordinary items.

Note: All oil company figures exclude excise taxes.

Source: U.S. Senate, 93rd Congress, Committee on Finance, Subcommittee on International Trade, *Multinational Corporations*; 26 February–6 March 1973 (Washington D.C., 1973) pp. 410–11.

TABLE V/G
Nations and Corporations

One way to show the size of today's large multinational corporations is to compare their gross annual sales with the gross national products of countries. This table uses 1970 figures for all except the centrally planned economies (excluding China) and General Motors Corp., for which 1969 figures are used. The amounts are shown in billions of dollars.

1. United States	. $974·10		51. Egypt	.	6·58
2. Soviet Union	. 504·70		52. Thailand	.	6·51
3. Japan	. 197·18		53. ITT	.	6·36
4. West Germany . .	. 186·35		54. TEXACO . . .	.	6·35
5. France	. 147·53		55. Portugal	.	6·22
6. Britain	. 121·02		56. New Zealand . . .	.	6·08
7. Italy	. 93·19		57. Peru	.	5·92
8. China . . .	. 82·50		58. WESTERN ELECTRIC .	.	5·86
9. Canada	. 80·38		59. Nigeria	.	5·80
10. India	. 52·92		60. Taiwan	.	5·46
11. Poland	. 42·32		61. GULF OIL . . .	.	5·40
12. East Germany . .	. 37·61		62. U.S. STEEL . . .	.	4·81
13. Australia . . .	. 36·10		63. Cuba	.	4·80
14. Brazil	. 34·60		64. Israel	.	4·39
15. Mexico	. 33·18		65. VOLKSWAGENWERK .	.	4·31
16. Sweden	. 32·58		66. WESTINGHOUSE ELEC	.	4·31
17. Spain	. 32·26		67. STANDARD OIL (Calif.)	.	4·19
18. Netherlands . . .	. 31·25		68. Algeria	.	4·18
19. Czechoslovakia . .	. 28·84		69. PHILIPS ELECTRIC .	.	4·16
20. Romania . . .	. 28·01		70. Ireland	.	4·10
21. Belgium . . .	. 25·70		71. BRITISH PETROLEUM .	.	4·06
22. Argentina . . .	. 25·42		72. Malaysia	.	3·84
23. GENERAL MOTORS .	. 24·30		73. LING-TEMCO-VOUGHT .	.	3·77
24. Switzerland . . .	. 20·48		74. STANDARD OIL (Ind.) .	.	3·73
25. Pakistan . . .	. 17·50		75. BOEING	.	3·68
26. South Africa . . .	. 16·69		76. DUPONT	.	3·62
27. STANDARD OIL (N.J.)	. 16·55		77. Hong Kong . . .	.	3·62
28. Denmark . . .	. 15·57		78. SHELL OIL . . .	.	3·59
29. FORD MOTOR . .	. 14·98		79. IMPERIAL CHEMICAL .	.	3·51
30. Austria . . .	. 14·31		80. BRITISH STEEL . .	.	3·50
31. Yugoslavia . . .	. 14·02		81. North Korea . . .	.	3·50
32. Indonesia . . .	. 12·60		82. GENERAL TELEPHONE .	.	3·44
33. Bulgaria . . .	. 11·82		83. NIPPON STEEL . .	.	3·40
34. Norway . . .	. 11·39		84. Morocco . . .	.	3·34
35. Hungary . . .	. 11·38		85. HITACHI . . .	.	3·33
36. ROYAL			86. RCA	.	3·30
DUTCH/SHELL .	. 10·80		87. GOODYEAR TYRE .	.	3·20
37. Philippines . .	. 10·23		88. SIEMENS . . .	.	3·20
38. Finland . . .	. 10·20		89. South Vietnam . .	.	3·20
39. Iran	. 10·18		90. Libya	.	3·14
40. Venezuela . . .	. 9·58		91. Saudi Arabia . . .	.	3·14
41. Greece	. 9·54		92. SWIFT	.	3·08
42. Turkey	. 9·04		93. FARBWERKE		
43. GENERAL ELECTRIC .	. 8·73		HOECHST . . .	.	3·03
44. South Korea . . .	. 8·21		94. UNION CARBIDE .	.	3·03
45. IBM	. 7·50		95. DAIMLER-BENZ . .	.	3·02
46. Chile	. 7·39		96. PROCTER & GAMBLE .	.	2·98
47. MOBIL OIL . . .	. 7·26		97. AUGUST THYSSEN-		
48. CHRYSLER . . .	. 7·00		HÜTTE . . .	.	2·96
49. UNILEVER . . .	. 6·88		98. BETHLEHEM STEEL .	.	2·94
50. Colombia . . .	. 6·61		99. BASF	.	2·87

Source: Lester Brown, 'The Interdependence of Nations'
Cited by SEnate Subcommittee on International Trade, 93rd Congress, 404.

Tables

TABLE VI
Plant and Equipment Expenditures by United States Domestic and Foreign-Based Manufacturing Firms, 1957–70

	Domestic firms		Foreign-based firms		Foreign as percentage of domestic
Year	Billion $	1957 = 100	Billion $	1957 = 100	
1957	16·5	100	1·3	100	7·9
1964	19·3	117	3·0	231	15·5
1968	28·4	172	4·2	323	14·8
1970	32·0	194	6·5	500	20·3

Sources:
Domestic Firms: *Economic Report of the President* (Washington, D.C., 1971), p. 239.
Foreign-Based Firms: *Survey of Current Business*, September 1965, p. 28; September 1966, p. 30; September 1971, p. 28.

TABLE VII
United States Portfolio Investments Abroad, 1950–70

Country	1950	1957	1964	1970*
Dollar Amounts (in billions)				
Canada	3·4	4·2	8·9	12·3
Latin America	0·4	1·0	2·3	3·4
Europe	1·4	1·8	5·4	5·1
Other	0·5	1·3	3·9	5·8
Total	5·7	8·3	20·5	26·6
Percentage to Total				
Canada	60	50	43	46
Latin America	7	11	11	13
Europe	25	22	26	20
Other	8	17	20	21
Total	100	100	100	100

Source: U.S. Dept. of Commerce, *Survey of Current Business* (various).
 * At this time, the U.K. portfolio investment overseas totalled 5550 (£ millions), Bank of England *Quarterly Bulletin*, vol. 12, no. 2 (June 1972), 214.

TABLE VIII/A

The Geographical Distribution and Employment of United States Foreign Aid, 1 July 1945 to 31 December 1970
($ millions and equivalents)

Country	Economic and technical assistance	Military supplies and services	Total
	(net)	*(net)*	*(net)*
Total, all areas	83,201	39,933	125,060
Austria	1,079	100	1,179
Belgium and Luxembourg	651	1,242	1,893
Denmark	260	620	880
Finland	42	–	42
France	4,123	4,206	8,329
Germany	2,849	858	3,707
Iceland	66	–	66
Ireland	146	–	146
Italy	3,028	2,369	5,397
Netherlands	761	1,246	2,007
Norway	229	901	1,130
Portugal	131	329	460
Spain	1,040	643	1,683
Sweden	99	–	99
United Kingdom	6,570	1,076	7,646
Yugoslavia	1,939	701	2,640
European E.E.C.	54	–	54
European Coal and Steel Community	51	–	51
European Payments Union	238	–	238
Other and unspecified	508	3,590	4,098
Total, Western Europe	23,865	17,880	41,745
Albania	20	–	20
Czechoslovakia	191	–	191
Eastern Germany	17	–	17
Hungary	20	–	20
Poland	945	–	945
Romania	33	–	33
U.S.S.R.	358	–	358
Total, Eastern Europe	1,584		1,584
Afghanistan	337	4	341
Ceylon	159	–	159

TABLE VIII/A *(continued)*

Country	Economic and technical assistance	Military supplies and services	Total
	(net)	*(net)*	*(net)*
Cyprus	24	–	24
Greece	1,673	1,985	3,658
India	8,228	–	8,228
Iran	971	841	1,812
Iraq	46	47	93
Israel	1,052	–	1,052
Jordan	589	57	646
Lebanon	103	9	112
Nepal	140	–	140
Pakistan	3,871	–	3,871
Saudi Arabia	85	36	121
Syria	56	–	56
Turkey	2,280	3,132	5,412
United Arab Republic	1,127	–	1,127
Yemen	48	–	48
UNRRA	550	–	550
Other and unspecified	171	*	171
Total, Near East and South Asia	21,510	6,110	27,620
Algeria	178	–	178
Cameroon	38	–	38
Congo, Democratic Republic of	364	27	391
Dahomey	11	–	11
Ethiopia	185	149	334
Ghana	223	–	223
Guinea	93	1	94
Ivory Coast	43	–	43
Kenya	68	–	68
Liberia	240	7	247
Libya	206	16	222
Maligasy Republic	14	–	14
Mali	19	3	22
Morocco	690	41	731
Nigeria	251	1	252
Senegal	33	3	36
Sierra Leone	44	–	44
Somali Republic	72	–	72
South Africa	92	–	92
Sudan	94	1	95
Tanzania	84	–	84
Togo	15	–	15

[*Continued overleaf*

TABLE VIII/A *(continued)*

Country	Economic and technical assistance	Military supplies and services	Total
	(net)	*(net)*	*(net)*
Tunisia	623	28	651
Uganda	33	–	33
Other and unspecified	285	38	323
Total, Africa	3,815	314	4,129
Australia	355	–	355
Burma	108	–	108
Cambodia	257	96	352
China (Taiwan)	2,245	3,676	5,921
Hong Kong	43	–	43
Indonesia	1,229	77	1,306
Japan	2,422	1,552	3,974
Korea, Republic of	4,885	3,134	8,019
Laos	697	–	697
Malaysia	83	1	84
New Zealand	50	3	53
Philippines	1,310	560	1,870
Ryukyu Islands	384	–	384
Thailand	544	607	1,151
The Trust Territory of the Pacific Islands	280	–	280
Vietnam	4,535	1,540	6,075
Other and unspecified	233	2,756*	2,989
Total, Far East and Pacific	19,662	13,998	33,660
Argentina	368	80	448
Bolivia	488	24	512
Brazil	2,440	242	2,682
Canada	12	9	21
Chile	1,187	117	1,304
Columbia	888	107	995
Costa Rica	151	2	153
Cuba	41	12	53
Dominican Republic	400	24	424
Ecuador	205	53	258
El Salvador	109	6	115
Guatemala	219	18	237
Guyana	40	–	40
Haiti	114	4	118

TABLE VIII/A *(continued)*

Country	Economic and technical assistance	Military supplies and services	Total
	(net)	*(net)*	*(net)*
Honduras	95	8	103
Jamaica	50	1	51
Mexico	575	2	577
Nicaragua	135	12	147
Panama	187	4	191
Paraguay	98	9	107
Peru	356	121	477
Surinam	9	–	9
Trinidad and Tobago	47	–	47
Uruguay	115	44	159
Venezuela	323	14	337
Other and unspecified	306	294	600
Total, Western Hemisphere	8,959	1,207	10,166
Other international organisations and unspecified areas	3,801	417	4,218
Investment in international agencies		1,928	1,928

Source: U.S. Government Printing Office, *Annual Report of Activities of the National Advisory Council on International Monetary and Financial Policies,* 92nd Congress, 2nd Session, House Docs., nos. 92–256, pp. 186–90.

*The source does not give a breakdown of the amount of 'Other' to be allocated between Near East-South Asia and Far East–Pacific. We have arbitrarily allocated all of the $2,756,000 to the latter.

Table VIII/B

United States Assistance Expenditures 1971–73 (in thousands of dollars)

	1971	1972	1973
Security Assistance			
Total	5,701,280	6,232,605	5,928,176
	(5,705,380)[1]	(6,236,805)[1]	(5,932,976)[1]
Military assistance program .	752,485	528,756	803,442
Military assistance service-funded .	2,325,900	2,339,400	2,055,000
MAAG administration and training	116,508	116,733	114,254
Transfer of defense stocks (excluding excess defense articles) .	278,428	462,086	105,800
Excess defense articles (legal value) .	118,399	185,000	245,000
Ships transfers (loans, leases) .	18,480	47,579	39,600
Real property transfers . .	217,009	740,651	485,680
Security supporting assistance .	572,971	598,100	874,500
FMS credit sales . . .	743,400	550,000	629,000
Export-Import Bank military sales	253,000	300,000	360,000
Public Law 480, sec. 104C . .	120,500	103,900	124,000
Purchase of local currency . .	184,200	260,400	91,900
Development and Humanitarian Assistance			
Total	2,762,454	3,189,908	3,763,765
	(3,017,073)[1]	(3,479,462)[1]	(4,191,295)[1]
Agency for International Development	1,257,345	1,420,446	1,598,976
International narcotics control and contingency fund . . .	26,242	50,291	72,800
Peace Corps	85,024	61,900	72,200
Public Law 480	1,138,843	1,249,966	1,099,789
Internation financial institutions .	255,000	407,305	920,000
Grand total, Foreign Assistance . . .	8,463,734	9,422,513	9,691,941
Export-Import Bank (other than military loans in security assistance)	2,880,800	7,331,800	7,331,800
Grand total, including Export-Import Bank . . .	11,344,534	16,754,313	17,023,741

[1] Figures in parentheses are those reported in S. Rept. 92-1231, p. 4; and in 'The Multinational Corporation and the World Economy', Senate Committee on Finance, U.S. Government Printing Office 90-604, p. 36. Difference from figures here due to minor revisions in agency estimates subsequent to submission of figures in documents cited.

Source: (1) Security Assistance: Department of Defence, estimates as of May 3, 1972. (2) Development and Humanitarian Assistance: AID, 1972 (spring). (3) Export-Import Bank: AID, 1972 (spring).

TABLE IX

The United States Contribution to International Financial and Monetary Institutions as at 30 June 1971 (in thousands of dollars)

1. *The International Monetary Fund*
   - Total — 28,490,000
   - U.S. quota — 6,700,000*
2. *The International Bank for Reconstruction and Development*
   - Subscribed total — 23,871,000
   - Paid total — 2,388,000
   - Paid U.S. portion — 635,000†
3. *The International Finance Corporation*
   - Total — 107,000
   - U.S. subscription — 35,000
4. *The International Development Association*
   - Total — 3,015,000
   - U.S. portion — 1,112,300
5. *The Inter-American Development Bank*
   - A. Ordinary capital resources
     - Total — 3,150,000
     - Paid total — 475,000
     - Paid U.S. portion — 150,000‡
   - B. Contributions to the fund for Special Operations
     - Total — 2,328,000
     - U.S. contribution — 1,800,000
6. *The Asian Development Bank*
   - Subscribed total — 1,005,000
   - U.S. subscription — 200,000

* 25% of this amount is in gold.

† The United States subscribed 6,350,000 (thousands of dollars).

‡ The United States subscribed 1,173,500 (thousands of dollars); the difference is 'callable' capital.

Source: U.S. Government Printing Office, *Annual Report of Activities of the National Advisory Council on International Monetary and Financial Policies*, 92nd Congress, 2nd Session, House Docs., nos. 92–256, pp. 212, 223, 234, 241, 246, 248, 253.

TABLE X
United States Gold Reserves vs Dollar Liabilities
(billions of dollars) 1950–70

End of year	Gold reserves of the United States	Percentage of the world's reserves held by the United States	Dollar assets held by foreigners
1950	22·7	63·7	6·9
1957	22·8	58·9	13·6
1964	15·4	35·9	26·5
1970	10·7	26·8	41·8

Sources:
U.S. bureau of the Census, *Statistical Abstract* (Washington, D.C., various).
Federal Reserve Bulletin (various).

The World's Merchant Fleets in 1970 (by number and kind of vessels)

Country of registry	Total		Type of vessel								Percentage of U.S. commerce carried by U.S. flag and foreign flag ships
			Combination passenger and cargo		Freighters		Bulk carriers*		Tankers		
	Number of ships	Percent of total world fleet	Number of ships	Percent of total	Number of ships	Percent of total freighters	Number of ships	Percent of total bulk carriers	Number of ships	Percent of total tankers	
U.S.A.	1,579	7·9	171	19·1	1,076	9·0	38	1·3	294	6·9	5·8
Privately-owned	793	4·0	19	2·1	475	4·0	37	1·3	262	6·2	n.a.
Government-owned	786	3·9	152	17·0	601	5·1	1	0·0	32	0·8	n.a.
Japan	2,109	10·6	28	3·1	1,284	10·8	429	14·5	368	8·7	5·7
U.S.S.R.	1,942	9·7	77	8·6	1,339	11·3	132	4·5	394	9·3	n.a.
Liberia	1,840	9·2	25	2·8	495	4·2	590	20·0	730	17·2	26·9
United Kingdom	1,772	8·9	75	8·4	967	8·1	296	10·0	434	10·3	7·8
Greece	1,195	6·0	45	5·0	757	6·4	177	6·0	216	5·1	5·3
Norway	1,173	5·9	27	3·0	442	3·7	341	11·5	363	8·6	12·6
West Germany	993	5·0	6	0·7	836	7·0	92	3·1	59	1·4	3·8
Panama	629	3·1	26	2·9	361	3·0	69	2·3	173	4·1	4·6
Italy	625	3·1	67	7·5	237	2·0	123	4·2	198	4·7	3·4
Netherlands	460	2·3	15	1·7	319	2·7	34	1·2	92	2·2	n.a.
France	457	2·3	19	2·1	242	2·0	61	2·1	135	3·2	n.a.
Spain	403	2·0	37	4·1	227	1·9	30	1·0	109	2·6	n.a.
Sweden	366	1·8	4	0·4	204	1·7	78	2·6	80	1·9	n.a.
Rest of World	2,858	14·3	102	11·5	2,037	17·1	426	14·4	293	6·8	24·1†
World	19,980	100·0	895	100·0	11,899	100·0	2,954	100·0	4,232	100·0	100·0

* Includes bulk/oil, ore/oil and ore/bulk/oil carriers.

† Including 9·1% carried by Canadian flag ships.   n.a. = not available.

Note: Percentage figures may not be additive due to rounding.

Sources: U.S. Department of Commerce, *A Statistical Analysis of the World's Merchant Fleets* (Washington, D.C., 1972); U.S. Department of Commerce, *The American Shipper and the U.S. Flag Merchant Fleet* (Washington, D.C., May 1972).

Figures for the distribution of world shipping in 1971 show the United States with 6·6 per cent; Liberia had 15·6 per cent, Japan 12·3 per cent, the United Kingdom 11·1 per cent and Norway 8·8 per cent. (For earlier figures see my *Impact of Western Man.*)

TABLE XII

The United States Merchant Marine 1789–1970

Year	Tonnage registered in foreign trade (tons to nearest thousand)	Tonnage registered in coastwise and internal trade (tons to nearest thousand)	Percentage of imports and exports carried in American vessels by value
1789	124,000	69,000	23·6
1800	667,000	272,000	89·0
1810	981,000	405,000	91·5
1820	584,000	588,000	89·5
1830	538,000	517,000	89·8
1840	763,000	1,177,000	82·9
1850	1,440,000	1,798,000	72·5
1860	2,379,000	2,645,000	66·5
1870	1,449,000	2,638,000	35·6
1880	1,314,000	2,638,000	17·6
1890	928,000	3,409,000	12·8
1900	817,000	4,287,000	9·3
1910	783,000	6,669,000	8·7
1920	9,925,000	6,358,000	43·0
1930	6,296,000	9,723,000	34·7
1940	3,047,000	10,654,000	28·7*
1950	19,154,000	12,048,000	39·3*
1960	14,737,000	13,833,000	12·3*
1970	18,423,000	Not available	5·6*†

* By cargo tonnage.

† The figure given by the U.S. Dept. of Commerce, *The American Shipper and the U.S. Flag Merchant Fleet*, May 1972, is 5·8%.

Sources:

U.S. Dept. of Commerce, *Historical Statistics of the United States, Colonial Times to 1957* (Washington, D.C., 1960), pp. 444–5, 452.

U.S. Dept. of Commerce, *Historical Statistics of the U.S., Continuation to 1962 and Revisions* (Washington, D.C., 1965) p. 63.

William Armstrong Fairburn, *Merchant Sail* (Center Lovell, Me., 1945–55) II 920, 958–9.

U.S. Dept. of Commerce, *Statistical Abstract* (Washington, D.C., various years).

TABLE XIII

Percentage of United States Total Shipping Tonnage Accounted for by Sail and Steam, 1810–1920

Year	Sail	Steam
1810	100·0	–
1820	99·5	0·5
1830	98·5	1·5
1840	96·5	3·5
1850	94·5	5·5
1860	90·0	10·0
1870	79·0	21·0
1880	60·0	40·0
1890	38·0	62·0
1900	20·0	80·0
1910	10·0	90·0
1920	5·0	95·0

Sources: William Armstrong Fairburn, *Merchant Sail* (Center Lovell, Me., 1945–55) II 1401, 1491. This table should be compared to that on pp. 444–5 of *Historical Statistics of the United States* which defines sail and steam differently.

TABLE XIV

United States Foreign Trade for Selected Years (in millions of dollars) 1790–1970

Year	Imports of merchandise	Exports of merchandise
1790	23	20
1806	129	102
1810	85	67
1812	77	39
1816	147	82
1820	74	70
1830	63	72
1834	109	102
1840	98	124
1850	174	144
1860	354	334
1870	436	393
1880	668	836
1890	789	858
1900	850	1,394
1914	1,894	2,365
1920	5,278	8,228
1929	4,399	5,241
1930	3,061	3,843
1939	2,318	3,177
1944	3,929	14,259
1950	8,852	10,275
1960	15,019	20,500
1970	39.963	43,226

Sources: *Historical Statistics of the United States* and *Statistical Abstract of the United States, 1970*. For the period prior to the Civil War, more refined figures have been prepared by D. C. North, 'The United States Balance of Payments, 1790–1860', *Trends in the American Economy in the Nineteenth Century* (Princeton, 1960) p. 577.

TABLE XV

United States Principal Imports by Economic Classes and by Selected Commodities (in percentages)

Economic Classes[1]	1821[2]	1830[2]	1840[2]	1850[2]	1851–1860	1861–1870	1871–1880	1881–1890	1891–1900	1901–1910	1911–1920	1921–1930	1931–1940	1941–1950	1951–1960	1961–1970
Finished manufactures	56·9	57·1	45·0	54·9	50·7	41·0	33·0	30·7	25·8	24·8	17·0	21·4	20·5	17·9	26·3	44·6
Semimanufactures	7·5	7·9	11·2	15·1	12·5	13·8	13·1	14·8	13·9	17·3	17·3	18·3	18·3	21·9	22·8	20·9
Crude materials	4·7	7·9	12·2	7·2	9·6	12·6	17·2	21·4	26·5	34·1	38·4	37·1	31·4	31·2	24·1	16·0
Crude foodstuffs	11·2	11·1	15·3	10·4	11·7	13·6	16·0	15·4	16·9	11·8	12·3	11·9	14·1	18·0	16·5	8·8
Manufactured foodstuffs	20·0	15·9	15·3	12·4	15·4	19·0	20·7	17·8	17·0	12·0	15·2	11·3	14·0	11·0	10·3	9·7

Selected Commodities[3]	1802–1804[4]	1807[4]	1815[4]	1821–1830	1831–1840	1841–1850	1851–1860	1861–1870	1871–1880	1881–1890	1891–1900	1901–1910	1911–1920	1921–1930	1931–1940	1941–1950	1951–1960	1961–1970
Alcoholic beverages	12·9	11·0	9·3	4·9	3·7													
Coffee	11·2	11·9	3·8	6·7	7·7	7·3	6·1	5·7	9·1	8·0	10·8	6·2	5·4	6·5	6·7	9·8	10·7	
Sugar	10·4	16·9	7·5	6·0	5·6	5·8	7·9	11·2	14·7	14·7	12·5	7·2	10·6	6·7	6·0	4·9	3·7	4·6
Tea	3·2																	
Molasses																		
Cotton manufactures				12·8	9·8	11·2	8·7	5·5	5·0	4·4	4·1	5·0						
Wool, mohair and manufactures				11·7	9·5	10·3	11·2	9·5	8·2	7·1	4·4							
Silk and manufactures				9·9	11·4	9·0	10·5	5·7	6·2	8·2	7·1							
Iron and steel manufactures				7·4	7·9	7·9	8·4	6·2	6·2	7·3	7·7							
Flax and manufactures				4·7	4·6	4·6	3·4	4·0	3·3	3·3								
Hides and skins											4·2	6·0	6·0	5·8	5·3	4·5	3·4	
Raw silk											4·2	4·8	5·8	9·6	6·7			
Crude rubber												4·0	5·4	6·5	6·7	10·2	3·4	
Forest products[5]													3·2	3·0	5·3	6·7	10·9	7·3
Petroleum and products													3·0	3·0	6·5	4·7	9·3	9·0
Non-ferrous base metals																10·7	10·1	5·2
Copper and manufactures[6]																3·0	3·1	
Tin, including ore																3·5	3·1	
Machinery																	3·0	9·2
Transport equipment																		8·3
Iron and steel products																		4·3
Chemicals																	3·0	3·9

Notes:

[1] General imports through 1932; imports for consumption 1933–64; general imports 1965–70.
[2] Prior to 1850, figures are available for selected years only.
[3] General imports through 1932; imports for consumption thereafter.
[4] Prior to 1821, figures are available for selected years only.
[5] Includes sawmill products, wood pulp, and paper and manufactures.
[6] Copper, including ore and manufactures since 1946.

Source: see Table XVI.

TABLE XVI

United States Principal Exports by Economic Classes and by Selected Commodities (in percentages)

Economic Classes[1]	1820	1830	1840	1850	1851–1860	1861–1870	1871–1880	1881–1890	1891–1900	1901–1910	1911–1920	1921–1930	1931–1940	1941–1950	1951–1960	1961–1970
Finished manufactures	5·7	8·5	9·8	12·7	12·3	16·3	15·1	15·7	18·5	25·6	37·1	41·0	48·6	63·4	60·5[2]	60·2[2]
Semimanufactures	9·4	6·8	4·5	4·5	4·0	5·2	4·6	5·2	8·0	12·8	15·4	13·3	17·5	10·3	13·5[2]	15·1[2]
Crude materials	60·6	62·7	67·9	62·4	61·7	38·8	38·6	36·0	30·0	31·0	21·5	25·9	23·4	10·2	12·9	10·7
Crude foodstuffs	4·8	5·1	4·5	5·6	6·6	19·7	19·7	18·0	18·1	10·6	9·1	11·7	3·8	6·3	7·3	8·6
Manufactured foodstuffs	19·5	17·0	14·3	14·8	15·4	24·1	22·0	25·3	25·6	20·1	16·8	11·7	6·8	10·8	5·8	5·5

Selected Commodities[3]	1790-4[4] 1792	1803–1810	1811–1820	1821–1830	1831–1840	1841–1850	1851–1860	1861–1870	1871–1880	1881–1890	1891–1900	1901–1910	1911–1920	1921–1930	1931–1940	1941–1950	1951–1960	1961–1970
Wheat and wheat flour	30·0	8·2	17·3	7·1	5·9	9·7	9·2	20·5	18·4	17·3	14·4	7·7	7·7	6·0	..	4·5	4·4	4·5
Unmanufactured leaf tobacco	20·0	8·2	10·3	8·2	7·8	6·9	5·7	8·8	4·1	..	..	..	..	3·5	4·1	..	..	..
Rice	10·0	..	..	3·2	..	..	..	..	..	..	..	..	..	..	..	..	..	..
Re-exports[5]	..	39·0	21·3	23·1	15·0	6·3	6·7	6·0	2·4	..	..	..	..	..	..	..	..	..
Unmanufactured cotton	..	13·7	26·9	36·9	51·0	46·2	49·6	42·6	33·0	29·0	22·0	23·9	14·8	17·1	12·4	3·8	4·5	..
Meat and meat products	..	..	..	..	..	..	..	11·7	13·6	13·6	13·9	11·1	8·3	..	..	..	..	..
Fish and fish products	..	5·5[6]	4·1	..	..	..	..	..	..	..	..	..	..	..	..	..	..	..
Petroleum and products	..	..	..	..	..	..	..	..	6·5	6·6	5·8	5·8	5·7	11·0	11·0	5·2	3·9	..
Sawmill and other wood products	..	..	..	..	..	..	..	..	..	..	5·3	5·0	3·0	..	..	..	..	..
Animal fats and oils	..	..	..	..	..	..	..	..	..	..	..	5·0	3·1	..	..	..	..	..
Machinery	..	..	..	..	..	..	..	..	..	4·8[8]	3·4	..	5·8	8·8	13·5	14·4	20·0	25·7
Copper and manufactures	..	..	..	..	..	..	..	..	..	..	..	5·9	3·7	3·1	..	..	..	..
Iron and steel mill products	..	..	..	..	..	..	..	..	..	..	..	4·7	6·8	6·4	6·3	5·3	5·5	2·2
Automobiles, parts and engines	..	..	..	..	..	..	..	..	..	..	..	..	..	3·7	8·3	5·8	6·9	7·3
Chemicals and related products	..	..	..	..	..	..	..	..	..	..	..	..	..	..	4·7	5·2	6·5	8·9
Fruits and nuts	..	..	..	..	..	..	..	..	..	..	..	..	..	..	3·3	3·0	..	..
Cotton manufactures	..	..	..	..	..	..	..	..	..	..	..	..	..	..	..	..	..	..
Coal and related fuels	..	..	..	..	..	..	..	..	..	..	..	..	..	..	..	..	3·0	..
Aircraft, parts and accessories	..	..	..	..	..	..	..	..	..	..	..	..	..	..	..	..	..	4·8

Notes:

¹Domestic exports.

²For security reasons, a small amount of semi-manufactures are included with finished manufactures.

³General exports through 1880; domestic exports thereafter.

⁴Prior to 1803, figures are available for selected years only.

⁵Re-exports of foreign origin.

⁶Includes beef, pork, tallow, hams, butter and cheese, lard, live cattle and horses. The major items were coffee, tea, sugar, and other primary produce.

⁷Based on figures for 1845–7, 1849 and 1850 only.

⁸Based on figures for 1882–90.

Sources for Tables XV and XVI:

For commodity groups by economic classes:

Bureau of the Census, *Historical Statistics of the United States, Colonial Times to 1957* (Washington, D.C., 1960; revised 1965).
Bureau of the Census, *Statistical Abstract of the United States* (Washington, D.C., annually); and
Bureau of International Commerce, *Overseas Business Reports* (April 1972), p. 3.

For selected commodities:

1790–1821: Timothy Pitkin, *Statistical View of the United States* (New York, 1817); U.S. Congress, *American State Papers: Commerce and Navigation*, 2 vols. (Washington, D.C., 1834); and *Historical Statistics*.

1822–1918: Division of Commerce and Navigation, Register of the Treasury, *Commerce and Navigation of the United States* (Washington, D.C., annually); U.S. Congress, *Executive Documents* (Washington, D.C., 1844–80); *Historical Statistics*; and *Statistical Abstract* (annually).

1918–1946: *Foreign Commerce and Navigation of the United States*; *Historical Statistics*; and *Statistical Abstract*.

1946–1970: *Historical Statistics and Statistical Abstract*.

TABLE XVII

United States Foreign Trade by Continents, 1821–1970

Percentage of United States Exports going to

Decennial Average	North America		South America	Europe	Asia	Australia and Oceania	Africa
	Northern	Southern					
1821–30	3·1	21·9	7·9	63·7	2·2		0·4
1831–40	3·5	17·5	5·2	72·1	1·3		0·5
1841–50	4·8	12·8	5·4	73·1	2·2		0·7
1851–60	8·5	8·9	4·6	76·1	1·8	1·4	0·8
1861–70	8·2	11·9	4·9	72·0	2·7	1·5	0·7
1871–80	5·7	6·3	3·7	81·7	1·4	1·0	0·5
1881–90	5·3	5·8	4·0	80·2	2·5	1·8	0·5
1891–1900	6·2	6·2	3·4	78·1	3·1	2·0	1·0
1901–10	9·4	7·7	3·9	70·3	5·4	1·9	1·5
1911–20	13·1	7·7	5·4	63·6	7·1	2·0	1·2
1921–30	15·9	9·3	8·1	49·8	11·7	3·5	2·0
1931–40	15·5	8·5	8·5	44·4	17·0	2·6	3·7
1941–50	15·1	9·1	9·8	44·1	12·0	2·5	6·8
1951–60	22·2	12·2	13·3	29·4	16·9	1·8	4·2
1961–70	21·1	7·7	8·6	33·5	22·0	2·8	4·3

Percentage of United States Imports coming from

Decennial Average	North America		South America	Europe	Asia	Australia and Oceania	Africa
	Northern	Southern					
1821–30	0·5	18·9	5·7	63·6	10·0	0·7	
1831–40	1·0	15·5	7·1	67·6	8·2	1·0	
1841–50	1·2	13·6	10·4	62·3	8·2	1·2	
1851–60	4·9	11·7	9·9	63·7	6·7	1·5	0·7
1861–70	8·9	15·1	9·5	56·3	6·0	1·4	1·0
1871–80	5·8	17·1	12·4	53·0	10·5	0·8	0·6
1881–90	6·0	14·1	11·5	55·6	10·5	2·0	0·6
1891–1900	4·8	13·3	14·0	51·6	12·7	2·6	1·0
1901–10	5·7	13·4	12·1	51·3	15·3	1·0	1·2
1911–20	10·2	16·0	15·2	33·5	21·5	1·6	2·1
1921–30	11·7	13·2	12·9	30·2	28·5	1·5	2·2
1931–40	14·3	10·1	14·0	27·7	30·2	1·2	2·6
1941–50	24·1	15·5	22·5	11·7	16·3	4·1	5·9
1951–60	21·8	11·8	19·6	23·5	16·3	2·0	4·9
1961–70	24·7	8·0	11·5	29·2	20·3	2·3	3·9

Note: The export percentages for 1950–64 were calculated from totals excluding exports of 'special category' commodities, which were not published for security reasons. The export percentages for 1965–70 were based upon totals including exports of 'special category' commodities, which were reported by continent but not by country.

Sources:

U.S. Bureau of the Census, *Historical Statistics of the United States, Colonial Times to 1957* (Washington, D.C., 1960), pp. 550–3.

U.S. Bureau of the Census, *Statistical Abstract of the United States* (Washington, D.C., various issues).

U.S. Bureau of Statistics, *Monthly Summary of Commerce and Finance of the United States* (June 1896), 1612, (August 1901), 610–44.

TABLE XVIII
UNITED STATES
Principal Imports for Selected Years 1821–1970
Approximate Percentage by Region of Provenance

Country or Area	1821							1840		
	Manufactures of cotton	Wool and manufactures	Silk and manufactures	Coffee	Alcoholic Beverages	Sugar	Flax and manufactures	Silk and manufactures	Coffee	Manufactures of iron and steel
1. Canada¹*	..	..	..	..	..	..	..	..		
Latin America										
2. Argentina				..	..	..	..	..	..	
3. West Indies			..	84·4	27·0	77·8⁹	..	..	38·4	..
4. Brazil			..	4·4	..	5·6	..	..	46·5	
5. Central American Republics²	..			..	..	..	..	..	..	
6. Chile	..		..	..	..	..	..	..	..	
7. Colombia	..		..	..	..	..	..	..	..	
8. Mexico	..		..	..	..	..	..	..	..	
9. Peru	..		..	..	..	..	..	..	..	
10. Venezuela	..		..	..	..	..	..	..	8·1	
Europe										
11. Belgium and Luxembourg	..		..		..		..	..		
12. France	..		46·7	..	21·6	..	7·7	70·3	..	..
13. Germany³	..		4·5	..	..	..	7·7	1·7	..	..
14. Italy⁴	..		4·5	..	2·7	..	..	1·7	..	..
15. Netherlands	..		..	..	5·4	..	..	..	..	
16. Portugal	..		..	..	2·7	..	..	..	..	
17. Spain	..		..	..	5·4	..	..	..	..	
18. Sweden⁵	..		..	..	..	..	..	..	..	16·4
19. Switzerland	..		..	..	..	..	..	..	..	
20. United Kingdom	90·4	97·2	4·5	..	5·4	..	84·6	17·0	..	75·3
21. USSR	..		..	..	..	..	..	..	..	6·9
Asia										
22. British East Indies⁶	2·7		..	6·7	..	..	5·6	..	1·1	..
23. China	..		..	28·9	..	..	..	..	7·6	..
24. Hong Kong	..		..	..	..	..	..	..	..	
25. Taiwan	..		..	..	..	..	..	..	..	
26. Indonesia⁷	..		..	..	..	..	..	..	2·8	
27. Japan	..		..	..	..	..	..	..	..	
28. Philippines	..		..	..	..	2·8	..	..	..	
Australasia										
29. Australia	..		..	..	..	..	..	..	..	
30. New Zealand	..		..	..	..	..	..	..	..	
Africa										
31. Angola	..		..	..	..	..	..	..	..	
32. Belgian Congo (Democratic) Republic	..		..	..	..	..	..	..	..	
33. British East Africa (Kenya)	..		..	..	..	..	..	..	..	
34. Ethiopia	..		..	..	..	..	..	..	..	
35. Union of South Africa (Republic)	..		..	..	..	..	..	..	..	
36. Other African	..		..	..	..	..	..	..	..	
37. Unspecified Countries	6·9	2·8	4·2	11·2	29·8⁸	8·2	..	0·6	4·2	1·4
38. Total Value in Millions of Dollars	7·3	7·2	4·5	4·5	3·7	3·6	2·6	11·8	8·6	7·3

* See p. 282 for footnotes and sources.

	1840				1860							1880		
	Wool and manufactures	*Manufactures of cotton*	*Sugar*	*Flax and manufactures*	*Wool and manufactures*	*Silk and manufactures*	*Manufactures of cotton*	*Sugar*	*Coffee*	*Manufactures of iron and steel*	*Flax and manufactures*	*Sugar*	*Coffee*	*Wool and manufactures*
	..	..	..	..	..	..	..	..	..	0·9	..	..	..	1·9
	..	..	..	..	..	..	..	..	..	..	..	..	..	2·8
	..	..	89·1	..	..	..	..	87·7	9·2	..	..	74·1	4·8	..
	..	..	5·5	..	..	..	..	4·5	78·0	..	..	7·5	63·2	..
	..	..	..	..	..	..	..	..	..	..	..	..	4·3	..
	..	..	..	..	..	..	..	..	..	..	..	..	3·3	..
	..	..	..	..	..	..	..	..	..	..	..	..	2·5	..
	..	..	..	..	..	..	..	..	6·0	..	..	..	8·3	..
	4·2	15·4	..	6·5	12·0	38·1	7·4	..	..	1·4	1·8	..	..	2·2
	..	10·8	..	4·4	16·2	4·7	9·9	..	..	2·8	..	..	..	19·1
	..	..	..	..	..	..	..	..	..	..	..	..	..	7·6
	..	..	..	..	..	..	..	..	..	..	..	..	..	..
	..	..	..	..	..	..	..	..	..	..	..	..	..	..
	..	..	..	..	..	..	..	..	..	2·4	..	..	..	..
	83·3	73·9	..	82·6	69·4	50·3	81·5	..	..	87·3	94·5	1·3	1·7	54·8
	..	..	..	6·5	..	..	..	..	..	0·9	0·9	..	..	..
	..	..	..	..	..	..	..	..	0·9	..	..	..	1·2	..
	..	..	..	..	..	5·5	..	..	..	..	..	..	..	..
	..	..	..	..	..	..	..	..	..	..	..	..	..	..
	..	..	..	..	..	..	..	..	2·3	..	..	1·4	8·0	..
	..	..	..	..	..	..	..	1·9	..	..	..	..	..	..
	..	..	..	..	..	..	..	2·6	..	..	..	..	..	..
	5·6	..	..	..	..	..	..	..	..	..	..	..	}	3·3
	..	..	..	..	..	..	..	..	..	..	..	..	}	
	..	..	..	..	..	..	..	..	..	..	..	..	..	..
	..	..	..	..	..	..	..	..	..	..	..	..	..	..
	..	..	..	..	..	..	..	..	..	..	..	..	..	..
	..	..	..	..	..	..	..	..	..	..	..	..	..	..
	..	..	..	..	..	..	..	..	..	..	..	..	..	..
	6·9[10]	..	5·4	..	2·4	1·4	1·2	3·3	3·6	4·3	2·8	15·7[11]	2·7	8·3[12]
	7·2	6·5	5·5	4·6	38	34	33	31	22	21	11	79	60	58

[*Continued overleaf*

TABLE XVIII – continued

Country or Area	1880			1900						1913
	Manufactures of Iron and Steel	Silk and manufactures	Manufactures of cotton	Sugar	Hides and skins	Coffee	Raw silk	Manufactures of cotton	Wool and manufactures	Coffee
1. Canada[1]*	2·8	..	..	..	2·5	..	..	..	1·4	..
Latin America										
2. Argentina	..	..	..	1·7	7·3	..	..	..	7·5	..
3. West Indies	..	..	..	29·3	..	..	..	..	..	..
4. Brazil	..	..	..	..	4·2	64·6	..	..	..	73·9
5. Central American Republics	..	..	..	..	..	8·0	..	..	..	2·9
6. Chile	..	..	..	..	..	..	..	..	..	..
7. Colombia	..	..	..	3·8	1·0	2·7	..	..	..	9·8
8. Mexico	..	..	..	..	4·1	6·3	..	..	..	3·5
9. Peru	..	..	..	1·4	2·7	..	..	..	..	..
10. Venezuela	..	..	..	..	..	6·7	..	..	..	5·9
Europe										
11. Belgium and Luxembourg	6·9	..	..	..	1·5	..	..	..	..	..
12. France	2·0	40·2	13·0	12·3	9·3	..	4·6	13·6	8·6	..
13. Germany[3]	5·7	18·4	31·7	..	8·5	..	..	21·6	10·0	..
14. Italy[4]	..	..	..	..	..	..	23·8	..	..	..
15. Netherlands	2·2	..	..	..	1·7	..	..	..	..	..
16. Portugal	..	..	..	..	..	..	..	..	..	..
17. Spain	..	..	..	..	..	..	..	..	..	..
18. Sweden[5]	..	..	..	..	..	..	..	..	..	..
19. Switzerland	..	..	..	..	..	..	..	21·8	..	..
20. United Kingdom	74·8	16·6	55·0	..	13·2	..	..	41·4	42·5	..
21. USSR	..	..	..	..	4·4	..	..	..	4·7	..
Asia										
22. British East Indies[6]	..	..	..	..	18·2	..	..	..	..	..
23. China	..	15·7	..	..	3·6	..	27·4	..	6·1	..
24. Hong Kong	..	..	..	..	a.	..	..	..	..	..
25. Taiwan	..	..	..	..	..	..	..	..	..	..
26. Indonesia[7]	..	..	..	24·2	..	5·5	..	..	..	1·0
27. Japan	..	8·2	..	..	..	..	43·7	..	2·2	..
28. Philippines	..	..	..	0·9	..	..	..	..	..	..
Australasia										
29. Australia	..	..	..	}	1·5	..	..	}	8·3	..
30. New Zealand	..	..	..	}		..	..	}		..
Africa										
31. Angola	..	..	..	..	..	..	..	..	..	..
32. Belgian Congo (Democratic Republic)	..	..	..	..	..	•	..	..	..	..
33. British East Africa (Kenya)	..	..	..	..	..	..	..	..	..	..
34. Ethiopia	..	..	..	..	..	..	..	..	..	..
35. Union of South Africa (Republic)	..	..	..	..	..	..	..	..	..	..
36. Other African	..	..	..	..	..	..	..	..	..	..
37. Unspecified Countries	8·4	0·9	0·3	26·4[13]	16·3[14]	6·2	0·5	1·6	8·7[15]	3·0
38. Total Value in Millions of Dollars	54	44	30	100	59	53	45	41	36	119

See page 282 for footnotes and sources.

TABLE XVIII—*continued*

| | 1913 | | | | | | | 1939 | | | | | | 1950 | |
Hides and skins	Sugar	Crude rubber	Raw silk	Wood and paper products	Crude rubber	Coffee	Sugar	Raw silk	Wool and Manufactures	Tin, including ore	Wood and paper products	Coffee	Petroleum and products
6·5	..	..	..	68·6	..	..	..	..	1·3	..	85·6	..	..
13·1	..	..	..	..	..	..	..	..	15·8	..	..	..	..
..	90·6	..	..	..	..	1·0	59·0	..	..	..	..	1·8	28·0
2·1	..	28·8	..	..	..	48·1	..	..	..	..	..	52·0	..
..	..	..	..	..	..	9·7	..	..	..	..	..	11·0	..
..	..	..	..	..	..	32·3	..	..	..	..	..	24·5	6·3
5·3	..	1·4	..	..	..	3·4	..	..	..	..	1·8	3·6	5·1
..	..	..	..	..	..	..	0·9	..	1·3	..	..	..	..
1·4	..	..	..	..	..	1·3	..	..	..	..	..	1·7	48·5
2·5	..	6·0	..	..	..	..	..	..	2·5	2·0	..	..	..
5·6	..	2·9	..	2·0	..	..	..	..	4·3	..	..	..	..
7·0	3·8	6·6	..	1·0	..	..	..	..	..	..	..	..	..
..	..	..	12·8	..	..	..	..	1·8	1·6	..	..	..	..
2·8	..	..	..	..	..	..	..	..	..	1·4	..	..	..
..	..	..	..	..	..	..	..	..	..	..	..	..	..
..	..	..	..	12·7	..	..	..	..	..	..	3·7	..	..
10·2	..	37·3	..	0·9	..	..	..	..	23·3	15·4	..	..	..
16·3	..	..	..	..	..	..	..	..	..	..	..	..	..
12·0[16]	..	13·1	..	..	55·5[18]	..	..	..	9·3[16]	66·3[18]	..	..	..
4·5	..	..	16·5	..	..	..	..	9·7	1·8	4·2	..	..	..
..	..	..	..	..	..	..	..	..	..	1·4	..	..	..
..	..	..	69·8	..	29·3	..	..	..	..	7·6	..	..	..
..	..	..	..	..	..	..	..	88·4	1·1	..	..	..	..
..	4·4	..	..	..	..	..	39·7	..	..	..	..	..	..
1·9	..	..	..	..	..	..	..	..	9·3	..	..	..	..
0·9	..	..	..	..	..	..	..	..	4·9	..	..	..	..
..	..	..	..	..	..	..	..	..	..	..	..	1·0	..
..	..	..	..	..	..	..	..	..	..	..	..	0·8	..
..	..	..	..	..	..	1·0	..	..	..	..	..	1·1	..
..	..	..	..	..	..	..	..	..	..	..	..	0·7	..
..	..	..	..	..	..	..	..	..	3·0	..	..	..	..
..	..	..	..	..	..	..	..	..	1·0	..	..	..	..
7·9	1·2	3·9	0·9	14·8[17]	15·2[19]	3·2	0·4	0·1	19·5[20]	1·7	8·9	1·8	12·1[21]
7	104	90	82	256	178	140	125	121	76	71	6113	1090	592

[*Continued overleaf*

TABLE XVIII – *continued*

Country or Area	1950 Wool and manufactures	Crude rubber	Sugar	Copper and manufactures	1970 Machinery and transport equipment Electrical	Non-electrical	Agricultural	Transport equipment	Total
1. Canada[1*]	1·0	..	..	15·7	14·4	26·7	69·7	53·7	39·4
Latin America									
2. Argentina	18·6	..	..	..	..	0·3	..	..	0·1
3. West Indies	..	..	86·2	3·4	0·5	..	..	..	0·1
4. Brazil	..	..	..	..	..	0·2	..	..	0·1
5. Central American Republics[2]	..	..	..	..	..	..	..	..	..
6. Chile	..	..	..	47·2	..	..	..	..	..
7. Colombia	..	..	..	..	..	..	..	..	..
8. Mexico	..	..	..	7·5	4·7	1·2	..	0·2	1·4
9. Peru	1·1	..	1·1	2·8	..	..	..	..	..
10. Venezuela	..	..	..	..	..	..	..	..	..
Europe									
11. Belgium and Luxembourg	1·9	..	..	..	0·3	1·0	3·4	2·1	1·5
12. France	1·0	..	..	..	1·7	2·9	1·5	1·3	1·8
13. Germany[3]	..	..	..	..	5·1	21·1	4·9	19·9	16·8
14. Italy[4]	1·4	..	..	..	2·4	5·5	3·0	1·1	2·8
15. Netherlands	..	..	..	..	2·3	1·9	0·8	0·2	1·0
16. Portugal	..	..	..	..	0·5	0·3	..	..	0·2
17. Spain	..	..	..	..	0·3	0·6	..	0·1	0·3
18. Sweden[5]	..	..	..	..	1·2	3·0	..	2·0	2·1
19. Switzerland	..	..	..	..	1·0	3·4	..	..	1·0
20. United Kingdom	10·5	..	..	..	3·4	13·4	11·7	4·1	6·5
21. USSR	..	..	..	..	..	..	..	..	..
Asia									
22. British East Indies[6]	1·6[22]	45·2[18]	..	..	..	..	..	..	..
23. China	4·5	..	..	..	..	..	..	..	..
24. Hong Kong	..	..	..	..	6·2	0·7	..	0·1	1·5
25. Taiwan	..	..	..	..	5·6	0·3	..	0·1	1·3
26. Indonesia[7]	..	24·3	..	..	..	..	..	..	..
27. Japan	0·9	..	..	7·0	43·3	15·4	3·0	14·1	20·1
28. Philippines	..	..	11·8	1·5	..	..	..	..	..
Australasia									
29. Australia	20·3	..	..	..	..	0·3	..	..	0·1
30. New Zealand	6·7	..	..	..	..	..	..	..	..
Africa									
31. Angola	..	..	..	..	..	..	..	..	..
32. Belgian Congo (Democratic Republic)	..	..	..	..	..	..	..	..	..
33. British East Africa (Kenya)	..	..	..	..	..	..	..	..	..
34. Ethiopia	..	..	..	..	..	..	..	..	..
35. Union of South Africa (Republic)	3·1	..	..	1·1	..	..	..	..	..
36. Other African	..	4·4	..	7·5	..	..	..	..	..
37. Unspecified Countries	27·4[23]	26·1[24]	0·9	6·3	6·6	1·8	2·0	0·4	1·9
38. Total Value in Millions of Dollars	542	459	380	243	2272	2753	264	5882	11171

See p. 282 for footnotes and sources.

TABLE XVIII—*continued*

1970

Petroleum and products	Wood and paper products	Iron and steel mill products	Coffee	Chemicals	Non-ferrous base metals
25·4	79·2	10·4	0·1	25·0	40·9
..	..	0·6	..	0·5	..
22·6	0·2	..	2·2	6·5	..
0·1	0·7	0·1	26·4	0·6	0·1
..	0·2	..	10·5	0·1	..
..	..	..	..	0·3	6·8
1·2	0·2	..	14·6	0·1	0·2
1·9	0·9	1·2	5·6	1·7	1·8
..	..	..	2·6	0·1	9·6
32·8	..	..	1·3	..	..
0·2	0·1	7·5	..	1·8	2·1
0·1	0·2	7·1	0·2	5·9	1·2
0·1	0·5	11·6	0·2	13·1	2·9
2·5	0·4	1·5	..	2·6	0·3
1·2	0·1	2·8	0·2	3·0	0·5
..	0·3	..	..	0·1	..
0·6	0·2	0·3	..	0·7	0·1
..	0·7	2·5	..	0·8	0·4
..	..	0·1	0·7	4·1	0·4
0·4	0·4	5·9	0·3	7·6	4·7
0·1	..	..	..	0·1	1·9
..	0·6	0·6	0·5	0·2	7·2
..	..	..	..	..	·:
..	0·2	..	..	0·1	..
..	1·9	0·2	..	0·5	..
1·9	..	..	2·9	0·1	0·3
0·1	4·3	44·0	..	12·1	4·5
..	1·5	..	..	..	..
..	..	0·4	..	5·4	1·9
..	..	..	..	1·0	..
..	..	..	5·3	..	..
..	..	..	0·7	0·1	1·0
..	..	..	0·9	..	..
..	..	..	5·4	..	..
..	0·4	1·3	..	0·4	3·2
3·5	0·2	0·1	15·8	0·2	0·3
5·3[25]	6·6[26]	1·8	3·6[27]	5·2	7·7
2770	2529	2032	1213	1450	1653

[*Continued overleaf*

TABLE XIX
UNITED STATES
Principal Exports for Selected Years 1821–1970
Approximate Percentage by Region of Destination

Country or Area	1821[8]			1840			1860			
	Raw cotton	Tobacco	Wheat and wheat flour	Raw cotton	Wheat and wheat flour	Tobacco	Raw cotton	Wheat and wheat flour	Produce of animals[9]	Tobacco
1. Canada	..	..	11·1	..	25·0	..	..	27·0	20·0	..
Latin America										
2. Argentina	..	..	..	..	..	..	..	..	..	..
3. Bermudas and Caribbean	..	..	51·1	1·6	16·7	1·0	..	10·5	21·0	..
4. Brazil	..	..	11·1	..	9·2	..	..	18·0	2·0	..
5. Chile	..	..	..	..	..	..	..	..	1·5	..
6. Columbia	..	..	..	..	..	..	..	..	..	..
7. Mexico	..	..	..	..	..	..	..	1·0	0·5	..
8. Panama	..	..	..	..	..	..	..	..	..	..
9. Peru	..	..	..	..	..	..	..	..	..	..
10. Venezuela	..	..	..	..	1·7	..	..	1·0	0·5	..
Europe										
11. Belgium and Luxembourg	..	..	..	1·6	..	2·0	1·0	..	..	2·5
12. Denmark	..	..	..	..	..	..	..	..	..	..
13. France	22·3	19·6	..	25·0	3·3	16·0	16·7	..	..	15·6
14. Germany[2]	..	..	..	1·6	..	15·0	3·7	1·0	1·5	17·5
15. Greece	..	..	..	..	..	..	..	..	..	..
16. Italy[3]	..	3·6	..	..	..	3·0	..	..	..	3·1
17. Netherlands	3·0	17·9	..	1·6	..	15·0	..	..	..	10·0
18. Portugal	..	..	2·2	..	..	..	..	..	..	..
19. Spain	..	3·6	..	..	..	1·0	2·6	..	..	5·0
20. Sweden[4]	..	1·8	..	..	..	..	..	..	..	..
21. Switzerland	..	..	..	..	..	..	..	..	..	..
22. Turkey	..	..	..	..	..	..	..	..	..	..
23. United Kingdom	68·3	44·6	11·1	65·3	33·3	32·0	69·8	22·5	43·0	28·1
24. USSR	..	..	..	..	..	..	1·6	..	..	..
Asia										
25. China	..	..	..	..	..	..	..	1·5	1·0	..
26. India[5]	..	..	..	..	..	..	..	..	..	..
27. Indonesia[6]	..	..	..	..	..	..	..	..	..	..
28. Israel	..	..	..	..	..	..	..	..	..	..
29. Japan	..	..	..	..	..	..	..	..	..	..
30. Pakistan	..	..	..	..	..	..	..	..	..	..
31. Philippines	..	..	..	..	..	..	..	..	..	..
32. Taiwan	..	..	..	..	..	..	..	..	..	..
Africa										
33. Union of South Africa (Republic)	..	..	..	..	..	..	..	..	..	..
Australasia										
34. Australia	..	..	..	..	..	..	..	4·0	..	..
35. New Zealand	..	..	..	..	..	..	..	..	..	..
36. Special Category[7]	..	..	..	..	..	..	..	..	..	..
37. Unspecified Countries	6·4	11·9	13·4	3·3	10·8	15·0	4·6	13·5	9·0	18·2
38. Total Value in Millions of Dollars	20·2	5·6	4·5	64·0	12·0	10·0	192	20	20	16

See p. 282 for footnotes and sources.

TABLE XIX—*continued*

1880					1900						1913	Machinery	
Wheat and wheat flour	Raw cotton	Meat products[10]	Corn and corn meal	Petroleum and products	Raw cotton	Meat products[10]	Wheat and wheat flour	Corn and corn meal	Petroleum and products	Machinery	Raw cotton	Electrical	Non-electrical
4·4	..	2·9	6·3	..	..	..	1·6	5·4	1·1	11·4	1·7	32·1	27·8
..	..	..	..	..	..	..	..	..	1·7	1·6	..	2·2	3·7
0·9	..	1·0	1·0	..	..	4·5	4·3	1·7	1·3	3·8	..	4·9	4·8
1·8	..	..	..	1·4	..	..	1·8	..	2·4	1·3	..	11·2	5·7
..	..	..	..	..	..	..	..	..	..	..	..	1·5	..
..	..	..	..	..	..	..	..	..	..	..	..	..	..
..	..	..	..	..	..	..	..	..	1·2	12·8	..	7·1	4·8
..	..	..	..	..	..	..	..	..	..	..	..	1·5	..
..	..	..	..	..	..	..	..	..	..	..	..	..	..
7·5	..	6·8	2·4	8·0	2·4	3·2	4·5	4·6	4·4	3·2	2·4	0·8	1·3
..	..	..	2·2	1·4	..	..	..	8·6	1·7	..	..	..	..
24·3	9·9	8·7	8·8	5·0	11·5	2·2	..	2·4	8·3	5·8	11·7	1·5	4·2
..	8·5	9·7	7·4	24·9	26·2	11·1	6·5	21·6	13·7	10·5	26·4	0·8	6·1
..	1·4	..	5·2	4·4	7·2	..	..	..	2·3	0·9	5·5	..	1·2
1·8	1·4	1·9	1·1	5·3	1·2	4·7	8·4	11·1	10·6	1·4	..	..	1·1
1·3	..	..	2·0	..	..	..	2·5	..	..	..	..	..	..
..	3·8	..	3·1	2·5	4·0	..	..	..	1·2	..	3·5	1·1	0·9
..	..	..	..	1·1	..	1·3	..	..	2·3	1·3	..	..	0·5
..	..	..	..	..	..	..	..	..	..	..	..	..	..
3·1	66·5	67·0	56·7	14·1	37·2	66·2	58·6	41·3	22·9	21·6	41·1	5·6	12·6
..	5·7	..	..	..	1·0	..	..	..	..	4·5	..	..	3·6
..	..	..	..	..	..	..	..	..	3·9	..	..	..	..
..	..	..	..	5·5	..	..	..	..	3·2	1·3	..	1·9	0·7
..	..	..	..	6·9	..	..	..	..	..	..	..	..	..
..	..	..	..	..	5·3	..	1·2	..	6·7	2·0	4·6	9·0	2·8
..	..	..	..	3·9	..	..	..	..	..	..	..	1·9	1·5
..	..	..	..	..	..	..	..	..	..	..	..	..	..
..	..	..	..	..	..	..	..	..	..	..	..	1·5	1·3
..	..	..	..	1·7	..	..	..	..	3·7[11]	5·6[11]	..	4·1	3·4
..	..	..	..	..	..	..	..	..	..	..	..	0·8	..
..	..	..	..	..	..	..	..	..	..	..	..	..	..
4·9	2·8	2·0	3·8	13·9	4·0	6·8	10·6	3·3	7·4	11·0	3·1	10·5	12·0
5	212	103	54	36	242	158	141	87	84	56	547	27	131

[*Continued overleaf*

TABLE XIX – *continued*

Country or Area	1913 Machinery: Agricultural machinery and implements[1,2]	Total	Iron and steel and manufactures	Meat products[1,3]	Petroleum and products	Copper and manufactures	Wheat and wheat flour	1939 Machinery: Electrical	Non-electrical	Agricultural[1,2]
1. Canada[1]*	17·2	26·3	41·5	4·7	9·5	5·3	0·9	17·4	12·5	30·6
Latin America										
2. Argentina	5·8	6·1	..	..	4·1	..	..	4·0	3·0	9·9
3. Bermudas and Carribbean	..	4·0	4·9	8·5	..	..	6·7	4·5	3·8	1·6
4. Brazil	0·7	5·6	4·3	..	3·4	..	2·2	8·6	3·3	2·3
5. Chile	..	..	2·4	..	2·0	..	..	1·6	0·9	1·0
6. Colombia	..	..	..	..	..	..	..	3·1	2·2	1·6
7. Mexico	1·5	4·6	5·5	1·1	1·4	2·2	..	4·2	2·6	2·9
8. Panama	..	..	5·5	1·3	..	..	..	..	..	..
9. Peru	..	..	..	..	..	..	..	0·8	0·8	0·6
10. Venezuela	..	..	..	..	..	..	..	3·5	3·5	1·7
Europe										
11. Belgium and Luxembourg	0·7	1·0	1·2	3·3	4·1	1·0	7·4	1·1	0·7	..
12. Denmark	1·7	0·5	..	0·8	1·4	..	1·2	..	..	..
13. France	8·4	4·6	..	2·0	7·5	14·8	3·5	1·7	7·3	1·7
14. Germany[2]	9·1	6·1	1·8	15·6	7·5	32·2	9·0	..	..	..
15. Greece	..	..	..	..	..	..	..	..	..	..
16. Italy[3]	1·2	1·0	2·4	1·4	2·7	5·2	5·3	0·5	0·6	0·6
17. Netherlands	1·0	1·0	..	10·4	6·8	19·7	13·4	1·4	1·2	0·9
18. Portugal	..	..	..	..	..	..	..	..	..	..
19. Spain	..	1·0	..	..	1·4	..	..	..	..	..
20. Sweden[4]	..	..	..	..	1·4	1·1	..	2·8	2·0	4·6
21. Switzerland	..	..	..	..	..	..	..	..	..	..
22. Turkey	..	..	..	..	..	..	..	..	..	..
23. United Kingdom	2·7	9·6	7·3	42·1	17·7	12·6	29·3	11·1	16·8	9·6
24. USSR	21·9	7·1	..	..	..	..	..	3·0	6·8	..
Asia										
25. China	..	..	..	..	4·1	..	..	1·0	..	..
26. India[5]	..	..	..	..	2·0	..	..	2·9	2·0	0·9
27. Indonesia[6]	..	..	..	..	..	..	..	1·1	2·2	0·6
28. Israel	..	..	..	..	..	..	..	..	..	..
29. Japan	..	3·0	4·3	..	4·1	..	4·9	1·0	8·5	..
30. Pakistan	..	..	..	..	..	..	..	..	..	..
31. Philippines	..	1·0	1·8	..	1·4	..	1·1	3·2	1·8	1·0
32. Taiwan	..	..	..	..	..	..	..	..	..	..
Africa										
33. Union of South Africa (Republic)	2·7	1·6	..	..	1·4	..	..	5·1	2·1	6·1
Australasia										
34. Australia	2·0	3·0	4·9	..	2·7	..	..	3·0	2·0	4·6
35. New Zealand	..	..	..	..	..	..	..	1·0	..	2·9
36. Special Category[7]	..	..	..	..	..	..	..	..	..	..
37. Unspecified Countries	13·4	12·9	12·2	8·8	13·4	5·9	15·1	12·4	13·4	14·3
38. Total Value in Millions of Dollars	41	199	164	152	147	143	142	105	328	69

See p. 282 for footnotes and sources.

...sport equipment (1939)								Machinery and transport equipment (1950)					
equipment	*Total*	*Petroleum and products*	*Raw cotton*	*Iron and steel mill products*	*Chemicals and related products*	*Wood and paper products*	*Copper and manufactures*	*Electrical*	*Non-electrical*	*Agricultural*	*Transport equipment*[12]	*Total*	*Raw cotton*
·9	14·2	13·2	6·2	12·8	17·6	16·8	..	17·2	18·4	41·1	18·0	18·8	6·3
·6	4·3	0·8	..	2·4	3·3	5·8	..	3·2	3·4	8·8	1·5	2·7	..
·5	2·7	6·8	..	4·0	5·2	7·1	..	7·0	3·0	2·5	5·1	4·5	..
·6	4·4	2·2	..	5·1	2·6	1·3	1·0	6·6	6·6	4·6	6·6	6·5	..
·0	1·1	1·2	..	1·7	1·0	..	..	1·5	1·3	0·6	0·7	1·0	..
·9	2·2	..	..	2·8	2·3	1·0	..	3·4	2·5	2·6	3·2	2·9	1·3
·4	3·6	1·1	..	3·4	4·3	3·4	..	6·7	7·3	7·3	6·1	6·7	..
..	..	..	..	..	..	..	..	..	..	..	5·2	2·5	..
·1	0·9	..	..	1·1	1·3	1·1	..	0·9	0·9	0·8	1·1	1·0	..
·2	2·8	..	..	3·7	2·0	1·9	..	5·9	4·0	2·0	4·5	4·4	..
·7	1·6	2·4	3·6	0·6	2·3	2·1	1·6	2·5	3·1	..	2·6	2·7	2·4
..	..	1·8	..	..	..	..	0·9	..	..	..	..	..	0·6
·8	8·2	8·8	8·3	..	3·1	1·7	17·6	3·7	6·7	1·6	1·0	3·6	10·7
..	..	3·6	3·8	..	2·2	..	5·5	..	1·1	..	..	..	11·2
..	..	..	..	..	..	..	..	0·9	0·9	0·6	0·5	0·7	..
..	..	3·6	8·2	3·1	0·9	1·3	6·6	1·6	5·9	..	0·8	2·8	10·1
·8	1·9	3·6	3·1	3·6	2·0	2·2	1·8	0·5	1·6	0·6	1·0	1·2	3·7
..	..	..	..	..	..	..	..	..	..	..	..	..	1·3
·3	2·9	3·6	4·6	3·0	2·6	..	6·0	0·7	1·7	..	0·9	1·2	1·0
..	..	..	..	..	..	..	..	1·1	1·0	..	0·8	0·9	..
..	..	..	..	..	..	..	..	1·1	0·9	3·5	1·0	1·1	..
·6	13·3	12·6	24·1	6·3	13·4	21·9	5·1	0·6	4·5	2·3	0·9	2·3	9·9
·8	3·2	..	..	0·9	..	..	6·4	..	..	..	..	..	..
·7	1·0	..	5·9	2·0	2·0	2·0	..	..	..	..	..	..	2·7
·0	2·0	1·2	..	..	2·9	0·9	1·3	1·0	2·6	0·6	1·2	1·7	7·2
·2	1·9	0·6	..	1·8	2·1	1·0	..	..	..	..	..	..	..
..	..	..	..	..	..	..	..	1·1	1·0	2·8	0·8	1·0	..
·4	4·3	11·8	17·8	19·4	4·8	3·6	29·5	..	..	..	..	..	21·4
·9	1·9	1·9	..	4·8	5·2	3·5	..	2·8	1·1	1·2	0·8	1·2	..
..	..	..	..	..	..	..	..	..	..	..	..	..	..
·9	4·0	1·1	..	1·7	2·0	3·4	..	1·5	1·7	2·0	1·9	1·7	..
·7	2·6	2·5	..	..	2·6	2·2	..	0·8	1·7	0·7	1·5	1·4	..
..	0·7	0·7	..	..	..	0·8	..	..	..	1·5	..	..	..
..	..	..	..	..	..	..	..	9·8	..	..	19·9	10·3	..
..	14·3	12·5	9·3	15·8	12·3	15·0	16·7	17·9	17·1	12·3	12·4	15·2	10·2
	896	383	239	236	164	100	97	438	1234	109	1450	3231	1024

[Continued overleaf

America's Impact on the World

TABLE XIX – continued

Country or Area	1950			1970 Machinery and transport equipment				
	Petroleum and products	Wheat and wheat flour	Iron and steel mill products	Electrical	Non-electrical	Agricultural[12]	Transport equipment	Total
1. Canada[1]*	31·8	1·0	26·3	20·1	19·8	28·0	37·4	27·2
Latin America								
2. Argentina	1·1	..	3·1	1·0	1·3	1·6	1·0	1·2
3. Bermudas and Caribbean	4·7	3·4	4·3	2·1	1·6	1·6	1·0	1·5
4. Brazil	2·1	2·2	3·4	1·6	2·4	7·2	1·4	2·1
5. Chile	0·9	..	1·8	0·7	0·9	1·0	0·8	0·9
6. Colombia	0·7	..	2·6	0·7	1·0	1·3	1·4	1·2
7. Mexico	5·6	6·3	7·9	6·5	3·9	6·4	3·7	4·5
8. Panama	..	..	..	0·4	0·3	0·6	0·5	0·4
9. Peru	..	1·8	0·7	0·4	0·6	0·5	0·5	0·5
10. Venezuela	..	1·3	3·9	2·0	2·2	2·1	1·6	2·0
Europe								
11. Belgium and Luxembourg	1·5	3·5	1·0	1·7	2·6	0·8	2·1	2·3
12. Denmark	0·6	..	1·0	0·6	0·4	0·3	0·2	0·4
13. France	2·2	..	2·0	4·5	4·5	3·2	2·8	4·0
14. Germany[2]	..	15·7	..	7·9	5·9	2·1	4·0	5·6
15. Greece	..	6·0	0·9	0·4	0·3	1·1	0·2	0·3
16. Italy[3]	1·9	4·0	3·4	3·0	2·6	0·6	2·2	2·5
17. Netherlands	1·0	8·1	2·9	2·8	2·4	0·5	1·2	2·1
18. Portugal	..	2·8	..	0·4	0·2	0·2	0·3	0·3
19. Spain	..	..	..	1·3	1·4	1·1	1·6	1·5
20. Sweden[4]	1·2	..	1·2	1·3	1·3	0·5	1·7	1·5
21. Switzerland	..	0·8	1·1	2·8	1·1	0·5	1·0	1·4
22. Turkey	..	..	2·5	0·7	0·4	0·3	0·5	0·5
23. United Kingdom	6·0	7·2	2·1	7·4	6·7	2·2	3·2	5·7
24. USSR	..	...	..	0·1	0·3	1·9	..	0·2
Asia								
25. China	..	..	..	..	..	..	..	..
26. India[5]	1·3	1·2	1·1	0·8	0·6	0·3	0·5	0·6
27. Indonesia[6]	..	..	..	0·3	0·5	1·9	0·5	0·5
28. Israel	..	1·4	2·8	1·7	0·6	0·8	0·8	0·9
29. Japan	..	14·5	..	8·0	7·2	3·3	4·4	6·4
30. Pakistan	..	..	..	0·3	0·5	0·5	0·8	0·6
31. Philippines	0·6	1·8	2·3	1·1	0·9	0·6	0·5	0·8
32. Taiwan	..	..	..	1·9	0·5	0·2	0·3	0·7
Africa								
33. Union of South Africa (Republic)	1·2	..	2·0	1·1	1·9	3·0	1·4	1·7
Australasia								
34. Australia	0·8	..	3·1	0·1	0·2	0·2	..	2·9
35. New Zealand	..	..	..	0·2	0·3	0·6	0·3	0·3
36. Special Category[7]	24·4	..	..	..	0·5	..	8·9	3·5
37. Unspecified Countries	10·4	17·0[14]	16·6	14·1	22·2	23·0	11·3	11·3
38. Total Value in Millions of Dollars	499	489	472	3000	8372	628	6504	17,875

See p. 282 for footnotes and sources.

Table XIX—*continued*

1970

Chemicals and related products	Wheat and wheat flour	Wood and paper products	Corn unmilled	Iron and steel mill products	Coal and related fuels
14·5	5·2	11·8	8·7	20·6	20·3
1·6	..	0·5	..	4·4	0·9
3·2	1·3	2·1	0·8	1·8	..
3·8	3·2	0·6	..	1·7	3·0
0·9	0·7	0·2	0·4	1·3	0·6
1·6	1·5	0·8	0·1	0·9	..
4·5	..	3·7	4·0	3·3	1·3
0·8	0·3	0·7	..	0·4	..
0·7	0·9	0·4	..	0·7	0·2
2·3	3·2	2·0	0·2	2·1	1·1
5·8	0·4	1·5	4·9	2·7	3·1
0·6	..	0·6	..	0·1	..
2·8	0·3	3·6	0·2	5·0	4·8
5·6	2·9	7·7	7·6	6·8	6·4
0·3	..	0·6	2·2	1·6	..
2·8	1·0	6·2	7·2	5·5	5·9
7·7	2·5	2·8	15·2	1·0	2·8
0·2	1·3	0·1	1·3	0·8	0·3
1·6	..	1·0	1·0	2·5	4·6
0·9	..	0·5	..	1·2	1·1
2·3	1·4	0·7	0·1	0·9	..
0·4	3·1	0·2	..	0·8	..
5·9	3·9	7·6	9·1	8·7	..
0·7	..	0·8	..	0·4	..
..	...	..	..	..	..
1·5	12·1	0·8	0·1	3·9	..
0·2	2·6	0·1	..	0·2	..
0·4	2·7	0·6	0·7	0·7	..
8·4	14·1	25·7	28·5	1·8	39·5
1·2	5·8	0·1	..	2·6	..
1·0	2·7	1·0	..	1·0	..
0·8	2·8	0·4	0·2	0·5	..
1·7	0·1	1·4	..	0·7	..
2·5	..	2·8	..	0·9	0·1
0·4	..	0·3	..	0·2	..
..	..	..	..	..	..
10·4	24·0[15]	10·1	7·5	12·3	4·0
3,826	1,112	1,818	824	1,270	1,044

FOOTNOTES AND SOURCES TO TABLES XVIII AND XIX

Table XVIII Footnotes:
[1] Prior to 1880, figures are given for British North American Possessions.
[2] Includes Costa Rica, Guatemala, Honduras, Nicaragua and Salvador.
[3] Figures are for the Hanse towns prior to 1880; for West Germany 1950–70.
[4] Figures are for the Papal States and the two Sicilies prior to 1870.
[5] Including Norway, prior to 1913.
[6] Includes British India and British Malaya; 1970 figures are for India and Malaysia.
[7] Netherlands East Indies prior to 1950.
[8] Including 8·1% from the Canary Islands, 5·4% each from Gibraltar and Madeira and 2·7% from the Azores.
[9] 75·0% from Cuba.
[10] Including 5·6% from Turkey.
[11] Including 5·2% from Hawaiian Islands.
[12] Including 2·9% from Uruguay.
[13] Including 20·4% from Hawaii and 2·1% from Austria–Hungary.
[14] Including 2·5% from Africa, 2·5% from Uruguay, 2·0% from Aden and 1·0% from Denmark.
[15] Including 8·1% from Turkey.
[16] British India only.
[17] Including 7·5% from Finland and 2·2% from Norway.
[18] British Malaya only.
[19] Including 7·2% from Ceylon and 5·2% from French Indochina.
[20] Including 3·4% from Iran and 2·5% from Syria.
[21] Including 7·0% from Kuwait and 4·0% from Saudi Arabia.
[22] India only.
[23] Including 15·9% from Uruguay, 2·0% from Iran, 1·7% from Syria, 1·2% from Iraq and 1·1% from Pakistan.
[24] Including 13·5% from Thailand, 9·0% from Ceylon, and 2·4% from French Indochina.
[25] Including 2·1% from Arabia Peninsula States not elsewhere classified (i.e. Yemen, Sultanate of Muscat and Oman, Trucial Sheikhs, Qatar and the neutral zone betweenKuwait and Saudi Arabia), 1·3% from Nigeria and 1·3% from Libya.
[26] Including 2·8% from Finland.
[27] Including 2·9% from Ecuador.

Table XIX Footnotes:
[1] Prior to 1880 figures are given for exports to British North American possessions.
[2] Hanse cities prior to 1880; West Germany 1950–70.
[3] Figures are for the Papal States and the two Sicilies prior to 1870.
[4] Prior to 1913 figures include both Sweden and Norway.
[5] British India prior to 1950.
[6] The Netherlands East Indies prior to 1950.
[7] For security reasons, country of destination information is not shown in export statistics for certain commodities, classified as 'Special Category' commodities.
[8] Regular annual reports on the destination of individual export items were not kept prior to 1821.
[9] 'Produce of Animals' includes beef, tallow, hides, horned cattle, butter, cheese, pork (pickled), hams and bacon, lard, wool, hogs, horses, mules and sheep.
[10] 'Meat Products' includes only beef, tallow, bacon, hams, pork and lard.

[11] Total for Australia and New Zealand.

[12] Tractors, parts and accessories are included in 'Transport Equipment' for 1950 and 1960, in 'Agricultural Machinery and Implements' for 1913, 1929, 1939 and 1965.

[13] 'Meat Products' includes beef, oleo oil, oleomargarine, tallow, bacon, hams, lard, pork, mutton, poultry and game, sausages and sausage casings and other meat products.

[14] Including 5·5% to Australia and 2·1% to Norway.

[15] Including 6·7% to Korea, 2·2% to Morocco, 1·5% to South Vietnam, 1·4% to Tunisia, 1·3% to Nigeria, and 1·3% to Algeria.

Sources: Tables XVIII and XIX

1821, *American State Papers*, 2 vols. (Washington, D.C., 1834).

1840–1913, United States Division of Commerce and Navigation, Register of the Treasury, *Commerce and Navigation of the United States* (Washington, D.C., annually).

1939, United States Division of Commerce and Navigation, Register of the Treasury, *Foreign Commerce and Navigation of the United States* (Washington, D.C., annually).

1950, United States Department of Commerce, *F.T. Reports* 110, 120, 410 and 420 (Washington, D.C., annually).

1970, United States Department of Commerce, *F.T. Reports* 135, 155, 410 and 455 (Washington, D.C., annually).

TABLE XX

United States Domestic Manufacturing Exports Compared with Sales from Foreign Investments ($ millions) 1957–70

Selected manufacturing industries	Exports from United States					Sales of Foreign Affiliates				
	1957	1964	1970	Increase	Index 1957–70 (1957=100)	1957	1964	1970	Increase	Index 1957–70 (1957=100)
Paper and allied products	223	374	622	399	279	881	1,595	2,898	2,017	329
Chemicals	1,457	2,364	3,826	2,369	263	2,411	5,903	12,972	10,561	538
Rubber products	161	161	186	25	116	968	1,582	2,779	1,811	287
Metals	1,881	1,864	2,978	1,097	158	1,548	2,940	8,282	6,734	535
Non-electrical machinery	3,102	4,860	8,677	5,575	280	1,903	4,592	12,094	10,191	636
Electrical machinery	874	1,665	3,000	2,126	343	2,047	3,579	9,364	7,317	457
Transportation equipment	1,784	2,844	6,199	4,415	347	4,228	9,466	18,951	14,723	448

Sources:
Exports: U.S. Bureau of the Census, *Statistical Abstract of the U.S.*, 1962, p. 879; U.S. Bureau of International Commerce, *Overseas Business Reports* (February 1971) pp. 6–9.
Sales of Foreign Bound U.S. Firms: *Survey of Current Business* (September 1962) p. 23; and October 1970, p. 19.
U.S. Tariff Commission, *Implications of Multinational Firms for World Trade and Investment and for U.S. Trade and Labor* (Washington, D.C., 1973) p. 444.

TABLE XXI

United States Manufactures: Foreign and Domestic Sales ($ billions) 1957–70

(1) Year	(2) Exports	(3) Sales by foreign-based U.S. firms	(4) Total foreign sales (2) plus (3)		(5) Sales of domestic manufactures	
			Absolute	1957 = 100	Absolute	1957 = 100
1957	16·2	18·3	34·5	100	147·8	100
1964	20·9	37·4	58·3	169	206·2	140
1968	28·4	59·7	88·1	255	285·3	193
1970	35·4	90·4	125·8	365	300·2	203

Sources:

Exports: U.S. Bureau of the Census, *Statistical Abstract of the U.S.*, 1962, p. 879; U.S. Bureau of International Commerce, *Overseas Business Reports*, February 1971, p. 3.

Sales of Foreign Bound U.S. Firms: *Survey of Current Business*, September 1962, p. 23; and October 1970, p. 18.

Sales of Domestic Firms: U.S. Bureau of the Census, *Annual Survey of Manufactures, 1964–5*, 1968 and 1971.

U.S. Tariff Commission, *Implications of Multinational Firms for World Trade and Investment and for U.S. Trade and Labor* (Washington, D.C., 1973) p. 432.

TABLE XXII

United States Share of World Exports
of Manufactured Goods (in percentages) 1899–1970

Country	1899	1913	1929	1937	1950	1967	1970
United States	11·7	13·0	20·4	19·2	26·6	20·6	18·9
United Kingdom	33·2	30·2	22·4	20·9	24·6	11·9	10·5
Germany	22·4	26·6	20·5	21·8	7·0*	19·7*	19·8*
France	14·4	12·1	10·9	5·8	9·6	8·5	8·7
Italy	3·6	3·3	3·7	3·5	3·6	7·0	7·2
Japan	1·5	2·3	3·9	6·9	3·4	9·9	11·7
Others	13·2	12·5	18·2	21·9	25·2	22·4	23·2
Total	100·0	100·0	100·0	100·0	100·0	100·0	100·0

* West Germany only.

Note: The figures for 1967 and 1970 differ slightly from those compiled by the British Department of Trade and Industry.

Source: A. Maizels, *Industrial Growth and World Trade* (Cambridge, Eng., 1963). Data for 1967 is from National Institute, *Economic Review* (February 1968). Data for 1970 is from United Nations, *Monthly Bulletin of Statistics* (September 1972) Special Table BI.

TABLE XXIII

United States Agricultural Exports, 1955–66
Financed by Foreign Aid

	Percentage of distribution government financed
All agricultural exports	30
Selected products	
Wheat and wheat flour	68
Milled rice	41
Cotton	32
Dairy products	57
Unmanufactured tobacco	14

Source: Economic Research Service, U.S. Department of Agriculture, *12 Years of Achievement under Public Law 480* (Washington, D.C., November 1967).

TABLE **XXIV**

Other United States Exports Financed by Foreign Aid, 1965

Commodity group	Percent of exports financed by aid
Machinery and equipment	5·3
Iron and steel mill products	24·4
Chemicals	5·5
Motor vehicles, engines and parts	4·6
Fertiliser	30·4
Non-ferrous metals	11·5
Rubber and products	9·6
Petroleum and products, excluding gas	7·5
Basic textiles	5·4
Railroad transportation equipment	29·5

Source: Charles D. Hyson and Alan M. Strout, 'Impact of Foreign Aid on U.S. Exports', *Harvard Business Review* (Jan–Feb 1968) p. 71.

TABLE XXV

United States Balance of Payments, 1790–1970
(In millions of dollars. For fiscal years, 1790–1900; calendar years, thereafter)

Type of transaction	1790[f]	1800	1810	1820	1830	1840	1850	1860
Exports of goods and services	29	107	117	84	86	160	166	438
Merchandise, adjusted[1]	21	74	68	70	74	133	153	401
Transportation	7	33	49	14	11	27	9	35
Foreign travel in the United States	..	..	..	..	1	1	4	2
Miscellaneous services	..	..	..	..	..	..	..	..
Military transactions	..	..	..	..	..	..	..	..
Income on investments	..	..	..	..	..	..	..	..
Imports of goods and services	30	108	110	84	79	134	210	438
Merchandise	24	93	91	75	71	109	185	376
Transportation	2	7	10	3	3	7	5	17
United States travel abroad	..	..	..	2	1	6	8	20
Miscellaneous services	1	4	4	..	..	..	..	..
Military expenditures	..	..	..	..	..	..	..	..
Income on investments[4]	4	5	6	5	5	12	12	25
Balance on goods and services	−1	−2	7	1	6	26	−44	−1
Unilateral transfers, net (to foreign countries [−])								
Private	..	..	..	1	2	4	20	8
Government	..	..	..	..	..	..	−4	..
United States capital, net (outflow of funds [−])								
Private	..	..	..	..	..	..	..	..
Government	..	..	..	..	..	..	..	..
United States and foreign capital, net (outflow of funds [−])[5]	1	2	−7	−1	−8	−31	29	−7
Foreign capital, other than liquid funds, net (outflow of funds [−])	..	..	..	..	..	..	..	..
Net unrecorded transactions[6]	..	..	..	..	..	..	..	..
Balance of payments, liquidity basis	n.a.	n.a.	n.a.	n.a.	n.a.	n.a.	n.a.	n.a.
Balanced by— monetary reserve assets (Increase [−])[7]	n.a.	n.a.	n.a.	n.a.	n.a.	n.a.	n.a.	n.a.
Foreign holdings of liquid dollar assets (decrease [−])	n.a.	n.a.	n.a.	n.a.	n.a.	n.a.	n.a.	n.a.
Balance on official reserve transactions basis[8]	n.a.	n.a.	n.a.	n.a.	n.a.	n.a.	n.a.	n.a.

1870	1880	1890	1900*	1900†	1910	1920	1930	1940	1950	1960	1970
507	963	960	1,578	1,686	2,160	10,264	5,448	5,355	13,807[2]	29,253[3]	63,578[3]
473	929	921	1,534	1,623	1,995	8,481	3,929	4,124	10,117	19,650	42,041
27	25	23	23	17	19	1,119	325	402	1,033	1,782	3,665
3	7	15	19	8	38	67	129	95	419	919	2,318
4	2	1	1	..	..	1	25	170	645	1,789	5,323
..	..	..	..	..	..	..	..	..	..	1,765	615
..	..	..	..	38	108	596	1,040	564	1,593	3,349	9,617
608	848	1,109	1,149	1,179	2,114	6,741	4,416	3,636	12,028	23,355	59,291
475	694	866	894	869	1,609	5,384	3,104	2,698	9,108	14,744	39,856
22	28	36	30	53	68	848	477	334	818	1,915	4,032
22	35	68	98	120	265	190	463	190	754	1,750	3,916
9	13	15	13	..	..	76	28	143	403	795	1,540
..	..	..	..	..	..	123	49	61	576	3,087	4,837
80	79	125	114	137	172	120	295	210	369	1,063	5,109
−101	114	−150	429	507	46	3,523	1,032	1,719	1,779	5,898	4,287
1	−4	−45	−54	−95	−204	−634	−306	−178	−444	−382	−925
..	..	..	..	..	..	−45	−36	−32	−3,563	−3,643	−2,724
..	..	..	..	−143	−90	−554	−555	245	−1,265	−3,878	−6,351
..	..	..	..	..	..	−175	77	−51	−156	−1,104	−1,588
100	30	194	−296	..	..	−278	66	−90	90	365	3,862
..	..	..	..	−75	345	..	..	..	..	..	..
..	..	..	..	−103	−26	−1,905	320	1,277	−21	−1,156	−1,274
n.a.	140	−1	78	91	71	−68	598	2,890	−3,580	−3,901	−3,848
n.a.	−140	1	−78	−91	−71	68	−310	−4,243	1,758	2,145	2,477
n.a.	n.a.	n.a.	n.a.	n.a.	n.a.	n.a.	−288	1,353	1,822	1,756	1,371
n.a.	n.a.	n.a.	n.a.	n.a.	n.a.	n.a.	n.a.	n.a.	n.a.	−3,403	−9,819[9]

Notes for Table XXV

.. Entry represents zero; n.a. = not available.

* Comparable to earlier years.

† Comparable to later years.

[1] Includes transfers of military supplies and services under grants for the years 1790–1910; merchandise figures for the period also include receipts from military cash and credit transactions. Figures for 1920–70 exclude military transfers under grants.

[2] Includes 'military transactions', not shown separately.

[3] Excludes military grants of $27,488 million in 1960 and $62,962 million in 1970.

[4] Net for 1790–1900.

[5] Following the procedure of Douglass North and Matthew Simon, these figures represent the balance of receipts and payments on account of merchandise trade, · transportation, travel, interest, dividends, and remittances which North and Simon assumed to indicate net flows of United States and foreign capital. Errors and omissions in the estimates of these items are reflected here. For the year 1900, the figures are in forms comparable to both earlier and later years.

[6] Includes 'errors and omissions'; it is believed to consist largely of unreported short-term capital flows.

[7] Includes gold, convertible currencies, and International Monetary Fund position. The estimates of gold movements in the period 1790–1870 are included with the merchandise data.

[8] Measured by changes in United States monetary reserve assets, in United States liquid liabilities to foreign official agencies, and in certain United States non-liquid liabilities to foreign official agencies.

[9] Includes allocations of special drawing rights of $867 million.

Sources for Table XXV

For 1790–1910: U.S. Bureau of the Census, *Historical Statistics of the United States, Colonial Times to 1957* (Washington, D.C., 1960) pp. 562–5.

For 1920–50: U.S. Bureau of the Census, *Statistical Abstract of the United States 1965* (Washington, D.C., 1965) p. 856.

For 1960 and 1970: U.S. Bureau of the Census, *Statistical Abstract of the United States 1971* (Washington, D.C., 1971) p. 753.

Index

291

292

Index